Yours for a complete obedience

Isa 1:19

Crowded to Christ

Crowded to Christ

by

L. E. Maxwell

Author of *Born Crucified*, etc.

Editor of *The Prairie Overcomer*,
PRINCIPAL, PRAIRIE BIBLE INSTITUTE
Three Hills, Alberta, Canada

WM. B. EERDMANS PUBLISHING COMPANY
Grand Rapids   1950   Michigan

DEDICATION

To the hundreds of our students in the
regions beyond, whose "obedience is
come abroad unto all men," this
book is gladly dedicated.

Foreword

Crowded to Christ is a trumpet call to Christians to dare to be "utterly believing believers" — New Testament Christians in this secular and carnal world. This book is a real book of the hour, calling orthodox Christians back to supernatural living. For Christians who are hungering and thirsting after the fulness of the Spirit this is a message for their hearts. Also for Christians and churches with "no fire" or with "wild fire" this book is a challenge to seek the "heavenly fire without the fanaticism of the flesh."

All are aware that there is a moral breakdown in America today; there is an apostasy also among religious leaders who deny the infallible Word of God. Not all are awake to the deadly foes in the camp of the orthodox who accept the Bible as God's infallible Word. On the one hand, there is a lack of the fire and passion of God in life and service; on the other hand, there is a cheap and easy "believism" that is blind to the terror and to the glory of God's moral standard.

One of the great missionary pioneers of the past generation, who day by day lived in the thick of the fight for souls in Africa, wrote me that he felt like writing to every Bible Institute in America to send them no more missionaries who made a boast of being "under grace," and having nothing to do with the law. This idea, he said, was working havoc in the training of native believers. About the same time one of the mightiest spiritual leaders in Latin America, a man who magnified the grace of God, told me that this new attitude toward the law of God and God's moral standard was a deadly thing in the right training of converts. Recently testimony has come from two leaders that the attitude of missionaries toward the observing of the Lord's Day has brought untold damage to the missionary work. Setting forth the true relation of the Christian to the law is one of the vital ministries of this book. It is a message that all of the great spiritual leaders of the church through the ages have agreed with. But our author has applied it in a magnificent way to the situation of our own day. More distinctly doctrinal and controversial aspects of law and grace are dealt with in five appendices which handle these problems in a warm and vital way.

Two things need to be added in this foreword by one who has received rich blessing and refreshment through reading the book. Its pages are filled with some of the choicest quotations and also outstanding experiences of many whom we consider spiritual giants and who considered themselves to be less than nothing before God: Rutherford, Spurgeon, Meyer, George Mueller, William Law, Robert Murray McCheyne, Pierson, Moody, Finney, Isaac Watts, A. J. Gordon, Goforth, Amy Carmichael, and a score of others.

Finally, I believe that the secret of the power of this volume is that it is more or less an autobiography of the spiritual experience of the writer. One of the modern miracles of God's supernatural working is the Prairie Bible Institute. This missionary training center sprang up on the prairies, not by magic, but by real faith and has already sent almost 500 Spirit-filled men and women to the uttermost parts of the earth. This book mentions quite incidentally the ministry of its author, but it is very evident that the vital power of the book springs out of an experience of living through the spiritual truths that are presented.

May God use this message of *Crowded to Christ* to stir multitudes of Christians to learn that the Christian life is intended to be a supernatural miracle, lived moment by moment in the power of the Holy Spirit. May it challenge Christian leaders to live a life like Paul, pressing on to real revival in our individual lives, in our churches, in our institutions, in the Body of Christ throughout the world — hastening on to the completion of Christ's Great Commission.

Columbia, South Carolina
June 1, 1950

ROBERT C. McQUILKIN,
President, Columbia Bible College

Author's Preface

A few years ago the Editor of *The Sunday School Times* published the following statement: "Leaders of the China Inland Mission, Unevangelized Fields Mission, and others, speak well of their missionaries who are graduates of the Prairie Bible Institute. What is the secret of its spiritual vitality? Undoubtedly one reason why the lives of many of the students and delegates to the three annual conferences are transformed is because of the emphasis upon the necessity for every believer to be identified with Christ in His death and resurrection."

The law is God's lariat in His great "round up" of sinners. But there are many other schoolmasters—pain, poverty, despair, death —whereby men are "Crowded to Christ." The aim of this book is to make clear that through the death-resurrection process God shuts men up to the blessed obedience of faith. Today we are inclined to overlook the fact that, whereas Paul's epistle to the Romans clearly sets forth salvation "by faith without the deeds of the law," the letter first speaks of *"obedience of faith* among all nations" (1:5, R.V.), and closes with the declaration that this Gospel, "according to the commandment of the eternal God, is made known unto all the nations unto *obedience of faith"* (16:26, R.V.).

The reader will note that the author does not follow the beaten track of this hour relative to the treatment of Law and Grace. The writer shares the alarm of godly men everywhere that such an over-emphasis has been placed on Grace that the principles of *"submission* to the righteousness of God" (Rom. 10:3) are fast disappearing from present-day Christianity. This book calls for an obedience that magnifies "the true grace of God."

May this book produce "obedience to the faith among all nations"—is the author's prayer.

Contents

Crowded to Christ

CHAPTER I

Shut Up to Faith

I AM ONE of the Jews who escaped from Germany," says Abraham Poljak. "I thank God for all the strokes with which I was driven from darkness to light. It is better that we arrive beaten and bleeding at the glorious goal than that we decay happily and contented in darkness. As long as things were all right with us, we did not know anything of God, and the salvation of our souls and the world beyond. Hitler's arrows and our misery have led us to the innermost heart. We have lost our earthly home but found the heavenly one. We have lost our economic support, but won the friendship of the ravens of Elijah. On the bitter ways of emigration we have found Jesus, the Riches of all worlds."

Our universe is confessedly one of mystery. Fallen man stalks selfishly and unfettered through the world. Though red-handed and highhanded, he is left to his own liberties. This is man's day. God seems to do nothing—so much so that men doubt whether or not He can. Let us who own His name, however, beware lest we, like the scoffer, charge God with folly. In the midst of mounting world misery and mystery there "runs one golden thread of purpose, not the iron thread of doom." God has gracious ends in view. There are things worse than trouble, worse than pain, worse than death. Sin, to God, is the only unendurable—more intolerable even than hell. Ah yes, God hates hell, hates it more than we do, but He hates sin more than He hates hell. If the world's mounting miseries will crowd men to Christ and make hell the emptier, they are better than sin. Such is the wisdom of God in a mystery.

Thistles, thorns, sweat—better than sin. Sorrows, sickness, suffering—better than sin. Pain, poverty, affliction—better than sin. Wars, plagues, famines, disease, destruction, death—better than sin. Endless tyranny, unpitied tears, broken hearts—better than sin.

15

"Ashes to ashes, dust to dust" our "mortal coil destined to the invasion of a million worms"—*all better than sin*. Such are the gracious and severe measures adopted by the All-wise in His zeal to recover lost man. Behold, therefore, the goodness and severity of God. Most of us, like Abraham Poljak, have to be "driven from darkness to light"; but once there, we confess with him that "it is better to arrive beaten and bleeding at the glorious goal than that we decay happily and contented in darkness."

Our own stupid and selfish hearts can bear shameful witness to the fact that God had to shut us up to faith in Jesus Christ. Certainly it is not to the credit of human nature that we must be thus "shut up" to the mercies of God—mercies so many, so grand, and so free. God has emptied heaven for us. Christ willingly gave us His all. Salvation is free and of infinite worth. Nevertheless, in spite of such mercies, we would, unless shut up to them, evade them and go on to our ruin as an ox to the slaughter. Recall how long we were in coming to the conviction that in ourselves there was no answer to the question, How shall a man be just with God? Though we tried many doors—the door of perfect duty, the door of good resolution, the door of baptism, the door of church membership—through none of them could we escape; for the doorway into the kingdom is "not of blood, nor of the will of the flesh, nor of the will of man, but of God." Finally—blessed *finally*—caught in the grip of failure and defeat and guilt and condemnation, we were shut up to one door, the only one, the doorway of faith in Christ. "Thus God, in His eagerness to drive us to faith in Himself, shuts every other door, that the soul weary, worn, fluttering, hard-pressed, may flee for refuge to the hope set before it, may be shut up to the faith which is revealed" (F. B. Meyer, in *Fire and Flood*). Throughout life the principle obtains. Faith is usually born of despair. We must be reduced again and again to the limit of all resolution and resources and be compelled by repeated failure to feel the need of Another's help and sufficiency. No one knows this fact more than the growing Christian.

The mark of a real Christian is a desire to "grow in grace." He cannot be satisfied with past experiences. He hungers and thirsts after righteousness, and to him, therefore, the promise is that he "shall be filled." However, in his determination to be humble, to love his enemies, to hate himself, to be more than conqueror—in other words, to be like Christ—the Christian may come sooner or later to a sense of crushing failure and defeat. In his honest endeavour to meet the high standards laid down by his Master, there dawns upon him the great gulf between his human capacity and Christ's exalted demands. At this stage some half-hearted saints resign themselves despairingly to their position of defeat. Others, thank God, cannot endure this double-mindedness; they look upon their unholy duplicity as a mockery of the grand and glorious promises of Christian victory, and feel that their lives are hollow hypocrisy. Moreover, they are not contented, as some, to blame all this on the devil, or on the weakness of the flesh, or on the "old man."

To such sincere souls it is cold comfort to be told that where sin abounds grace does much more abound. Are they then to continue in sin that grace may abound? Their whole regenerate beings cry out, "Perish the thought." Nor can they blunt the edge of conscience by maintaining that "It is no more I that do it, but sin that dwelleth in me." They rightly feel the personal responsibility for this overmastering power of evil. They can neither deny this sinfulness nor shake off the responsibility for the same. Still the muddy stream of their mixed lives only darkens and deepens. Sin becomes enormous, infamous, "exceeding sinful." Oh, what disclosures may yet come to these determined and zealous souls! Not having made Paul's deep discovery, "I know that in me (that is, in my flesh,) dwelleth no good thing," they redouble their efforts. They do not utterly despair of themselves. They think that if they are only more watchful, more prayerful, more diligent, they will yet be able to attain. They strive and struggle; they fight and fast; they yearn and pray. How many have gone through it—yes, thank God, *clear through it!* Hudson Taylor speaks of his unquenchable yearnings for more holiness and life and power in his soul:

> I felt the ingratitude, the danger, the sin of not living near to God. I prayed, agonized, strove, fasted, made resolutions, read the Word of God more diligently, sought more time for meditation and prayer—but all was without effect. Every day, almost every hour, the consciousness of sin oppressed me. I knew if I could only abide in *Christ* all would be well,

but I *could not* . . . each day brought its register of sin and
failure, of lack of power. To will was indeed present with me,
but how to perform I found not. Then came the question, Is
there no rescue? Must it be thus to the end—constant conflict and, instead of victory, too often defeat . . . I hated myself; I hated my sin; and yet, I gained no strength against
it. I felt I was a child of God: His Spirit in my heart would
cry: "Abba, Father"; but to rise to my privileges as a child
I was utterly powerless.

> "*God is a tower without a stair*
> *And His perfection loves despair.*"

Like Hudson Taylor, a host of others have found themselves thus
shut up to despair and death—death with Christ on the Cross. Did
One die for all, in the room and stead of all?—then all died, died
in His death once for all. However, not until they had come to an
end of all self-righteousness and satisfaction in themselves, not until all their peace and joy and strength of will and resolution and
purpose had been "slain by the law," could faith stretch forth her
hands for victory. Only when they sensed the tragedy, the futility,
the folly and failure of every human attempt to overcome the law
of sin and death, were they shut up to Him who not only "justifies
the ungodly" but "quickens the dead." It is a blessed day—and
with many persons it is a blessed crisis, a crisis followed by a process—when they thus die and are shut up to their union with Christ
in death and resurrection.

Most Christians are not brought into the overcoming life without passing through afflictions, both external and internal. This
happens through two chief causes, viz., ignorance and self-will. More
generally it is through the latter. We are slow to learn what is
to be done, but still more reluctant to submit to its being done.
While most Christians would like to have full enjoyment of Christ,
they want other enjoyments as well; and therefore attach their affections first to one object and then to another. All the time they long
to have the benefits of reckoning themselves dead indeed unto sin
through Jesus Christ, they are secretly bowing to some idol seen
or unseen. From this they refuse to be detached—"and there they
remain for a time, fixed, obstinate, inflexible." How blessed that
our God is patient and loving and determined! If He sees that He

can utterly detach us from every earthly tie and fuse us into a living union with Himself through the Crucified, His love will not shrink from reducing us to the very dust of despair and death. He will apply the sword to every tie that binds us to the world. He will spoil all our pharisaical foliage. He will lay the axe of the Cross to the very root of the tree of self. We may find the whole inward fabric of our lives overwhelmed and burned and blasted to the very extremity of endurance. Shrink not, fearful soul. This is God's undoing of the old life. Remember that we can enjoy the new only as we learn to put off the old. In the midst of all this dreadful baptism God is teaching you to unlearn self and learn Christ. *Who teacheth like Him?*

The old natural life is contrary to faith. The whole of our natural life is dominated by self-love, self-centeredness, and self-confidence—in a single term, *selfishness*. The process, therefore, of unlearning self and learning Christ will be for every believer a painful process. Natural ambitions and natural aspirations enter so largely into our Christian life and service that God has all He can do to uproot and cut off these myriad branchings of the life of nature. Simon Peter was a man of strong impulses, a man in whom nature flourished to the full. As spokesman for a group of men who were ambitious for thrones and favours in Messiah's kingdom, men who had left all to follow Christ, he was perhaps more consecrated than most of us. Nevertheless the life of nature was still dominant in him. These mixed ambitions were not unknown to Christ's great arch enemy, and the accuser of the brethren knew he had some place, some ground of accusation, in Peter. Christ, furthermore, could not deny Satan's territorial rights in this blustering and self-confident disciple, but He would bring Peter to an undoing of himself and rid him of this filthy wretchedness. Here watch infinite Wisdom at work: "Simon, Simon, behold, Satan asked to have you, that he might sift you as wheat" (Luke 22:31, R.V.). Peter must come to know how wretched and miserable and poor and blind and naked he really is. He must come to a true self-disclosure, as Satan's sifting winnows out the chaff of the natural life. With what frightful exposure and shame and pain was Peter finally driven from his unbounded confidence in the flesh!

Let us go back to Abraham, the very father of faith, and notice how he had to learn these lessons after the same fashion. Most of his life was made up of "going out" from the natural, of leaving the natural to learn the supernatural. He left his home, his kindred, and his country. He left Lot the first choice of the land. He left Lot. He left the spoils of battle to the king of Sodom. At each of these steps of faith he acted contrary to nature, while every atom and instinct of his natural life must have shrunk from such obedience. As he was forever leaving the natural whether of affection, of choice, or of possession, the old patriarch could look up and say,

> *He emptied my hands of my treasure store,*
> *And His covenant grace revealed;*
> *There was not a wound in my aching heart*
> *But the balm of His breath had healed.*
> *Oh! tender and true was the chastening sore*
> *In wisdom that taught and tried,*
> *Till the soul that He sought was trusting in Him*
> *And nothing on earth beside.*
>
> —Selected

There were still greater tests ahead for the father of faith. He had been leaning on Eliezer, hoping that he might be the father of the covenant heir, until that door was closed. Next he had listened to Sarah's fleshly suggestion, but that did not better his position; for "what saith the scripture? Cast out the bondwoman and her son." Finally, when ninety years old and nine, with his own vital powers withered and decayed, "under hopeless circumstances, he hopefully believed." With every door in nature closed, Abraham at last was shut up to faith. Out of this very despair a superhuman hope was born for a supernatural son.

Faith works better when there is no natural hope. If there be but a straw for sight to cling to, then faith finds difficulty. George Mueller says, "Remember it is the very time for faith to work when sight ceases. The greater the difficulties, the easier for faith; as long as there remain certain natural prospects, faith does not get on as easily as where natural prospects fail." During one of our times of trial when our enemies sought to extort from us $9,000 for supposed damages in a truck accident, one of our board members said, "Thank God, if they were suing us for $2,000 we would try to figure out how to pay it, but since it's for $9,000 there is no hope. *We will have to trust God.*" Needless to say, God saw us through, because we could not see our own way through. When we were at wit's end corner of desperation, right there God revealed His power. Faith is usually born of despair.

While we are dwelling on the necessity of the cutting off of the old natural life, we cannot leave the subject without dwelling upon the matter of faith vs. feelings. In certain religious circles there is an icy formalism that is without a sign of fervour or feeling; doubt and death dominate the situation. At the other extreme the pendulum has swung completely over to sensation, sentiment, and soulishness. In this latter circle there are many godly souls who have unfortunately been led into a system of living by special manifestations and feelings — a position not conducive to solid Christian growth and character. Between the extremes of *no fire* and *wild fire* there is a golden balance. It is our desire to help every honest soul who wants heavenly fire without the fanaticism of the flesh.

While the Christian life is emphatically a *life of faith*, it is not altogether without feelings and manifestations. These, however, must be kept in their place, and we must understand that they furnish no ground whatever as a basis of our acceptance or favour or fellowship with God. Many fervent Christians have been so poorly instructed on this essential matter of living by faith that they seem unable and unwilling to make a complete surrender and consecration unless God first gives them some joyous feeling, some specific manifestation, or some inward or outward sign. They feel that some such manifestation is necessary before they can believe that they are fully consecrated and filled with the Spirit. Such souls would reverse the Scripture, "He that believeth on the Son of God hath the witness in himself," to read, "He that hath the witness in himself believeth." As a result, such persons suffer many mental and emotional reactions, and their lives exhibit a miserable "alternation of elevations and depressions—of the joyful and of the terrific—of rapture and of wretchedness" (Upham). Such a life is freighted with the gravest dangers of darkness and deception and demonic power.

Those who insist on living a life of specific feelings and manifestations, great or small, need to realize that they are cherishing and keeping alive a selfish principle. They are like spoiled children who must have a stick of candy when they are in a bad humour. All unconsciously they are dictating terms to God—laying down conditions, which God must meet, before they will believe Him. In thus feeding and keeping alive the life of nature, they are refusing the way of the Cross, which is essentially the way of self-renunciation and faith. Those who demand signs and wonders know not how subtle is the wicked unbelief which asks, How do you know you have been filled with the Spirit unless you have such and such rhapsodies? Poor foolish souls! Were they saved by their feelings or by Christ? Certainly we can all agree that we were justified by faith. As poor sinners in our ungodliness and darkness we were compelled to stake our all in naked faith on God's promise of salvation through Christ. Dare we now turn back in unbelief and deny that the just shall live by faith? Is the whole Christian life not a life of faith? Surely we walk by faith, not by sight. By faith we stand. We are kept by the power of God through faith. We are to fight the good fight of faith and, finally, through faith and patience inherit the promises. How sweeping is the phrase that "without faith it is impossible to please Him." The demand for signs, therefore, is everywhere spoken of in the Bible as a proof of unbelief. Should we not then as believers "receive the promise of the Spirit *through faith*" (Gal. 3:14)?

Take the example of Gideon. Having already asked and received one sign to help his poor wavering faith, he knew that God might well smite him for demanding further signs. It is precisely in connection with this principle of faith vs. signs that Paul rebukes the Corinthians: "In the law it is written, With men of other tongues and other lips will I speak unto this people; and yet for all that will they not hear Me, saith the Lord. Wherefore tongues are for a sign, not to them that believe, but to them that believe not: but prophesying serveth not for them that believe not, but for them which believe" (I Cor. 14: 21,22). Note that this was written to God's unbelieving people and not to the unsaved of the world. (Paul says the same chaotic unbelief obtained in Isaiah's day. The prophet rebuked God's unbelieving people that they could not be spoken to except through the lash and lip of the Assyrian armies, i.e., mere externals, "other tongues." Yet for all that they would not believe.)

All this reminds us of the silly bride who is not sure that she has a husband unless she has a ring on her finger; it would seem that she prefers the ring to the husband. We fear that the Bride of Christ is made up of many such. Oh, for a living faith in a living God whose living word can never die!

If you, my reader, are bent on becoming an utterly believing believer, one who pins all his confidence upon the veracity of God's naked Word, then hesitate not to take the simple and crucifying, the humbling and purifying way of faith—the only way in which prophets and apostles and martyrs have trod. Ask God to "put a thorn in every enjoyment, a worm in every gourd," that would either prevent your being wholly Christ's or would in any measure retard your growth in faith. Submit yourself to the divine will and let God cut every idolatrous prop away, whether of feeling or emotion or manifestation. Why demand to *see* your own faith, or *feel* His presence? Those who have done exploits in the Church of Christ have often experienced the greatest inner desolations.

CHAPTER II

Shut up to Faith (continued)

MANY PERSONS keep themselves in a perpetual foment through hoping they will get into a situation where they can enjoy a better Christian life. They feel enclosed in a net of circumstances which they cannot accept. They are so wearied and baffled and beaten by the continuous pressure about them that they wish and itch for things to be different, quite sure that if things were only different Christ would be more real. It has never dawned upon them that at the heart of these very circumstances they are to find Christ, find His grace sufficient, find the life more abundant. From various translations we paraphrase Paul's experiences as recorded in II Cor. 4:8, 9: On every side hard pressed—but not hemmed in; without a way—but not without a by-way; put to it—but not put out; in desperate plight—yet not despairing; close pursued—but not abandoned (not left in the enemy's hands); beaten to the earth—yet never destroyed. Paul says in summary: "Always bearing about in the body the dying of the Lord Jesus, that the life also of Jesus might be made manifest in our body." It was a perpetual, a never-ending, a continuous process. "Perpetually in peril, he had a perpetual series of escapes; perpetually at his wits' end, his way perpetually opened before him" (Denney).

Why the perpetual perils, the hot pursuits, the unrelenting pressure?—why the long unending succession? Is it mere incident and accident? Nay! the purpose is "that *the life* of Jesus might be made manifest." Unless Paul be in peril, how can he experience God's escape? Unless exposed to danger and death, how can he enjoy God's deliverance? Unless he be pressed out of measure, how can he appreciate relief? Unless battered down, how can he be lifted up in the life all-divine?

"In spite of care and prayer," do things go wrong day after day in never-ending succession? Are you desperately holding out against the process, praying that the thorn may be removed—only to be crowned with more? Worst of all, you know that you can neither manage nor control the forces arrayed against you. Why then not just settle down and settle in? Accept the fact that this is your lot for life—and neither accidental nor incidental. Cease hoping for things to be otherwise, and cease itching to be otherwhere; for you are not moving on, not moving out. This is life; this is "home." You may just as well unpack. In your weariest and weakest and most bewildered moment, simply say, "Now, Lord, here is my chance, and Thine—my chance to die, Thy chance to manifest the life of Jesus."

Our mortal life is full of testings—testings in the home, in business, in public life, in ministerial life. That we may not think them strange, God in His great mercy has given us in the Scriptures detailed experiences of certain characters whose spiritual history is much like our own. One such character is Jacob, who well illustrates the career of some of God's best men and women. In our inclination to reflect upon Jacob as the supplanter, the trickster, the manipulator, let us not forget that it was Esau who despised his birthright and sold it for a mess of pottage, that it was Esau who is called a profane person. It was Jacob, remember, who coveted the blessings of the covenant; it was Jacob who acted on God's promises; and it was Jacob who acted on the heavenly vision. Jacob is therefore a singular illustration of God's nobility, a man who covets the highest and whose motive is the best. Nevertheless this very man Jacob is forced to confess at the last of his life, "Few and evil have the days of the years of my life been." What was it that so saddened his later life and experience? Was it not his lifelong seeking to bring about by human manipulation and contrivance the plans and purposes of God? Yet with all his management and manipulation he brought himself only sorrow and worry and misery. He was putting God's covenant and kingdom first, yet he dared not let God manage matters to suit Himself; he refused to leave the fulfillment of the promises in divine hands. God, however, patiently pursued him. Let us notice how He finally managed to catch up with him after twenty years.

By divine direction and encouragement, Jacob begins his journey back to Bethel. "The LORD said unto Jacob, Return unto the land of thy fathers, and to thy kindred; and I will be with thee" (Gen. 31:3). Testings follow him, however, for ere long he is pursued by his old enemy, Laban; and no sooner is Laban pacified than Esau comes to meet him with four hundred men. Recall that Jacob has now become a man of substance; he has been a good manager, and God has been with him and blessed him. He has possessions and cattle, so long served for and so dearly earned through twenty years of toil and sweat—twenty years of nomadic shepherd life, during which time Laban had changed his wages ten times. Recounting these miseries, Jacob cries, "Thus I was; in the day the drought consumed me, and the frost by night; and my sleep departed from mine eyes" (Gen. 31:40). Yet with all that discipline of twenty years behind him Jacob is still Jacob, not an Israelite indeed in whom is no guile. Now that Esau is about to kill him, what will he do? Whither can he turn? How can he manage? Avoid Esau he cannot; face him he must. Therefore he must hatch another plan. First, last, and always, his thought was *a plan*. He at once divides his company into two bands; then after managing details as well as he can, he falls on his knees in his desperation and tries to commit all to the Lord:

> And Jacob said, O God of my father Abraham, and God of my father Isaac, the LORD which saidst unto me, Return unto thy country, and to thy kindred, and I will deal well with thee:
>
> I am not worthy of the least of all the mercies, and of all the truth, which Thou hast shewed unto Thy servant; for with my staff I passed over this Jordan; and now I am become two bands.
>
> Deliver me, I pray Thee, from the hand of my brother, from the hand of Esau: for I fear him, lest he will come and smite me, and the mother with the children.
>
> And Thou saidst, I will surely do thee good, and make thy seed as the sand of the sea, which cannot be numbered for multitude.
>
> (Gen. 32:9-12)

Note that with all the proofs of God's past faithfulness and with all the assuring promises of divine protection spoken from the very gate of heaven, Jacob is nevertheless fearful and afraid, a veritable victim of his wicked unbelief. Yet he pleads all the divine promises with all the decision and detail of the most orthodox.

How like the prayers of so many good Christians who are yet mastered by unbelief and fearfulness of heart! They too are continually managing and manipulating, and then religiously committing all to the Lord. Many splendid Christians, worthy successors of Jacob in their zeal to promote the fundamentals of the faith, come before God in this selfsame way. With the same inner sense of contamination and condemnation, they come before the throne reminding God that He looks at them only through Christ, that they are complete in Christ, that His promises of their safekeeping in Christ are sure, and that they have been blessed with all spiritual blessings in the heavenly places in Christ. The analogy is perfect between Jacob and his Christian successors. O fatal self-hood! how cruel! "Myself arch traitor to myself!"

Such Christians, like Jacob, cannot draw near in full assurance of faith with their hearts sprinkled from an evil conscience. They have no confidence toward God, and cannot therefore ask and receive that their joy may be full. Mastered by self and unbelief, they first manage and plan, then would fain persuade themselves that they are trusting God when they plead with prayers and divine promises of protection—only to rise from their knees, like Jacob, and hatch another plan, devise a different scheme. "I will appease him [Esau] with a present." Jacob's confidence was in his scheming; but God catches the wise in the midst of their craftiness, and that night He caught up with Jacob. When Jacob's desperation had reached the point of despair, the Divine Wrestler seized upon him, that giant of unbroken health and vigour, and left him ere dawn a poor, lame, halting man. Hear the strengthless and clinging cripple as he cries, "I will not let *Thee* go." In order to break Jacob's pride in his own natural power, the angel had been forced to touch the hollow of his thigh so that the sinew shrank. It is better to "enter into life *halt*." Jacob had at last— how late!—entered into a more abundant life. His name was changed to Israel, "a prince with God," for he had power with God and men, and prevailed. God now made even his enemy Esau to be at peace with him.

Beloved reader, have you met your Esau? Has God been able to catch up with you? shut you in? hedge up your way? shut you up to faith? You may be a business man. Do you drive hard bargains? Is your dealing a bit shady? Do you excuse yourself that "business is business?" You may be a mother in the home. Are you like Rebecca? Does your husband, Isaac, have his pet, Esau? Of course you must outmanage him, so what can you do but manipulate for your Jacob! Maybe you only make matches for a son or daughter, unable to let God arrange these affairs. If anyone should inquire how you manage so well to get the "venison," like a pious fraud you will join Jacob saying, "The Lord thy God helped me." You may, like another mother, push your own children to the front: "Grant that these my two sons may sit, the one on Thy right hand, and the other on the left, in Thy kingdom" (Matt. 20:21). Through some such fleshly favouritism you cannot leave your itchy fingers off. What a grief to God are the many manipulating wives and mothers!

You may be a minister. If you are indeed like Jacob, you cannot say with Paul that you have "bidden farewell to the things of shame." You manage, manipulate, promote, pull wires; you know how to "put it over." Professor Denney says of some ministers: "They have recourse to arts which shame bids them conceal; they become diplomatists and strategists . . .; they manipulate their message . . . contrive to put something of their own between their hearers and the gospel . . . wish to conciliate a class or an interest; create an opinion in favour of their own learning, ability, or eloquence; enlist sympathy for a cause or an institution which is only accidentally connected with the gospel." In conversation once with "an Israelite indeed" I mentioned that certain leaders wished me to get together with them in order that we might frame our policy. To my remark this man of God replied, "Brother, these men have something to promote. You and I have nothing to promote but Christ."

May I ask again, Have you met your Esau? Has your desperation reached the point of despair? With Jacob you may recall the discipline of twenty years of trouble. Perhaps in the midst of some frightful illness or agony once you cried desperately to high heaven, reminding God of all His promises—yes, even making Him some promises, if only He would deliver you, deliver your wife, deliver your child. As a businessman you have known what it is to face the darkness of an uncertain tomorrow or the torture of an unavoidable turn in business. Whatever your lot now, or whatever your troubles may have been in the checkered past, have you ever met your Esau? and your God? Have you ever had God lay hold of you in the wee hours and reduce you until you had

> "Nothing left to do but fling
> Care aside and simply *cling?*"

No longer anxious about tomorrow's Esau, have you as a poor clinging cripple cried and prayed and prevailed?

Thank God for a host of such men who have become princes with God. They are in every walk of life, in business, in the pulpit, and in out-of-the-way places. Through means rough and rugged they have learned in all their ways to acknowledge Him that He might direct their paths. They have ceased from the efforts and strivings and manipulations of the flesh; their eyes have ceased to look upon *causes*, upon *conditions*, upon *consequences*, upon *supplies*. Their strength and wisdom now match that of Jehoshaphat, who cried in his despair, "O our God, . . . we have *no might* against this great company . . .; *neither know we* what to do: but our eyes are upon Thee" (II Chron. 20:12). To such souls God has entrusted the keys of the kingdom. They are heaven's own messengers, shut in with Christ, sealed, anointed, knighted. Needless to say, such spiritual giants are not produced by schools or councils or any other combination of men; but, as a modern soul-winner has observed, "by many prayers, and tears, and confessions of sin, and heart-searchings and humblings before God, and self-surrender, and a courageous sacrifice of every idol, and a bold and deathless and uncompromising and uncomplaining embracing of the Cross, and an eternal, unfaltering looking unto Jesus crucified."

Such men, moreover, will be the first to admit that they have never ceased to meet that which answers to Esau. Trials great and small have become their meat and drink; they have "unpacked"; they have found their home in seas of trouble.

> *One billow passed—another rolls to meet thee*
>   *Across thine onward track;*
> *On every side new trials seem to greet thee,*
>   *As if to turn thee back.*
> *Until thy soul, o'erwhelmed, in darkness sinking,*
>   *Can raise submissive eyes;*
> *Yield to His Will, and, while thy flesh is shrinking,*
>   *His purpose recognize.*
>
> —Selected

Hudson Taylor was one of those tested and trusted and triumphant souls. He had learned to trust God in many ways for *himself*, but the process of a deeper dying and rising again was yet to be his. Death was working in him that life might come to China. His great question was how to trust God to keep *others* and provide for them. He says, "I feared that in the midst of the dangers, difficulties, and trials which would necessarily be connected with such a work [and he knew how great these were], some who were comparatively inexperienced Christians might break down, and bitterly reproach me for having encouraged them to undertake an enterprise for which they were unequal." Thus Hudson Taylor could say with the Psalmist, "I am shut up, and I cannot come forth." So binding was the burden and the sense of blood-guiltiness which was borne in upon this already battle-scarred veteran that he was continually hearing these words: "If thou forbear to deliver them that are drawn unto death, and those that are ready to be slain; . . . . doth not He that pondereth the heart consider it? and He that keepeth thy soul, doth not He know it? and shall not He render to every man according to his works?" (Prov. 24:11,12). Thus the perishing tens of thousands passing away into Christless graves were dependent upon this man who was yet struggling to believe God for the supply of workers. He says:

> Perishing China so filled my heart and mind that there was no rest by day, and little sleep by night, until health broke

down. For two or three months the conflict was intense. I scarcely slept night or day for more than an hour at a time, and feared I should lose my reason. Yet I did not give in. To no one could I speak freely, not even to my dear wife. She doubtless saw that something was going on, but I felt I must refrain as long as possible from laying upon her a burden so crushing—these souls, and what eternity must mean for every one of them, and what the gospel might do, would do, for all who believe, if we would take it to them.

At this stage Hudson Taylor was invited by a friend to spend a few days at Brighton Beach. There upon the sands of the sea-shore the poor haunted and tried missionary met God face to face, and the China Inland Mission was born. In his own words he says:

On Sunday, June 25th, 1865, unable to bear the sight of a congregation of a thousand or more Christian people rejoicing in their own security, while millions were perishing for lack of knowledge, I wandered out on the sands alone, in great spiritual agony; and there the Lord conquered my unbelief, and I surrendered myself for this service. I told Him that all the responsibility as to issues and consequences must rest with Him, that as His servant, it was mine to obey and follow Him—His, to direct, to care for, and to guide me and those who might labour with me.

My remarks thus far may have seemed especially to the minister and missionary, and truly how my heart goes out to all such that they may find the keys not only to an abundant life but also to abounding fruitfulness. God, however, is no respecter of persons. The wind bloweth where it listeth, and revivals have often begun with laymen. It was to a fisherman that the keys were first given. Let us then turn aside and listen to the rather detailed account of a layman, James McConkey, who learned in the school of circumstances the blessedness of being shut up to faith.

In my early life I entered into a partnership with a friend in the wholesale ice business. Both of us were young men and we embarked all we had, and considerably more, in the business. As time passed on we met with disappointments. For two seasons in succession our ice was swept away by winter freshets. Things had come to a serious pass. It seemed very necessary that we should have ice in the winter of which I now speak. The weather became very cold. The ice formed and

grew thicker and thicker, until it was fit to gather. I remember the joy that came into our hearts one afternoon when there
came an order for thousands of tons of ice which would lift
us entirely out from our financial stress. Not long before God
had let me see the truth of committal. He showed me that it
was His will that I should commit my business to Him and
trust Him with it absolutely. As best I knew how I had
done so. I never dreamed what testing was coming. And so
I lay down that Saturday night in quietness. But, at midnight
there came an ominous sound — that of rain. By morning
it was pouring in torrents. I looked out upon the river from
my home upon the village hillside. Yellow streaks of water
were creeping over the ice. I knew what that meant. The
water was at flood stage. That condition had swept away our
ice twice before. By noon the storm was raging in all its
violence. By afternoon I had come into a great spiritual
crisis in my life.

That might seem strange—to come into a spiritual crisis
over a seemingly trivial matter. But I have learned this: A
matter may be seemingly trivial, but the crisis that turns upon
a small matter may be a profound and far-reaching one in
our lives. And so it was with me. For by mid-afternoon that
day I had come face to face with the tremendous fact that
down deep in my heart was a spirit of rebellion against God.
And that rebelliousness seemed to develop in a suggestion to
my heart like this:

"You gave all to God. You say you are going to trust God
with your business. This is the way He requites you. Your
business will be swept away, and tomorrow you will come into
a place of desperate financial stress." And I found my heart
growing bitter at the thought that God should take away my
business when I wanted it only for legitimate purposes.

Then another voice seemed to speak: "My child, did you
mean it when you said you would trust Me? Can you not
trust Me in the dark as well as in the light? Would I do anything, or suffer anything to come into your life which will
not work out good for you?" And then came that other voice:

"But it is hard. *Why* should not God spare your ice? *Why*
should He take your business when it is clean and honest and
you want to use it aright?" It was a very plausible sort of
voice, and for the moment I did not detect the serpent hiss
that was in it—in that word, "Why."

Still back and forth with ever-increasing intensity, waged
one of the greatest spiritual battles of my life. At the end of
two hours, by the grace of God, I was able to cry out, "Take

the business; take the ice; take everything; only give me the supreme blessing of an absolutely submitted will to Thee." And then came peace.

The storm was still beating upon the earth and upon my ice. But it did not seem to make any difference whether it rained or ceased. Then and there I discovered that the secret of anxious care is not in surroundings, but in the failure of allowing life and will to be wholly given up to Him amid all circumstances and surroundings.

That night I lay down to rest in perfect peace, but with the rain pouring torrents upon my field of ice, and with every prospect that my business would lie in wreck the next morning. But it did not. By midnight there came another sound, that of wind. By morning the bitterest blizzard of the year was upon us. By evening the mercury had fallen to the zero point. And in a few days we were harvesting the finest ice we ever had. God did not want my ice. But He did want my yielded will, and my absolute trust in Him, and when that was settled, He gave back the ice; He blessed the business; and He led me on and out, until He guided me from it entirely, into the place He had for me from the beginning—that of a teacher of His Word.

CHAPTER III

The Ways of God

A<small>N</small> O<small>FFICER</small> in the American Flying Corps says:

I was out over the ocean alone, and I saw in the distance, coming rapidly toward me, a storm that was blacker than midnight; the black inky clouds seemed to be coming on with lightning rapidity. I knew I could not reach shore ahead of the storm. I looked down to the ocean to see if I could go underneath it, and perhaps alight on the sea, but the ocean was already boiling with fury. Knowing that the only thing to do was to rise above it, I turned my frail craft straight up toward the sky, and I let her mount 1,000, 2,000, 2,500, 3,000, 3,500 feet, and then the storm struck me.

It was a hurricane and a cyclone and a typhoon all in one. The sky became as black as midnight. I never saw blackness like that. I could not see a thing. Rain came in torrents, the snow began to fly, the hail struck like bullets. I was 4,000 feet up in the air. I know there was only one thing to do, and that was to keep on climbing. So I climbed to 6,500 feet, and then, suddenly, I was swept out into sunlight and glory such as I never saw in this world before. The clouds were all below me. The sapphire sky was bending low above me in amazing splendour. It seemed the glory of another world, and I immediately began to repeat Scripture to myself, and, in the heavens above the clouds, I worshipped God. —*S. S. Times*

The way out for that man was up! Now let us see in Psalm 77 the secret of deliverance in despair, of triumph in trial. The Psalmist says there that the ways of God are two: "Thy way is in the sanctuary" and "Thy way is in the sea." As we study the Psalm, however, we see that these two, though different, are after all only one.

The context carries us back to Israel at the Red Sea. Hemmed in on all sides, the Israelites were so seized with terror and consternation that they wished themselves back in their bondage.

"Stand still, and see the salvation of the LORD," cried Moses. Here is God's first word to the believer who is caught in the storm of providential circumstances. On the one hand is an insurmountable mountain; on the other is the world's fortified frontier. Before him lies the impassable sea; behind him lie all the forces of hell in hot pursuit. Blocked to the right and blocked to the left, death facing them and death pursuing them — in this dilemma consider God's first command, "Stand still." Is not that exactly the last thing in the world that anyone can do at such a time? Yet God commands the impossible. It is a working principle of divine Wisdom to shut us up to faith. God's four walls of trial, circumstance, disappointment, and despair all serve to shut us up and keep us in ward until we are willing to take the way of faith. God's first task at such times is to kill the panic in His people, for to them how terrific is the word, "Be still and know that I am God," — "Stand still, and see the salvation of the LORD."

Spurgeon once summarized the various recourses of the flesh at such times, as follows:

> *Despair* whispers, "Lie down and die; give it all up."
> *Cowardice* says, "Retreat; go back to the worldling's way of action; you cannot play the Christian's part; it is too difficult. Relinquish your principles."
> *Precipitancy* cries, "Do something; stir yourself; to stand still and wait is sheer idleness."
> *Presumption* boasts, "If the sea be before you, march into it, and expect a miracle."
> But faith listens neither to Presumption nor to Despair nor to Cowardice nor to Precipitancy, but it hears God say, "Stand still," and immovable as a rock it stands.
>
> *—Streams in the Desert*

In these days of hurry and worry nothing is more difficult than to stand still; in fact it is impossible to the natural. Hemmed in on four sides, frightened flesh must hear God say, Neither by *flight* nor by *fight* will you be delivered. There is only one way out, and it is *not forward* through the sea, but *upward* through the heavens. In all God's ways His purpose is to draw us off and away from every earthly prop, to let all refuge fail us, to shut us up to faith. An old writer says:

Again and again does God rifle our hearts of their best and dearest treasures, desolate our homes of those who made it dear and precious, and dry up our earthly streams of joy, and blessing, and comfort—and why? Only to *force* us to seek the eternal Fountainhead, from whence alone all lasting and satisfying joy, and pleasure, and blessing flow.

Old John Vassar, that great soldier and soul-winner, said, "When I laid little Jimmie down out of my arms into the arms of the dear Saviour, this world and I forever parted company."

We have just heard Moses commanding the children of Israel to stand still and see the salvation of the Lord. The next moment we hear Moses crying heavenward. No, we do not exactly hear him, but we hear Heaven's response to his agony: "Wherefore criest thou unto Me?" Or, as the Chaldee explains it, "I have accepted thy prayer." In his utter desperation Moses has gotten the ear of God. This brings us to the first of God's ways, as found in v. 13 of Psalm 77. The poor Psalmist has cried unto God and has been heard. He bursts out as he comes forth again into heaven's sunlight, "Thy way, O God, is in the sanctuary." Out of the depths he lifted his voice, and in his despair has been heard.

God's first way is in the sanctuary, in the holiest of all, i.e., He gets us into His presence. "In Thy light we see light." "In Thy presence is fullness of joy." "The darkness and the light are both alike to Thee." When we get still, get into the sanctuary, get away from the felt and the tangible and the terrorizing — when we see things from Heaven's viewpoint — then what a difference! The situation itself may not have changed, but the fret, the worry, and the anxiety are all hushed. We become soul-conscious that He has the key, that He knows and sees it all.

Under different but difficult circumstances the same Psalmist confessed, "Until I went into the sanctuary of God I was baffled, beaten; my feet were almost gone; my steps had well nigh slipped." As he beheld the prosperity of the wicked, he saw

> *"Truth forever on the scaffold*
> *Wrong forever on the throne."*

At this he well nigh tumbled to his downfall, but when he got into the sanctuary of God's presence he saw the solution: *"Then under-*

stood I their end." From *Things New and Old* Spurgeon quotes this appropriate paragraph on Psalms 73 and 77:

> In Psalm 73 the soul looks *out*, and reasons on what it sees there, namely, successful wickedness and suffering righteousness. What is the conclusion? "I have cleansed my heart in vain." So much for looking about. In Psalm 77 the soul looks *in*, and reasons on what it finds there. What is the conclusion? "Hath God forgotten to be gracious?" So much for looking in. Where, then, should we look? Look *up*, straight up, and *believe* what you see there. What will be the conclusion? You will understand the *"end"* of man, and trace the *"way"* of God.

Note that when Asaph breaks forth (77:13), "Thy way, O God, is in the sanctuary," he follows with this instant burst of praise: "Who is so great a God as our God?" Once he gets into God's presence, darkness and difficulty vanish; for as soon as he sees that God is *good*, he can easily believe that God is *great* and that nothing is too hard for Him.

Many Christians miss the way just at this point. They have been reduced to great straits, so bound as with fetters of iron that they cry in unbelief, "I am shut up, and I cannot come forth." In their grief and bondage they pray for an increase of faith, convinced that if they could only believe in the *greatness* of God then they could trust Him to handle their difficulties. They therefore struggle for greater faith, but this does not bring them into God's presence. They somehow do not enter within the veil, for they proceed on the wrong basis. Most likely they have not credited God with being *good* in bringing them into this shut-up condition. How quickly they could believe in the greatness of God if only they would tell Him how good He has been in allowing them to fall into all this trouble. We repeat: When we believe that God is *good*, then we can believe that God is *great*. When we credit Him with goodness in having tried us, then faith immediately beholds God abundantly able to deliver us.

"Who is so great a God as our God? Thou art the God that doest wonders." Had he said, *Thou art the God that hast done wonders*, he would have seen God only as the "I Was" of former days and miracles; but he says, *Thou art the God that doest wonders,* i.e., Thou art the great "I AM" of my present difficulty.

God's way is in the sanctuary, and His way is also in the sea. Now it is time for God to give His orders: "Speak unto the children of Israel, that they go *forward*." *Heavenward* first, then *forward; upward,* then *onward.* God first walls us up to heaven that we may reach the throne in prayer; then, but not until then, can He give us His command to go forward. God's way is therefore first in the sanctuary, and then His way is in the sea. Both shut us up to faith.

"In the sanctuary" all is transparent, light, and clear. In God's presence darkness and difficulty dissolve like mist before the rising sun; every entangling problem is undone in heaven's own sunlight. There are no mistakes and no second causes as we mount high into that bright world above. "In the sea," on the other hand, every-thing is intricate and complex, insoluble and unfathomable — a veritable night of mystery. Such was Israel's night of mystery and darkness — a situation sunless, starless, and pathless. Yet it was right through the impassable Red Sea that God chose His highway for the redeemed. "Thus saith the LORD, which maketh a way in the sea, and a path in the mighty waters; . . . that hath made the depths of the sea a way for the ransomed to pass over" (Isa. 43:16, 51:10). No sooner had the Psalmist come through his own recent Red Sea than he saw in Israel's ancient experience a parable of the divine plan, a parable of purpose and wisdom. He saw that God must secure our confidence, and that He tries us in order to make us *trust* where we cannot *trace.* Without faith it is impossible to please Him. "Thy way is in the sea." While, there-fore, He has no pleasure in our agony and perplexity, He knows that it is in the trackless and traceless sea of trouble that we come to trust.

This is all easy to write about, perhaps easier to talk about; but it is only those who have faced the agony and have felt the pain of the unsolved that understand. When the natural man or the Chris-tian living in the power of the flesh faces the forces which shut him up to faith, he becomes dumb with grief and rage. It is said of a certain man of God that he wrote the following phrase in his journal just after he had received at the hands of his doctors the medical verdict which was to him the *arrest of death*:

On waking it seemed to me that I was staring into the future with startled eyes. Is it indeed to me that these things apply? Incessant and growing humiliation, my slavery becoming heavier, my circle of actions steadily narrower. What is hateful in my situation is that deliverance can never be hoped for and that one misery will succeed another in such a way as to leave me no breathing space, not even in the future, not even in hope. All possibilities are closed to me, one by one.

This poor imprisoned soul felt it difficult to escape from a dumb rage against all this. Amy Carmichael, writing in *Gold by Moonlight*, comments thus on this quotation: "It is indeed not only difficult, it is impossible." But God's ways have never ceased to be through the impassable and the impossible. Terror and rage must give place to trust. To be wrecked aright brings relief — relief instead of rage.

Wrecked outright on Jesus' breast;
Only *wrecked* souls thus can sing;
Little boats that hug the shore,
Fearing what the storm may bring,
Never find on Jesus' breast
All that wrecked souls mean by rest.

Wrecked outright. 'Twas purest gain:
Henceforth other craft can see
That the storm may be a boon,
That, however rough the sea,
God Himself doth watchful stand—
For the wreck is in His hand.
　　　　　　　　　　　—M. E. Barbour

Perhaps the first marvel to one unused to the sea is that he sees no path, no landmark, no sign of shore. No previous ship has left a trace in the watery deep; the sea is as pathless, as trackless, as traceless as though no ship had ever gone that way. Fresh from his recent Red Sea experience and swallowed up not with his former darkness but with the Divine Presence, the Psalmist cries out: "Thy way is in the sea, and Thy path in the great waters, and Thy footsteps are not known." This is just another way of saying, "O the

depth of the riches both of the wisdom and knowledge of God! how
unsearchable are His judgments, and His ways past finding out!"
(Rom. 11:33). Here our own wisdom is undone; it cannot plumb
such depths. Here faith becomes good common sense. The key
to all enigma, the chart for every pathless sea is with our Captain.
All clues and keys are His, and they will all our life remain in
higher, holier, hidden hands. From first to last, from infancy to
old age, let it be forever settled in my mind that

> Before me lies an unknown sea,
>   The past I leave behind;
> Strong waves are foaming at the prow,
>   The sail bends to the wind.
> Sometime, I know not when or how,
>   All things will be revealed,—
> And *until then* content am I
>   To sail with *orders sealed*.
>   —Selected

Inquiring and well-meaning persons often ask us how to set about
a new work, hoping that we can help them. How do we know what
to say? We can only relate a bit of God's doings and dealings with
us. The experiences of one may help another, but, after all, each
one must find his own way through. Too many of us would like
to see our way through before ever starting new enterprises, but
the way lies in the traceless sea. Ours has always been an untried
path. Let us quote, regarding the founding of the Prairie Bible
Institute, from our own booklet, *Hoping for Nothing*.

Whoever heard of such a thing? A Bible School in a
country district—what folly and presumption! To our knowledge it had never been done. It was a new thing and different.
The path was untried. It was all contrary to nature. We
naturally want to see where we are going, but the obedience of
faith never becomes real until it ventures forth where it cannot
understand. God must take us out beyond the apparent and
reasonable . . . Such is our experience. We have been thus
in days past, have been there often—are there now. As we
write there are perplexities and embarrassing circumstances.
Our path is still untried. Does the reader ask, What are your
plans? Do you still intend to build? How much larger will
you grow? How will the money be provided? Dear friends,
we do not know. We are still following.

How comforting in this connection has been the story of Pastor Louis Harms of Germany. To this man of God the path was utterly untried, but he had been strongly moved of God to encourage simple and spiritual men of low educational attainments, who felt a distinct call, to carry the gospel to the heathen. On account of this vision for the lost he was much spoken against. A. J. Gordon says:

> Thus he was straitly shut up to God, and thus was he brought into that travail of decision, which crisis he has so vividly described: I have knocked at men's doors and found them shut; and yet the plan was manifestly good and for the glory of God. What was to be done? *'Straightforward makes the best runner.'* I prayed fervently to the Lord, laid the matter in His hand, and as I rose up at midnight from my knees, I said in a voice that almost startled me in the quiet room, *'Forward now, in God's name!'* From that moment there never came the thought of doubt into my mind. (Quoted from *The Holy Spirit in Missions*)

At the end of thirty-one years this man of God had trained and sent forth in utterly untried ways no less than 350 missionaries. "The secret of the LORD is with them that fear Him."

Seldom do we feel more helpless and stupid than when someone asks advice about a new venture of faith. In fact we feel so ignorant that we seem to disappoint almost every inquiring soul. Helpful advice is almost impossible to give because each person must face his own Red Sea. God's way is first in the sanctuary, and then in the sea. Those who get forward into God's plan and path must first get upward, get above all low-hanging clouds of doubt and darkness and unbelief. In some instances we have felt that inquiring persons have yet to be shut up to Heaven, shut up to the pattern in the Mount, shut up to the faith which will afterward be revealed. The following lines may be helpful to all such souls:

> Have you come to the Red Sea place in your life,
>   Where, in spite of all you do,
> There is no way out, there is no way back,
>   There is no other way but through?
> Then wait on the Lord with a trust serene
>   Till the night of your fear is gone;
> He will send the wind, He will heap the floods,
>   When He says to your soul, "Go on."

And His hand will lead you through—clear through—
Ere the watery walls roll down;
No foe can reach you, no wave can touch
No mightiest sea can drown;
The tossing billows may rear their crests,
Their foam at your feet may break,
But over their bed you shall walk dry shod
In the path that your Lord will make.

—Annie Johnson Flint

I cannot close this chapter without a word of comfort for those who may be victims of the great accuser. How fiery are his darts! How strategic are his attacks! How plausible and agonizing are his "ifs" and "whys." *If* God loves you, *why* so many trials: *If* you were in His will, *why* that accident? Your child died. Why was the doctor late in coming? If the medicine had only arrived! Maybe the diet was not correct. Who has not felt the pain and torture of second causes? Is God's way in the sea? His path in the great waters? His footstep unknown? Yea, verily, but that is not the last word. Listen to the Psalmist's conclusion: "Thou leddest thy people like a flock." Though God's way is in the sea, He still leads and feeds His flock like a Shepherd; He still gathers the lambs with His arm, still carries them as of old in His bosom.

Her child had just died — only a bereft mother can understand. Of course the slanderer came, came with his "buts" and "whys," suggesting that God was cruel. The poor mother listened and wondered and froze. To her the heavens became brass. So binding was her grief that she could not even say, "I am shut up, and I cannot come forth." There was neither entrance nor exit to her life; she uttered no word and shed no tear. Out of very fear her husband called the doctor, who advised him to take her away as soon as possible, to travel, to give her a change — lest her mind snap. The advice was the best his prudence could offer.

The travels of these two took them to the Holy Land, where they visited the ancient sights and looked on sacred scenes. They roamed the Judaean hills and relived Bible days, seeking to forget their grief. They were especially interested in the shepherds. One day their attention was drawn to a faithful shepherd tending his flock. He sought to persuade an old mother sheep to cross the stream, but she held back, set herself, and stubbornly tossed her head, first to the right and then to the left. Stiffly she refused to go over. At length the shepherd, with a wisdom proven and true and tender, took her little lamb on his shoulders and himself waded the stream. Of course the old mother sheep took it all in. When she saw her little one on the other side, with a toss or two of her head she plunged into the water and crossed to the other bank.

Another mother seated on the hillside also took it all in, and when she saw that old stubborn sheep cease tossing her head, saw her plunge into the water, and saw her follow to the shore beyond, she burst into a flood of tears — the first she had shed since she had been shut up. Until then she had been shut up, not to faith, but only in her grief. Now, it was to the faith which was so blessedly revealed. The heavens opened, and the sea — and of course she recovered. The Heavenly Physician and Shepherd had her case in hand.

Such are the ways of God, such is the way of faith, and such is the way to happiness and holiness and heaven. As for God, His way is perfect.

> *God moves in a mysterious way,*
> *His wonders to perform:*
> *He plants His footsteps in the sea,*
> *And rides upon the storm.*
>
> —Cowper

CHAPTER IV

Sabbath of the Soul

SOUL-REST — what a sweet word. God's saints long for rest of soul, for the blessed rest of faith. In Hebrews 3:7-4:13 the writer warns the Hebrew believers not to come short of the Promised Rest. In dealing with his subject, he speaks successively of the Rest of Canaan, the Rest of God, and then finally the blessed Rest that remaineth for the children of God. This last Rest he terms "a Sabbath Rest." As such it has been called "the Sabbath of the soul."

Before dwelling upon this portion, however, we would turn to the Saviour's sublime offer of rest as it is recorded in Matt. 11:28-30.

> Come unto Me, all ye that labour and are heavy laden, and I will give you rest.
> Take My yoke upon you, and learn of Me; for I am meek and lowly in heart: and ye shall find rest unto your souls.
> For My yoke is easy, and My burden is light.

Christ's incomparable invitation to those toiling under the burden and bondage of sin is *"Come* unto Me." Here Christ promises rest from sin's penalty and condemnation, a rest we might speak of as *initial* rest from the guilt and bondage of sin. Then Jesus added another significant phrase which has special application to those who have already come and have experienced initial rest: "Take My yoke upon you, and learn of Me; for I am meek and lowly in heart: and ye shall find rest unto your souls. For My yoke is easy, and My burden is light." Here is suggested a two-fold rest, as many commentators note — the one from sin's penalty, the other from sin's power; the one the rest of salvation, the other the rest of consecration; the one bringing us out of bondage, the other bringing us into Canaan rest; the one giving us peace with God, the other giving us the peace of God. The first aspect of rest, the rest of *com-*

ing, is to be followed by that deeper rest, the rest of *taking* and *learning*.

In this passage the Saviour furnishes a link between the initial rest of conscience and the soul-rest promised in the last part of His invitation, therein disclosing the precious secret of entering into the Sabbath of the soul. This link Jesus calls My yoke, My burden. It is one thing for us to experience the initial joy of our salvation, to enjoy the sweetness of God's forgiveness and the blessedness of deliverance from bondage, yet all the while to think little of the will of God — too blissfully happy to consider what God expects of us. At this stage we do not look upon the Christian life as a life of doing the *will* of our Father which is in heaven. While, therefore, it is one thing to be brought out of Egyptian bondage, it is quite another to be brought into the land of our inheritance, into the land of abiding rest and obedience. In rehearsing God's dealings with Israel Moses declared, "He brought us out from thence (Egypt), that He might bring us in, to give us the land which He sware unto our fathers" (Deut. 6:23). While Israel as a whole experienced the initial rest of deliverance, we read that the majority of those who were brought out of Egypt failed to enter into their inheritance. Similarly, God has brought us *out* that He might bring us *in;* and, like Israel of old, the initial rest of deliverance we experience, but the promised abiding rest most saints know little about. When they hear Paul saying, "We which have believed do enter into rest," they sigh and wish they could believe so as to enter into rest.

As mentioned above, Jesus furnishes us the clue to that abiding rest in the words, "Take My yoke upon you and learn of Me." A brother minister, commenting once upon this passage, mentioned that it requires more than one figure in Scripture to show forth a truth, for which reason Scripture uses many figurative conceptions. For example, believers are likened to living stones, to branches, and often to sheep. We seem to like this last figure especially, because we need tending and attention, and we love to think of the tenderness and care and laid-down life of the Great Shepherd. Christ also uses many figures in speaking of Himself; for example, He likens Himself to bread, to a vine, to a door, and to a shepherd, as we have just noted. In Matt. 11:28-30, He is apparently likening

Himself to the burden-bearing ox under the master's yoke when He speaks of "My yoke" (the yoke I wear) and "My burden" (the burden I bear).

While it may be very beautiful to consider the yoking of two oxen together, the one bearing the heavy end of the yoke and the other the light, we are inclined to believe that the Saviour was not here telling us as disciples to take the other end of the yoke, but to take His yoke — "Take *My* yoke." And what was His yoke? It was to do the Father's will. His delightful yoke and burden were the doing of God's will: "My meat is to do the will of Him that sent Me, and to accomplish His work" (John 4:34, R.V.).

Why is it then that most Christians are forever tossed and feverish and restless? Why are they forever in an agonized and unsettled state of soul? The answer is just this — they are like bullocks unbroken and unaccustomed to the yoke, never having learned the meaning of "It is good for a man that he bear the yoke in his youth" (Lam. 3:27). In the very "youth" of their Christian experience they should have been led to bow their necks in full surrender to Christ's "yoke"; they should have been harnessed, broken, and yoked to service. But they prefer to be sheep, loving to be fed and gently led. What is more, many leaders verily believe that Christians must be fed for a long time before they can expect to serve. Ere long they become restless, and an easy prey to various slants and twists of prophecy or even of deeper-life teaching. They long for better things, for the fruits of Canaan, but they do not know how to enter into rest. They are not furnished as they should be with this blessed link of the Saviour's yoke; they have not been led to embrace the whole will of God in a once-for-all and delightful surrender. To all such Christ's service seems burdensome; they believe His yoke is hard, His burden heavy. They think it is hard work to please God, and speak of cross-bearing with a deep sigh. These souls need to be taught not only to sing, "His yoke is easy, His burden is light," but to believe that it is so.

For a moment let us observe the connection between the Cross and the will of God. When Jesus came into the world He said, "Lo, I come to do Thy will, O my God." His lifelong obedience was climaxed when He became "obedient even unto death." At the

Cross He embraced the Father's yoke in its most supreme expression, saying, "Not My will, but Thine, be done." He had come to put an end to sin. And what is the essence of sin? "The whole evil and ruin of sin is that man turned from God's will to do his own. The redemption of Christ had no reason, no object, and no possibility of success except in restoring man *to do God's will.* It was for this Jesus died. He gave up His own will; He gave His life, rather than do His own will" (Andrew Murray). As sinners we come, first of all, believing on Christ crucified — coming for initial rest from sin's condemnation — but also embracing Him in the fellowship of His selfless and laid-down life. Now the Cross, when embraced by the believer, is heavy only to the life of nature, to the life of the flesh, to life outside the will of God. The Cross is that on which nature dies; it kills off that to which it seems heavy. Christ's yoke hard? His burden heavy? Never! The burden of obedience to God's will, the burden of doing His commandments, *is not heavy — "His commandments are not grievous."* Samuel Rutherford said, "Christ's Cross is the sweetest burden that ever I bare; it is such a burden as wings are to a bird, or sails to a ship, to carry me forward to my harbour."

As long as we believe that Christ's yoke is hard and His burden heavy, we will be as restless as Sabbathless Satan. The Saviour, however, says that if we would find our soul's true rest we must, after *coming* to Him, *take from* Him His own yoke and enter into "His rest." From the bottom of our hearts we must pray the Saviour's own prayer to His Father, "Lo, I come to do Thy will, O My God." That yoke we must take from Him; that will we must embrace. In spite of all our feelings and appearances, and contrary to all self-interests, we must believe that the land of our inheritance, the land of rest and blessing, is a good and acceptable and perfect abiding place. Few of us really do believe that serving God can be a delight; we cannot bring ourselves to "serve the Lord with gladness." Somehow we refuse to link up the land of perfect rest with the place of complete obedience, yet these two are one. The will of God, heartily and wholly embraced, becomes to us good and acceptable and perfect — a delightsome land" (Mal. 3:12). The Saviour furnishes us with the link between deliverance from bondage and entrance into Canaan when He says, My yoke — in other words, if Canaan is to become your place of rest, it must be entered as the land of complete obedience. To Israel of old it was the same: "If ye be willing and obedient, ye shall eat the good of the land."

A word of warning is in order here. After pointing out the wicked refusal of the Israelites at Kadesh-Barnea to enter into Canaan, the writer to the Hebrews warns all New Testament believers: "Let us labour therefore to enter into that rest, lest any man fall after the same example of *unbelief*" (Heb. 4:11). Notice that "unbelief" is translated in the margin "disobedience." Now faith is no mere beautiful attitude of mind, and unbelief is no mere mental attitude, no little failure, no slight weakness. It is a wicked principle of heart, a denial of divine ownership, a making of God a liar. It provokes the most High. "I sware in My wrath, They shall not enter into My rest" is God's reaction to such willful and wanton wickedness. To refuse to embrace God's good will and enter into His blessed land of obedience is nothing short of high-handed rebellion and anarchy. Dare we vainly think that it is mere option with us whether or not we embrace the will of God? Can we pick and choose as we like? Are we free to accept or reject? True, we must choose, but we have no option but to choose the best and to submit to the will of God. In that will is rest — complete rest, rest from wandering, God's own rest. In God's will we find God's rest. To refuse to enter into that rest is to trifle with unbelief, i.e., disobedience. We are shut up to faith. The warning is: "Take heed, brethren, lest there be in any of you an evil heart of unbelief, in departing from the living God" (Heb. 3:12).

Once we have embraced the divine will, *taken* Christ's yoke, then there follows the lifelong learning. "*Learn* of Me; for I am meek and lowly in heart: and ye shall find rest unto your souls." It is one thing to *become* obedient under Christ's yoke; it is another thing to "*learn* obedience." To *become* is to begin; to *learn* is to continue. To enter into rest is one thing; to abide in Christ is another. It is, therefore, one thing to become bullocks with our necks beneath the yoke; it is a lifelong experience to wear the yoke, to bear the burden, i.e., to learn obedience by the things which we suffer. Christ became obedient, and then all His life "He learned obedience." We, too, will learn obedience only in the way He learned it, by having our own wills crossed. When we suffer — and that is the last thing we ever want — then and only then is our obedience tested. Let us therefore *learn* from Him. We shall suffer many things before we become like our Master, "meek and lowly in heart," but such is the place of abiding rest.

From this point our aim is to bring definite help to those sincere saints who need encouragement. There are many servants of the Lord who, as far as they know, are in the center of God's will, but who nevertheless know little of the "Sabbath of the soul." They are tireless in their fidelity to the tasks committed to them; they are true to their Master, true to His cause, true to His people. No one would question their consecration and zeal. One would never think of classing them with the lazy and indolent souls who imagine resting in the Lord as a kind of passive and peaceful self-enjoyment, nor with those who sit down and enjoy the mystic musings of a select few. Regarding this last class, a word of explanation and warning may be helpful. Many little groups are forming over the country who are separatists in outlook, who live and think within their own little "holier-than-thou" clique. They cannot associate even with a good fundamental and aggressive ministry. Beware of such, for their fellowship is an end in itself. They focus within their own circle, imagining they have a spiritual paradise unknown to others. Their slogan is, We have the message; yet they know little of the aggressive warfare of winning the lost, for they do not focus in that direction. Beware of groupings and groups that wall you off from other fellowships and attach you exclusively to themselves in their "deeper life" or other special teachings.

We here seek to help those who desire the widest possible service and who want to work most effectually for their Lord and Redeemer. Many of these do not know how to distinguish between work done in the energy of the flesh and that done in the power of the Spirit. Are you, my reader, in that class? Have you begun to awaken to the shallowness, the hollowness, the deadness, of your own mixed and double-minded life? You long to know how you may be delivered from doing dead works that you may serve the living God. It is still a great mystery to you how to be at rest in the

midst of work, how to say, "I laboured more abundantly than they
all: yet not I, but the grace of God which was with me." You are
among the many who find themselves just where that aggressive
missionary leader, A. B. Simpson, found himself before he could
write the great hymn entitled, "Himself," in which he says,

> *Once it was my working,*
> *His it hence shall be;*
> *Once I tried to use Him,*
> *Now He uses me.*

Many souls can bear tearful witness to months and years of at-
tempting to work *for* God, but at length they sensed that self was the
center of all their doings. Self was on the throne and would not
abdicate; self worked for God and then stole the glory, yea, vaunted
itself in God's very presence. The stink of a foul and fleshly self-
life contaminated all their best efforts. After multiplied and painful failures, such souls have been driven to despair of and to cease
from their own works. They then enter into soul-rest, a rest hitherto
unknown to them. There they find the new power for work through
letting God work in them both to will and to do of His good pleasure.

When we were saved, we were saved from hell in an instant. It
seems to take longer, however, for us as saints to be saved from ourselves, to be emancipated from our own self-righteousness—in a
word, to unlearn self. In this mixed and muddled condition, where
self obtrudes its ugly head into every well-meant effort, we fight
like Trojans to bring ourselves into a state of quiet and restful
faith. Self has hard work indeed to cast out self! We have in
mind a young man, energetically consecrated to God, who stren-
uously sought to get over the pride of his own works. He refused
to sing in public, refrained from taking part in anything that gave
him prominence, and declined every service that might feed or fos-
ter his vainglory. His motive may have been right, but his method
was hopeless. His sanctimoniousness did not forward his sanctification. He might as well have put vermin in his undergarments
to make him humble, as did a certain Dean of Canterbury in days
gone by. Oh, the myriad forms of legalistic self-improvement re-
sorted to in order to obtain rest and victory in personal experience!
Concerning all such attempts to bring ourselves into the blessed

rest, the rest that can come only through simple faith, an old writer says:

> Not penal sufferings, not mortifications of any sort, not anything that we have, not grace already received, not anything we are or can be, not death or purgatory, no, not the purgatory of all our doings and sufferings and strivings put together [brings rest from sin]. No, no! Christ is the procuring, meritorious Cause of all our salvation . . . *Faith is the only condition and shares in the Omnipotence it dares to trust.*

The many means contrived by the flesh to win the way into rest only increase the power of our conceited Phariseeism; they only trim the myriad branches of the fleshly life of nature, thereby throwing the full strength back into the trunk of self and leaving the taproot of the ego yet more firmly rooted in its own self-righteousness. If you are one of those sincere souls filled with earnest strivings and endless strugglings, then truly yours is a wilderness wandering. You are ceaseless in your efforts, and restless—forever going without arriving. Your experience has been well described by Saphir as "motion without progress, journey without end, toil without reward, question without answer."

Though you may have awakened to your deep need of rest and victory, you may not yet be prepared to cease from your own works. Your fleshly resolutions may take a turn in another direction, namely, that of grasping truth to give you rest. In the energy of the natural mind you will attempt to lay hold of *light* which may not have become *life*. In time you may find yourself among those who are "ever learning, but never able to come to the knowledge of the truth." Finally, your mental gyrations, added to your fleshly devotions and dry-as-dust doings, continue to carry you into a still further circle of confusion. The vital trouble may be defined as simply an unwillingness yet to enter into God's rest, a rest abundantly provided "from the foundation of the world" (Heb. 4:3 and Rev. 13:8). The fact is, my friend, that the entire fabric of your inner self-life has not yet been broken down. The mystery of the *inward* as well as the *outward* cross you do not understand. It is very true that we are not to crucify ourselves, for God did that work when He crucified us "together with Christ"; but the power of

Christ's almighty death, generated and released at Calvary, must make a death-dealing impact on your old self-life. God dare not let you rest satisfied in the flesh, for the whole of your natural life is a sworn enemy of faith. Therefore, before you can trust God fully and enter into His rest, you must come to an end of all your filthy self-righteousness, all fleshly resolution, and all smug self-satisfaction. You may indeed find all past peace and joy and hope take wings and fly away. Certainly you must find that all your own righteousnesses are as filthy rags and that your own strength of will and purpose is only so much opposition to God. Not until you have been thus smitten and peeled within and without and thereby brought to deplore and abhor yourself, will you be ready to believe fully in your Joshua to lead you into "the Sabbath Rest of the Soul." What a wonderful day of emancipation when you come to the end of your own deadly doings and find yourself shut up to Christ and His resurrection rest! Whereas you had wailed in a veritable paroxysm of soul, "Oh that I had wings like a dove! for then would I fly away, and be at rest," you now find your rest is near at hand, nearer than breathing, closer than hands and feet. You find your all "in Christ," and *there* you are. The boat of your life which, with all your toiling and rowing had been brought no nearer its haven of rest, has immediately arrived at the land. In His immediate presence with its fullness of joy there is "no absence, no distance, no departure, no separation."

CHAPTER V

Sabbath of the Soul (continued)

ARE You, my reader, still wondering whether you can ever cease from your own doings and inner strivings and be free from the dominion of self? Are you asking, Is there deliverance for me? Yes, my friend, there is deliverance, and it is found through our identification with Christ. As Christians we have already been united to Christ in His death and resurrection. "Reckon ye also yourselves to be dead unto sin, but alive unto God in Jesus Christ (Rom. 6:11, R.V.). Believe that the death of Christ in all its omnipotent power can cut you off not only from all past failure but also from the ceaseless and foul strivings of self. In the power of Christ's death, cease from your own dead works. In a certain sense this can be fulfilled in you: "Blessed are the dead which die in the Lord . . . Yea, saith the Spirit, that they may rest from their labours" (Rev. 14:13). God will make crystal clear to you the difference between your own self-efforts and the working of Christ in you "both to will and to do of His good pleasure." Then you will be able to say with Paul, "I labour, striving according to His working, who worketh in me with might" (lit. "agonizing according to His energy who energizes in me with might").

The writer to the Hebrews says concerning this Sabbath rest, the rest here and now to be entered into by the people of God, "He that is entered into His [God's] rest, he also hath ceased from his own works, as God did from His." Just as God finished His six days of creative work and entered into His Sabbath rest, so must the believer cease from his own works to rest in the finished work of Christ. Herein we discovered the divine meaning of the Sabbath incorporated into Israel's national life. This portion of Hebrews cannot, therefore, be studied intelligently apart from the meaning of the Sabbath as set forth in Ex. 31:12-17.

The LORD spake unto Moses, saying,

Speak thou also unto the children of Israel, saying, Verily my sabbaths ye shall keep: for it is a sign between Me and you throughout your generations; that ye may know that I am the LORD *that doth sanctify you.*

Ye shall keep the sabbath therefore; for it is holy unto you: every one that defileth it shall surely be put to death: for whosoever doeth any work therein, that soul shall be cut off from among his people.

Six days may work be done; but in the seventh is the sabbath of rest, holy [Heb. holiness] to the LORD: whosoever doeth any work in the sabbath day, he shall surely be put to death.

In this passage two things stand out, namely, *significance* and *severity.* The significance appears in v. 13 in the phrase, "that ye may know that I am the LORD that doth sanctify you." In their observance of the Sabbath, the Israelites would be distinguished from other nations as sanctified, separated unto the Lord, a people peculiarly His own possession. Had God Himself entered into rest after His work of creation? He would have His own enter with Him into "His rest." When the Spirit of God, speaking in Hebrews 4, says, "His rest," "My rest," and "God rested," He is designating that divine rest into which we as believers enter, and of which we partake when we enter into the Sabbath of the soul.

Let us examine those things that made the Sabbath so significant to Israel. It might be observed at the outset that this significance was largely lost to the carnal masses of the nation, for then as now only the little flock entered into its true meaning. When any spiritual Israelite, however, came into the Sabbath, he could sense that he was entering into God's own rest, a provision all divine and antedating "the foundation of the world" in the "Lamb slain." As God had ceased from "His own works," so did the Israelite in whom was no guile. This Sabbath he was to keep, the Lord said, "that ye may know that I am the LORD that doth sanctify you." The Sabbath of "God's rest" set forth their sanctification "in the LORD." Such Israelites learned thereby to "rest in the LORD." It was as though the Lord had said to them: In entering "My rest," you may know that in Me you have been severed from all your own works, cut off from all your own ways, and so restfully separated unto Myself that you may turn away "from doing thy pleasure on My holy day; and call the sabbath a delight, the holy of the Lord, honourable; and shalt honour Him, not doing thine own ways, nor finding thine own pleasure, nor speaking thine own words: Then shalt thou delight thyself in the Lord" (Isa. 58:13,14).

These considerations lend understanding and deepest spiritual meaning to the severity of the warnings coupled herewith regarding the defiling of the Sabbath. A person doing any work on the Sabbath would "surely be put to death . . . cut off from among the people." By dragging their labours into "His rest," Israel would be denying "the Lord that doth sanctify," denying Him who had redeemed them to be all His, denying Him, their King and Redeemer and Sanctifier. If they would thus defile and dishonour Him in His "finished work," they could expect nothing short of death; the man who so much as gathered his firewood on the Sabbath was stoned to death. Likewise all labour, all deadly doings of the flesh, must be shut out of the God-given Sabbath of the soul. In what a fearful light does this severity set off the abomination with which God views all the fleshly doings which spring from the foul root of our own self-righteousness! Nothing is more defiling to the Sabbath of the soul.

How beautifully this harmonizes with our entrance into "His rest" in this present age, a rest that cannot be entered with any of our own works! It is only through the death and resurrection of Christ that we may enter into God's rest; to presume to enter the Sabbath of the soul otherwise is to be "hung up" at once and consigned to the Cross. The Crucified is made unto us sanctification, and anything short of resting in Him is to be found accursed. The doorway of entrance into Him is only through Calvary. At the Cross we find ourselves severed forever from all our own works, and separated entirely unto Him. In vain can we drag into His glorious rest anything of the old creation. Calvary terminates the heaving seas of the old life. Heaven's death-stroke at Golgotha answers precisely to the severity attached to the old Sabbath. Neither the Israelites nor we can enter God's rest with anything that defileth.

The symbolic meaning of circumcision sets forth the same significance and severity in our entering into the Sabbath of the soul. Circumcision was on the eighth day, a reminder of the first day of the week, the Lord's Day. How beautifully, then, the Lord's Day of our dispensation symbolizes the same Sabbatical rest as was symbolized by the seventh day Sabbath of old. This distinction needs to be observed. Paul tells the Colossians that the Sabbath, among other observances, was a shadow of things to come, "but the body is of Christ." As one travels toward the sunrising, he is in the shadow of that body which is between him and the dawn. Once he arrives at "the body," the shadow is no more; where the shadow leaves off, the body is found. We have found Him; we have believed *into* Him; we are alive in Him, "joined unto the Lord in one Spirit." If any man be "in Christ" he is a new creature. Old things have passed away; behold, all things have become new. Quickened from the dead, we are alive in Him.

Few of us realize, however, the implications of our life-union with Christ. Union with the Risen One is a glorious truth, but what a severing it involved! In order to cut us away from our old ruined race—"our old man was crucified together with Him"— Christ was Himself cut off out of the land of the living. There He severed our tie with the past, severed us from sin, severed us from self. By the "immeasurable depths of Calvary's annihilations" (Huegel) He condemned to death and crucified "the flesh with its affections and lusts." By His divine dying He brought us to an ignominious undoing. Our position in Him is nothing short of "dead indeed unto sin."

Let the reader see how clean-cut and complete is his break with the past. "In whom also ye are circumcised with the circumcision made without hands, in putting off the body of the sins of the flesh *by the circumcision of Christ*" (Col. 2:11). What does circumcision mean but the excision of the flesh, the cutting off of the old, our old man crucified together with Him. As sons of the flesh we were circumcised, crucified, shorn of the old life; our old fleshly self-life, so restless and foul and fretful, was cut off, nailed to the Cross, severed completely and forever. The flesh profiteth nothing; it is fit for nothing but the tomb. How can this foul protrusion ever inherit with the Spirit? It cannot, dare not, "shall not be heir" with our heavenly Isaac. Ishmael must go out and stay out. What saith the Scripture? Cast him out. Remember, dear fellow believer, that you cannot rest except in a realized union with Christ risen. As He entered that risen life only through death, so must you. Would you share with Him in glory? Come, then, and share His tomb. You came into Christ only through His Cross, through a divine dying with Him. There you left the old life—the restlessness, the fuss, the fret, and the fuming. Do you consent to such a break with the past, such a severing from the flesh, such a cutting off from the old self-life? Such consent is indispensable to vital faith.

We which have believed do enter into rest. We are the circumcision which worship God in the Spirit and rejoice in Christ Jesus and have no confidence in the flesh. This is rest indeed. Oh to believe, to enter in, to rejoice with joy unspeakable and full of glory! "If thou canst believe, all things are possible to him that believeth."

We which have believed do enter into rest. In summary, let us see again the three simple conditions.

1. *Enter in by faith.* This utterly simple condition implies a despairing heart and an open hand to take God's rest as your very own.

2. *Enter as you are.* Drag none of your filthy works into God's Sabbath rest. Come unimproved or you will never enter. If rest is by faith, you must enter it as you are, ceasing from your own works.

3. *Enter today.* The Holy Ghost says, *"Today."* If rest is *by faith* and you enter *as you are,* then rest may be yours here and now. This blessed threefold cord of faith cannot be broken. Therefore begin today to experience the Sabbath of the soul.

We cannot better illustrate all that has been said than by recording in part J. Hudson Taylor's experience confirming this rest that may become ours today. This testimony was written from China in a letter to his sister in 1869.

As to work—mine was never so plentiful, so responsible, or so difficult, but the weight and strain are all *gone*. The last month or more has been, perhaps, the happiest of my life, and I long to tell you a little of what the Lord has done for my soul. I do not know how far I may be able to make myself intelligible about it, for there is nothing new or strange or wonderful—and yet, all is new! . . .

Perhaps I may make myself more clear if I go back a little. My mind has been greatly exercised for six or eight months past, feeling the need, personally and for our Mission, of more holiness, life, power in our souls. But personal need stood first and was the greatest. I felt the ingratitude, the danger, the sin of not living nearer to God. I prayed, agonized, fasted, strove, made resolutions, read the Word more diligently, sought more time for meditation—but all without avail. Every day, almost every hour, the consciousness of sin oppressed me.

I knew that if only I could abide in Christ all would be well, but I could not. I would begin the day with prayer, determined not to take my eye off Him for a moment, but pressure of duties, sometimes very trying, and constant interruptions apt to be so wearing, caused me to forget Him. Then one's nerves get so fretted in this climate that temptations to irritability, hard thoughts, and sometimes unkind words are all the more difficult to control. Each day brought its register of sin and failure, of lack of power. To will was indeed "present with me," but how to perform I found not.

Then came the question, Is there no rescue? Must it be thus to the end—constant conflict, and too often defeat? Instead of growing stronger, I seemed to be getting weaker and to have less power against sin; and no wonder, for faith and even hope were getting low. I hated myself, I hated my sin, yet gained no strength against it. I felt I *was* a child of God. His Spirit in my heart would cry, in spite of all, "Abba, Father." But to rise to my privileges as a child, I was utterly powerless.

All the time I felt assured that there was in Christ all I needed, but the practical question was—how to get it *out*. I knew full well that there was in the root, the stem, abundant fatness, but how to get it into my puny little branch was the question. As gradually light dawned, I saw that faith was the only requisite—was the hand to lay hold on His fullness and make it mine. But I had not this faith.

I strove for faith, but it would not come; I tried to exercise it, but in vain. Seeing more and more the wondrous supply of grace laid up in Jesus, the fullness of our precious Saviour, my guilt and helplessness seemed to increase. Sins committed appeared but as trifles compared with the sin of unbelief which was their cause, which could not or would not take God at His word, but rather made Him a liar! Unbelief was, I felt, *the* damning sin of the world; yet I indulged in it. I prayed for faith, but it came not. What was I to do?

When my agony of soul was at its height, a sentence in a letter was used to remove the scales from my eyes, and the Spirit of God revealed to me the truth of our *oneness with Jesus* as I had never known it before: "But how to get faith strengthened? Not by striving after faith, but by resting on the Faithful One."

As I read, I saw it all! Ah, *there* is rest! I thought. I have striven in vain to rest in Him. I'll strive no more. For has not *He* promised to abide with *me*—never to leave me, never to fail me?

CHAPTER VI

Death-Resurrection Process

"THERE WAS A DAY when I died, *utterly died*, died to George Mueller, his opinions, preferences, tastes, and will—died to the world, its approval or censure—died to the approval or blame even of my brethren and friends—and since then I have studied only to show myself approved unto God." Thus answered George Mueller when asked for the secret of his successful service.

While it is never wise to set up any personal experience as a pattern for others, there is back of all successful spiritual service that which answers in some practical way to the above—namely, a surrender, a voluntary consent to the frightful and blessed implications of the Cross. With many Christians this surrender is a definite crisis in their Christian experience. Countless Christians, on the other hand evade this concrete, crisis-identification with Christ in death and resurrection, fearing that it savours of fanaticism; and therefore prefer to continue in a kind of indefinite and ineffective Christian life. Have they not been saved out of Egypt? To them that is the one all-important thing. As to their Christian inheritance they remain lazy, hazy, and indefinite—living a life of little fruit and less fight. While they feel that they would like to enjoy an abundant life, they consider the terms too severe, and therefore oppose any crisis. They refuse to consent to their crucifixion with Christ.

The hosts of Israel were encamped just outside Canaan on Jordan's eastern shore. The divine command was, "Now therefore arise, go over this Jordan"— notwithstanding the Jordan at that time of the year "overfloweth all his banks." Nevertheless Joshua had been told, "Thou shalt cause them to inherit the land," and plainly enough the pathway into Canaan, into the land of promised rest and victory, lay through Jordan's swollen waters. Obedient to

60

Joshua's command, Israel's officers informed the people, "Within three days ye shall pass over this Jordan, to go in to possess the land, which the LORD your God giveth you to possess it" (Josh. 1:11).

What is meant by this three-day pause? It is evidently the period of death and resurrection. The Lord Jesus said, "As Jonah was three days and three nights in the belly of the sea-monster (R.V., marg.), so shall the Son of man be three days and three nights in the heart of the earth." Even in the Old Testament we read, "On the third day He will raise us up, and we shall live before Him" (Hosea 6:2). It was beautifully fitting, therefore, that a three-day pause should precede Israel's passing through Jordan as symbolic of the death-road over into resurrection territory. Recall that such were Jordan's floods at this season that, ever after, Israel's overwhelming troubles were likened to "the swellings of Jordan." During these three days of pause Israel could contemplate the very deliberate and definite step she was to take into and through these flooding waters. Certainly the very consideration served to shrivel the energies of the flesh and prepared them for this definite act of faith. How well they knew that only through these fordless and flooding depths could they enter into their inheritance. Between them and the promised land came burial and resurrection. The gateway to their goal lay through nothing short of a grave.

The pathway into the Christian's Canaan is marked out through death and resurrection. "Know ye not, that so many of us as were baptized into Jesus Christ were baptized into His death? Therefore we are buried with Him by baptism into death: that like as Christ was raised up from the dead by the glory of the Father, even so we also should walk in newness of life" (Rom. 6:3,4). Christ's pathway back to glory could have been by no other way than through death and resurrection. Neither can mine, for the servant is not above his Lord. Certainly He has brought me *out* of Egypt that He might bring me *into* the land, the land of the abundant and blessed life, the land of overflowing fruitfulness. Into this land He Himself has led the way, and He has opened it up for me in His death. If I have Christ at all I must have Him in His death

and resurrection. Did He die for me? Then I died with Him.
One died for all—all died.

As those redeemed from Egypt we are bidden to cross over into
Canaan. Our heavenly Joshua is commissioned, "Thou shalt cause
them to inherit the land." Between us and our inheritance, however, lies death and resurrection. Are we nevertheless determined
not to "come short" of our promised possession? Would we inherit
with Him? We shall indeed be with Him in the likeness of His
resurrection, *if* we have been planted together in the likeness of
His death. George Mueller must have had something like this in
mind when he said, "There was a day when I died, *utterly died*,"
etc. Thereby he entered into the land of complete obedience, dying
to every consideration of the world behind him, before him, and
around him.

Come again to Jordan's eastern bank, and there behold Israel's
priests as they dip their feet into Jordan's floods. The ark of the
Lord goes with them. How majestic is the statement, "Behold, the
ark of the covenant of the Lord of all the earth passeth over before you into Jordan." When He puts forth His own He goeth
before. The ark was, of course, a type of Christ, and symbolic of
that kingly Presence in their midst. Above the ark was the mercy-
seat. "There," He said, "I will meet with thee." Identified with
Him, God's people entered into the very depths and stood with their
Lord in the midst of the fleeing waters. In meditation upon that
marvel and miracle, the Psalmist cried, "What ailed thee, O thou
Jordan?" Jointly-buried with their Lord down in Jordan Israel
learned afresh the meaning of Moses' exhortation, "Cleave unto
Him: for He is thy *life*." In the midst of Jordan's threatening
depths, the Lord alone was their life; to them He was now indeed
very breath of their breath, life of their life—their all. Buried between those banks, and (but for mercy) beneath those billowy
waves, none knew better than Israel that theirs was a life in union
with Another. Certainly mercy—not merit—"cut off" those waters.
Of what avail now were all their efforts? Neither by resolution of
will, nor by effort of the flesh, nor by all their agonies or strivings
put together could they claim an entrance into Canaan. Only by

mercy and by miracle and by the merits of Another were they carried through. Hallelujah, what a Saviour!

The lessons here seem self-evident. Our entrance into the Blessed Life is through union with Him who united us with Himself when He dipped His feet into Calvary's floods of death. We have been crucified, "cut off" from every engulfing force, whether of sin or self or the world. In identification with Him we have passed through death over to resurrection ground. We are "children of the resurrection." Hallelujah! Ours is the land of promise, of rest, of victory.

Remember at this point that you can no more reach this blessed land through the resolutions of either your bad self or your good self than Israel could wade into the promised land. The floods of death stand between you and that land, and the sentence of doom is written over every bit of your fleshly strength and natural energy. The impassable depth of death, death to every breath of the natural, is the divine highway between you and all that blessedness. Only the supernatural and almighty death of the Redeemer can carry you through; only your heavenly Joshua can cause you to possess your possessions. If you have come to feel, through ever-recurring misery and defeat, that unless Another shall lead you into the land of fruitful obedience your whole Christian career will be a spiritual and moral chaos, then perhaps you are ready to venture your all upon your union with Christ in death and resurrection.

Are you, my reader, sick of the half-hearted shallows and shoals of the Christian life? You know there are depths of blessedness which you have scarcely tasted, and you realize through repeated and tragic failure that Another must lead you into the land of fruitful obedience. Your natural strength has been spent, and you have come to the end of yourself. What you would, you do not, and what you would not, that you do. You realize how far short of your inheritance you have come; in fact you now see no other way into the land of rest and victory except through the overflowing floods of Calvary. Your life has already been a living death. You may long have cried, "Who shall deliver me from the body of this death." You have therefore been made ready to say, I can but perish if I go. Come, then, and sink your self-life into Calvary's floods and follow Him all the way. Remember that all God's billows and waves have gone over Him once for all. In His ignominious departure, your self-life was done to death, cut off. Are you united to Christ and therefore a partaker of Christ? Then you are one with Him in all the unplumbed power generated at Calvary. That is *potential*. However, your position calls for your cordial consent to your co-crucifixion with Christ that the power of His death may be yours. Cut yourself off. Pass the death sentence upon yourself. Consent to your once-for-all death with Christ. Let your objective crucifixion with Christ become a subjective and personal experience. Dip your own two feet into this Jordan, that passing through this death-resurrection road you may possess moment by moment your heavenly inheritance. By an act of sheer faith, apart from any feelings, be "planted together with Him in the likeness of His death." Only thus will you experience "the likeness of His resurrection"; only thus can you reach resurrection ground. *Reckon* on your life-union with Him. *Reject* the old life, and reckon until He makes real your resurrection position.

Do not forget that you must plant your feet upon the truth. However fearful and afraid you may feel, venture by faith into that awful river, the river of death, and it will become as true of you as of Israel: "[Their] feet stood firm on dry ground in the midst of Jordan." So will yours—until you have "passed clean over Jordan."

"What mean these stones?" By divine command twelve stones were brought up from Jordan's depths where the priests' feet had stood firm, and these stones were pitched on resurrection ground "for a memorial unto the children of Israel forever."

> "In Him we died, in Him we rose,
> In Him we triumphed o'er our foes;
> In Him in heaven we took our seat,
> And heaven rejoiced o'er earth's defeat."

The twelve stones on the bank, a stone for each tribe, symbolize the emergence of each believer with Christ in glorious resurrection. We remember Paul's word, "One died for all, therefore all died; and He died for all, that they which live should no longer live unto themselves, but unto Him who for their sakes died and rose again" (II Cor. 5:14, 15, R.V.).

We could call in witness after witness of this yet-not-I kind of death-resurrection life. Regardless of their ecclesiastical connection and differing phraseology—hungry hearts outrun doctrinal quibblers—these great saints agree that we can cross over into the blessed land of obedience only through an inner crucifixion that will cut us off not only from Egypt, but also from the wilderness wanderings of the double-minded. George Mueller's testimony we have quoted. Let us bring in one other. Dr. A. B. Simpson possessed the same secret of the blessed life, and that secret can doubtless be traced to what he himself describes as follows: "I look back with unutterable gratitude to the lonely and sorrowful night when, mistaken in many things and imperfect in all, and not knowing but that it would be death in the most literal sense before the morning light, my heart's first full consecration was made, and with unreserved surrender I first could say:

> *'Jesus, I my cross have taken,*
> *All to leave and follow Thee,*
> *Destitute, despised, forsaken,*
> *Thou, from hence, my all shalt be.'* "

Thus far we have dwelt only upon our death-resurrection *position*. To continue, let us now consider the *process* which necessarily follows, for the position is of little use apart from the process. We hasten to say that many persons who know the truth of the death-resurrection position seem to know little of practical victory because they fail in the process. Unable to forget the things that are behind and stretch forth unto the things that are before, they forever hark back to some experience or crisis instead of going on.

This brings us to note that another pile of twelve stones was set up "in the midst of Jordan, in the place where the feet of the priests which bare the ark of the covenant stood." We have observed that the stones on the bank declared that Israel had entered once for all into the land of milk and honey. Now what mean these other twelve stones buried back in Jordan's depths? Do they not mean that our *abiding in Canaan* is no mere once-for-all passage through death and resurrection? "Israel cannot abide in Canaan without a constant abiding in death through the twelve symbolic stones, buried in the stream" (F. J. Huegel). There is the death-resurrection position which is taken once for all; and there is the death-resurrection process which lasts all our days. The process conditions our abiding in the blessed life, and that process is continuous, without intermission, lifelong.

At the close of his life the apostle Paul hungers to "know Christ and the power of His resurrection, and the fellowship of His sufferings, *being made conformable unto His death*." Some years after Paul wrote "I have been crucified together with Christ," we find him here laying down as the one condition of knowing Christ and the power of His resurrection that he must be more and more assimilated into and "conformed unto His death." Paul well knew that the experimental efficacy of Christ's resurrection power was in proportion to his own conformity to Christ's death. Paul had long known the Spirit-filled life, deliverance from sin's dominion, as well as long and victorious Christian service. He gloried in the law of the Spirit of life in Christ Jesus, which had made him free from the law of sin and death. Late in life, however, we find Paul hungering to know more of *"His death."* He knew that the condition of realizing the efficacy of Christ's glorious resurrection was coming into deeper conformity to *His death*. "The climax of the risen life gravitates, strange to say, back to the Cross" (C. A. Fox).

Let us now note how the continual application of the Cross worked out in Paul's life. Paul's whole life, like that of his Master, was a continuous cross. Who can question that Golgotha was the logical goal and terminus of the Saviour's life? In His crucifixion we behold the bright outshining of the entire principle of His life: He saved others, Himself He cannot save. Thus it was also with the great Apostle. In reminding the Corinthians of one of his extremities he said, "We ourselves have had the answer of death within ourselves, that we should not trust in ourselves, but in God which raiseth the dead" (II Cor. 1:9, R.V.). The Apostle had been so weighed down and reduced that he despaired even of life. When he looked to the right, his whole being answered, Death.

When he looked to the left, the answer was the same. When he looked ahead, Death stared him in the face. The one voice that cried to Paul wherever he looked was, Death, Death, Death—Death everywhere, Death all around, Death within. And to what purpose? That Paul might not trust in himself, but in God, who raises the dead. The Apostle was compelled to cast himself upon Him who alone can raise dead men. Paul was brought perpetually to his wit's end that he might prove Christ's resurrection power. He says, "For we which live are always delivered unto death for Jesus' sake, that the life also of Jesus may be manifested in our mortal flesh" (II Cor. 4:11, R.V.).

Paul calls this the "putting to death of Jesus" (II Cor. 4:9, Roth.). He does not say "the death of Jesus," but rather "the process which produces death" (Denney). In his pains, perplexities, perils—to say nought of the care and pressure from all the churches—Paul senses the fellowship of Christ's sufferings. He calls these dangers and "deaths oft" the process which produces death. Nevertheless, in spite of this daily dying he lived. "Perpetually in peril, he had a perpetual series of escapes; perpetually at his wit's end, his way perpetually opened before him" (Denney). What is the explanation? "That the [resurrected] life also of Jesus may be manifested in our mortal flesh." Paul's perpetual danger and despair furnished occasion for resurrection life—yea, necessitated his receiving life from the dead. He was perpetually shut up to the Lord of death and life. From these perils and sufferings and exposures to death, Paul experienced repeated escapes and restorations and manifestations of newness of life. Such was his lifelong experience, a process at once both spiritual and physical. This everlasting cycle became to the Apostle "a series of resurrections."

The Apostle now goes further and says, "So then death worketh in us, but life in you" (II Cor. 4:12). Here is set forth the positive outcome and purpose of daily deliverance unto death for Jesus' sake—namely, death works in us for the sake of life in others. The death-resurrection process, then, is not only that we may unlearn self and become the recipients of personal resurrection life, but also that by means of our own weakness and self-sacrifice and selflessness and suffering, the life of Christ may be imparted to others. Life then for the consecrated and cross-centered Christian is to be a whole series of deaths and resurrections that life may come to others. It is once again the "corn-of-wheat" program, the only program which insures success. How very far, by the way, is all this from the usual conception of the victorious life—a life of pleasure under a palm tree, of feasting on grapes and pomegranates, and even of settling down to a fleshly soft life! Let us never forget the saying of C. A. Fox: "The climax of the risen life gravitates, strange to say, back to the Cross." Be this our life-long attitude!

Such is the process by which God makes His kings and priests for the coming resurrection ages. Would we reign with the Greater Son of David and sit down with Him on His throne? Then let us remember the condition: "Even as I also overcame and am set down with my Father on His throne." Recall how David reached the throne and how other saints came to be exalted in due time. In *Bone of His Bone*, F. J. Huegel says:

> David does not come to the throne until in the caves of the Philistines, where he was hunted down like a dog by the infuriated Saul, he dies—deaths innumerable. The Psalms, so adapted to human woe . . . could not have been, but for the inner crucifixion in the heart of the sweet singer of Israel, brought about by the mad persecutions of Saul . . . Jeremiah dies a thousand deaths as he weeps over the chosen people. Jonah is pitched into the sea and is swallowed by a whale—even then he does not come forth wholly purged from self. God's people have never in any age come to the mountain-peak of spiritual attainment, the glory of unbroken communion with the Most High, without having the "self-life," the "flesh-life," brought again and again to the dust of death.

Lord, evermore give us this Bread.

CHAPTER VII

Flesh and Spirit

THE WRITER had a godly associate who used to say, "I didn't know I had a temper until after I was saved." Until then the house of her own life had not been divided, even as "Satan is not divided against himself." There had been no dispute, since she was the sole occupant and proprietor. Blissfully self-satisfied she had had her own way; she had held sway over all her little world. But when the Spirit of God gave her a new life in Christ, war began —civil war. The flesh lusted against the Spirit and the Spirit against the flesh, and these are contrary the one to the other.

The Saviour stated a great basic fact when He said, "That which is born of the flesh is flesh"—nothing comes of it but flesh. It never enters the realm of the Spirit. Hence the absolute necessity of being born again, born anew, born a new creature through union with Jesus Christ. "That which is born of the Spirit is spirit." It was as a new creature in Christ that Paul said, "I delight in the law of God after the inward man."

It is a real mark of my regeneration that I begin to hunger and thirst after righteousness. In my pursuit after righteousness, however, I sooner or later make the great and shocking discovery that the flesh profiteth nothing, even though I am regenerated. I find "that in me, that is, in my flesh, dwelleth no good thing." Although redeemed from Egypt, I have not entered into the land of milk and honey—at least I do not dwell there. I find my habitat in the wilderness of a divided affection. As I wander in this mixed and muddled state, my very virtues are all tainted with the flesh, the touch of death corrupts all I do, and my best deeds seem "only taught practices grafted on a corrupt bottom." Speaking of this state William Law says,

> Everything that you do will be a mixture of good and bad;
> your humility will help you to pride; your charity to others
> will give nourishment to your own self-love, and as your
> prayers increase so will the opinion of your own sanctity.

A vivid portrayal of this warfare is set forth in Exodus 17. God's
people had long been enslaved under cruel bondage in Egypt, but
sheltered beneath the blood and redeemed by mighty power, they
had come forth in triumph as Jehovah's purchased people. Blessedly refreshed from the smitten rock—"that rock was Christ"—they
were suddenly and subtly fallen upon from the rear. "Then came
Amalek, and fought with Israel in Rephidim." Thus the Christian,
redeemed from death, regenerated, and renewed in the Holy Spirit,
awakes sooner or later to the fact that in *the flesh* which he has
with him he is being hotly pursued by a besetting and tireless antagonist. Amalek represents the flesh in its warfare against the
Spirit. In the very nature of the case there is no possible recon-
ciliation between these two.

The flesh has almost infinite forms. It may not always appear
devilish, deceitful, and hateful; on the contrary, it may be cultured,
educated, refined, and religious. In fact it may so play possum as
to lead you to think that it is dead. It thrives in any soil, and
under the shades of earthly sorrow as well as in the sunshine of
prosperity. Whatever its behaviour, however, it is still changeless
flesh, "unimprovable, incorrigible, incurable . . . There remains,
then, no remedy but that which God has provided—condemnation,
crucifixion, death with Christ" (Mantle). The only trade-mark
becoming to the flesh is the death-mark of the Cross.

We are slow to learn, and the last thing we even want to learn
is the unlearning of self. The thought of self-discovery and self-
disclosure terrifies us. We have been so long addicted to self-love,
so long and so blissfully fixed upon this false center that it is no
mere child's play or the lesson of a day to unlearn this domination.

Self is the last idol to fall. Eve ate the forbidden fruit that she
might better herself. Adam sinned because he deliberately chose
self. Cain killed Abel because he preferred his own envy and pride,
the pride of self. And what of David, the "man after God's own
heart"? Samuel Rutherford says:

What was the hook that took David and snared him first in adultery, but his *self-lust?* and then in murder, but his *self-credit* and *self-honour?* What led Peter on to deny his Lord? Was it not a piece of *himself*, and *self-love* to a whole skin? What made Judas sell his Master for thirty pieces of silver, but the idolizing and avaricious *self?* What made Demas go off the way of the Gospel to embrace the present world? Even *self-love* and a love of gain for *himself*. Every man blameth the devil for his sins; but the great devil, the house-devil of every man, the house-devil that eateth and lieth in every man's bosom, is that idol that killeth all, *himself*. Oh! blessed are they who can deny themselves, and put Christ in the room of themselves! O sweet word: I live no more, but Christ liveth in me! (Quoted by Mantle in *The Way of the Cross*).

Self-love is so blind, so subtle, and so strong that it will lead a man into a fool's paradise and leave him there till the searchlight of God locates him and spoils his vain opinion of himself. Until a Christian is thus located and given a death-dealing self-disclosure, he will know little of God's mighty inward redemption from the power of the flesh. Even Paul, that spiritual giant, went through untold agonies before he finally cried out, "O wretched man that I am! who shall deliver me from the body of this death?" While there is no scriptural reason why we as new converts should not at once enter into the Christian victory of Romans 6, the fact remains that most of us do not come quickly to the place of utter self-despair, not until we pass through repeated agonies, miseries, and failures. Only thus do we come to believe what Paul finally learned, namely, "that in me (that is, in my flesh,) dwelleth no good thing." When at length we are ready to cry, "who shall deliver me?" only then can we reckon ourselves "dead indeed unto sin, but alive unto God through Jesus Christ our Lord." Not until we feel our deep need and tragic defeat can we say in faith, "Thanks be unto God who giveth us the victory through our Lord Jesus Christ—I live no more, but Christ liveth in me." Thus, when Israel was pounced upon by Amalek, her only help was from heaven, through the intervention of Another. Moses' uplifted hands signified victory given, heaven-sent and free. "This is the victory that overcometh the world [including the flesh and the devil], even our faith" (I John 5:4).

On this first occasion of Amalek's relentless antagonism against
God's people, Heaven's doom was pronounced upon the Amalekites.
"Because the hand of Amalek is against the throne of the LORD,
therefore the LORD will have war with Amalek from generation
to generation" (Ex. 17:16, marg.). Likewise, in his last charge
to Israel Moses said, "Remember what Amalek did unto thee by
the way, when ye were come forth out of Egypt; How he met thee
by the way, and smote the hindmost of thee, even all that were
feeble behind thee, when thou wast faint and weary; and he feared
not God. Therefore it shall be, . . that thou shalt blot out the re-
membrance of Amalek from under heaven; *thou shalt not forget it*"
(Deut. 25:17-19).

With these pronouncements in mind, notice in I Sam. 15 the
commission given to King Saul: "Go and smite Amalek, and utterly destroy all that they have, and spare them not" (v. 3). There-
upon Saul went forth and gained a wonderful victory. So fully
did he obey that he "utterly destroyed all the *people* with the edge
of the sword" (v. 8). Nevertheless, he did not utterly destroy *all*,
even though his victory had been so sweeping that he boasted of
complete obedience. True, "every thing that was vile and refuse,
that they destroyed utterly" (v. 9), but in this he did only what
most Christians do when it comes to the flesh—namely, he destroyed
the worthless and kept alive the good; for "Saul and the people
spared Agag, and the best of the sheep, . . and all that was good, and
would not utterly destroy them" (v. 9). The average Christian
sees at once that he should destroy the wicked, the worthless, and
the vile, i.e., all lust, drunkenness, murder, adultery, and such like.
Saul's subtle temptation is ours—to keep alive the refined forms
and virtues of the flesh, the attractive bearing, the cultured kindness, the studied smile, the fair show in the flesh. How difficult
for the saint to see that the flesh in every form, though it be cultured, and religious, and kind, is as doomed to the stroke of death
as all obviously wicked "works of the flesh." The whole of our
"old man was crucified with Christ." It is not over a part but
over the whole of our old natural life that it is written, "They that
are Christ's have crucified the flesh with the affections and lusts"
(Gal. 5:24).

Notice that the king of the Amalekites was called Agag, perhaps an imperial name, or a throne title such as the name Pharaoh. Sir Henry Rawlinson says that this title means "Venerable King." Agag, then, was the Venerable King of all Amalek. Likewise, fallen flesh also has a king, King Self, a king regarded universally as most "venerable." It is as difficult for us to consign self to the Cross as it was for Saul to put the sword to Agag, for we read that Saul spared that "venerable king." Was he not manifestly a king, cultured and courtly and refined? Spared and in chains, Agag became the exhibition of Saul's victory, a victory to the glory and praise of Saul. To the Lord, however, Agag in chains was the exhibition of Saul's own pride and disobedience, for Agag represented self spared, self allowed to live, self escaping the edge of the sword, self conquering self, self still king.

Now watch Samuel, the prophet of God, deal with this trophy of Saul's conquest. "Bring ye hither to me Agag the king of the Amalekites. And Agag came unto him *delicately* [cheerfully]. And Agag said, Surely the bitterness of death is past" (I Sam. 15:32). Agag was delighted, and came up *cheerfully*, thinking, If only I may escape the edge of that sword and live! Samuel looks like a gracious and godly old fellow—surely he too will spare me. He is so holy that he must be harmless and brotherly, not brutal. If I only escape I will behave from now on. What a perfect picture of Self! Someone has well said:

> The last enemy destroyed in the believer is self. It dies hard. It will make any concessions if allowed to live. Self will permit the believer to do anything, give anything, sacrifice anything, suffer anything, be anything, go anywhere, take any liberties, bear any crosses, afflict soul and body to any degree—anything if it can only live. It will consent to live in a hovel, in a garret, in the slums, in far-away heathendom, if only its life can be spared.

For Agag, however, the bitterness of death was not past. The sword of the Lord, a "two-edged sword, of heavenly temper keen," was in the hand of God's prophet, and "Samuel hewed Agag in pieces before the LORD." In sparing Agag, Saul had tried to spare

himself; furthermore, he was courting the favour of his followers
by furnishing them with "the best of the sheep," and he was pam-
pering his pride by keeping Agag for display. Obviously he had
never put the sword to his own vainglorious self-life. As Samuel
showed Agag no mercy, even so the Cross does not stop short of an
inner crucifixion of self, thereby laying the axe to the root of the
tree. God spared not His only Son, as in Christ He executed you
and me.

> *If Christ would live and reign in me,*
> *I must die;*
> *With Him I crucified must be;*
> *I must die;*
> *Lord drive the nails, nor heed the groans,*
> *My flesh may writhe and make its moans,*
> *But in this way, and this alone*
> *I must die.*
>
> —Selected

Take heed, dear fellow believer, and be well warned against pam-
pering a proud self-life.

The very sword with which Saul should have slain Agag became
the instrument of his own destruction. "Saul took his sword, and
fell upon it" (I Sam. 31:4, R.V.). What but his own inner self-
life, the Agag within, slew God's anointed? When Saul spared Agag
he sealed his own doom. At that moment he came under the curse
later pronounced by Jeremiah against the Chaldeans should they
execute less than unsparing judgment upon the proud Moabites:
"Cursed be he that doeth the work of the LORD negligently; and
cursed be he that keepeth back his sword from blood" (Jer. 48:10,
R.V.). Did Saul spare Agag? keep back his sword from blood?
do the work of the Lord negligently? Did he not rather spare himself, pamper his own pride, and bring a sword and curse upon himself? How are the mighty fallen! Heaven's curse fell upon him
through his own foul hand—all because of his own unbloody sword.
Thus with the sword of his own disobedience he slew himself. O
fatal self-love! How cruel are thy ways!

It appears that at least one of Agag's royal household must have
escaped, for nearly six hundred years later his posterity comes to

light in the person of "Haman the son of Hammedatha the *Agagite*" (Esther 3:1). We read that Haman was promoted above all the princes of the Persian king, and everybody bowed to him and did him reverence, "for the king had so commanded concerning him." Among God's scattered people, however, was a little Jew by the name of Mordecai, who "bowed not, nor did him reverence." Mordecai was apparently an offspring of Saul's own people, "the son of Kish a Benjamite." At this time the Jews were scattered all over the Persian Empire. The scene centered about Shushan the palace. In fiendish glee this Amalekite had consigned God's people to utter destruction. The king of the flesh was on the throne. The houses of Saul and Agag stood face to face once more. In Haman is photographed the unslain and fleshly self-life that will tolerate no rival; it reigns king over all until dethroned at the Cross.

In Mordecai, however, Haman met a nobler than Saul. When Mordecai bowed not nor did him reverence, then was "Haman full of wrath." This ugly unbending Jew he could not endure. Although immensely elated that he was the only and honoured guest of Queen Esther, he said, "Yet all this availeth me nothing, so long as I see Mordecai the Jew sitting at the king's gate." Nothing would do but that a gallows eighty feet high be erected on which to hang this despised Jew. He would build it high so that Mordecai might be disgraced to the limit in his death, and Mordecai's people could all see what would shortly come to them.

In Mordecai we see a man who defied all edicts even to transgressing the king's commandment. He "stood not up, nor moved" for Haman. His unyielding obstinacy not only endangered his own life but also brought the whole Jewish nation to the verge of extermination. Had he but bowed ever so little, reverenced Haman at least as became his position, or even ceased to slight and insult and despise him, he could have saved his own life and that of all his people. But Mordecai would let God bear the consequences. In his unbending determination Mordecai declared that the Lord "hath indignation against Amalek forever." Like his cousin, Queen Esther, he declared, "If I perish, I perish."

Think you, my reader, that it was Haman who built the eighty-foot gallows? Nay, verily. It was that unbending, insignificant, despised little Jew, the man who died to self, forfeited his life, and so enraged that Agagite that his wrath knew no bounds. Mordecai reminds us of three other unbending Jews who once defied King Nebuchadnezzar. Recall their carefree contempt of the king: "We are not careful to answer thee in this matter. If it be so, our God whom we serve is able to deliver us from the burning fiery furnace, and He will deliver us out of thine hand, O king. But if not, be it known unto thee, O king, that we will not serve thy gods, nor worship the golden image which thou hast set up" (Dan. 3:16-18). The fiery furnace was at once made ready, seven times hotter than usual. By whom? By the three Hebrews, unbent and tempered in the fires of affliction. Through their unbending and uncompromising stand, they themselves had fired the furnace for their own death.

I know my God is able to deliver;
Able to save from direst human ill;
Able, as when He saved the Hebrew children—
  Almighty still.

But if, perchance, His plans are not my plans;
If hid in darkness should my pathway be;
If when I plead He does not seem to answer,
  Nor care for me—

Then, though men scoff and bitterly deride me—
Listen! I fling my challenge to the sky!
God may deliver, but if not, I'll trust Him,
  And trusting, die!

—M. Mannington Dexter

Then came Heaven's turn to laugh, as God burned up His enemies in their own furnace of fire. It would have been too bad indeed had not those Jews kindled that fire, for then wherein and how would their enemies have been consumed?

Let God's servants who are determined to die to the flesh and live only unto Him lay hold of this profound principle. Many a Mordecai is needed to prepare a "royal" hanging for Haman. We dare to believe that God has little trouble hanging Hamans. He can at any moment use even a sleepless king to turn the scales.

Heaven's issues seem to hinge around His key men, men like Mordecai who by death to self build gallows on which to hang the Hamans. When some Mordecai dies utterly to all self-preservation, whether of himself or of his family or of his friends, then God has *the whereon* to hang the flesh. *Mordecai furnished God the gallows.*

There are many middle-of-the-road ministers who may be excused for wishing that God would hang all the modernists, but there is first an Agag to be hanged in the fundamentalist. The sinful self-life in the fundamentalist is of all modernists the worst. Martin Luther said, "I am more afraid of my own heart than of the Pope and all his cardinals. I have within me that great Pope, Self." If the fundamentalist, whether within or without the modernistic machine, persists in saving self, in living for and bowing to self, on what is God to hang these modern Hamans? Haman builds gallows only when he finds an unbending Mordecai. The orthodox man who *moves* for Haman, *bows* to him a little, and *bends* a bit is not dangerous. Haman can tolerate a harmless compromiser, and can afford to let him live.

The three unbending and carefree Hebrew children prepared a fire in Babylon such as God's enemies had not felt before, and it was the fiery zeal of the Lord of Hosts in those three Hebrews that kindled that fire. We are convinced from Scripture that if fighting, militant, and daring fundamentalists would only sink into a selfless, carefree contempt for their own lives, forgetting their reputation and position, their cause and kingdom, and be willing to expose themselves to every battery the devil can muster against them we have little doubt that God could and perhaps would burn up His enemies round about and hang the Hamans of today as easily as He handled matters for Mordecai. Remember, my friend, you and I must furnish the gallows, and fleshly energy, method, and ambition—killing Egyptians and cutting off ears—have nothing to do with building gallows.

Parents dealing with children need to understand this principle. Here is a parent who hopes God will get hold of his child, yet as soon as this parent faces the accusation of being narrow-minded, bigoted, and too hard on this youngster, he tries to save face. In doing so he bows a little here and bends a little there. The youngster knows it, and God knows it. "No man ever yet hated his own flesh." Not having learned the meaning of "Henceforth know we no man after the flesh," the parent naturally regards his child with the affection of the flesh; he has not learned to say with Paul, "I have you in my heart to *die and live* with you"—God's order. He has his child in his heart to *live and die* with him—the fleshly order. Since, therefore, the child has no gallows on which to die to the flesh, how can God get hold of him? If the parent had but kept to his identification with Christ crucified—the Cross is God's gallows for the flesh—then God would have been able to bring the youngster to the death of his self-will and rebellion. Would you have Christ crucified revealed to your child? Carefully read God's word to the mother of Jesus in Luke 2:35. Then remember that a sword must pierce thine own soul also, *that the thoughts of thy child may be revealed.*

There are friendships in the flesh that are very dangerous. A few times—thank God very few—some students of the "holier-than-thou" type have come to a very intimate mutual understanding of spiritual conditions at P.B.I. They forthwith have a deeply spiritual prayer meeting of the private kind for the select few, because as someone subtly put it, "We can pray over things more freely where there are only a few of us." Thank God one of their classmates, with a sword in his soul, hooked two of these young fellows and brought them into the office to be dealt with. Thereafter, both of these young men made Christian workers. And the method?—"not peace, but a sword."

Then there is the friendship that shields rather than exposes the wrongdoer. What is this but sparing our own flesh the embarrassment and fear of losing a friend? Love like that is not without hypocrisy; what is more, it is as cruel as death. True love, on the other hand, while far more costly is kindness indeed. An instance of false friendship occurred in the life of Kohila, who for a time fell into "shielding a wrongdoer."

A special friend of Kohila's caused a younger one to stumble by teaching her to deceive. Kohila's judgment was influenced by her fondness for her friend. She admitted the [friend's] wrong-doing but condoned it. She did what Samuel refused to do for Saul. [After Saul's disobedience and rejection he so feared public disgrace that he cried, Honour me now, I pray thee, before the elders of my people.] She forgot her Lord's solemn words about "the millstone" and "the sea." Her sympathy was rather with the offender than with Him who was offended in the offense done to His little one. But syrupy affection never yet led to spiritual integrity. And though it looks so like the charity which is greater than faith and hope that it is "admired of many," it is not admirable. It is sin.

Kohila, by Amy Carmichael

From subtle love of softening things,
From easy choices, weakenings,
From all that dims Thy Calvary,
O, Lamb of God, deliver me.
—A. C.

There is also a feigned love which is wickedly hypocritical. In *By My Spirit* Dr. Jonathan Goforth of China tells of a Chinese elder who "had flown into a rage and denounced the whole presbytery." After his suspension from that mission, he was taken up by another group and appointed principal of a large high school. However, he was still an unrepentant man. About the third day of the meetings in this school, it became quite evident that the Holy Spirit was working among the scholars; yet whenever a boy made a confession this principal would immediately pray, "O Lord, comfort his heart. He's a good boy. He has really nothing to worry about." The battle became terrific. The boys of the school became incensed when Dr. Goforth publicly "questioned the veracity of their principal. Shouting and yelling and kicking they left the church." But the Spirit of God gave those boys a terrible searching. Many of them could not sleep at night. Later they stood to their feet and openly acknowledged their sin. Dr. Goforth says, "And, to crown the devil's defeat, the principal himself came to the front, weeping and confessed his sin."

Such is the battle-front warfare so sorely needed in many orthodox churches. Where the flesh is enthroned, some anointed and unbending soul must question its veracity and expose its carnality, though a storm of fury be raised. A storm is far better than "distilled death"; riots and revivals were partners in Paul's experience.

Where are the Goforths to put the sword to such hypocritical professors?

To every reader who is bent on buying gold tried in the fire, though that fire be "seven times hotter," and who will sell his very garment to buy a "soul with a sword," we would commend the noble reply of the missionaries who, when confronted with the challenge, "Are you ready to die?" were able to answer, "We died before we left home." Such is the secret of the Lord that is indeed with them that fear Him.

> *Men return again and again to the few who have mastered the spiritual secret, whose life has been hid with Christ in God. These are of the old-time religion, hung to the nails of the Cross.*
>
> —Robert Murray McCheyne

CHAPTER VIII

Above Only—Not Beneath

Denis Diderot, the French atheist, cried out: "To be, amid pain and weeping, the plaything of uncertainty, of error, of want, of sickness, and of passion—every step, from the moment when we learn to lisp, to the time of departure when our voice falters—this is life." From the morass of rank atheism, Diderot saw man a mere victim in the net of nature. Man's life was a world upon which the Sun of righteousness had never risen. Brilliant Bertrand Russell confirms the creed of men who live "under the sun" when he says: "The life of man is a long march through the night, surrounded by invisible foes, tortured by weariness and pain, towards a goal that few can hope to reach, and where none may tarry long. One by one as they march, our comrades vanish from our sight, seized by the silent orders of omnipotent Death."

Certainly man was not made to be either a prisoner of death, or the plaything of uncertainty. He was made to have dominion. He was created for kingship. It was not the design of Deity that man should wander in a starless night of mystery and misery. Fresh from the hand of his Creator man was commissioned a king. His freedom and royalty (though under the government of God) were without limitation. Thou "hast crowned him with glory and honour. Thou madest him to have dominion over the works of Thy hands; Thou hast put all things under his feet" (Psa. 8:5,6). Yet man in his first disobedience forfeited this royalty, lost this dominion, and sold his kingdom. When he threw off the yoke that was easy and the burden that was light, he unfitted himself for dominion and was "sold under sin." Out of harmony with Heaven man drove himself from the place of true possession, true dominion, and true authority. A fugitive from justice he became a vagabond in the earth. Therefore, unless man ceased to be dominated by his sinful self-assertion, he could never be trusted with position, power, or responsibility.

However, still instinct with the desire to rule, a desire perverted and dangerous, each man scrambles over his fellows to found his little kingdom and gain the dominion. There is scarcely any lust, including the love of money, that can equal the passion of man for mastery, for ascendancy, for power. Yet it is this selfish and foul perversion of his highest instinct that has created for man a night utterly starless and hopeless—"That which is crooked cannot be made straight" (Eccl. 1:15).

What true Christian, beholding all the world's insoluble problems and perplexities and desolations, can have less than a sympathetic weeping with those who weep? For the Christian not only sees all these knotty and stubborn facts of the curse, but he also has the sharp knife that cuts the Gordian knot of the world's mystery and misery. That some Christians enter more deeply and sympathetically into the world's travail, let Dr. A. B. Davidson, a great Hebrew scholar, testify. "Do you ever," he asked an intimate friend, "without any special reason for grief, fall into uncontrollable weeping?" Then after a pause he added: "Just the other day I was alone; and there came such a sense of the mystery, the uncertainty, the loneliness, the pathos of life that I was for a long time shaken by sobs which I was unable to control" (D. M. Panton).

In the face of all these "sufferings of this present time," whether of tribulation, or perplexity, or persecution, or famine, or nakedness, or peril, or sword, Paul cries out in exultation, "In all these things we are more than conquerors through Him that loved us." And to the Corinthians he boldly says, "All things are yours; whether . . . the world, or life, or death, or things present, or things to come; all are yours" (I Cor. 3:21, 22). Diderot and Russell, on the other hand, having shut out the God of light and revelation, behold man beset with numberless calamities, the mere plaything of uncertainty, and conclude with Solomon that, under the sun, "all is vanity and vexation of spirit" so that an untimely birth is better than life. Without Heaven's solution Solomon's summary is inevitable. Human reason might exclaim, What risks (of chance, of misunderstanding, of criticism) God seems to have taken! Did

man, in the midst of a veritable Eden of plenty and perfect, fail
and forfeit all kingship? Indeed man came from the hand of the
Creator every inch a king. Then if, as a perfect being, in the fullness of manhood, and in perfect circumstances, man was so completely overcome and undone for dominion, what would be the
likelihood that he would ever conquer in this wilderness outfield
of sin, death, corruption, and multiplied misery? What chance
has poor man in the grip of iron law with his whole career crowned
with thorns and thistles, and with the whole hierarchy of hell arrayed against him, of overcoming a thousand moral deficiencies or
of finding his way back to dominion? As a result of his fall (and
the consequent curse) man must pass through troops of evil, and
a life of labour to a destiny in the dust, only to be seized upon at
last "by the silent orders of omnipotent Death." What a prospect!

Beneath the sun the prospect is truly hopeless. God means it
to be so. Divine wisdom dare not permit unregenerate man to
build a heaven on earth with a little hell at its heart. Man must be
compelled to feel that it is an evil thing and bitter that he has forsaken the Lord. He must learn that life "under the sun" is indeed
an uncertainty, a failure, a chaos, a curse. What, then, is the prospect for the future? As bright as the promises of God. The utterance of Him who cannot lie is that ere long "there shall be *no curse
any more.*" Christ must reign until He has put all enemies under
His feet. And the last enemy that shall be destroyed is death. Such
a prospect is sufficient and has been the sure foundation, the promise immutable, to all God's pilgrims. They lodge their entire
fortune and future on what God has said. They have checked, dare
I say, clear through to the New Jerusalem. Behind them they see
Christ's empty tomb; before them they grasp His soon return. Such
glorious facts give them a farsighted calculation that makes them
carefree in the present and that shapes all their future.

Becoming deeper infidel with every passing year, this present
world abominates such a visionary prospect. Its motto is, Get all
you can, and get it now. The Communist's creed, therefore, cuts
right across the Christian's faith. On the other hand, the Christian

knows that "faith at its worst is better than the world at its best."
He can well afford in this life to be "of all men most miserable,"
for the time is coming when "God shall wipe away all tears from
their eyes; and there shall be no more death, neither sorrow, nor
crying, neither shall there be any more pain: for the former things
are passed away" (Rev. 21:4).

Such a future reign of God on earth is dimly glimpsed in the
ancient nation of Israel. As she stood on the threshold of the
kingdom and beheld the land of her inheritance, Moses said, "The
LORD shall make thee the head, and not the tail; *and thou shalt be
above only, and thou shalt not be beneath*" (Deut. 28:13). Theirs
was the Sovereign of all sovereigns, the invisible King, Christ.
Through Him they were more than conquerors over nations "greater
and mightier" than they. Israel's high privilege was "to bind their
kings with chains, and their nobles with fetters of iron; To execute upon them the judgment written" (Psa. 149:8,9). Israel was
to be *above only—not beneath.*

But such a kingdom is not now; it is yet to come. That the
saints are now utterly set at nought, counted as sheep for the slaughter, done to death all the day long is a fact frightfully real in much
of the world. Our only hope of a kingdom is in the coming King.
What, then, is our own prospect for the present? Must we merely
submit and succumb? Must we be depleted and defeated? Surely
our New Testament breathes a better prospect. Surely the over-
comers of all the ages have been ablaze with the spirit of conquest
and possession, even as Paul assured the Corinthians: "Ye are
Christ's . . . *all* things are yours."

There can be a kingship under such a curse. This fact is not
new, for if it were new it would not be true; and if true, it cannot be new. 'Tis the old, old story. Through the Cross there
comes the kingship. Our dominion is returned to us again, but
only through the accursed Tree, only through the Son of God on
the Cross. Someone says, "No cross—no crown"—even for Omnipotence. Therefore give the winds a mighty voice: "Say unto
the people, the LORD *reigneth from the Tree*" (Psa. 96:10, old
Latin version).

> The truth that David learned to sing,
> Its deep fulfillment here attains:
> "Tell all the earth the Lord is King!"
> Lo, *from the Cross*, a King *He reigns!*
> —*Mrs. Charles*

From the Tree Christ holds sway. And for every follower of His the law is the same. With every rebel against the throne of Heaven, the government of God over his soul must begin at Golgotha. What power, what dominion, what authority can be trusted to the foul and selfish hands of man until he is transfixed to the Tree. At the Cross Christ, "obedient unto death," triumphed over all the powers of darkness and brought to an end man's reign of pride. Under complete subjection to His Father—"Thy will be done, not Mine"—Christ condemned and exposed every false dominion. The Cross pronounces "a judgment so adverse to the soul's selfish interests that it spells death" (Huegel); nevertheless its revolutionary power captures us, subdues us, and unseats us from the throne of every earthly ambition. At the Cross we become His captives. Was man created a king? Calvary creates a better. Did we lose kingship in Adam? Through the last Adam God creates us kings and priests. Did man lose kingship in Paradise? In this world's wilderness he must learn to be a king, must learn the meaning of "Ye are Christ's . . . all things are yours."

Let us now note the context of the phrase, "Ye are Christ's . . . all things are yours." The Corinthian believers were split up into sectarian factions, some claiming to belong to Paul, others to Apollos, and still others to Cephas. Paul scorned this sectarian spirit on the basis that each and every believer belongs directly and only to Christ. There is but one Lord, Jesus Christ, and He is Lord of all. In effect, Paul says: You Corinthians are bought with a price. Be not ye the slaves of men. Has Christ not seized upon you, subdued you, and by His own death made you wholly and only His? Then beware lest you own any other master. "One is your Master, even Christ." We apostles are but your ministers, not your masters; your servants, not your lords. We preach Christ Jesus as Lord, and ourselves your servants. Beware of saying you belong to any other than Christ. "For all things are yours; Wheth-

er Paul, or Apollos, or Cephas." They all belong to you, each
has a contribution to make to you, own them all for your good.
They are all your *servants*, but not your *lords*. You belong to
Christ; and they belong to you, not you to them. Each of these ministers is your servant to do you good. Learn to say, then, in deepest meaning,

> *I own no other Master,*
> *My heart shall be Thy throne,*
> *My life I give, henceforth to live,*
> *O Christ, for Thee alone.*
> —Thos. O. Chisholm

Now let us note the entire sweep of the Christian's possessions
as set forth in I Cor. 3:21-23, R. V.

> All things are yours;
> Whether Paul, or Apollos, or Cephas, or the world, or life,
>   or death, or things present, or things to come; all are yours;
> And ye are Christ's; and Christ is God's.

In these verses Paul says to all believers: Do you belong to Christ?
Do you serve Him? Then you are lords of all, whether of men,
of the world, of life or death, of time or eternity. Through union
with Christ believers are servants and lords—servants of Christ,
lords of all beside.

"All things are yours—*the world*." Here Paul doubtless is referring to the external, material universe. As servants of the last
Adam we are reinstated to that kingship which was lost to us in
the first Adam. This does not mean, of course, that we are pro-
prietors of the world—at least, not yet. Nor does it mean that we
are merely joint-heirs with Christ, or that we are the coming heirs
of the world. To most of us it is familiar truth that in due time the
saints shall reign with Christ. But in this passage Paul is insisting
that we *here and now* possess our possessions, and make all things
our servants.

We would hasten to add that the man who has come to forfeit and
despise and trample the world under his feet is the only man who
owns the world. One can never truly possess until he is dispossessed.
The law of possession in Christ's kingdom is poverty. Not riches,
but poverty is the pathway to possession, to power, to kingship.

Until this lesson is learned, all men are like the rich fool who says, My house, my goods, my barns, my fruits, my soul. We cannot possess the world until we have been mastered by Christ. The world lords it over us, masters us, dictates to us, enslaves us until then. Those who truly possess the world make it their servant. Blessed are such paupers, for theirs *is* the kingdom. Though they are earth's blessed poor, yet they make many rich. In them is fulfilled: "As having nothing, and yet possessing all things."

Do you possess the world? Or does the world possess you? Is it your servant or your lord? your minister or your master? Remember, he who drags his chain has not escaped. Boast not of your possessions if you are still a slave of self and sin. Loaded down with lands and houses, some poor souls still hug their chains. They vainly imagine they are kings of all creation (at least in their little circle); but their vaunted freedom is only boast and bondage.

A. J. Gordon said concerning the great soul-winner, John Vassar: "I am sure I do not exaggerate when I say there was nothing in this world, from riches to bodily comfort, from reputation to personal gratification, that had the slightest attraction for him." John Vassar's life was lived according to the Saviour's directions in the parable of the unjust steward. We read that "the lord commended the unjust steward, because he had done wisely: for the children of this world are in their generation wiser than the children of light." Before being dismissed, the unjust steward very skillfully managed his present stewardship in order to "feather his nest" for the future. He made the present serve the highest future advantage. During the last few days of his stewardship he "made himself friends" in order that they, in grateful return for his consideration, might receive him into their homes. In His application of this parable Jesus said: "I say unto you, Make to yourselves friends by means of the mammon of unrighteousness;"—i.e., make use of the material world to make to yourselves friends— "that, when it shall fail, they"—souls saved from every land through your means and already on yonder shore—"may receive you into the eternal tabernacles" (Luke 16:9, R.V.).

My mind recalls the history of Grandma and Grandpa Kirk (as we knew them), who lived on a poor Ontario farm with a modest family of ten children. Yet they managed to give hundreds of dollars to missions. Their children were brought up on mush and missions. (Of course they all came to Christ.) Years later, after the Kirks and their children had moved to the vicinity of Three Hills, one of their sons (now a member of the Sudan Interior Mission) left his quarter section to Grandma and Grandpa to live on. They were too old to farm it, yet with their cows and chickens they managed to give to missions several thousand dollars. They were still making themselves friends by means of the mammon of unrighteousness. During one year alone, after they were seventy years of age, they gave one thousand dollars to foreign missions and spent only eighty dollars on themselves. How many friends Grandma and Grandpa must have had to greet them on yonder shore with the words, Come in, thou blessed of the Lord; we are part of that host of friends you made by means of that world you were *using* and others *abusing!*

Kingship over material things as manifested by these old patriarchs of the faith reminds us of a Cambridge graduate, Robert Arthington of Leeds, who lived in a single room, cooked his own meals, and gave to foreign missions five million dollars on condition that it be spent for pioneer work within twenty-five years. After his death a slip of paper was found on which he had written these words: "Gladly would I make the floor my bed, a box my chair, and another box my table rather than that men should perish for the want of the knowledge of Christ." Robert Arthington possessed his world. Do you possess yours? Or does it possess you? Thou shalt be above only — not beneath.

"All things are yours—*life.*" With Christ as my Master, life is *mine.* Let me ask just here, Do you serve life, or does your life serve you? Is life your minister or your master? Is it your servant or your lord? Only those who have yielded their lives utterly to Christ, i.e., have not lost them, have found life in its true meaning. Life has become their servant, serving them for time and eternity. "Ye are Christ's"—life is yours.

"My thought is now for the souls of men;
I have lost my life to find it again,
Ere since one day in a quiet place
I met my Master face to face."

The secret of possessing life is to own no other master but Christ.
But until Christ is Lord of my life, I cannot make life my servant.
When I can say, "I have been crucified with Christ," then I can
add with joyful assurance "nevertheless I live"; yes, I truly live,
making this present life my servant indeed. Paul goes on to un-
fold the mystery by saying, "Yet not I, but Christ liveth in me."
When Christ is enthroned I am freed to make life my servant, to
make it of use to God, to souls, and actually to myself. This is the
law of recompense. This is a principle of life. This is law, inexorable and unbreakable—that he who selfishly saves his life shall
lose it. But make life yours by losing it, then life will be a romance
of ceaseless miracle and marvel.

This principle finds illustration in two young men who stood on
the dock. The one was using his life to serve his Lord and Master,
for he was about to go forth as a missionary to minister to lost
men. "You are a fool," cried his friend. "You are going out
to that heathen land, and the cannibals will eat you." "And who
will eat you?" retorted the hilarious missionary. After a few
thoughtful moments came the solemn answer: "The worms, I suppose." To this the missionary answered, "Well, take your choice
of the cannibals or the worms!" This missionary owned his life.
He had already lost it to find it again.

We are reminded here of the martyr missionary, Katar Singh
of Tibet, who, after he had been sewn up in a wet yak skin and
been exposed all day to the blistering sun, died an excruciating
death. But before his sun had set he called for a writing tablet
and wrote the following lines:

I give to Him, who gave to me
My life, my all, His all to be;
My debt to Him, how can I pay
Though I should live to endless day?

I ask not one, but thousand lives
For Him and His own sacrifice;
Oh, will I then not gladly die
For Jesus' sake, and ask not why?

"All things are yours—*death.*" Death, as well as life, belongs
to me. As Paul gives us the inventory of the Christian's possessions, he uses the wildest extravagance. Because these things are
true, his language is without stint or limit. Yet how is it possible
that death can be mine? my minister? my servant? Surely no
man can be lord of death as well as life. In the face of this last
enemy that shall be destroyed, how helpless we all are! Who can
command this awful force? Who can say him nay? "Death is an
enemy—an enemy universal, imminent, irresistible, authorized, inexorable, horrible, always lurking round the corner; death is the
wolf that tears the flesh from our bones, the sight from our eyes,
the pulse from our heart, the loved ones from our arms" (D. M.
Panton). How can any Christian, then, dare to say, "Death is
mine"? Hallelujah! The Lord of life and death once pulled the
fangs of the very king of terrors. Christ is Lord both of the dead
and living. He makes it gloriously possible for the believer to say,
"Whether we live, we live unto the Lord; and whether we die, we
die unto the Lord: whether we live therefore, or die, we are *the*
Lord's" (Rom. 14:8). We belong not to life, not to death. We
belong to Christ. All things are ours, whether life or death.

"Why are you martyrs so bent upon death?" cried an official to
Pionius of Smyrna, "You are so bent upon death that you make
nothing of it." The noble martyr replied, "We are bent not upon
death, but upon life." Verily, the poor, blind, persecuting world
has never heard the whisper of Christ to the martyr-heart: "Be
thou faithful unto death, and I will give thee a crown of life" (Rev.
2:10). The martyred missionary, J. W. Vinson, when asked by
his captor-bandits if he was afraid to die, replied: "No, if you
shoot, I go straight to heaven." Later, his body was found decapi-
tated. His fellow missionary, Mr. Hamilton, was inspired to write
the following lines:

Afraid? Of What?
To feel the spirit's glad release?
To pass from pain to perfect peace,
The strife and strain of life to cease?
    Afraid?—of that?

Afraid? Of What?
Afraid to see the Saviour's face,
To hear His welcome, and to trace
The glory gleam from wounds of grace?
    Afraid?—of that?

Afraid? Of What?
A flash—a crash—a pierced heart;
Darkness—light—O heaven's art!
A wound, of His a counterpart!
    Afraid?—of that?

Afraid? Of What?
To do by death what life could not—
Baptize with blood a stony plot,
Till souls shall blossom from the spot?
    Afraid?—of that?
            —C. H. Hamilton

Death was Vinson's servant. To die was gain. Death opened the door and sent Vinson to his Master. By death he did what life could not. Martyrs' deaths have proved to be God's greatest and most final argument with the rebel world, for the blood of the martyrs is the seed of the Church. O death, where is thy sting? O grave, where is thy victory? Since I belong to Him who died and rose again, O death, thou art mine.

CHAPTER IX

Above Only—Not Beneath (continued)

STUNNED and indignant, the people of Constantinople were ready to create a disturbance because they could not bear the thought of banishment for their faithful preacher, John Chrysostom. Triumphantly he exclaimed to the agitated crowd: "What should I fear? *Death?* Christ is my life! *Banishment?* All the earth is the Lord's! *The seizure of my worldly goods?* I brought nothing into the world; what should I take out with me? I despise the world's terrors, and mock at all its splendours." Later, when recalled from his first banishment, Chrysostom said to his people, "Banished from among you, I praised God; given back to you, once more I do the same. The courage of the faithful Pilot is not weakened by the calm, any more than it is shaken by the storm!"

Let me ask: Who was really emperor in those days? Was not Chrysostom? Banished? The whole world was his fatherland. His goods confiscated? He only held them to give away to the poor. The Roman Emperor would take away his life? He already hated "his own life also." Christ was so much his life that to kill him would be gain, not for the emperor, but for Chrysostom. Truly he lived "as having nothing, yet possessing all things." He possessed the world, possessed his chains, possessed his goods, possessed the land of his banishment, possessed any and all circumstances, yea, possessed even the Roman Emperor himelf, for that tyrant was too baffled and beaten to know what to do with this emancipated and all-victorious martyr. During one banishment Chrysostom had said: "Since Heaven is become my country, the whole world is a place of exile; Constantinople is no nearer Paradise than the desert to which they have sent me." Throughout life, and in death his motto was: "God be praised for every thing."

"All things are yours—*things present.*" Having been ourselves mastered by Christ, we Christians are to master every present thing, whether of place or condition or circumstance. Things present are to be not our masters, but our ministers.

> *"Say not, my soul, 'From whence*
> *Can God relieve my care?*
> *Remember that Omnipotence*
> *Has servants everywhere."*

Each "thing present" is the servant of Omnipotence, so that it is not for us to reason whether God or the devil sent it. Circumstances may be providential, or may be forced upon us, or may be of our own creation. In any case let us settle on this one thing: God is eager to use them for our good. In no instance should we allow them to becloud the face of God even as Dr. Holden once said, "Circumstances have proved to be not hiding places from God, but meeting places with God."

Nor is it ours to itch for a change of conditions. The sinning and selfish world is forever crying out against its circumstances, and most of us saints do little better. We cannot say, "I have learned in whatsoever state I am, therewith to be content." Restless and fretting, we chafe for a change. We wish ourselves "otherwhere" than where we are. Yet until we are willing and determined to win the victory in the midst of present circumstances, whether they be good or evil, what reason have we to suppose that we would ever win the victory in any other circumstances?

But how can we win the victory? Not by fretting or fighting, not by setting our teeth to grin and bear it, not by dogged determination to wait for the suffering to pass, not by a mere negative silence and submission—not by any and all these fleshly energies. Victory comes only by a deliberate acceptance of these things from the hand of our loving Father. "To them that love God all things work together for good." A saintly old farmer understood this truth and put the text, "God is love," on his weathercock. Mr. Spurgeon queried, "Do you mean that God's love is as changeable as the wind?" To this the godly man replied, "No; whichever way the wind blows, God is love." To the man who loves God every weather is right. Then let me know no gain nor loss. Let my hopes be fulfilled or dashed to the ground. Let my prayers be answered or unanswered. Whenever I am tempted to say, "Surely the darkness shall cover me"; behold, "even the night shall be light about me. Yea, the darkness hideth not from Thee; but the night shineth as the day: the darkness and the light are *both alike to Thee*"—and may be both alike to *me*, bless God. George Mueller used to say: "In 1,000 things it is not 999 of them which work together for good, but 999 plus one." Many of us are able to thank God for many things, perhaps even for a few hard things. We are able to see how these few hard things do us good. But can we thank God for the thing which is, to every appearance, against us? What is our "plus one?" *There* God "gets us." *There* we meet Him in grace.

In *By My Spirit* Dr. Goforth recounts the experience of a lady missionary to whom a printed motto had been given which read something like this: "Whatever my Father sends me, be it joy or disappointment, no matter how hard it may be to bear, since I know it comes from my Father, I am going to receive it with both hands joyfully." During Dr. Goforth's subsequent meetings at her station, this missionary was disappointed and defeated in her expectations of revival. One afternoon during her absence one of her colleagues repainted her motto and, she says, "hung it on the wall opposite the door of my room, so that I would be certain to see it as soon as I entered. Well, when I opened the door and saw that motto hanging there—it was just too much. I went right over and turned its face to the wall. I simply couldn't for the moment bring myself to receive such a disappointment as this 'with both hands joyfully.'" This missionary refused, for the moment, to possess her disappointment. Ere long, however, she repented and since that time has been used mightily in all parts of China for the deepening of the spiritual life. Her distressing disappointment she made her servant by taking it *joyfully with both hands*. She made it *hers*, and thereby ceased to be "under the circumstances." She was above only—not beneath.

Yet how do Christians get out from beneath their circumstances to the position of "above only?" Many defeated souls hope for a better, brighter day when they will find themselves borne on eagles' wings by the mystic joys of faith. How it shall come to pass they know not, but they do hope to discover the mystic key whereby they will find themselves, as if by magic, on top. Most assuredly they will find themselves in the same defeated condition in the coming years unless some action is taken. But how shall they act? Where shall they begin? To get the victory in the midst of present circumstances there is no remedy but to begin here and now. Remember that Christ triumphed over all in His supreme weakness. In His death He slew the whole hierarchy of hell—*"triumphing over them in it"* (Col. 2:15). To the followers of the Crucified there is the assurance of victory in "things present," neither by fleeing from them, nor by evading them, nor yet by escaping them, but by triumphing *"in"* all these things. Christ promises to be with us "in trouble." Someone has wisely said: "Jesus Christ is no security *against* storms, but He is perfect security *in* storms. He has never promised you an easy passage, only a safe landing."

Begin then to obey the command, *"In every thing give thanks."* More practical still, begin "giving thanks *always* for all things." Without even wishing for a change of circumstances, begin to thank God for the trial, the sickness, the insult. Remember that, if you are ever to learn to be more than conqueror, you must learn it *soon*, for, ere long, you will be where you can never learn for His sake to be "killed all the day long." If you have failed to learn to be victor in the midst of present circumstances, yours will be a great shame before Christ at His coming.

When Paul began to pray thrice that his "thorn" in the flesh might depart from him, he almost missed the Lord and His way in trial. For this thorn was intended to be "the messenger of Satan" for the express purpose of buffeting him. How reasonable it was to pray that it might depart! But Christ's answer changed Paul's outlook, for He said: "My grace is sufficient for thee: for My strength is made perfect in weakness." Instead of resisting his thorn and frantically fighting this messenger of Satan, Paul said: "I take pleasure in being without strength, in insults, in being pinched, in being chased about, in being cooped up in a corner for Christ's sake; for when I am without strength, then am I dynamite" (lit. trans.).

The blind preacher of Scotland, George Matheson, took this same position when he said: "My God, I have never thanked Thee for my thorn. I have thanked Thee a thousand times for my roses, but not once for my thorn. I have been looking forward to a world where I shall get compensation for my cross; but I have never thought of my cross as itself a present glory. Teach me the glory of my cross; teach me the value of my thorn. Show me that I have climbed to Thee by the path of pain. Show me that my tears have made my rainbows" (*Streams in the Desert*). The following words quoted from the same book are appropriate:

> One who was passing through deep waters of affliction wrote to a friend: "Is it not a glorious thing to know that no matter how unjust a thing may be, or how absolutely it may seem to be from Satan, *by the time it reaches us, it is God's will for us,* and will work for good to us."

Even when Satan entered into Judas the betrayer, Christ said: "The cup which My Father hath given Me, shall I not drink it?" And, again, when Pilate boasted of his authority, He said: "Thou couldest have no power at all against Me, except it were given thee from above." If we, too, would only take up the "thing" with both hands joyfully, many a trouble, many a sickness, and many a devilish deed would become "a royal diadem in the hand of our God"—our meeting place with God. If we are not mistaken, days of persecution are beginning to return even to our own land. It is high time that we so learn to "quit ourselves like men" that down deep in our hearts we can love the shadow of the Cross. All who wish to live victoriously and die triumphantly should read *Foxe's Book of Martyrs*, for its pages are brimful of the triumphs of prisoners who, like the apostle Paul, belonged neither to Caesar nor to any circumstance, and so could say, "I therefore, the prisoner of the Lord." Verily, they owned no other master but Christ, so that things present, including Caesar, belonged to them.

The great Apostle called himself
"The prisoner of the Lord";
He was not held by Roman chains,
Nor kept in Caesar's ward;
Constrained by love alone,
By cords of kindness bound,
The bondslave of the living Christ,
True liberty he found.

Oh, happy those who see
In poverty and pain,
In weakness and in toil,
Their Father's golden chain;
Who feel no prison walls
Though shut in narrow ways,
And though in darkness fettered fast
Can still rejoice and praise;
From sin's dread bondage bought,
They own their Master's ward,
They bear the brand of Christ,
Blest prisoners of the Lord!

—Author Unknown

Paul had a worthy follower in George Fox. When falsely accused, he was thrust into a horrible dungeon among felons and moss-troopers and loathsome surroundings. He says, "A filthy, nasty place it was, where men and women were put together in a very uncivil manner. Yet, bad as the place was, the prisoners were all made very loving and subject to me, and some of them were convinced of the Truth . . . I was never in prison that it was not the means of bringing multitudes out of their prisons" (From *Kohila* by Amy Carmichael).

Has my reader been caught in an inescapable net? Have your hopes been blasted? Are you the victim of an incurable disability? Have you been caused to suffer for righteousness' sake? Do you feel you are as much in prison as Paul or George Fox? Why not begin to "count it all joy," i.e., put it to your credit in the "joy column." By a deliberate act of faith accept your condition as the cup which your Father has given you. All things are yours, even your present prison. So improve the present that you will be able to say hereafter "I was never in prison but that it was the means of bringing multitudes out of their prisons."

To my desk as I write, a similar word comes from Africa from Hector Kirk. Concerning the consecration, disappointment, and suffering of his mother (Grandma Kirk, as we knew her), he writes:

> A book which came into her hand at that time, and which greatly influenced her life, was *The Christian's Secret of a Happy Life*. Its development of the truth that *all* things—even the wrongs and meannesses of fellow-Christians, as well as our own mistakes—God can and does work together for our good, gripped her, and gave her the Christian's heritage indeed, a happy life under any circumstances.

As a result from her prison of incapacity and ill health Grandma Kirk, through her children and grandchildren who are serving God in many places, brought multitudes out of their prisons. To the faithful intercession of this mother in Israel the Prairie Bible Institute owes much. Who follows in her train?

Is there some reader who, like Grandma Kirk, has no public ministry? Come with me to Bedford jail, and hear how John Bunyan, the tinker, felt as he wrote his immortal allegories: "I was at home in prison; and I sat me down and wrote and wrote, for joy did make me write." Perhaps in your "prison" God means you also to have a private ministry. Or come to another prison and learn from one who spent many years behind the bars at the hands of Rome:

> A little bird I am,
>   Shut from the fields of air;
> And in my cage I sit and sing
>   To Him who placed me there;
> Well pleased a prisoner to be,
> *Because, my God, it pleases Thee.*
>
> Nought have I else to do;
>   I sing the whole day long;
> And He whom most I love to please,
>   Doth listen to my song;
> He caught and bound my wandering wing,
> But still He bends to hear me sing.

My cage confines me round:
　Abroad I cannot fly;
But, though my wing is closely bound,
　My heart's at liberty.
My prison walls can not control
The flight, the freedom of the soul.

Oh! it is good to soar
　These bolts and bars above,
To Him whose purpose I adore,
　Whose providence I love;
And in Thy mighty will to find
The joy, the freedom of the mind.

But what shall I more say? Has God given us all things "in Christ"? Let us begin to possess, you in your small corner and I in mine. Convert every foe into a friend. Let even the wrath of man praise God. Are there great giants in your land? Do not complain, with Jacob, and say, "All these things are against me." Since all things work together for good that thought is a lie. Romans 8:28 is no less true than John 3:16. "They are bread" for you. Moabites and Ammonites? God will cause these, who have agreed together to put you out of your inheritance, to fight one another; then you can come along and "gather much spoil." Winds of adversity are against you? Our God "maketh the clouds His chariot"; He "walketh upon the wings of the wind." It is high time you climb aboard and ride with Him to victory. Do not hope to get through life *somehow*. Get through "not somehow, but triumphantly." He has springs for you in the rocky place. Like Samson you can gather honey from the entrails of a lion. Your valley of Achor will yet prove to be the door of hope. God can make your foes fight for you. Though the Philistines were Israel's deadly foes, yet the prophet Isaiah looked forward to the day when Israel would "fly upon the shoulders of the Philistines." Not only is Israel to conquer her foes, but she is to use them as horses and chariots to carry God's Israel to further victories.

O fellow believer, will you still choose to be poor in the midst of riches—in the midst of so many "things present" that are all working together as servants for your good? Listen: "He, that hath so many causes for joy and so great, is very much in love with sorrow and peevishness who loses all these pleasures, and chooses to sit down on his little handful of thorns" (From *Gold by Moonlight*, by Amy Carmichael).

"All things are yours—*things to come*." The unknown and uncontrollable future is *ours*. We belong to Him who is the first and the last. Because we are His who holds the key to all the future, "things to come" are ours. Today as of old, He himself knows what He will do. To Peter, in his perplexity concerning the present, Jesus said, "What I do thou knowest not now; but thou shalt understand hereafter" (John 13:7, R.V.).

The great apostle Paul had unmoved confidence for the future. As he went bound in the Spirit to Jerusalem, not knowing the things that would befall him there, he learned that bonds and afflictions awaited him. To all these warnings and forebodings he replied: "None of these things move me, neither count I my life dear unto myself, so that I might finish my course with joy" (Acts 20:24). And herein lay his secret: "Neither count I my life dear unto myself." Those who love not their lives unto the death give no place to the devil. In spite of the uncertain future they are not afraid. With the poet Lowell they well know:

Careless seems the great Avenger; history's pages but record
One death-grapple in the darkness 'twixt old systems and the Word;
Truth forever on the scaffold, Wrong forever on the throne—
Yet that scaffold sways the Future, and, behind the dim unknown,
Standeth God within the shadow, keeping watch above His own.

O fellow believer, the world is yours; life is yours; death is yours; things present and things to come, yea, "all things are yours." God has begun to give them to you. You begin to possess. Since every place that the sole of your foot shall tread upon shall be yours, let your foot of faith begin to tread heavily. Be above only—not beneath. In due time Love's great promise shall be fulfilled to you: "He that overcometh shall inherit these things; and I will be his God, and he shall be My son" (Rev. 21:7, marg.). Be content until that glorious day with such things as ye have: "As poor, yet making many rich; *as having nothing, and yet possessing all things*" (II Cor. 6:10).

CHAPTER X

Shut Up in Unbelief or Kadesh-Barnea

H E HAD BEEN in the ministry for some twenty-six years. In the midst of a Sunday evening service God laid hold of him and broke his proud heart. He went down to the church vestry, locked the door, and threw himself on his face on the rug in front of the mantelpiece. His church was full. His church relationships were good. He loved his people and they loved him. He could say, "I have not known a Sunday for fifteen years without conversions." He could not, therefore, be reckoned otherwise than a most successful minister of the gospel. That night his wife came to him in the study and said, "We are waiting for you to come to supper." "You must not wait for me; I have a broken heart. You don't know what I mean, do you? Wait till you get it." His testimony continues somewhat as follows:

That night God laid His hand on a proud minister and told him he had not gone far enough; there were reservations in his surrender; that he wanted Him to be pleased with the work which he had been trying to evade by making others do it. I would not give in. It took over four months for the truth to get home to me—to break me down. I knew that God was right and that I was wrong, but I was not prepared to pay the price. Christmas time came; it was the most miserable Christmas I ever had. I knew what Jesus wanted. He gave me a picture of a congregation with myself in the midst. I saw myself praying with my own people that I had preached to for fifteen years, and they had not been saved. I said, But, Lord, You know that is not my work; do not give me that; it will kill me. I cannot come out of the pulpit and plead with the people; it is against my temperament; and You made me!

At the end of January I saw well that it was Jacob struggling instead of clinging. I thought what was wrong was my circumstances; but what was really wrong was myself. After four months of struggling, there came a crisis. On the Saturday night I wrote my resignation to my church, marked with tears. I loved that church, but I felt I could not go on preaching when I had a contention with God. I went to bed, but could not sleep; then I arose and came out of the bedroom, and in doing so, I stumbled over my dog, Mike, at the door. He knelt at the side of his master and licked his face, thinking I was ill. I knelt there for three minutes, and then I found myself in the bosom of Jesus Christ forever, and ever, and ever; and all power and all joy and all blessedness rolled in like a deluge. I looked up, and it was two o'clock in the morning. I knew what Jesus wanted, and it was so kind of Him to have waited four months for a man like me.

Thereafter this man of God entered into a great inheritance among the fisher folk of the old land. His sermons were simple, but powerful. Hundreds and hundreds were saved. Every place that the sole of his foot trod upon was his. For four months, however, he had stood at his Kadesh-Barnea. That point was to him either "a gateway or a goal." There faced him the impossible barrier of his own proud and unbelieving heart. A great conquest lay before him, souls to conquer for Christ. He was about to quit the ministry and turn back into the wilderness. His willful and proud unbelief almost overthrew him; but at length the Spirit of God won through and brought him into the dust of death, the death of self. Out from his innermost being there flowed rivers of living water, and wherever that river went there sprang up an abundance of fruit.

Come now to Kadesh-Barnea, that we may consider the issues of that crisis hour as it applies to God's people of all ages. Having been redeemed from Egypt "by a mighty hand," the Israelites have come to the end of a long trek. "We went through all that great and terrible wilderness," said Moses, "and we came to Kadesh-Barnea." With redemption behind them and with a glorious inheritance before them, they belonged, with all God's people, "not to their past but to their future." God brought them *out* to bring them *in*. "Behold, the Lord thy God hath set the land before thee: go up and possess it, as the Lord God of thy fathers hath said unto thee; fear not, neither be discouraged" (Deut. 1:21). Kadesh-Barnea was Israel's gateway into the kingdom. It was the last post on the long trek, the gateway to great things for God's people. Theirs was a call to conquer, to inherit, to enter into God's rest.

From Moses' admonition to the new and disciplined generation some forty years later, we may gather, however, how gigantic were the tribes, how impregnable the fortresses, and how terrific the odds which faced Israel at Kadesh-Barnea: "Hear, O Israel: thou art to pass over Jordan this day, to go in to possess nations greater and mightier than thyself, cities great and fenced up to heaven, A people great and tall, the children of the Anakims, whom thou knowest, and of whom thou hast heard say, Who can stand before the children of Anak!" (Deut. 9:1, 2).

For their assurance in the face of such overwhelming odds, Israel was told to "well remember" plagued and smitten Egypt, the signs at the Red Sea, the drowning hosts of Pharaoh. The voice of the past was sufficient. Pursued by one long succession of miracles, Israel's memory could furnish all manner of food for faith. Had they hungered? Manna had rained from heaven. Had they thirsted? Waters had gushed from the rock. Had they faced warring Amalek? Through uplifted hands the weak had taken the prey. Had they needed guidance? Day and night the cloud had been there. Had they themselves fallen into idolatry and lust? "With mercy and with judgment" they had learned the terrible consequences of disobedience. With many signs in mind and with Sinai's awful demonstrations yet fresh upon their memories, Israel came to Kadesh-Barnea. It was an hour of choice, an hour solemn, revealing, decisive. So severe was the test that the result would be nothing short of tragedy or triumph. But with such a marvelous past behind her and such a glorious land before her, Israel could well have said, in the language of the Ethiopian proverb· *"Hats off to the past; coats off to the future."*

But God's people were weighed in the balances and found wanting. The hour was one of supreme testing and discovery. The walled cities, the sons of Anak, the impregnable fortresses, the "seven nations greater and mightier"—all these insurmountable odds found faith wanting. God's people were both discovered and uncovered. They could not enter in because of unbelief. They had either to go on or to go back—and they, therefore, "in their hearts turned back again into Egypt."

Let us consider some of those things which might answer to "the seven nations greater and mightier" than God's Israel and which in every age prevent His people from entering into their inheritance. Let us set out seven insurmountables "greater and mightier" than Canaan's condemned giants.

Unbelief

The first of these is that age-old sin, the sin of unbelief. This is the sin charged upon Israel. Unbelief is no mere negative evil. It is a positive rejection of God—His claims, His commands, His truth. Israel rebelled against the Lord. So terrible and provoking was their sin that God said, "I sware in my wrath, They shall not enter into My rest." A thousand years later Nehemiah said that they "refused to obey, neither were mindful of Thy wonders that Thou didst among them; and hardened their necks, and in their rebellion appointed a captain to return to their bondage" (Neh. 9:17).

Moses accused Israel: "*In this thing* ye did not believe in the LORD your God." We are like Israel. We doubt not that God can do great and wonderful things. We are fundamental. We can subscribe to the entire range of miracle. It can be said of us as of Israel: "They saw My work." But, dominated by unbelief, we too refuse to believe that God *can now do* the impossible. In the given thing, the present crisis, we do not believe. Israel "entered not in," not because of Anak or any seven nations, but "because of unbelief." It is the same with us. In unbelief we balk. Far "greater and mightier" than any son of Anak is the power of unbelief in the heart. Hence the frightful admonition: "Today if ye will hear His voice, Harden not your hearts . . . lest any man fall after the same example of unbelief [disobedience]." Can it be that the reader has come to some definite issue? some mountain of difficulty? Some unrelenting opposition? some impossible witness for Christ? some insurmountable? Has God written it against you that *in this thing* ye did not believe in the Lord your God?" What is your issue? Beware—this may be your Kadesh-Barnea.

Listen to Hudson Taylor as God was calling him to enter into the land of rest and blessing and bounty both for himself and for China:

> As the light gradually dawned on me, I saw that faith was the only pre-requisite, was the hand to lay hold on His fulness and make it my own. *But I had not this faith.* I strove for it, but it would not come; tried to exercise it, but in vain. Seeing more and more the wondrous supply laid up in Jesus, the fulness of our precious Saviour—my helplessness and guilt seemed to increase. Sins committed seemed but as trifles compared with the sin of unbelief which was their cause, which could not, or would not, take God at His word, but rather made Him a liar. Unbelief was, I felt, the damning sin of the world —yet, I indulged in it.

SIN

A certain Christian lady was seeking in vain to know the Spirit-filled life. She seemed unable to believe the promises of God and receive by faith the Spirit's fullness. After some dealing and probing it was discovered that she had "ought against" her brother. She insisted that she could not forgive him unless he came and confessed his sin. It was pointed out that she must first go and be reconciled and forgive, even as she had been forgiven. With contrition and tears she confessed her sin, and set out to obey God— that she might obtain forgiveness. How quickly faith sprang up in her heart. She was able to believe the promises and claim the Comforter's gracious infilling. Ere long she was rejoicing with joy unspeakable and full of glory. To Timothy Paul spoke of "holding the mystery of the faith in a pure conscience." Someone says, "A pure conscience is the home of faith. There she abides. Let conscience be defiled, and faith disappears."

Beware of minimizing the *size* of sin. Do not excuse yourself by saying, "Oh, it is such a little thing." There are no little sins. Regardless of the size, remember that each sin is one of those mighty insurmountables, so much "greater than thou" that by comparison all the sons of Anak dwarf into grasshoppers.

Sin! How short the word! How brief the sound! But oh, the length and breadth and depth and height of sin! Who can fathom its birth? Who can trace its death? It scaled the infinite heights and turned Heaven's archangel into the prince of darkness. It prepared the prison house of hell for the devil and his angels. It kindled the flames unquenchable. "It forged the chains which bind lost sinners to their burning beds." It was sin that raised man's rebel hand against God. It is still sin that lays Christ's honour in the dust. What then have saints to do with sin! Jesus came to save His people *from* their sins.

There is no taskmaster like sin. Blame not your lack of victory on the flesh or the old man. If you are having difficulty getting into the possession of the abundant life, the reason may not be far to seek. Is there some unforsaken sin? some unforgiven wrong? some unheeded command? some uncorrected statement? some unpaid debt? It may be that you have ceased—or have you ever begun?—to go and humble yourself and confess your sinful pride of heart to those you have wronged. Although quite unaware of your state, you may be miles from the place of blessing. Perhaps you came to Kadesh months or years ago. Take heed lest you be "hardened through the deceitfulness of sin." Get desperate, get definite, get down and dig that dirty sin out and do it to death.

FLESH

Scripture says they that are in the flesh cannot please God. Flesh and faith are in direct antagonism. Paul says, "The carnal mind [the minding of the flesh, Gr.] is enmity against God: for it is not subject to the law of God, neither indeed can be" (Rom. 8:7). Having been cut off from the old Adam at the Cross, and having been grafted into the new Adam, believers are said to be "not in the flesh, but in the Spirit." But who can doubt the nearly almighty power of the flesh in its dominating thralldom over God's people? Scripture speaks of many forms of the flesh. Space will allow us to touch upon only those forms suggested by the murmuring, complaining people of God at Kadesh-Barnea. We read that "the mixt multitude that was among them fell a lusting [lusted a lust] : and the children of Israel also wept again, and said, Who shall give us flesh to eat? We remember the fish, which we did eat in Egypt freely; the cucumbers, and the melons, and the leeks, and the onions, and the garlick: But now our soul is dried away: there is nothing at all, beside this manna, before our eyes" (Num. 11:4-6). They murmured, "Wherefore have ye brought us up out of Egypt to die in the wilderness? for there is no bread, neither is there any water; and our soul loatheth this light bread." The Psalmist says that they "lusted exceedingly in the wilderness, and tempted God in the desert. And He gave them their request; but sent leanness into their soul" (Psa. 106:14, 15). And their wicked fleshliness showed itself in all its virulence at Kadesh-Barnea when they feigned a special affection for their wives and children, and made God out to be a tyrant for having brought them forth to die in the wilderness.

Until saints realize the power of the flesh, how can they believe God? All man's natural powers, whether of mind or emotion or will, are under the dominion of the flesh. In this day of cultured, refined, and educated flesh, there is nothing quite so subtle as the thinking and willing and planning of fleshly Christians. Shall we set out a few?

Think of the schemes of raising money to forward the cause of Christ. What has the Holy Spirit to do with these manipulations, which have the marks of the flesh?

Note the young people's gatherings where the flesh is whipped up to "fall in love with Jesus." Mistake us not. Let us encourage every effort to rescue the young, but let leaders cease to cater to the flesh in order to do the work of the Spirit.

One of the subtlest forms of flesh is in connection with unregulated human affections. What have all these premature engagements and marriages to do with getting the gospel to the heathen world? Hundreds of these young people might have obtained the heathen for their inheritance, but the flesh has blocked and bound them. They cannot enter in.

Think of the many homes where Christians manifestly live to eat. Their excesses could almost support a missionary—while the heathen wait and die and perish. Recall what Paul says about those "whose God is their belly."

Consider the superfluity not only of finery and food, but also of furnishings and extravagances in the homes of many Christians. A. T. Pierson once said: "There is buried in gold and silver plate and useless ornaments, within Christian homes, enough to build a fleet of fifty thousand vessels, ballast them with Bibles and crowd them with missionaries; build a church in every destitute hamlet, and supply every living soul with the gospel within a score of years."

While God's people thus continue to bow and serve and cater to the flesh, how shall they ever be able to believe God and enter in?

If Thou, O God, wilt make my spirit free,
　　Then will that darkened soul be free indeed;
I cannot break my bonds apart from Thee;
　　Without Thy help I bow, and serve, and bleed.

Arise, O Lord, and, in Thy matchless strength,
　　Asunder rend the links my heart that bind;
And liberate, and raise, and save, at length,
　　My long-enthralled and subjugated mind.
　　　　　　　　　　　　　—Author Unknown

WORLDLINESS

Closely related to the flesh is worldliness. It has three chief roots, "the lust of the flesh, and the lust of the eyes, and the vainglory of life"; yet how ramified are the myriad branchings of this deep-rooted tyranny. The Church of Jesus Christ for the most part is dominated by the world. She is subject to the world's maxims and slogans, its standards and fashions, its principles and opinions. The poison of the prince of this world has so penetrated church life as to paralyze faith. Think of the religious world, much of which is bound with its traditional and ecclesiastical domination, its exclusiveness and caste, its subtle aims and promotional interests. Note how we hasten to bow and pay homage to the lettered and the influential. When the world's wisdom erects her image and sends forth all kinds of janglings — such as, "scholarship is agreed" — behold how quickly the church leaders, fearing to be reckoned among us "ignorant and unlearned," begin to trim and square their creed to suit the world's vain conceit. We need ministers with such a holy and courageous defiance of all the world's idolatry that they will answer with the three Hebrews: "Be it known unto thee, . . . that we will not serve thy gods, nor worship the golden image which thou hast set up" (Dan. 3:18).

What kind of world rises up and bids defiance to the reader? What is it that paralyzes you with fear? Or what is your subtle and soft little world, unknown to anyone else, that hugs and holds you back from your inheritance? Whatever her form, whether fair or foul or frightful, beware of her. She is "greater and mightier than thou." Many strong men have fallen before her. Even Paul lamented: "Damas hath forsaken me, having loved this present world." Jesus warned men: "No man, having put his hand to the plow, and looking back, is fit for the kingdom of God."

However, let us also be encouraged. The world was crucified, put to a hanged-man's doom. It is a victim of the Cross. Christ assures us, "I have overcome the world." Thank God, then, we are well able to overcome it — this is the victory that overcometh the world, even our *faith*. Before the "mustard seed" this mountain will fall.

PRIDE

Many professors, teachers, and Christian workers are bound by pride. They will not humble themselves and take the place of a learner. Seldom does one hear a teacher or professor or minister admit his own need except in the most vague and general terms; and even such admissions build up and "save face," rather than lose it. Do such men wonder why they seem never to enter in by faith? "How can ye believe, which receive honour one of another, and seek not the honour that cometh from God only?" (John 5:44).

There is a mighty connection between a humble attitude and a living faith that can enter in and cast out the mountain of pride. We verily believe if many of God's children would cease telling God about their high and holy aspirations and would begin to tell Him the truth regarding their stinking pride and vanity and a thousand other unmanageable things in their secret lives, they would soon be able to stretch forth the hands of faith and take territory they have hitherto been unable to claim.

COVETOUSNESS

One of our graduates (whom we shall call Mr. Smith) had just been called into work among a tribal people.   Before he could speak the tribal language, he began conducting a short-term Bible School with a tribal brother as interpreter.   This tribal evangelist told Mr. Smith that the leading deacon in the local church was a man given to wine and was, moreover, a man with a fierce temper, to which he often gave way.   This deacon's life was felt to be a definite hindrance to blessing in that church.   Now, according to custom visitors were entertained in the various Christians' homes.   The first night they were invited to the deacon's house.   To accept such hospitality was to give public endorsement of the deacon.   Mr. Smith and the evangelist were uneasy about the matter, but they accepted the hospitality offered.   As Mr. Smith sat down to the table and began to swallow his first mouthful of rice, a verse came to him as from God:

> "But now I have written unto you not to keep company, if any man that is called a brother be a fornicator, or covetous, or an idolater, or a railer, or a *drunkard*, or an extortioner; *with such an one no not to eat*" (I Cor. 5:11).

Mr. Smith said later that he felt he would have choked had he tried to eat.   Then he did a thing which was the height of discourtesy; had he risen and deliberately slapped his host's face it would not have been less shocking to the oriental sense of propriety.   Without a word of explanation he arose and left his host's table and went out.   The deacon turned to the evangelist for explanation — and the evangelist had to tell him.   The deacon was furious and threatened a lawsuit against the church.   Mr. Smith spent that night in the woods praying.   In the morning the proud deacon came with burning tears of repentance, and publicly confessed his sin and got right with God.

But let the reader notice that between the "fornicator" and the "drunkard," concerning whom Paul says "with such an one no not to eat," he names both the "covetous" and the "idolater." Elsewhere Paul speaks of a covetous man as an idolater. Many Christians are doubtless forbidden entrance into their inheritance for the reason that they are covetous — i.e., plain idolaters. Perhaps many of these would enter in, as did the deacon, were they as faithfully dealt with as the deacon was. Has the reader ever heard of a Christian worker refusing endorsement of some covetous Christian by refusing to eat with him? Why not? Was the worker himself coveting the favour or the cash of the covetous brother?

Let it be remembered that there are many forms of covetousness — that the monster is hydra-headed. Christians covet not only cash and things but also fame and honour. A news item states that a certain Governor of Hong Kong was entertaining a lady at the Government House. The latter was quite aggrieved to find herself on the Governor's left instead of his right. Although she broached her grievance obliquely, she made her covetousness of position obvious. Finally she remarked: "I suppose it is very difficult for your aide-de-camp always to put your guests in their right places?" "Not at all," said the Governor blandly; "those who matter don't mind, and those who mind don't matter."

In Romans 7 Paul calls all this the sin that indwells the believer. He says, "I had not known lust, except the law had said, *Thou shalt not covet.*" He finally found himself full of this slimy protrusion which brought him into complete captivity. "What I would, that do I not; but what I hate, that do I." Until the covetousness of evil desire was dealt with, Paul could not enter into the land of rest and victory. Covetousness blocked his way, a "greater and mightier" than Paul.

SELF

Self cannot cast out self, nor can self ever believe God. Until a Christian in some measure sees by the illumination of the Spirit that he is hopelessly enslaved to himself, and until he despairs of any deliverance apart from Christ, he will find his way into the land of promise blocked.

Myself, arch traitor to myself;
   My hollowest friend, my deadliest foe,
My clog whatever road I go.

                                    —Rossetti

"Sin arises from the erection of self into the supreme power within us. And self will reign until a Mightier One occupy the throne it has usurped" (Beet). The all-pervading plague of man is the plague of self. Behold a man full of leprosy, the leprosy of self. Paul lays down the only possible escape from sin: "Reckon ye *yourselves also to be dead indeed unto sin,* but alive unto God through Jesus Christ our Lord." The Cross is the end of me in my relation to sin. Sin and self expired together. Our old man was crucified with Him. As Paul puts it elsewhere, "I have been crucified together with Christ." Yet again he says, "One died for all, therefore all died; . . that they that live should no longer live unto themselves, but unto Him who for their sakes died and rose again" (II Cor. 5:14, 15, R.V.).

At this point let us detect the deep-seatedness of secret self uncovered at Kadesh-Barnea. Here the heart of man, so given to concealment and hypocrisy, declares itself in all its blackness, rebellion, and murder. Its terms are unmistakable. With no mere impulsive madness or unbridled passion did the Israelites cry, "Would to God we had died in the land of Egypt!" or "Would to God we had died in this wilderness!" Herein they uttered their considered and deliberate heart attitude. The dreadful fact dawned upon them that there was no possibility of entering the land but by faith in God. They were shut up to faith; but, since they were wrong in heart, they had shut themselves up in unbelief. They were caught and uncovered. The one thing they could not and would not do was believe God. "So we see they could not enter in because of unbelief." They faced the absolute necessity of dying to stubborn self in order to trust God. Yet God's claims were clear-cut. They could inherit through faith or die. It was as if they said, *"Would to God we had died already* — If it is a question of death to self or physical death, we declare ourselves as unqualifiedly in favour of physical death rather than letting God have all His way with us."

They actually said that they preferred to have died in Egypt during the slaughter of the first-born, or even to have died in the wilderness under the divinely sent plague upon those who lusted.   They preferred the plague of physical death under divine judgment "rather than run the hazard of making a descent upon Canaan." They wished rather to die criminals under God's justice than to live conquerors in His favour.   As proof that they preferred physical death to the death of self — the grave instead of grace — they daringly, impudently risked their all by going up presumptuously "in the morning" to fight their own way into Canaan.   They had, however, shut themselves up in unbelief — and God shut them out.

In addition to this daring impudence they level another charge, not against Moses but directly against the Lord (even though in so doing they recognize that it was the Lord indeed who had miraculously brought them all the way thus far): "Wherefore hath the LORD brought us unto this land, to fall by the sword, that our wives and our children should be a prey? were it not better for us to return into Egypt?   And they said one to another, Let us make a captain, and let us return into Egypt" (Num. 14:3, 4). When self flames forth, it can do nought but make God a tyrant, a cheat, a liar.   In effect God answers: You prefer the *grave* to meeting Me in *grace?*   You wish to die?   Then die you shall.   You will not enter in?   Enter in you shall not.   You have expressed your deliberate decision.   It is ratified in Heaven.   I swear in My wrath you shall not enter in!

Kadesh-Barnea became not a gateway, but a goal — a grave.

They came to the gates of Canaan,
But they never entered in;
They came to the very threshold,
But they perished in their sin.
                                            —A. B. Simpson

CHAPTER XI

The Fear of God

IT MAY BE that the atomic bomb is the 'good news of damnation,' " said Dr. Robert M. Hutchins of Chicago University shortly after the first atomic bomb was dropped on Hiroshima, "that it may frighten us into that Christian character and those righteous actions and those positive political steps necessary to the creation of a world society — not a thousand or five hundred years hence, but now." Similarly in his book, *This Atomic Age and the Word of God*, Dr. Wilbur M. Smith has pointed out that ours might easily have been an age to a large extent without fear. Modern medicine has virtually eliminated the dread of pain and sudden death by disease; improved cultivation has eliminated the fear of famine, at least on this continent; democracy has eliminated any immediate dread of the dictator; social insurance has eliminated fear of insecurity in old age; and the United Nations, it was hoped, would eliminate war. President Roosevelt's "four freedoms," deemed essential to a peace-time millennium, included freedom from fear — not in some dim and distant future but "in our own time and generation."

It is remarkable, therefore, that, at the very time when so many causes of fear seem to have been eliminated, the most frightful form of fear ever to make men afraid — the fear of sudden, unannounced, and entire "liquidation" — is being heralded from the housetops. In his frank and famous confession entitled, "I am a Frightened Man," Professor Harold C. Urey, one of the leading scientists in connection with the atomic bomb, said, "I write this to frighten you. I am a frightened man myself. All the scientists I know are frightened — frightened for their lives — and frightened for *your* life."

Perhaps it is to our generation especially that Paul's character sketch of the ungodly applies, "There is no fear of God before their eyes." Could it be that the All-wise is not going to permit our prodigal world to plunge into the far country of indulgence and infidelity to find there a peace-time of plenty and pleasure with all fear removed? Has the most High reserved this discovery of such frightful forces to be Heaven's final and universal hold on an otherwise fear-less and care-less and care-free humanity?

In calling the atomic bomb "the good news of damnation," Dr. Hutchins manifestly hopes that human nature may be frightened into some form of good behaviour. Is it not a remarkable fact, then, that most educators discredit fear as a motive worthy of creating faith and moving men heavenward? Many of the overwise of this generation — those wise above that which is written — would deny to fear any genuine virtue as a force in divine-human relationships. Nevertheless in matters of everyday life these same men make use of the motive of fear. See them fear the uniformity of the laws of nature and obey them; see them fear the danger of stepping off a hundred-foot building because they believe in the law of gravitation and fear it with profound respect; see them fear in some measure the laws of the land. In manifold ways men bow the knee to fear.

Yet in spite of this fact theologians unite with educators in the silly and popular fashion of discrediting fear utterly when it comes to higher realms of ethics. If the laws of the universe are so fixed and stable as to defy disrespect, then how much greater are the laws in the higher realm of morality and righteousness! When, with a lofty air of superiority, conceited men waive aside the terror of the Lord as a superstition or a relic of the Middle Ages, they reveal their inconsistency and contempt for God. Even the great poet, Goldsmith, said, "Fear guides more to their duty than gratitude. For one man who is virtuous from the love of virtue, from the obligation which he thinks he lies under to the Giver of all, there are ten thousand who are good only from their apprehension of punishment."

That any fear that merely frightens, startles, or dismays can have no lasting moral effect is generally agreed. Such fear has only torment and breeds bondage. Even fear of the atomic bomb can neither check nor chain human depravity and sin. All such hopes for lasting transformations are doomed to most tragic disappointment. Had there ever been any hope in that direction, then surely the discovery of gunpowder, of dynamite, of TNT, and of poison gas would long ere this have been the good news of damnation that would perform a mighty gospelizing of the nations. But it has not been so. Only by the fear of God men depart from evil. Dread of His wrath and His displeasure is indeed "the beginning of wisdom."

To ascertain the motives that move men and women Godward, we have conducted an annual survey of our incoming Bible School classes for several years. This survey is an astonishing reflection and revelation of how the poison of "no fear" has virtually paralyzed effective testimony. In this day when God's servants are continually being reproached for not preaching more of the *love* of God, and when we are told that this modern age has outgrown appeals of this kind, it is more than merely interesting and shocking to note how great a percentage of each Bible School class here was moved to flee to Christ for safety by the powerful influence of some form of fear. We herewith present the result of this survey covering the past eighteen years:

Year	No. in Class	Percentage Moved by Fear	Percentage Moved by Love
1931-32	86	76.8	7
1932-33	100	75	3
1933-34	122	73.3	5
1934-35	88	60	8
1935-36	72	67	1.4
1936-37	110	71	10
1937-38	103	63	7
1938-39	128	60	8
1939-40	125	50	6
1940-41	157	60.5	6
1941-42	137	60	9
1942-43	117	60	6
1943-44	108	66.6	--
1944-45	134	60	3.7
1945-46	134	63.4	9.7
1946-47	259	62.5	12.7
1947-48	266	64.3	6
1948-49	261	58.6	10.4

It will be noted that of these 2507 students almost two-thirds of them (65%) were moved through the motive of fear alone, whereas those who were moved by the motive of love averaged only a little more than six percent of the total. (Other motives such as desire for peace, joy, and satisfaction claimed a small percentage, while some, having come to Christ at an early age, knew not the motive that moved them.) These facts, startling and undisputed accord with those ascertained on one occasion in the Old Country. A missionary writing to the *Evangelical Christian* in May, 1931, says:

Your article on "the fear of the Lord" reminds me of an incident in 1920 or 1921. A three day's conference met in London to consider the Person and Work of the Holy Spirit. The conference was convened by the late Dr. F. B. Meyer. About four hundred Christian workers remained to tea one of the days when Dr. Meyer conducted a tea-table conference. After testing those present as to the period in life of their conversion, he tested to get the agencies most used and the kind of message. Dr. Meyer was surprised, as were all of us present, to find that not only were the large majority of those present brought to the Lord as a result of the regular work of the church rather than special missions, etc., but also that an overwhelming number testified that it was because of some message or influence of the *Terror* of the Lord—*fear* of consequences against refusing the Lord's grace. Fewer were brought to faith and trust in Christ by the message of the *Love* of God! Dr. Meyer remarked in words something like this: "Oh, this is more than interesting and astonishing, especially in these days when we are rebuked often for not preaching more of the Love of God! Christian workers, ministers, and missionaries, take note of this; you will need to remember it as you go to your work."

Is the majesty of the Moral Ruler to meet with no respect? Is the authority of His law of no consequence? "Is there nothing in God to fear?" An effete dilettantism would feign tell us so. Nevertheless all history and Scripture and experience cry out against such an emasculated and effeminate theology. In the Middle Ages there may have been a disproportionate prominence given to the contemplation of the inexorable Judge. Men so feared that they were almost unable to believe the Gospel's good news. Even Christ was almost unapproachable. But oh how far we have departed from those days! Today the pendulum has swung to an extreme that is infinitely more dangerous and deadly, for there is "no fear of God" before our eyes. Today conscience is so seared that God is no longer a "consuming fire" who can "by no means clear the guilty."

If it is not already manifest, the future may make it clear as the noonday sun that the greatest crime committed against this generation has been the stubborn and stupid extermination of *fear* from the churches. Modernism is perhaps largely responsible for this eradication of the terror of the Lord. Dean Inge, the man who declares that the doctrine of hell is a "blasphemy," is quoted by D. M. Panton as saying, "There never was a time when the fear of God played so small a part in men's and women's real religion as it does now. We are not afraid, as earlier generations were afraid, of God's judgment. The decay of fear as an element in vital religion is one of the most significant features of our time. The disappearance of threats from the pulpit is a very remarkable phenomenon, however we may account for it, and whether we approve it or not. The modern churchgoer is not much afraid when he listens to the warnings of God's judgment." Isn't it lamentable that this modernist was so utterly blind that he could not recognize the outcome of his own deadly doings? Having sown to his modern "wind of doctrine," he failed to recognize the whirlwind.

Not all men, however, are quite so blind as to what it is that is creating so many delinquents, and emptying the churches of young people. Clear-thinking, front-rank intellectuals know we are watering down our gospel and tempering truth to suit the age. Even *The London Times* (May 22, 1943) says, "Among the causes of the drift away from churchgoing and of the relaxation of moral standards which have come about within living memory, there can be little doubt that one of the chief has been the disappearance of the belief in eternal punishment. Rightly or wrongly, men are not afraid of God as they used to be, and have cast off the restraints which fear imposed."

Evangelist Oscar Lowry writes of a preacher who was robbed on the road by his one-time servant. The man was arrested and sentenced to a long punishment. Thinking he would try to touch the condemned man's conscience, the preacher queried, "How could you be so base as to rob your kind old employer?" The man's reply utterly silenced him: "You yourself tempted me to commit this offense against the law. I often heard you say both in public and in private that all men will enjoy everlasting bliss after death and that there is no such thing as eternal punishment or hell in the next world. Since you have removed my greatest fear, why should I dread the lesser one?"

Passing by Modernism's responsibility and guilt in eradicating man's fear, let us observe how this iniquitous absence of fear has largely devitalized and stripped present-day orthodoxy of its most powerful weapon. Listen to Dr. Timothy Dwight, the founder of Yale University: "Few, very few, are ever awakened or convinced by the encouragements and promises of the gospel, but almost all by the denunciations of the law. The blessings of immortality and the glories of heaven are usually, to say the least, preached with little efficacy to an assembly of sinners." Such was the wisdom vouchsafed to the original founders of our great institutions of education. What a frightful and wholesome sense of the majesty of the most High possessed these mighty men of God!

How differently men of a more stalwart generation warned the ungodly to flee from the wrath to come! For instance, the great hymn writer, Dr. Isaac Watts, whose hymns bear a depth and a dignity that shames the jazz and jingo of modern hymns, said, "I never knew but one person in the whole course of my ministry who acknowledged that the first motions of religion in his own heart arose from a sense of the goodness of God, 'What shall I render to the Lord, who hath dealt so bountifully with me?' But I think all besides who have come within my notice have rather been first awakened to fly from the wrath to come by the passion of fear."

These testimonies indicate that, with each succeeding age since their day, our gospel message has become poorer, more worthless, and more powerless in proportion as we have had the weapon of fear filched from us. Whereas the results of the above survey may startle some of us because of the proportion of our students moved by the motive of fear, our alarm should rather be that fear did not claim a still greater proportion. Indeed it ought to be observed that with the increasing lawlessness of the past twenty years the proportion has been decreasing.

My friends in the ministry will recollect that the old theologians of the Reformation had a wholesome sense of the fear of God. Their appreciation of fear was linked with the fact that, unlike many today, they did not belittle the Mosaic revelation. Recall that it was when Sinai's law was thundered from the Mount, causing the Israelites to quake and cringe in mortal terror, that Moses explained the meaning of that ministry: "God is come to prove you, and that *His fear* may be before your faces, *that ye sin not*" (Ex. 20:20). On the other hand, through no-law preaching extreme dispensationalists have not only contributed to lawlessness but as a consequence have also swung from a true understanding of the important place that fear should exercise in their ministry. Since in their theology Moses is largely tabooed, how can they conveniently drive home the terrors of a broken law? If the avenger of blood be not on the sinner's trail, why should he flee for safety to the city of refuge? With the neglecting of the law's curse there has developed not unnaturally a corresponding criminal failure to preach the wrath and judgment of the New Testament. The result is that people in the pew are led to feel that the consequences of disobedience are no longer to be dreaded as they once were. If "by the law is the *knowledge* of sin," it is not at all strange that there develops before us a growing insensibility to sin. It can scarcely be denied that the theology of extreme dispensationalism leads us still farther away from the fear and dread of God.

Perhaps some reader is not unlike an orthodox preacher of the writer's acquaintance, a man who has been rescued from ultra-dispensationalism. Back in the days of the depression this man of God came to feel that if he should preach judgment it would only harden his hearers. He felt that those troubles were already testing men beyond what they could endure. At that time, however, as he was making a study of the book of Revelation, he could not help but be thunderstruck with the message from the angelic trumpeter during the great tribulation (a time of trouble such as has never been nor ever again will be) when Antichrist will demand an undivided worship upon pain and penalty of death. Just when righteous judgments are falling in swift succession, and when the beast demands the bent knee of every man and his mark on every brow, Heaven's only "everlasting gospel" will thunder from the ether: "*Fear God*, and give glory to Him; for the hour of His judgment is come: and worship Him that made heaven, and earth, and the sea, and the fountains of waters" (14:7). My preacher friend also noted that there would follow the most fearful angelic warning ever yet heard in this world, a warning that will reach far beyond this frightful earthly visitation of divine wrath. For even in the midst of threatened starvation, and death in its most frightful forms, if any man dares to save life and limb by bowing to the beast, "he shall be tormented with fire and brimstone in the presence of the holy angels, and in the presence of the Lamb." Should we be surprised that this preacher who had begun to grow soft and sympathetic with sinners, in a sympathy at once foul and false and which failed to endorse the methods of God in His dealings with men, was cured of his tendency to qualify and emasculate the fearful threatenings of Scripture? "When we step back from identification with God's interest in others into sympathy with them, the vital connection with God has gone; we have put our sympathy, our consideration for them, in the way; and this is a deliberate rebuke to God" (Chambers).

Let us turn to the sequel of this heavenly warning, to the tribulation saints who fear God. How satisfying to finish reading the account (Rev. 15:2-4) of these tribulation saints who heeded this everlasting gospel and are enrolled forever as "them that had gotten the victory over the beast, and over his image, and over his mark, and over the number of his name"! These victors on the sea of glass sing "the song of Moses the servant of God, and the song of the Lamb," with that mighty burst of assurance for a finale: "Who shall not fear Thee, O Lord, and glorify Thy name? for Thou only art holy: for all nations shall come and worship before Thee; for Thy judgments are made manifest."

It is difficult for most of us to believe that to concur with these conclusions regarding the important place of fear depends upon depth of fellowship with God. To be entrusted with these dreadful and divine secrets requires a consecration to the death and a

courageous faith. Only men who have had a vision of God and
of themselves, and who have come through appalling humiliations
and heart-breaks and confessions will be able to pour forth a message compounded of the terror of the Lord and constraining love.
Enoch and Noah, the only two men of whom it is specifically said
that they "walked with God," were preachers of coming judgment.
But what reason are we given why Noah by faith prepared an ark
to the saving of his household? He was *"moved with fear."* The
conviction that a flood was coming so overwhelmed this "preacher
of righteousness" that he "moved" out to obey God in the face of
all the ridicule and reproach heaped upon him daily by a mocking,
scoffing world. God's warning voice stirred that old preacher to
build the ark. Cannot Christ still anoint men so that they too may
"walk with God" and bring to bear upon a silly and wicked generation the appalling sense of a judgment to come, a hell to escape,
and a coming deluge of fire from which men need to flee?

William Bramwell was one such preacher. With the dread of
these coming mysteries upon him and with a language almost inspired he came forth to manifest the awe of the divine majesty. The
one who preached his funeral sermon before a weeping audience
of ten thousand declared concerning him:

> Never did I behold a fallen child of Adam whose moral
> renovation was so complete, nor one who was so angelic and
> saintly. He appeared to be everything the Lord designed him
> to be.

This same William Bramwell wrote to a friend:

> You know I have been about three months in the furnace.
> This mystery of God I know not now, but I know He was with
> me. The glory I experienced was beyond all I can now relate.
> I was filled with mercy; I could have shouted mercy contin-
> ually. *Yet I never had so clear a view of the torments of the
> damned.*

Yet, again, in writing to another friend, he said:

> Though I have been in the furnace, yet I can assure you I
> have had such views of the glory of heaven and the torments
> of the damned that, if I have strength, I shall pour out such
> blessings and curses as I have never done before (Quoted in
> *Dynamic of Life,* by Wilkes).

At this point let us observe briefly the "fear nots" of Scripture as they are addressed to the saints. What a comfort to myriads of souls these have been! To the martyr role of all the tortured, how cheering has been this word of our Lord: *"Fear* none of those things which thou shalt suffer;" *"fear not,* neither be dismayed;" *"fear* thou not; for I am with thee." For the encouragement and confidence of needy souls who live in closest intimacy with God comes the assuring word: "There is *no fear* in love, but perfect love casteth out fear: because fear hath torment. He that feareth is not made perfect in love" (I John 4:18). What a goal! What a fellowship! What an attainment! Yet be assured that between most of us and such a vital experience much ground lies untaken. On the rugged road leading to such reality we have ignored many necessary and wholesome scripture portions on the fear of the Lord. They who by-pass the Scriptures bidding them to "fear" gather cold comfort from the Saviour's "fear nots." Paget Wilkes says, "It is eminently true that . . . those who have walked in closest fellowship with God have had more fearful visions of the wrath to come than are vouchsafed to the ordinary Christian." So, between an awful and reverential fear of God and John's "perfect love," where is there really any inconsistency or conflict? Our fault has been that we have dwelt at length on the "fear nots" for the saints, whereas the Scriptures, New as well as Old Testament, emphasize the impelling motive of fear. Four great impelling motives move men to action: Fear, Hope, Faith, and Love — these four, but the greatest of these is Fear. Fear is first in order, first in force, first in fruit. Indeed fear *is* "the beginning of wisdom."

Does it surprise my reader to learn that the Lord Jesus used the motive of fear more freely than any other? Who was it that spoke of the quenchless flame, the undying worm, the never forgiveness, the body and soul plunged in Gehenna? Indeed it was the One who was incarnate tenderness, and who "offered a perfect escape from hell to every sinning soul, and who died in order to secure it" (Moses Stewart). No less solemnly did the Saviour handle this subject of fear when addressing His own disciples, as recorded in Luke 12. Jesus "began to say unto His disciples first of all, Beware ye of the leaven of the Pharisees, which is hypocrisy"

(v. 1). Beware — lest you pretend to be what you are not, or conceal what you are. Be afraid — of being a hypocrite. Why? "For there is nothing covered, that shall not be revealed; neither hid, that shall not be known" (v. 2). The mask is coming off. Nothing can be finally concealed. Unlimited exposure of every hidden thing, be it evil or good, is the ultimate purpose of God. The Saviour urged such teaching in order to create fear in His "disciples" — fear of exposure, fear of shame, fear of public disgrace.

Having warned His disciples to be afraid (of hypocrisy), Jesus next utters a forbidden fear. Again He is addressing His own: "I say unto you, *My friends*, Be not afraid of them that kill the body, and after that have no more that they can do" (v. 4). Men may kill the body; then their venom is spent and their power ends. "After that" they can do "no more." He therefore forbids His friends to fear those who kill the body. Such freedom as this from false fear would be utterly impossible were it not for the commanded and true fear: "But I will forewarn you whom ye shall fear: Fear Him [God], which after He hath killed hath power to cast into hell; yea, I say unto you, Fear Him" (v. 5). Three times in one verse there is the repetition of the word *fear*. The emphasis is clear. "Only the fear of the Greater will effectually expel the fear of the less" (David Brown). It would be impossible not to be afraid of those who kill the body except for the truth of the little phrase, *"and after that* have no more that they can do."* The power for this victory over false fear "has nothing to do with the *act* of dying, but solely with what lies *beyond death*" (Panton). Only the finalities of the eternal future can master our fears. The more awful fear of God, the God of the hereafter, drives out the present fear of man.

Reversing the order the Saviour now voices another "Fear not." He says, "Are not five sparrows sold for two farthings, and not one of them is forgotten before God. But even the very hairs of your head are all numbered. Fear not therefore: ye are of more value than many sparrows" (vv. 6,7). Surely false fear is as needless as it is foolish. Has God power after death to cast into hell? No less has He power on earth to protect and preserve, even to the hairs of our head.

We are here reminded of a crisis in Judah's history during the days when wicked Ahaz was reigning over the southern kingdom. The northern kingdom of Israel was confederate with Syria against Judah. Concerning Ahaz we read that "his heart was moved, . . . as the trees of the wood are moved with the wind" (Isa. 7:2). Paralyzed with fear, this wicked king was determined to flee not to God but to Assyria for help. But God's word to Judah was, "Sanctify the LORD of hosts Himself; and let Him be your fear, and let Him be your dread. And He shall be for a sanctuary" (Isa. 8:13, 14). It was as though God said: Let the wholesome and awful dread of My displeasure expel your dread of these two kings; then you will prove that My presence "shall be for a sanctuary." Make Me your fear and you will experience My fellowship, My presence, My protection.

An excellent illustration of sanctifying the Lord of Hosts is the experience of the three Hebrew children. These three valiant soldiers feared God so much that they feared not the power of Nebuchadnezzar. To them God had always been a consuming fire. They feared Him more than they feared any furnace that might be heated seven-fold. Because they let Him be their fear and their dread, they could tell that mighty Babylonian monarch: "We are not careful to answer thee in this matter." Into the furnace they were thrown, but there they proved the truth of the word, "He shall be for a sanctuary." There the three walked with Him, walled in by fire and in fellowship divine. The form of the fourth was like unto the Son of God. "Nor was an hair of their head singed." Just 500 years later the Saviour said, "Even the very hairs of your head are all numbered. Fear not therefore: ye are of more value than many sparrows."

Lastly, Jesus comes to the very point of this whole discourse on *fear*. Keep in mind throughout that He is addressing "His disciples" (v. 1) and His "friends" (v. 4) — those to whom God is Father (v. 30), and Christ is Lord (v. 36), and who will therefore as servants have to render an account (v. 47). Christ has already bidden these men beware of hypocrisy, whether of pretense or of concealment. Now, as His followers, He especially warns them against the latter, of *concealing what they are*: His *disciples*, His *friends*. "I say unto you, Whosoever shall confess Me before men, shall the Son of man also confess before the angels of God: But he that denieth Me before men shall be denied before the angels of God" (vv. 8, 9). Thus in "His disciples *first of all*" the Lord Jesus sought to produce such a wise and holy fear that before a hostile and persecuting world they would come out into open and bold confession of Him.

It then comes to this: Disciples must be taught to fear. Christian workers who fail to instruct the churches in a wholesome and holy fear of God are guilty of unfaithfulness. They have missed the mind of their Master. Let us then as saints take care lest we be so encouraged to *fear not* that we find ourselves minus that stern and soul-purifying motive of fear which the Lord Jesus in wisdom laid down for "His disciples first of all."

Should anyone insist that this teaching of Jesus was before Calvary — a strange and illogical argument — then let us move forward to Paul's word to the Ephesians: "Be filled with the Spirit . . . subjecting yourselves one to another in *the fear of Christ*" (Eph. 5:18, 21, R.V.). Take his word to the Corinthians: "Having therefore these promises, dearly beloved, let us cleanse ourselves from all filthiness of the flesh and spirit, perfecting holiness in *the fear of God*" (II Cor. 7:1). Or note his admonition to the Philippians: "Work out your own salvation *with fear and trembling*" (Phil. 2:12). Finally, observe his warning to the sagging Hebrew saints: "*Let us therefore fear*, lest, a promise being left us of entering into His rest, any of you should seem to come short of it" (Heb. 4:1). God does delight to have His people enter into rest, enter into full assurance of faith and into a sense of their safekeeping in Christ. (It is pathetic how backslidden people are forever shaken over the pit at their annual camp meetings in some circles. This is a deplorable state of affairs. How our hearts have ached for them!) However, for the benefit of the rest of us who have swung to the opposite extreme of "no fear of God" someone pointedly says: "There never was a day when we needed more to beware of a teaching that encourages us to rejoice without trembling, that bids us walk in the comfort of the Holy Ghost unmindful of the fear of God, or serve the Lord with thanksgiving without reverence and godly awe." If there is such a thing as having "the cart before the horse" in things theological, we fundamentalists are guilty, verily guilty. That we have put the "cart" of spiritual *comfort* before the "horse" of holy *fear* cannot be denied.

Early church leaders were not so stupid and blind as we are. They warned the saints to "rejoice *with trembling.*" The great apostle Paul does indeed declare: "The love of Christ constraineth us." But, while we today still emphasize that constraint, we carefully overlook how Paul, like Noah, was first "moved with fear." "Knowing therefore the terror of the Lord," he persuaded men (II Cor. 5:11, 14). The early churches were edified and multiplied by walking in the fear of the Lord, and in the comfort of the Holy Ghost. They went forward in abounding power and multiplication under two great working principles (note their Scriptural order and logical connection), *"walking in the fear of the Lord, and in the comfort of the Holy Ghost"* (Acts 9:31). Does not our having ignored the combination of these two master-principles of the ministry account to a great degree for our loss of power and influence with men?

CHAPTER XII

Sin Finding Us Out

SADHU SUNDAR SINGH was once traveling in the mountains with a Tibetan companion on a bitterly cold day when snow was falling. Both men were so nearly frozen to death that they despaired of arriving at their destination alive. About that time they stumbled over a man half buried in the snow, unconscious and nearly dead from exposure. The Sàdhu suggested that they carry the unfortunate man to shelter, but the Tibetan refused to help, insisting that they would have all that they could do to save themselves. While the Tibetan passed on his way, the Sàdhu shouldered the man and with great difficulty managed to struggle on with his heavy burden. Through his extra exertion, Sundar began to warm up, and before long the nearly frozen fellow hanging on his shoulders began to share his warmth. Soon the Sàdhu came upon the body of the Tibetan, frozen to death. By the time Sundar had arrived at the village, the half-dead man had recovered consciousness. With a full heart, Sundar thought of the words of his Master: "Whosoever will save his life shall lose it: and whosoever will lose his life for My sake shall find it."

This experience of Sundar Singh perfectly illustrates the principle that he who loves his life and selfishly saves it will lose it. To be self-centered is to be self-destroyed. "Myself, arch-traitor to myself." Self carries within itself the element of its own destruction. When I think of my family, my home, my cash, my church, my denomination, my little kingdom, in terms of self — whatever constitutes my life, its enjoyment and end — that is spiritual suicide. It is law, law in its very essence, law inexorable, that the preservation of self is the surest path to self-destruction. On the contrary, the law of love, which is "the law of Christ," is to forfeit life, to lay it down, to lose it. To deny this working principle

128

is to deny the very foundations of our salvation. When Jesus faced the Cross, He said He *must* go, *must* suffer, *must* be killed. In that *must* was embodied love's law, a principle inevitable, abiding, ageless.

The words cast at Christ on the Cross, "He saved others; Himself He cannot save," express the profoundest truth. In order to save us He must stay there on the Cross, *must die*. He could not save Himself and others. Nor was this principle of laying down His life confined to His death. His was a *life* of poverty. He was poor, very poor; not merely "poor in spirit," but *literally poor*. His whole life from the filthy stable at His birth to the borrowed tomb at His death was one of privation, weakness, sorrow, suffering, one of spending and being spent for others. The only way He could save men, whether in life or in death, was by the sacrifice of Himself — "He saved others; Himself He cannot save." He recognized it as the very principle of life, as Heaven's own law of propagation: "Verily, verily, I say unto you, Except a corn of wheat fall into the ground and die, it abideth alone: but if it die, it bringeth forth much fruit. He that loveth his life shall lose it; and he that hateth his life in this world shall keep it unto life eternal" (John 12:24,25).

A missionary tells of his boyhood days back in Wisconsin when the family was pursued by the wolf, hunger. His old father brought out of the cellar the few potatoes that were left and said, "Mother, we've got to plant these." Mother cried, "Daddy, we just can't do it; we'll have nothing to eat." But the father insisted. The mother stood there with tears streaming down her cheeks as she saw those few potatoes being cut to pieces and buried in the ground. However, in the fall there was a great ingathering of potatoes — food for many days. His mother would have kept them and consumed them — and starved, possibly. His father lost them to find them again, find them all new and multiplied. The lesson is plain. We parents, as well as our children, need to be taken right out of our personal "cellar," taken out of the dark of a self-centered life — perhaps out of cold storage — and cut into a thousand pieces and planted and exposed to the disintegrating forces of death. Such is God's only law of multiplication. We cannot improve on Heaven's "corn-of-wheat" program.

> *"The corn of wheat to multiply*
> *Must fall into the ground and die."*

Our obedience to this law is not only the one imperative for multiplication but also our only assurance of personal safety and survival. A crisis in Israel's early history vividly illustrates this fact. The nation was about to enter upon the conquest of Canaan and take possession of that land. She had already taken the territory on the east side of Jordan. On the west side of the river lay the promised land challenging conquest, for it was full of Israel's enemies. Then there arose a question, a problem, a crisis. Two of their tribes, Reuben and Gad, possessed great herds of cattle, and therefore requested that they might settle down on the already conquered pasture land east of Jordan. But the other tribes had not yet been brought into their territory and inheritance; Palestine proper had yet to be conquered and divided among the other ten tribes. Moses therefore sternly rebuked Reuben and Gad, warning them that if they failed to go across Jordan with the others they would not only incur the anger of the most High but also "destroy *all* the people," including themselves. At length the two tribes consented to go over and fight on until all the people had come to their God-given inheritance. Here was their reply: "We ourselves will go ready armed . . . until we have brought them unto their place: . . . We will not return unto our houses, until the children of Israel have inherited every man his inheritance" (Num. 32:17, 18). The two tribes thus agreed that they would neither rest nor settle down until every man had come into his possession. This agreement satisfied the divine demand, and Moses' word of assurance to them was: "Afterward ye shall return, and be guiltless before the LORD, and before Israel; and this land [east of Jordan] shall be your possession before the LORD. But if ye will not do so, behold, ye have sinned against the LORD: and *be sure your sin will find you out*" (vv. 22, 23).

These two tribes learned that day that their only personal safety and their only assurance of possessing their own possessions lay in their first bringing the rest of Israel into their promised inheritance. They were furthermore warned that any failure to do so would mean that they had "sinned against the LORD." Concerning such sin and its consequences they were not left in the dark: *"Be sure your sin will find you out."* What a solemn warning for God's people! This passage is commonly taken to apply only to sinners, but in its immediate context it has to do with the failure of God's people to bring others into the land of promise, the sin and consequence of omitting known duty. Herein lies the most profound principle of missions. If we fail to "go armed before the LORD to war," as Israel was bidden to do, until we win the lost of other nations and bring them into their inheritance and in' to their possessions in Christ, then the word of warning still applies: "If ye will not do so, behold, ye have sinned against the LORD: and *be sure your sin will find you out.*"

History teems with instances of churches which, when faced with obedience to the spirit of missions, refused to go forward — and died. North Africa was once ablaze with gospel light, but the church of those areas took to controversy instead of taking territory farther inland. She failed to bring Africa's unreached millions to their gospel possessions. For this criminal neglect Christ removed her candlestick. Having lost her savour, she was trodden under foot by the Mohammedan scourge. Her sin found her out. Think too of the Armenian Christians. How miserably they failed to take the gospel to the Turks! They spared themselves the pains and sacrifices necessary to go to their cruel neighbours and win them for Christ. For this omission of duty they brought upon themselves from those very Turks an unspeakable baptism of blood, a virtual extinction. Their sin found them out. Coming closer home, we may note how Ontario Christians have not carried Christ to nearby Quebec, that great mission field always lying right at their door. Now Ontario is being taken over by the Catholics. Be sure, Ontario, your sin will find you out. Such is the law of retribution — retroactive and righteous. If this is indeed the law of life, and especially of church life, when will the Church obediently believe it?

We turn to more easily perceived and vivid experiences for concrete illustration of this law. Before World War II many Christian parents had been reluctant to surrender their boys to go to the missionary fronts and capture men for Christ, but the governments wrung from them and their sons an obedience which hitherto they had refused to yield to the Captain of their salvation. Instead of going abroad voluntarily to carry the good news to needy neighbours — we are thinking of Japan especially — these very sons were compelled in self-defense to carry death and destruction to these very nations. Many such soldiers — all thanks to their heroic sacrifices on our behalf — seemed to be little more than fodder for foreign guns. Were those guns but the backfire of disobedience, the disobedience of those Christian soldiers to an earlier and higher summons?

Failure to abide by these principles of gospel propagation has been the source of untold national woes as well as the cause of our own moral deterioration and spiritual death. Subsequent to the war the American Baptist Foreign Missionary Society published a frank acknowledgment of its own fall-off in foreign missions, admitting therein: "We have taken the war seriously. We have all but ignored that program which, if we had taken it seriously, would have made the war impossible."

Concerning the one business of the Church, somebody says, "It is Evangelize or Fossilize." Government leaders know that their whole financial power and life depend upon the amount of business done abroad. The motto therefore of many nations today is: "Export — or Die." Herein the children of this world are again demonstrated to be "wiser than the children of light," for to the Christian Church there is no surer road to bankruptcy and ruin than to fail to export. Our spiritual assets and reserves are only in the proportion that we get our gospel goods abroad. "There is that scattereth, and yet increaseth; and there is that withholdeth more than is meet, but it tendeth to poverty" (Prov. 11:24). The nations are only acting on gospel and missionary principle when they adopt the slogan, "Export — or Die."

This principle finds illustration all around us. Modern warfare makes it necessary that leading nations exercise vigilance as to their outposts, their advance air bases, their military missions. This is their first and highest kind of military strategy. America knows, we are told, that her only safety at home lies in advancing her military missions abroad. Herein lies a lesson for the Church. Instead of retrenching and recalling our missionaries (thinking thereby to save our falling budget, save our home churches, save our denominational lives), we should still keep the frontiers manned and press on into further untaken territory. Our only safety at home lies in aggressive advancement abroad. Foreign missions is not only our supreme obligation, but also (and for that very reason) our highest form of divine strategy.

In view of these vital principles of law and life and multiplication, how must fundamental churches face the crying need of a thousand million still shrouded in darkness? Many orthodox groups are full of splendid people, old as well as young, who need to "lose," i.e., lay down, their lives. If the corn-of-wheat program is not followed, those churches will soon become like great grain containers full of musty, mouldy, worm-eaten wheat — unplanted grain. For very survival, as well as for fruitfulness, they must send forth their young people to light up the regions beyond, lest their own light be turned into darkness — "and how great is that darkness!" As I write, the wires are hot with the report that, having tapped new and wealthy oil reserves in Alberta, the Imperial Oil Company is putting a pipe-line right across the country to the head of the Great Lakes. Big oil business gets busy at once to see that the oil gets flowing out across the waters to light up and build up other lands. The Church is shamed again and again by men of the world who for mere gain will obediently brave all manner of hardship to land their wares on foreign soils. "A missionary writing from Manchuria," says Dr. Glover, "told of seeing displayed by a Standard Oil Depot in that faraway country the ambitious slogan: 'Get the light to every dark corner of the world.' "

Abraham Lincoln, the great emancipator, is reported to have said: "Those who deny freedom to others deserve it not for themselves, and, under a just God, cannot long retain it." On more than one occasion Jesus laid down this principle concerning the use and abuse of gospel gifts and privileges: "For whosoever hath [made gain], to him shall be given [still more to invest], and he shall have more abundance; but whosoever hath not [made gain], from him shall be taken away even that he hath." It is as though He had said, Make gain with your spiritual gifts, your earthly riches, your gospel freedoms — pass them on to others. *Use* them, or *lose* them — it is divine law.

> *"Shall we, whose souls are lighted*
> *With wisdom from on high,*
> *Shall we to men benighted*
> *The lamp of life deny?"*

An English clergyman once asked the Duke of Wellington, "Will it do any good to try to evangelize these people of India?" To this that noble soldier replied, "What are your orders, Sir?" One would suppose that nothing more is needed to make us move than the marching orders, the plain, explicit, oft-repeated command of Christ's "Go ye." The spirit of missions is simply the spirit of obedience to command. However, in spite of all we have said about our sin finding us out, there may be those who, in some form or another and perhaps all unconsciously, have hold of a darling little lie by which they excuse themselves from their missionary obligations. Certain subtle reasonings have crept in which kill a sense of responsibility and cut the nerve of missionary endeavour. Let us examine a few of these.

1. Many Christians hold to the lie that the heathen are not lost because they have never heard the gospel. It is said that once a student asked Charles Spurgeon if he thought that the heathen who had never heard the gospel would be saved. He answered, "It is more of a question with me whether we who have had the gospel and fail to give it to those who have it not can be saved." It has been my own personal conviction that for us as believers it is not so much a question of what God is going to do with the heathen who have not heard as it is a question of how He will adjudicate upon saints who have disobeyed more light than the heathen have, who with such amazing privileges have trampled them under foot.

If for the heathen the entrance into heaven be through the doorway of ignorance, then it would indeed be folly for them to be wise. In fact, were that so, the only reason millions on *this* continent are lost would be that they have heard the gospel. The fact is the heathen are lost not because they have not heard the gospel, but because of known light, the light of Conscience and Creation, that they have disobeyed. Anyone reading Romans 1 and 2 can see that the heathen are consciously under "wrath" and "without excuse."

That great missionary leader, Dr. A. B. Simpson, founder of the Christian and Missionary Alliance, has declared:

> The heathen pass out of wretched existence here, into a darker future beyond. Do you say you do not believe this? that God is too merciful to let them be lost, and that there must be some other way of hope and salvation for them? Beloved, this settled unbelief of God's Word is probably the secret of most of our sinful neglect of the heathen world. We are pillowing our conscience on a lie. God has solemnly told us in His word that there is no other name under heaven given amongst men whereby we must be saved but the name of Jesus. The tenderest voice that ever spake on earth declared, "Except a man be born again, he cannot enter the kingdom of God." If God would have saved men in any easier way, He would never have given His Son to the horrors of Calvary.

The question actually comes down to this: "Shall I charge the Son of God with the unbelievable and unparalleled folly of having come all the way from heaven's glory to be made sin and die under the wrath of Heaven, to save from outer darkness and damnation a people in no danger of ever going there? Shall I further charge the risen Christ, who urged it upon His apostles and disciples to *go* and preach this gospel to every creature, with ignorance of the uncondemned condition of the heathen? And, finally, was that greatest of all missionaries only self-deceived when in his zeal for lost men everywhere he cried, "Woe is unto me if I preach not the gospel"? Space forbids our dwelling longer upon this lie. Let any man read his Bible in subjection to its plain declarations and he will know that men without Christ are without God and without hope either in this world or in the world to come.

One of our own graduates, Earl Carlson, was bitten as a young Christian with this lie that the heathen would be saved because they had not heard. When, under the providence of God, he was later labouring with Filipinos in Alaska, he said to himself: Now these are the men who have never heard the gospel; they therefore go to heaven when they die. But before long he came to the conclusion that if these were the men who were going to heaven he did not want to go there. His simple conclusion — one he might easily have reached had he read his Bible aright — was that sinful men are not fit for God's holy presence. He was converted at once to what the Scripture says about the condition of the heathen. Mr. Carlson early burned out for God among the hill tribes of China. A worthy pioneer of that land said of this young man: "A better missionary than Earl Carlson never went to any foreign land." However, unless he had become convinced of the lostness of the heathen, he would have made no missionary worthy of the name.

2. Another error which has gained some currency among orthodox believers (manifestly among those inclined to evade their responsibilities to missions), is the assumption that the heathen, whether at home or abroad, will be given a second chance, and that Christ will hereafter be proclaimed to all such. Such a belief is based upon what seems to be a twisted view of one portion of Scripture. We believe that the much-disputed passage (II Pet. 3:18-4:6) refers not to the preaching made by Christ to people after death, but to the time when "the longsuffering of God waited in the days of Noah, while the ark was a preparing." This is manifestly the sense of 4:6 where those "that are [now] dead," having had the gospel preached to them during their lifetime, will be "judged according to men in the flesh." Noah was "a preacher of righteousness" (II Pet. 2:5), and Peter informs us that it was "in the Spirit" with resurrection power that Christ "preached" through Noah to the men who are now "spirits in prison" awaiting judgment (cf. Eph. 2:17). Only those who lack the spirit and "woe" of missions can be contented to leave the eternal destinies of lost men to an assumed after-death preaching of the gospel. Certainly the general teaching and tone of all Scripture is that man's state after death is fixed, final, irreversible. The rich man in hell was told of "a great gulf fixed" and impassable. Believers are to exhort others daily "while it is called To day" (Heb. 3:13). How

plain is the warning that "whatsoever a man soweth [in time], that shall he also reap [in eternity]" (Gal. 6:8). Nor does the Scripture say "after death a second chance," but rather "after this the judgment" (Heb. 9:27). Where is there any Scripture proof of probation and second chance after death? Surely the present life determines the final and fixed state of every man. "In the place where the tree falleth, there it shall be" (Eccl. 11:3). So Judas went "to his own place." And John's last word seems conclusive: "He that is unjust, let him be unjust still: and he which is filthy, let him be filthy still: and he that is righteous, let him be righteous still: and he that is holy, let him be holy still" (Rev. 22:11).

A certain (professedly) fundamental missionary virtually advocated a second chance in his reply to the question of earnest converts relative to their heathen ancestors. To such inquiries he offered the following: "God, who knows the end from the beginning as well as every heart of man, knows therefore who would have believed, if the opportunity had been given to them." Commenting upon his solution he added: "If such a reply be a right one, we may believe that through the atoning sacrifice of Christ countless numbers from other lands and from bygone days will be found praising God around His Throne." Such an assumption denies the necessity of the present proclamation of the gospel and kills missionary zeal. What is this but an after-death kind of salvation?

If there be no positive danger of endless punishment awaiting those who die out of Christ — certainly there is no salvation apart from Christ — then our gospel is neither imperative nor necessary. The inexpressible gravity of our message cannot be vindicated apart from the positive danger of eternal woe. That the missionary nerve has been severed among those who fail in these convictions is manifest by the poverty of missionary effort among all such. (We are not here dealing with false sects which manifest a fleshly zeal "not according to knowledge." Nor are we discussing the varying degrees of punishment according to light and opportunity — Rom. 2:11-15).

3. Other orthodox leaders are heard to say: Had God chosen the angels to evangelize the world, heaven would have been emp-

tied in five minutes; but for some strange reason He has not been pleased to employ them to do this missionary work. While we do not presume to know aught of Heaven's reasons for so ordering this missionary program, neither dare we imply that God has arbitrarily — "for some strange reason" — given us the privilege (privilege verily it is, and a glorious one) of doing this task, whereas He might have chosen any one of several, and possibly better, methods. Certainly the tone of all Scripture is to the effect that Christ has not only commanded us, but that He is also *shut up to His own redeemed people*, those who know salvation's story, to carry out world-wide evangelization. If it were only for some strange reason, presumably whimsical and arbitrary on God's part, that He has chosen us to do such holy work, then I at once begin to feel that I need not become too much concerned, much less "beside myself," to get souls saved or to reach the heathen with the gospel, since God has always had other ways of accomplishing this task. Does the writer not know a score of missionary-minded men who would not conceal one least means of winning others? With such frightful and everlasting issues at stake, would these men permit either whim or fancy to determine their choice of instruments to rescue the lost? Would not they seek by the best means, yes, "by all means," to save some? Can such men possibly be more concerned than God is? Beloved reader, we must come to this conclusion: *God is shut up to men to win men.*

4. An intimate missionary friend was doing his best to interest a thrifty business man in the claims of Christ for Africa. After listening to my friend for some time, the business man bluntly retorted, "Don't you know that after the Church has been translated the Jewish remnant will do a much better job of preaching 'the gospel of the kingdom' than we have ever done?" This man had followed to its logical conclusion the teaching that Matthew (including the Great Commission) is for the Jews and that the "Jewish remnant" will do in a few months what we as a Church have failed to do in two thousand years. He was unconcerned about the multitudes perishing here and now. He had found an excuse that seemed to relieve him of present missionary responsibility. His

lack of conviction regarding Christ's last command arose from an ultra-dispensational handling of the Scriptures which furnishes Christians with an excuse from the obligations of obedience.

It was the writer's rare privilege to have as one of his personal friends the late Dr. Robert H. Glover, one of the world's great missionary statesmen. In order to confirm the above conclusions regarding the detrimental effect of these extreme teachings of dispensationalism, we quote from his valuable book, *The Bible Basis of Missions*, a book which should be in the hands of every Christian worker.

> Another view which sadly militates against a united and wholehearted effort by the true Church of Christ to carry out to a finish in this day the evangelization of the world is that advanced by certain gifted teachers of prophecy for whom we have high regard, but with whom we must frankly disagree upon one important point. While holding firmly the truth of the Lord's premillennial coming, they yet relegate to a future company of Jews, subsequent to the rapture of the Church, the task of proclaiming the gospel to the whole world, and accordingly they relieve the Church today of this responsibility . . . While some who thus teach are missionary minded because of their love for the Lord, the natural result upon those who accept this teaching and apply it consistently is to cut the nerve of missionary concern and effort. What the Church fails to do in its day will be done by the "Jewish remnant" after the Church has been taken away!
> . . . We must say that we believe the prodigious achievement attributed to this "Jewish remnant" rests largely upon mere inference rather than upon any clear and explicit Bible statement, and that by this line of teaching the responsibility which Christ laid upon His Church for this age is shifted to others, wrongly and with most unfortunate results.

Before leaving the consideration of how extreme dispensationalism militates against a wholehearted enthusiasm for missions we should observe that the Great Commission is recorded not only in all four Gospels but also in the first chapter of Acts. Let us briefly observe the first few verses of Acts 1 in their missionary outlook and dispensational connection. The risen Christ was about to be taken up into heaven, but before His departure He would give His disciples their marching orders. Two angelic beings were near by about to announce the return of "this same Jesus," the inference being that while He is away the Church will be completing the one and only task left her to accomplish. Thus Missions and the Second Coming are properly and practically linked the one to the other. Concerning this instance Dr. Glover says:

> The risen Lord comes upon His apostles engaged in what would today be termed a dispensational discussion. They ask Him, "Lord, dost Thou at this time restore the kingdom to Israel?"—a very natural question for them, as Jews, to ask. But His reply is, "It is not for you to know times or seasons, which the Father hath set within His own authority. But . . ." But what? "But ye shall be my witnesses . . . unto the uttermost part of the earth."
>
> Can anyone fail to see the point? The Lord brushes aside their discussion about "times and seasons" as irrelevant for the time being, and presses home the thing that *was* relevant, and of vital importance, namely, that they give themselves unreservedly to the one great business and prime objective of the Church for the present age, the evangelization of the entire world. Is this not a word in season to the Lord's people today, and to certain of their leaders in particular, bidding them give less attention to "times and seasons," or, in other words, to profound but largely academic discussions and controversies over various fine points of prophetic interpretation, about which there have always been differences of opinion and always will be, and to devote their time and talents more to the practical aspect of the subject, the carrying out to completion of their risen Lord's last expressed wish and command?

These are wise words from a discerning and Spirit-taught man of God. Yet I have before me as I write a whole volume of sermons delivered at a great Congress on Prophecy, thirty-three sermons in all, each by some well-known and esteemed prophetic teacher; yet in not one of the many mentions of "end time" things is there reference to the speeding up of Christ's own missionary program before His return. Concerning such amazing omissions (*o-missions* indeed) in the thinking of great evangelicals, Dr. Glover most graciously expressed only this much of his personal grief:

We well remember one particular instance when we listened to a masterful address on *The Signs of the Second Coming of Christ*, in which, however, no mention of the missionary sign was made. When we afterwards called the speaker's attention to this, sincerely thinking that the omission was purely from lack of time (for the hour was late), he expressed surprise and very frankly said that he did not believe missions had anything whatever to do with the return of Christ.

We are by no means disposed to overlook such signs as the steady increase of lawlessness, the rise of political dictatorships, the persecution of the Jews, the growing religious apostasy, and so on. But we would call attention to the fact that these are matters about which, despite our feeling of deep concern, we can do little or nothing, whereas promoting the spread of the gospel to the ends of the earth is something in which all Christians can have an active and effective part.

5. Here is another specious bit of sophistry. Missionary appeals to young people for service often run something like this: If you do not go, God will get someone else to do your job, but you will miss the blessing. While we grant that there are multitudes of saints who miss the blessing of obedience (to say nothing of the corruption they will reap for their disobedience), it is with the first part of this kind of appeal that we are here concerned. If it be true, my reader, that "God will get someone else to do your job," how is it that half of the world does not have the gospel? It is apparent that God is not getting someone else to do your work. If he does his own, will he not have all he can do? If, therefore, you do not do your own work, who will?

Perhaps there are few theologians in our Calvinistic circles who would today join hands with the venerable Moderator of the Nottingham meeting of Baptist ministers in his cold and callous indifference to Christ's last command. It will be recalled that when young William Carey made his passionate appeal for the spread of the gospel among the heathen, the Chairman shouted out this stern rebuke: "Sit down, young man, you are a miserable enthusiast for proposing such a question. When God pleases to convert the heathen He will do it without your aid or mine." We have been compelled to admit that the Scriptural plan for reaching the heathen includes "human processes" (R. H. Glover) as the God-chosen and indispensable *means* to the *end* of man's salvation.

Consider several illustrations in point: Many generations of Haitians, within close proximity to American and Canadian Christians, lived and died in the deepest degradation and sin. However, some of our graduates have recently gone to Haiti. Because of this effort over 50,000 souls have been converted during the past few years. Christians today will agree that there was a necessary connection between the obedience of these missionaries and the recent conversion of these thousands of lost souls. But then there comes that inevitable and embarrassing moment, that moment of shame and pain, when native Christians begin to question the missionary after the manner of an old Mohammedan woman in Bengal: "How long is it since Jesus died for sinful people? Look at me; I am old; I have prayed, given alms, gone to the holy shrines, become as dust from fasting, and all this is useless. Where have you been all this time?"

The same cry was echoed from the icy shores of the farthest Northwest Territory. An old Eskimo said to the Bishop of Selkirk, "You have been many moons in this land. Did you know this good news then? Since you were a boy? And your father knew? Then why did you not come sooner?"

Again, in the snowy heights of the Andes a Peruvian asked, "How is it that during all the years of my life I have never before heard that Jesus Christ spoke those precious words?"

It was repeated in the white streets of Casablanca, North Africa. "Why have you not run everywhere with this Book?" said a Moor to a Bible seller. "Why do so many of my people not know of the Jesus whom it proclaims? Why have you hoarded it to yourselves? Shame on you!"

A missionary in Egypt was telling a woman the story of the love of Jesus, and at the close she said, "It is a wonderful story. Do the women in your country believe it?" "Yes!" said the missionary. After a moment's reflection the woman replied, "I don't think they can believe it, or they would not have been so long in coming to tell us."

A noble pioneer, L. L. Legters, was once preaching the gospel to a group of Latin-American Indians from one of the many totally unevangelized tribes. As he told of how the Son of God died on a cross of His own free will that they and all others might escape eternal punishment, one man, who had listened with intense interest, interrupted him: "Senor, when did this One die for us of whom we have never heard? Was it as long as twenty-five years ago?" He stepped back in blank amazement when the answer came, "It was two thousand years ago."

On another occasion as Mr. Legters was talking to an old Indian chief in South America, the latter said, "White man, how long since you knew this Jesus way?" "Chief, it has been a long time." "How long since your father knew this way?" "Oh, it was a long time." "How long since his father knew this way?" Mr. Legters could only reply, "Oh, it was long ago." Finally the old chief, folding his blanket about him, doubtingly concluded, "White man, you wait too long, you wait too long." The old Indian's reasoning was good. "How do you expect us to believe this news, so good beyond all reckoning, when you have waited 'too long'?"

"So you have come at last," said a Taoist priest as the missionary entered the Chinese temple. The latter had seen the priest listening attentively in the open air service. The man had long been hungry to know the truth. In some kind of vision he had been impressed that "some day messengers would come from far away lands." Was it necessary for him to have waited about eighteen long years?

Finally, in *The Growth of a Soul* (published by the China Inland Mission) occurs this reproaching witness against the Church: In talking with Hudson Taylor, Mr. Nyi, a Chinese Christian, unexpectedly raised a question, the pain of which was not easily forgotten. "How long have you had the Glad Tidings in England?" he asked all unsuspectingly. The young missionary was ashamed to tell him, and vaguely replied that it was several hundred years. "What," exclaimed Mr. Nyi in astonishment, "several hundreds of years! Is it possible that you have known about Jesus so long, and only now have come to tell us? My father sought the truth for more than twenty years," he continued sadly, "and died without finding it. *Oh, why did you not come sooner?*"

What shall I more say? Time after time from our own conference platform missionaries confess their experiences of pain as their native Christians fire the questions: "What about my father? my grandfather? You say that God is 'not willing that any should perish.' But *somebody was.* Where were your Christians during all that time?" The thrust goes home. The missionary cannot make excuses. No doctrinal hideout will help him. He hangs his head; his heart bleeds; his mouth is closed. He can only bear his share of the criminal neglect and blood-guiltiness of those Christians who denied the past generations the gospel. He feels what Dr. A. B. Simpson felt after God had given him a missionary heart:

> *"O Church of Christ, what wilt thou say*
> *When in that awful judgment day*
> *He charge thee with their doom?"*

We cannot close without considering Jonah, that runaway missionary of Old Testament times. Nineveh's judgment lay just ahead of a *silent* forty days. By this time the disobedient prophet had experienced such mingled miseries and mercy that he had become willing to be recommissioned. Arriving at Nineveh, he cried up and down her streets, and by warning men of their impending doom brought a million souls to repentance. Then we find that pouting prophet in his little booth outside the city sitting out those forty days wondering whether or not God would turn that whole city to a cinder. He was far more concerned over his own comfort, and over the end time of Nineveh and the fulfillment of prophecy — "yet forty days, and Nineveh shall be overthrown" — than he was over Nineveh's escape from doom. How we abominate the mean, narrow, and bigoted attitude of this man! Yet how he is a photograph of the Church today!

True Christians everywhere profess to believe with Jonah that judgment awaits all men outside of Christ, that there are cities whose days are numbered, sinners whose cup of iniquity is fast filling, souls whose destiny will soon be sealed. Yet we sit in our little religious booths intensely interested in sermons on prophecy and the ten toes of Daniel's image, whereas a message on missionary endeavour to spare doomed myriads from judgment is uninteresting. We do next to nothing to send earth's millions the message that would bring them eternal salvation. We seem unconcerned even to deliver our own souls from blood-guiltiness. Yet all the while we *say* we believe that *our silence will seal their fate* — so subtle and hidden heart-unbelief can be. We stand rebuked by the words of a gifted and noted unbeliever who said:

> Were I a religionist, did I truly, firmly, *consistently believe,* as millions say they do, that the knowledge and the practice of religion in this life influences destiny in another, the Spirit of truth be my witness, religion should be to me *everything.* I would cast aside earthly enjoyments as dross, earthly cares as follies, and earthly thoughts and feelings as less than vanity. Religion should be my first waking thought, and my last image when sleep sunk me in unconsciousness. I would labour in *her* cause alone. I would not labour for the meat that perisheth, nor for the treasure on earth, where moth and rust corrupt, and thieves break through and steal; but only for a crown of glory in heavenly regions, where treasure and happiness are alike beyond the reach of time or chance. I would take thought for the morrow of eternity alone. I would esteem *one* soul gained to heaven worth a life of suffering. There should be neither worldly prudence nor calculating circumspection in my engrossing zeal. Earthly consequence should never stay my hand nor seal my lips. I would speak to the imagination, awaken the feelings, stir up the passions, arouse the fancy. Earth, its joys and its griefs, should occupy no moments of my thoughts; for these are but the affairs of a portion of eternity so small that no language can express its comparatively infinite littleness. I would strive to look *but on eternity,* and on the immortal souls around me, soon to be everlastingly miserable or everlastingly happy. I would deem all who thought only of this world, merely seeking to increase temporal happiness, and labouring to obtain temporal goods, pure madmen. I would go forth to the world, and preach to it, in season and out of season; and my text should be, "What shall it profit a man, if he shall gain the whole world, and lose his own soul?" (A. S. Ormsby in *Alone With God*).

The mystery is how we can read such words and still sit like Jonah in our little booths, comfortable and content to let earth's Ninevehs — millions without Christ in every land — sink into a lost eternity, yes, sink and be forever lost, not because God did not choose to save them but because we denied them deliverance. Oh the crime of it all, this criminal silence! Face it, my reader. What sin can compare with the sin of omission — the criminal silence, the shameful evasion of responsibility, the wicked contentment to let men be swept down into the abyss as though they were only so many autumn leaves!

At the conclusion of a message on Jonah wherein we likened him to the present-day believer, one of our students (now a foreign missionary) wrote the following appropriate lines:

Jonah built a little booth,
A shelter from the heat.
A gourd-vine grew, protection from
The wind that on him beat.

Jonah rejoiced, exceeding glad
For this convenient gourd—
Espec'lly since this comfort was
Provided by the Lord!

"I thank Thee, Lord, Thou hast been good
To my dear wife and me;
We're glad we're in a peaceful land
Of great prosperity.

It makes us feel so good—
This little bungalow—
The kitchenette, the living room,
The rug, so soft you know.

We love our children, ev'ry one;
We keep them home for God:
The homeland needs them just as much
As mission fields abroad.

And fundamentalists are we,
My children, wife and I—
So thankful that we're saved by grace,
Secure until we die!

What didst Thou say? Oh—Nineveh?—
Well, that's another thing.
Right now we want to praise our God
We're sheltered 'neath His wing!"

Thus fundamental Jonahs to
The Lord their praises tell.
They'll sing "We're saved and satisfied,"
Till Nineveh goes to hell! — Ted Laskowski

The word of warning to ancient Israel rings again in our ears: "Ye have sinned against the Lord: and *be sure your sins will find you out.*"

Turning from all the carnal contentments and excuse-making of this carefree generation of Christians, it is a great relief to bow the shoulder and bear the burden of the word of the Lord. It is indeed better to be obedient than disobedient. Obedience at its worst, cost what it may, is worlds ahead of an easy-going believism at its best. It is better, yea very much better, to be burdened and borne down with a great and crushing sense of responsibility for the blood of others than to seek to escape the obligations of an obedient faith. His commandments are not grievous. Like the dew of the morning, like a drink of cold water, like sunshine after rain, come the words of Hudson Taylor as he battled through and embraced the burden of the Lord on Brighton Beach in 1865:

> Unable to bear the sight of a congregation of a thousand or more Christian people rejoicing in their own security while millions were perishing for lack of knowledge, I wandered out on the sands alone, in great spiritual agony; there the Lord conquered my unbelief, and I surrendered myself for this service.

Let me plead with you, my reader, to let no worldliness, no selfishness, no manner of excuse or lie of the devil stand between you and complete obedience to the Saviour's last command. God warns: "If thou forbear to deliver them that are drawn unto death, and those that are ready to be slain [those slipping to the slaughter — (Young)]; If thou sayest, Behold, we knew it not; doth not He that pondereth the heart consider it? and He that keepeth thy soul, doth not He know it? and shall not He render to every man according to his works?" (Prov. 24:11, 12).

Let every reader *go* or *let go* or *help go*. As much as in us lies let us rise up and pay our just debt to the last man on earth. Else — how shall we escape

SIN FINDING US OUT?

CHAPTER XIII

From Death To Life

A BASHFUL young farmer out in the West,* who was utterly unfamiliar with religious meetings, was challenged by Dr. H. C. Mabie to come to a prayer meeting that evening in a neighbouring farmhouse and openly confess Christ. The young man replied, "I never could stand up and talk in that way before people, even though I wanted to; it would kill me to do it."

"Well," Dr. Mabie replied, "die then . . . Christ commands the impossible . . . He commands you to confess Him before men, and I shall expect you to do it tonight, even though you die in doing it."

To the meeting that timid young man came. As he rose to his feet, labouring as if he were Atlas lifting the world on his shoulders, the very effort crushing him, he confessed with his mouth "Jesus as Lord." Before he sat down, he was thanking God for the new life. By faith he had fulfilled the principle of "This do, and thou shalt live."

Some might argue that Dr. Mabie should have shown this young man how to believe instead of stipulating this condition of confession. However, it was divine wisdom that led this soul-winner to press the issue at the very point where the Spirit of God was already at work in this young man. Dr. Mabie did not make conversion easy. Facing the lost man squarely, he demanded of him the thing impossible, the thing most difficult for him to do. The young man admitted that it would kill him to do it. He did the impossible; died, as it were, and lived anew.

In circles where religious softness reigns it is often said: "Well, you know, God is very kind and loving; He would never ask anyone to do anything he could not do. Such circles know little of the ways of God or the commands of Christ. The Lord Jesus was

---

* A full account of this story appears at the close of appendix D.

ever facing men with some impossible obedience. He always brought souls face to face with some command which was impossible to the flesh and demanded action at that point. God is still testing men by such principles. Man has gone astray; he has willfully turned to his own way. God must therefore cross man's will, bring him face to face with some one thing which well-nigh paralyzes him, and there bring the sinner into submission.

Mr. Moody once had some 5,000 atheists in a meeting in London. When he gave the appeal for "whosoever will," one leader shouted out, "I won't." The evangelist then showed that the dreadful alternative facing every man in that hall was "I will" or "I won't." Then Mr. Moody cried, "Men, you have your champion in the middle of the hall, the man who said 'I won't.' I want every man here who believes that man is right to follow him, and to rise and say 'I won't.' " Not a man responded. When Mr. Moody next entered a plea for "I will," some 500 men responded, and those infidel clubs of London never recovered. The battle always rages right there, namely, around the will. God "*willeth* that all men should be saved" (I Tim. 2:4, R.V.) ; man must *will* the same or send himself to hell. Mr. Moody used to observe that the elect were the "whosoever will's" and the non-elect were the "whosoever won't's."

Charles Finney, that successful revivalist, always sought to get sinners to act. He well knew that men were saved only by grace through faith and that no amount of works could help one iota toward any man's salvation. Thank God, however, he was not afflicted with that modern softness which has made so much gospel work ineffective. Mr. Finney was forever seeking to find where sinners were entrenched, face them there with the truth, and get them started out of their hiding places. He found that his methods differed with varying circumstances and individuals. Concerning a new method adopted at Rochester, N. Y., he says:

> I had never, I believe, except in rare instances, until I went to Rochester, used as a means of promoting revivals, what has since been called "the anxious seat." I had sometimes asked persons in the congregation to stand up; but this I had not frequently done. However, in studying upon the

subject, I had often felt the necessity of some measure that would bring sinners to a stand. I had found that with the higher classes especially the greatest obstacle to be overcome was their fear of being known as anxious inquirers. They were too proud to take any position that would reveal them to others as anxious for their souls. When I called them simply to stand up in the congregation, I found that this had a very good effect; and so far as it went, it answered the purpose for which it was intended. But, after all, something more was necessary to bring them out from among the mass of the ungodly to a public renunciation of their sinful ways and a public committal of themselves to God.

Evangelists have debated whether or not they should have an altar call. Some have contended for an idealistic "just-let-the-Word-of-God-do-the-work" kind of appeal. They can cite proof from experience that God has honoured their method. Others contend that the anxious seat, or the sawdust trail, or the altar call, or the mourner's bench, is necessary, and that by this method they have won their thousands. Actually there is no cause for an argument over these matters; the fact is that God has no unvarying rule or method in His dealings with men. When the Lord Jesus dealt with souls, His method was adapted to the need of the individual. However, it is remarkable that almost invariably He brought souls face to face with some one thing which in their own strength they could not do, and there demanded an act of obedience. In the realm of physical disability Jesus commanded the utterly impossible. Likewise in the realm of spiritual disability He gave commands which were sky-high, unbearable, utterly unattainable, completely out of the reach of the natural. His ethics are so utterly contrary to nature that they are humiliating and undoing. Let any man in the flesh touch one of Christ's commands and find how killing it is.

In order to create a sense of sin and a need of divine strength Jesus gave command just where men were inclined to wander or argue or excuse themselves. He anticipated these individual tendencies and gave commands that would run counter to the human will and bring a crushing sense of conviction and need of grace. Since human nature is still the same and since salvation is a matter of the will, God must often lay upon the sinner some command, obedience to which will demand faith. Around that issue of command the individual will believe or reject Christ. "He that believeth on the Son hath eternal life; but he that *obeyeth not the Son* shall not see life, but the wrath of God abideth on him" (John 3:36, R.V.).

When Mr. Finney was converted, he went out into a grove to pray. Several other souls did likewise and found peace with God. But a certain old squire argued that he had a parlour in which to pray. He would be different. Around this issue, so insignificant and immaterial in itself, was the point where he fortified himself in his pride. He would pray, pray all night in his parlour, only to find himself the more distressed. He even became angry that God did not hear his prayer, and was tempted to kill himself. After returning from meeting one evening, he was so impressed with his pride that he was determined to make himself and God believe that he was not proud. That he might demonstrate that it was not pride which kept him from going into the grove to pray, he sought for a mud puddle in which to kneel down. Frustrated, he finally yielded, went to the grove, and there met God in wonderful grace. His confession later was that as soon as he gave up to God on that point, and went into the woods, there the Spirit of God filled him with joy unspeakable.

A similar story comes from a seeker after Christ in Massachusetts. D. M. Panton tells of a lady who had a strong prejudice against the penitent form. She argued — and rightly so — that God's grace can be found in one seat quite as well as in another. She declared, "I will *never* go to a penitent form to be converted." So for *five years* she prayed and wept, and prayed and wept, yet received no salvation. During the visit of an evangelist a large number of her friends were saved, including nearly all of the choir of which she was a prominent member. In these meetings she was sometimes annoyed, sometimes in tears, but still she said, "I will not go to the penitent form." Desperate, she at last dropped her controversy with God, and came all the way down the aisle, *only to find that the penitent form was full.* She turned to a little bench nearby, and was hardly seated before she was conscious that Christ had saved her. As a matter of fact, she had found Christ *without* coming actually to the penitent form, but not until she had expressed her willingness *to come.*

Mr. Panton also tells of a teacher in a New York college who, becoming anxious, determined that he would come *secretly* to Christ, and that until he knew his sins were forgiven he would tell no one. To those who spoke to him about his soul, he betrayed no concern, but secretly wrestled and prayed for weeks. He was willing to give up every sin and to consecrate all to Christ, but he was unwilling for God to *save him in Heaven's own way*. As he sat one evening alone in his study, this fact suddenly broke upon him. He said to himself, "I must take care. I *cannot* be saved because I am unwilling to let it be known or to ask anyone to pray for me." At once he started out to find someone, but *before he had reached the stairs* God gave him the consciousness of perfect forgiveness. He had had a contention with God. His unsurrendered will had fortified itself within one certain spot. *There* he would still be king and dictate conditions. But when it dawned upon him that the whole horror of hell was wrapped up in this one thing, he submitted to God.

We have mentioned that God often paralyzes man with some impossible command and thereby shocks him into conviction. Mr. Finney tells how a wealthy and influential man in Buffalo, a man of good morals and high standing, came to broken-hearted penitence as a sinner. At first he stoutly opposed Mr. Finney's revival. In his self-righteousness and non-submission he found himself in company with the scoffers who were taking refuge behind him. This greatly humiliated him, for he was not of that class. Finally God smote him with conviction. After a sleepless night he stole away into the woods to kneel down and pray only to find that he had no words. His heart was like flint. In his desperation it occurred to him that he might say the Lord's Prayer. As he uttered each successive phrase, he became so shocked that he almost choked. At length he came to "Thy will be done in earth, as it is in heaven." Against this his heart rose up and he could not say it. Here he was brought face to face with God's will. Before that time he could not be made to believe that he was at war with the will of God. Now on his knees he saw that his opposition to God, to His law, to His will, to His claims, was the one obstacle in the way of his conversion. His heart's rebellion rose up in all its enormity. Finally, in an agony of despair and repentance, he cried aloud, "Thy will be done." He made a full surrender to God and accepted Christ just as He was offered in the gospel. Sweet peace filled his soul. Finney's preaching and the Lord's Prayer had been Heaven's schoolmasters to shut him up to Christ.

Let us now turn to the context of the phrase "This do, and thou shalt live" (Luke 10:25-37). The lawyer came "tempting" Jesus. His intention was to test the Lord Jesus as to His knowledge of eternal life: "Master, what shall I do to inherit eternal life?" The lawyer was full of the old Judaistic notion that eternal life could be earned as the reward of works. Yet it is surprising withal what a true technical knowledge he had both of the spirit and letter of the law. Knowing there could be no higher commandment than the all-embracing comprehensiveness of love to God and man, he answered, "Thou shalt love the Lord thy God with all thy heart, and with all thy soul, and with all thy strength, and with all thy mind; and thy neighbour as thyself." In spite of his spiritually-correct understanding of the law, however, he found himself trapped when Jesus stamped his answer with approval: "Thou hast answered right: *this* do, and thou shalt live." Obviously apart from the possession of eternal life no man could exercise perfect love to God and man. Thus Christ forced the lawyer to face obedience to what he knew. "But he, desiring to justify himself, said unto Jesus, And who is my neighbour?" (v. 29, R.V.). Jesus must lead this proud pretender to condemn himself. The lawyer's desire to justify himself proved that he was not at the end of himself, that he had not come to "the end of the law for righteousness." He fell into his own trap and sought to escape before conviction fastened upon him.

To bring the lawyer to judge himself, the Saviour answered his self-justifying question "And who is my neighbour?" with the parable of the Good Samaritan. Both the priest and the Levite, representing all self-righteous religion, avoided the poor half-dead man who had fallen among thieves. In order to present an utter contrast to the priest and Levite, Jesus introduced a half-heathen Samaritan, who was not only a stranger but one despised by the Jews. Jews had no dealings with low-down Samaritans. On one occasion when the Pharisees had lost their argument with Jesus, they retorted: "Say we not well that thou art a Samaritan, and hast a devil?" (John 8:48). Thus to them the word Samaritan was "synonymous with heretic and devil." Did the lawyer wish to know whom he was to love as neighbour? The Saviour would help him answer his own question. Pointedly He asked which one of these three showed the love of a neighbour. At this the poor, proud lawyer could not bring himself even to say the word "Samaritan." That would have been too belittling, too humiliating. The most he could say was: "He that showed mercy on him." In his answer he was forced to a condemnation of his own Jewish nation and especially of those leaders of his own class and station. Better still, he had to commend the outcast Samaritan for having been a neighbour to a Jew who hated and despised him. Thus the lawyer was smitten and stunned, though not sufficiently shut up to find the door into eternal life. When the Lord Jesus said unto him, "Go, and do thou likewise," He said in substance: Humble thyself in utter confession of thy lovelessness and lack of the basic principle of life eternal. If ever you find the doorway into the kingdom, you will have to be reduced from your haughty hypocrisy to the confession that you have less likelihood of finding eternal life than your despised Samaritan neighbour. Thus the Saviour dealt with the real difficulty in the lawyer. He sought to paralyze him into sinnerhood and bring him to the need of grace.

After this public exposure we can almost hear the lawyer muttering to himself: What! Does it come to this, that we are no better than the Samaritans? What advantage then have we Jews? "Go, and do thou likewise!" — am I and my fellows then "in the same condemnation," and must we be identified with dogs and half-dogs? I asked Him for some *doing*, but certainly for no such *undoing*. If eternal life is to be had only on such a condition, I'll have none of it. I'd rather die than be so reduced and killed off to all that is worth while in the way of Jewish advantage.

Thus the lawyer chose to depart with the curse of the broken law "working wrath" upon his hard and impenitent heart. We hope that ere long he cried out, "God be merciful to me the sinner," and, no longer desirous of justifying himself, he went down to his house *justified*.

Some may wonder why the Saviour did not declare His deity to the lawyer and insist that he believe on Him and thereby experience the new birth. Why did Jesus not explain to him that he could not love the Lord with all his heart and his neighbour as himself until he had been born again? Why did He not explain that salvation is not by doing but by believing? or that He himself is "the end of the law for righteousness to every one that believeth"? Notice that throughout the passage the principle of faith is not stressed, but, on the contrary, the principle of law. The little word "do" is indicative:

> "What shall I *do* to inherit eternal life?"
> "This *do*, and thou shalt live."
> "Go, and *do* thou likewise."

The most that some extreme dispensationalists can make of such language is that salvation was still being held forth on the basis of merit. (The fact is, of course, that salvation was *never* offered on the basis of meritorious self-righteousness.) As the Great Physician, did the Lord Jesus not know what He was doing? Did He not know how to give a proper and effective application of the law that would bring this fellow to an end of himself and thus to "the end of the law for righteousness"? How useless and ineffectual it would have been for the Saviour to tell this unconvicted and self-righteous lawyer just to believe. Christ is indeed "the end of the law for righteousness to every one that believeth," but the lawyer had not come to the end of himself. The end or aim of the law had therefore not been reached. Before ever he could believe, the lawyer had to be reduced to despair, where he would pour contempt on all his pride. To such men Jesus once said, "How can ye believe which receive honour one of another?"

The only "good news" — good for this lawyer in his condition — was that which Jesus gave him. He needed to be given what has been termed "a sweat-bath of anguish and sorrow" under an application of law. It needs to be emphasized today that many persons in the pew have been given such an unvarying repetition of the good news about just believing in Christ that they have lost all appreciation of the true gospel. Further comment regarding the place of "fear" in the preaching of the gospel appears in Chapter XI.

The various methods employed by Jesus in dealing with souls should correct any tendency among us to catalogue and contrast various gospels. There are indeed differing descriptive terms, such as "the gospel of the kingdom," "the gospel of grace," etc.; but this does not mean that we must fall into a fixed routine or an unvarying repetition. In a limited sense every Spirit-led preacher preaches the gospel as Jesus did, adapting it to his audience and to the occasion. He may use the method of Moses in shutting men up under conviction and condemnation without giving them for the moment one hope of release. At another time he may hold out nothing but pure grace and love. At still another time he may adapt the changeless and "everlasting gospel" by proclaiming the coming reign of Christ on earth. After all, there need not be such a hair-splitting and cataloguing of the good news into a great variety of gospels.

There is a growing tendency among ultra-dispensationalists to read the New Testament in the letter, even as there has been a propensity among many to misunderstand the spirituality of the Old Testament. With this tendency there has developed a fixedness of gospel formula, from which no man dare depart or else he is reckoned ill instructed and poorly taught. Do we forget that the gospel was preached before unto Abraham? (Gal. 3:8). Furthermore, the gospel must have been given to Israel of old, for the writer to the Hebrews says, "Unto us was the gospel preached, as well as unto them" (Heb. 4:2). The only reason it did not profit some of them was that they did not believe it. Of course, no one will deny that the terms used to express and to adapt God's gospel differed greatly in the various dispensations. But when men chop up the Bible so as to make the first book of the New Testament "the Law according to Matthew" instead of "the Gospel according to Matthew," then it becomes manifest that we are handling the Book with a carnal wisdom such as makes the Word of God of none effect.

We recall the experience of a splendid, zealous young missionary who went out to India with the unvarying prescription of "just believe." Before long he had gathered together great masses of "believing" church members. They had long been used to believing. They had been afflicted for centuries with religion. When

they heard the beautiful news about this wonderful Jesus, they believed some more but — with no more effect. In the course of
time, however, this missionary became desperate to account for the
lack of growth in grace on the part of the churches. When he
turned "to the law and to the testimony" to find out what was
wrong, he learned that he had omitted an essential and preparatory
ministry for the gospel — he had utterly omitted repentance. Unlike his Master he had not called "sinners to repentance." He had
not warned them: "Except ye repent, ye shall all likewise perish."
His gospel, unlike that of the greatest of all missionaries, had not
included both "repentance toward God, and faith toward our Lord
Jesus Christ" (Acts 20:21).* He had preached only the latter half
of Paul's compound message. Had not his school of thought at
home told him times without number that repentance was for the
Jews and not for the Gentiles? that John's gospel and the book of
Romans emphasize faith? He therefore unconsciously omitted
giving those people of India the kind of message that was required
in their case to produce conviction of sin. His gospel was so soft
and convictionless that he had multitudes of church members with
no heart experience of having passed from death unto life. He was
forced to disfellowship all his churches and begin again at the bottom to build on solid foundations. Some soft armchair professor
at home was chiefly to blame for this chaos.

Dr. I. S. Spencer gives an account of a meeting so awfully solemn
that there was a tomb-like silence resting on the assembly. Each
of the hundred persons knelt in prayer. As he slipped around from
soul to soul, one young man despairingly said, "I can't repent."
Here is the conversation (abbreviated) that took place between Dr.
Spencer and this soul:

---

* It is true that in a few theological circles repentance has been aimed at
as something meritorious to commend the sinner to God. True repentance is
but a simple acknowledgment of a deeply felt need. Perversions of true
repentance have led some to swing to the opposite extreme of preaching the
gospel of free grace to men who have no sense of their sinful and lost condition. But a few perversions of true repentance can scarcely compare with
the disastrous results of mere mental assent to doctrinal statements. Orthodox
leaders today might well believe that their chaotic church conditions are due
to the shallow, cheap, easy-going "believism" of this present hour.

"What an awfully wicked heart you must have! You can't
repent! — you love sin so well that you cannot be sorry for it —
you cannot forsake it—you cannot hate it—you must be in
an awful condition indeed! You are so much the enemy of
God that you cannot cease to contend against Him, that you
cannot cease to resist the Holy Spirit—you must have an
awfully depraved heart!"

"I can't repent," said he again (with an accent of grief and
intolerable vexation)—"I can't repent, with such a heart! I
should if I could"—and the tears rolled down his cheeks.

"You would if you could; it is only a self-righteous and
self-justifying excuse. Your deceitful heart means by it that
you are not so wicked as to continue in your impenitence
willingly. It means that you are willing to repent, but you
cannot. You are deceived. You are not willing. You think
you are, but you are in an error. You say you are not to be
blamed because you can't repent. God blames you! the whole
Bible blames you! Your own conscience, though you strive
to silence it, blames you! This excuse will not stand."

"I *can't repent!*" said he again as if in anger.

"Then God can't save you, for He cannot lie, and He has
said the impenitent shall be destroyed! *You* say you cannot
repent. *He* has not said so. He commands you to repent."

With much agitation, but in a subdued tone the young man
replied, "I am sure I have tried long; and my mind has been
greatly tormented. All has done no good. I do not see as I
can repent!"

To which I replied, "Other people have repented . . . Such
is the call of the Bible: 'Turn ye, turn ye, for why will ye
die? Repent, and turn yourselves from all your transgressions; so iniquity shall not be your ruin.'"

"Do you think I am self-righteous?" he asked.

"I *know* you are. That is your grand difficulty. You have
been trying to save yourself. You are trying now. When you
tried to repent, *your heart aimed after repentance as something to recommend you to God,* and constitute a reason why
He should forgive and save you. It was just an operation of
self-righteousness instead of relying by faith on Jesus Christ,
to be saved from wrath through Him. You are trying to be
righteous before God, not through your reformations and
duties, but through your painful attempts and convictions.
You ought to go to the Lord Jesus Christ as a poor, guilty,
undone sinner, to be saved by Him alone—saved by grace.
You ought to go to Him, just as you are, to be washed in His
blood, to be clothed in His righteousness, to be sheltered from

the thunders of God's eternal law, in the security of His all-sufficient atonement."

"But," said he, "I can't repent and come to Christ *of my-self.*"

"I certainly never said you could, and never wished you to think you could. In my opinion, God does not wish you to think so. And if you have found out that you cannot repent of yourself, you have found out an important truth. Most certainly God does not tell you to repent of yourself. God never expects you to repent without His help, but with it. He knows you are too wicked to do it, that you are without strength, helpless, undone, a *lost* sinner! You have been trying to repent in a way that God never told you, just by your own powers, instead of getting to God and asking Him to have mercy upon you and save you. When He commands you to repent, He does not tell you to rely upon your own shattered strength; but you have done so. Then you complain that you can't repent. You have rejected His help. And for this reason you will be the more criminal if you do *not* repent. His Spirit is your only hope. If He leaves you to yourself, you are lost—eternally lost! Tread softly. Let not the Holy Spirit bear witness against you in the day of the final judgment: 'because I have called and ye refused!' "

The young man cried to God for help and was happily saved. Let the reader note the divine wisdom given Dr. Spencer to insist and to keep insisting that this young man repent, even though he was going about to establish his own religious self-righteousness. Making full use of the principle of law, Dr. Spencer continued to crowd him until he was crushed to an acknowledgment of his own sinful self-righteousness. Had he in this instance released the fellow from the lash of law, he might never have come to a saving faith in Christ.

Dr. Harry Ironside well says: "Shallow preaching that does not grapple with the terrible fact of man's sinfulness and guilt, calling on 'all men everywhere to repent,' results in shallow conversions; and so we have myriads of glib-tongued professors today who give no evidence of regeneration whatever. Prating of salvation by grace, they manifest no grace in their lives." Then this same writer notes that some earnest gospel preachers are almost afraid of the terms "repent" and "repentance" lest their hearers misunderstand these terms as implying something meritorious on the part of the sinner.

But such is not the case. It is no merit to recognize our need. "They that be whole need not a physician, but they that are sick." It is no merit for the sick man to call the doctor. He but recognizes his need of a physician. There was no merit on the part of the prodigal to say, "Father, I have sinned against heaven, and in Thy sight, and am no more worthy to be called Thy son." His repentance merited no pardon, but it did put him in a place to receive one. It was only when he confessed and forsook his sin that he received the Father's waiting and gracious forgiveness. As certainly as no sinner was ever saved apart from the grace of God, no less surely can a sinner ever receive that grace who does not first recognize his need, i.e., repentance. This is neither contrary to grace nor the limiting of grace; it is preparing the way for grace. In this day of mounting lawlessness and shameless impenitence, Heaven knows that we need some John the Baptist to go up and down the land in all the fury of Sinai's thunders and terrors, calling on men to repent, in preparation for that great and notable day of the Lord. It is high time that preachers cease to prattle about law itself being such an enemy of grace. Do preachers not know that the reason why the grace of God is having so little effect today is that their church members have not been crushed into broken-hearted submission through the terrors of law and the obligations of obedience? Such is the appalling ignorance that is plaguing both pulpit and pew today. Preachers are saving their own skins instead of holding sinners to the point where the Holy Ghost is shutting them up to judgment.

One such preacher is, we fear, making a wicked provision for the flesh when he gives as the reason why the precepts of the Sermon on the Mount are "so universally ignored" that they "belong to conditions obtaining in another age." As a further root of escape for fleshly disobedience he goes on to ask, "Will not the exalted demands of the Sermon on the Mount be more easily obeyed when earthly conditions are changed [in the millennium], as they will be?" This teacher's own question discloses why these sublime Beatitudes are today so "universally ignored," viz., that the natural man wants an ethical standard not too high in its "exalted de-

mands," and prefers some indefinite or far-off day when such demands can be "more easily obeyed." But we ask again: Were any
of Christ's teachings ever meant to be acceptable to the flesh? Had
the early Christian martyrs followed this subtle reasoning, they
might have muzzled their open confession of Christ until that demand could have been "more easily obeyed." Why should they have
endured the lion's gory mane? Should they not have waited until the millennial age when "the lion shall eat straw like the ox"?
A relaxed, easy-going, flesh-loving believism prepares no saints for
soldiery or for sacrifice, much less for martyrdom.

As a final illustration, we remember a young man in our own
town who had been listening to the gospel as preached by our own
students on the streets of Three Hills. He had been smitten with
conviction and felt that he ought to become a Christian, but he was
not yet ready to pay the price. He called on one of the local ministers, an easy-going orthodox man, and said something like this:
"I would like to become a Christian, but I do not want to be one
like the folks at the Bible School." To this the learned physician-
of-no-value replied, "Well, you can become a Christian without being like those folks." Note that God had seized upon this young
man's heart with the challenge: Would you inherit eternal life? believe on My Son? become a Christian? The Spirit's insistence was:
This do, go stand on the street, confess Christ openly, be unashamed
of the Saviour. Then the young man saw himself a public spectacle,
an object of reproach and contempt in his own home town. The
soft preacher, unlike Dr. Spencer, released the young fellow where
God had sought to shut him up to faith. This poor, unwise minister, himself evading the Cross in all its supremacy, presumed to
show him how to "believe" without meeting his issue. But on this
issue hung the young man's believing, yea, his whole eternal destiny. There he faced God's "this-do-and-thou-shalt-live," and there
he rebelled. As far as we know he has never come to Christ.

Perhaps there never was a time when we needed to insist so much
that Christian workers get away from an unvarying literalism, and
learn how to adapt the gospel to meet the manifold needs of many-

sided sinners. We insist that we must begin to learn the meaning of Paul's words: "Which things also we speak, not in the words which man's wisdom teacheth, but which the Holy Ghost teacheth; comparing spiritual things with spiritual" (I Cor. 2:13). Thus we shall learn the mind of God and come to have the particular "this-do" of the Spirit which will bring the repentant sinner to saving faith in Christ.

CHAPTER XIV

The Rich Young Ruler

S TRAYING into a church, Francis of Assisi heard Christ's word
of command to the rich young ruler: Sell all thou hast, and distribute unto the poor. Such words seized hold of his conscience.
They haunted him. They tormented him. Then he sold every thing
but the bare garment which clothed him. Yet still his obedience
seemed to fall short of the Saviour's command. He therefore
stripped himself even of his poor raiment, and for very shame was
clothed there in the church in a peasant's tunic, which he wore
unto death (J. B. Brown).

This account reminds us of the exchange which once took place
between Thomas Aquinas and the Pope. As he was showing Thomas the glories of the Vatican, the Pope remarked: "We cannot say
with St. Peter of old, 'Silver and gold have I none.'" To this
Thomas replied, "Nor can we say, 'Such as I have give I thee: In
the name of Jesus Christ of Nazareth rise up and walk.'" It seems
there may have been some connection between Thomas' voluntary
poverty and his power — between his *poverty* of spirit and his *power* of discernment. The Pope had the gold; Thomas had God.

What revolutions in religious thinking lie between the world of
that day and ours! Protestantism today must needs react against
Rome in its practice of poverty, for of course Rome's friars and
mendicants went to ridiculous and unscriptural lengths. They made
it chiefly a matter of merit, of winning their way to heaven. But
we Protestants have swung to an opposite extreme. We are rich
and increased with goods and have need of nothing; we steer clear
of any literal application of forsaking all; we believe in doing everything *in spirit*; to us poverty of spirit is beautiful to hear about,
pleasant to think about, easy to preach about, but in the least outward correspondence thereto — extremely unnecessary. Today

poverty is as abominated by Protestants as ever it was boasted of by the orders of Rome.

Let us now briefly consider the incident of the rich young ruler to whom Christ gave His command to forsake all. The first thing that strikes us about the young ruler is his transparent honesty and genuine earnestness. Although he undoubtedly had a clean record, he was not apparently self-sufficient; although rich, he was not proud. Boldly and publicly he knelt in humility before Jesus to learn the *how* of eternal life. In spite of being a ruler of the Jews, he came running to Jesus and sincerely inquired about the one good thing he might *do* to inherit eternal life. His thought was that there must be some one great and good thing which, if done, would win everlasting life. His intense earnestness indicated that he was prepared to make no small effort to win that reward. Nor did he raise any dispute, as did the lawyer concerning who was his neighbour.

In spite of all this, the Saviour counters the ruler's "Good Master" with "why callest thou Me good? there is none good but one, that is, God." In other words Christ said, "If I am not God, I am not good." To be assured of eternal life the young ruler needed, of course, to see and believe in Jesus Christ as the Son of God. But how did the "Good Master" undertake to bring this splendid specimen of humanity to this insight and this confession? Stand to one side and listen in to the Great Physician of souls. He did not proceed with technical explanations or doctrinal assertions of His own deity, such as we might have expected. Nor did He seek to correct the zealot's utter misapprehension that eternal life could be obtained by *doing* rather than by *believing*. "Thou knowest the commandments." Keep them if thou wilt enter into life. "Commandments? Which?" responded the young man. "Name me the one I have not already kept." Then Jesus quickly ran through the second table of the law, summing it up with the single and positive statement: "Thou shalt love thy neighbour as thyself." But like Saul of Tarsus, "touching the righteousness which is in the law," the young ruler was blameless. Yet withal he continued to have a misgiving that all was not well and under a sense of dissatisfaction cried out, "All these things have I kept from my youth

up: what lack I yet?" — what can it be that I lack? "Then Jesus
beholding him loved him." Was he not perfectly sincere? Did
not his sense of failure bring him to Jesus to inquire about this felt
lack? Jesus "looked lovingly upon him." But note that Jesus did
not congratulate him nor tell him, "What a fine young man you
are!" Did the young man feel that some one good thing might
meet his need? The Saviour would take him on this ground: If
thou wilt be perfect and have the one good thing thou lackest, then
here it is: Go and sell that thou hast, and give to the poor, and
thou shalt have treasure in heaven: and come, take up the cross, and
follow Me. Mark tells us how at that saying "he was sad," i.e.,
he was "astonished and confounded." Such a thing was never
dreamed of as a demand of the "Good Master." It shocked him. It
paralyzed him. It dealt a death blow to his stocks and bonds, to his
god of gold. Jesus had shattered his entire list of virtues. In lacking
the one thing, the man lacked everything. Even as Napoleon, who
said, "I always master the worst first; then I know that I have
mastered all that is less than the worst," so Christ aimed at the
ruler's heart, which was "deceitful above all things and desperately
wicked." To destroy the deeds of a man of high merit is difficult.
He dies hard, but die he must. The divine wisdom must force such
a man to move out of the natural. He has done so much good that he
must be stunned and startled and made aware of that which nature
cannot do.

Had this young man been told to be temperate and chaste and
fair in his dealings, or had he been directed to help some poor
wounded and half-dead man on the way to Jericho, he would have
done that. Human nature could have done such things, and perhaps had done them already. But the Saviour's "one thing," namely, "Go . . . sell . . . distribute . . . come . . . take up the cross
. . . follow Me," plumbed the depths of his heart. Alas, alas, for
this poor rich man! He could give alms and pay tithes. Ah yes!
But complete poverty? Horrible! Among the Jews, Edersheim tells
us, poverty "was worse than all the plagues of Egypt put together,
worse than all other miseries; the worst affliction that could befall
a man" (*Life and Times of Jesus*, Vol. II). Christ's command to
become a *pauper* was paralyzing, a veritable sentence of death to

all his life. With an awful sense of his unmet need, the rich man went away very poor. Jesus had laid upon him the supreme demand, the one thing needful, and had pressed the point where he must pass from death unto life. This final word of command had shut him up to the end of the law for righteousness. But the rich young ruler would not submit himself to "the righteousness of God." He refused Christ's "This *do*, and thou shalt *live*."

It has often been pointed out that the Old Testament gospel was comprehended in the phrase, "Do and live," while the New Testament gospel is comprehended in the reverse phrase, "Live and do." This is true in a very real sense. We must remember, however, that it was the same unchanging God who said both. "Unto *us* [of New Testament times] was the gospel preached, as well as unto *them* [of Old Testament times]: but the word preached did not profit them, not being mixed with faith in them that heard it" (Heb. 4:2).

The same God who said to the Israelite "Do and live" also said to him, "I kill, and I make alive; I wound, and I heal." He demanded obedience or death simply in order to shut a man up, to kill him off to all his own ability, and bring him at last to the despairing cry, "God be merciful to me a sinner." Only such a man could then *live* with the ability to *do*. God's special means in New Testament times of letting a man see what a sinful wretch he is, and where his own foul red-handed rebellion would place the "Fairest Flower" of heaven, is an uplifted and rejected Christ on a cross. Be it noted that if a man takes a square look at the Crucified without condemning himself, then he is self-condemned to the nethermost hell. The first look at Calvary should both crush a man into broken-hearted repentance and also cause him to come to life. Sinners look, then *live*, and then proceed to *do*. In making a man a new creature this New Testament gospel, then, also has a killing and a bringing to life. Even so the Old Testament gospel first crushed the man with an unbearable doom in order that he might be granted *repentance unto life*. Only then would he be able truly to do. The God of the Old Testament who said, "I kill, and I make alive," says in the New Testament, "One died for all; therefore all died; and He died for all, that they which live should no longer live unto themselves, but unto Him who for their sakes died and rose again" (II Cor. 5:14, 15, R.V.). When we were born again, we were born at the Cross, born crucified. Through death we came to life. Whether in the dispensation of *law* or in this age of the especially manifested *grace* of God, death is God's gateway to life.

Take another study of the sentence, *"This* do, and thou shalt live." When "this do" refers to Christ's single and specific command to an individual, it really means "this *death*, and thou shalt live." This pointed demand sums up all the potency of a death-dealing command, a command that in the same stroke will kill and also make a-live. It is the very same principle which had held true in the ministry of John the Baptist. When he laid the axe to the root of the tree, people utterly selfish and sinful cried out, "What shall we do then?" John answered, "He that hath two coats, let him impart to him that hath none; and he that hath meat, let him do likewise." That they might come to repentance, John crossed the wills of these selfish sinners. When the publicans also cried, "Master, what shall we do?" note the wisdom in John's answer, "Exact no more than that which is appointed you." That command would kill any publican. Why was he a publican at all except to exact more than that which was due? The soldiers likewise demanded, "What shall we do?" Again came the pointed word, "Do violence to no man, neither accuse any falsely; and be content with your wages." Such conditions ran counter to every soldier's misbehaviour. John's whole ministry countered and crossed each sinner just where he lived in order that the "one thing" might bring him to the very dust of death, the death of self.

Jesus often made use of the same principle of law. Was it necessary with this young ruler that he should actually go and part with all that he had? The Saviour said so. His bulging pockets would never allow him to get through the doorway into the Kingdom. It was, of course, a heart matter. "What was an *outward*, was also, as we perceive it, an *inward* necessity" (Edersheim). But might it not have seemed enough for Christ to have given this young man some directions about holding his possessions as a trust from God to be carefully and wisely distributed to the needy? Could not the Lord take the *will* for the *deed?* This may be all that is necessary for some souls but not for the rich young ruler. He must needs go and sell and distribute and come and take up his cross and follow Christ. No link in the chain could be omitted. We hasten to ask: If one well-off man is commanded thus, why not others? How few of us ever use this drastic and death-dealing weapon with today's well-fixed folk! Are we afraid to offend them? Or are we after some of their cash? Have we so "left all" ourselves that we can lay such a command upon others? A Christian man, who is well acquainted with the insurance business, has divulged the fact that some leading fundamental preachers are eagerly laying up treasure on earth — laying up for the family, laying up for the "rainy day." Will God be forced to see that their rainy day comes?

Regarding these purse-shattering words to the rich young ruler, Alexander Maclaren says, "Though no doubt the spirit, and not the letter, is the universal element in them, there are far more of us than we are willing to confess who need to obey the letter in order to keep the spirit." How wickedly we wiggle away from such Scriptures so as to apply them only "in spirit." Real sacrifice and literal self-denial and voluntary poverty can prove to be the very gateway into life for many souls who are bound by "the things that are in the world."

Let me ask my reader, Have you never said as you have been forced to face some impossible command, "I'd rather die than do that"? Have you never come to a gateway of death in your life? Recall my mention of the bashful young farmer who was commanded to stand up and confess Jesus Christ as his Saviour. His complaint was, "It would kill me to do it." Remember also the argument of the preacher who was asked to come down out of his pulpit and talk to the people in the pew: "But Lord, you know that is not my work; do not give me that; it will kill me." It was just at the point of argument that the Lord got both the farmer and the preacher. At what point will the Lord get you, my reader? Only Heaven knows. He may get at you through demanding an uttermost consecration of your life to go "anywhere with Jesus." Maybe you have said, "Anywhere but there, Lord." Not a few young folks have said, "Anywhere but to Africa." But God urges that it be Africa. Maybe the reader has said, "I can love anybody

but so-and-so." Yet the Spirit still insists that you love your enemy, love your neighbour, love the unlovely. Perhaps you have said
that you are willing to give much to God, even the half of your
goods to missions. God says, "Give all." Or "this do" may mean
"this do *without*, and thou shalt live." Right there you discover
your selfishness. Your Master was the poorest of the poor. Are
you His servant? Or, are you one servant that is above his Lord
— careful that the Saviour's command is kept only in *spirit?* Do
you call Him "Lord, Lord," but do not *the thing* He commands you?
Sometimes "this do *without*," may mean a farm, a bank account,
a nest egg. Hath not God chosen the poor of this world? Most
of God's work has been done by God's poor. Or if you are a parent, "this do without" may mean a son, a daughter, or both. Have
you said, "I'll give all my goods, but not my child"?

The issue varies with each individual; but wherever the point at
issue is, there you are commanded to obey. You reply, "I would
rather die than do it." God answers, "Do both. Die in doing it.
This do, die here, and thou shalt live. Only at this point shalt thou
come to life. Just where your rocky heart breaks, the living waters
will begin to flow." It seems so often as if it "needed not only
the Word of God but a stroke of some Moses' rod to make the
water gush forth from the rock" (Edersheim). Around perhaps
some seemingly small and immaterial thing you will either believe
unto righteousness or wither away in your death and unbelief.

Does someone reply, Oh how much simpler is the New Testament
righteousness of "just believe"? Yes, it is true that when the multitudes asked Jesus, "What shall we do, that we might work the
works of God?" He replied, "This is the work of God, that ye believe on Him whom He hath sent." All this seems so very simple,
even though it is called "the work of God." Nothing more was required than to "just believe." That was all. But believe what?
Just believe that that insignificant, despised Nazarene, the Root out
of a dry ground, without form or comeliness, was the sealed of God,
the Sent-One of Heaven. There He stood before them. When they
saw Him, there was no beauty that they should desire Him. All
they had to do was just believe that this (to them) inconspicuous
specimen of humanity was the Giver of the ever-enduring bread.

They had just to believe He was far greater than Moses, who had given them bread not for only one day but for forty long years. All these disciples had to do — nothing more! — was just to believe that here was an infinitely greater than Moses. Easy? No! Who can but exclaim, "This is *the work of God,* that ye believe on Him whom He hath sent"? These multitudes had seen the miraculous feeding of the thousands and had eaten the bread. Now the command comes: Believe the True Bread. Such a word of demand was just as contradicting and crushing to their carnality as the word of command laid upon the rich young ruler. Whether it was the word of *demand* laid on these multitudes or the word of *command* laid on the rich young ruler, both were calculated to shut them up to faith, to cause them to pass from death unto life. Both the *demand* and the *command* were addressed to the heart. In both instances Christ's word was specific and carried with it a promise of life everlasting. The rich young ruler had an outward condition as a point of issue; the multitudes had no such external condition. Christ's word of command to the rich young ruler was *no less "spirit and life"* than was the demand of simple faith laid down to the multitudes.

Just here in John 6:28, 29 we have a bright illustration of "the bond of union between Paul and James . . ." of the faith of Paul being in fact the work of James, i.e., the work of God" (Godet by Schaff). It has been said that in the statement of the Lord Jesus, "This is the work of God, that ye believe on Him whom He hath sent," we have the clearest proof that all eternal life proceeds from nought but faith in Christ. How true! When was it ever otherwise, whether under Moses or Paul or James? Manifestly the method of Jesus with the ruler differed from that which He used with the bread-hungry multitude. While it may be said that the former was the method of law and that the latter was the method of grace, let us be sure to keep it clear in our thinking that in both instances "the end" was Christ and righteousness through faith in Him.

In a single verse Paul brings both of these methods together when he says, "If thou shalt confess with thy mouth Jesus as Lord [a single and simple condition of an obedient faith], and shalt be-

lieve in thy heart that God raised Him from the dead" [a heart-believing which is indeed the work of God], most assuredly "thou
shalt be saved" (Rom. 10:9, R.V.). Man believes with the heart;
man confesses with the mouth. Would a man attempt to believe
with his heart and conceal that faith, i.e., remain a secret believer?
Is he believingly submitted to Jesus as Lord? His mouth will say
so. Heart-believing apart from works is indeed the single and sole
condition of salvation, but such a heart submission will issue in
open confession. The man who claims he is submitted to Christ
while refusing open confession has no Scriptural ground to back up
such believing.

This passage indicates clearly that in Scriptural salvation (there
is no other), the man must not only inwardly believe, but must regardless of all consequences express the lordship of Jesus openly.
Surely this present world is relentless in its hostility to Christ. If
any man should desire to be saved, let him know how he will in-
volve himself before such a world. His confession may cost him
everything. Therefore when the condition is laid before the sinner: "If thou shalt confess with thy mouth Jesus as Lord, . . ." at
once the whole issue may hinge upon a heart submission that will
produce a mouth confession. How *can* the man believe with his
heart while holding out against confession with his mouth? Paul's
"word of faith" is here shown to include submission of both the
heart and the mouth with reference to Jesus as Lord. Both believing and confessing blend into a beautiful harmony and include
the harmonious and simultaneous consent of heart and mouth. Both
represent the two-fold emphasis and method of reaching the gospel
righteousness of faith. Did Moses assure Israel that God's word of
demand was "nigh" unto them, in the *mouth* and in the *heart,* only
to be embraced by an obedient faith? Paul says that the same
"word" which he preaches is likewise in the mouth and in the
heart, a word calling for an undivided heart-and-mouth subjection
to Jesus as Lord.

Would some theologian argue that Paul's stipulated condition
to the sinner to "confess with the mouth the Lord Jesus" refers to
his confessing to God alone that he believes on Christ as Saviour?
Does such a theologian fear that Paul's simple test of an obedient

faith may jeopardize the blessed doctrine of salvation by grace a-
lone? Let such a one consider that in the next phrase Paul clearly
implies public confession before others, "Whosoever believeth on
Him shall *not be ashamed.*" Seek not to divorce the mouth from
the heart, the confession from the believing. "The heart and the
mouth are the fountain and the river the light and its rays, the root
and the flower, the fire and the flame" (D. M. Panton). Heart and
mouth go together in what might be termed the twin method of
bringing men to the one and only salvation.

"A dumb faith is no faith," said Olshausen. As faith without
works is dead, so faith without confession is either dead or dying.
Confession without heart belief is hypocritical lip service. Heart
faith must issue in some form of confession. Faith and confession
are as connected as heart and mouth. Be the consequences what they
may, the believing heart will express its full acknowledgment that
Jesus Christ is Lord in some manifest way. Of course confession
with the mouth may not necessarily be the *sine qua non* of salvation, for circumstances can most assuredly alter the method of ac-
knowledging Him. "Christ declares baptism, as the appointed means
of confession, to be necessary (Mark 16:16); not, however, as a
sine qua non, but as a command, the obligation of which providential dispensations may remove, as in the case of the thief on the
cross" (Hodge). This thief acknowledged "Jesus as Lord" and
King of his life in the face of the public repudiation and crucifixion of Christ, and while still exposed to the uttermost shame. The
chapter on "Salvation and Baptism" clarifies other points in this
connection.

Should my reader still be inclined to argue that New Testament
believing is so much easier than we have pictured it to be in these
pages, reflect again on the soft and shallow "believism" of this
present day. By contrast note the believing of New Testament times,
when, says Tertullian, "Not the name of any crime stands against
us, but only the crime of a Name."

> *And so to the wild wolf Hate*
> *Was sacrificed*
> *The panting huddling flock*
> *Whose crime was Christ.* —Selected

Of those early Christians all that was required was simple faith. How blessedly true! *All* they had to do was to "just believe." But no sooner do they believe than they (and we) are "crucified together with Christ." This was self-evident, of course, even to the heathen onlooker. Before ever they considered salvation, they sat down to count the cost: Did One die for all? Then "all died." If ever they became identified with Christ, how well they knew that they would be as-good-as-dead men! Thus *from* death and often *through* death they passed into life. Now ask yourself, Were they saved by faith alone? Indeed they were. But was it all so very simple? All they had to do in the face of martyr fires was "just believe" — and, "just die." How strange such theology sounds to this shallow-pan generation! How far we have wandered! What far distances lie between us and such a divine dominion! The rich young ruler rejected that reign. And in most "believers" of today that dominion wields no sceptre, controls no career, governs no purse.

Finally, come now to Mulheim, Germany, and take a leaf from the life of that saint of only two and a half centuries ago, Gerhardt Ter Steegen. In his teens he entered deeply into the power and passion of Christ. The Spirit of God so mightily possessed him that he spent whole nights in prayer and supplication. Then he renounced his wealth and comfort to minister to the poor. He was indeed a rich young ruler who followed Christ literally because he sensed he needed "to obey the letter in order to keep the spirit." After his utter abandonment to his Master, luke-warm Christians deserted him, shunned him, and derided him as a fanatic. Though once the possessor of wealth, he became so reduced to destitution that for a time he lay alone in an attic burning up with a fever, neglected from morning till night, and with no one to bring him even so much as a cup of cold water. Dr. A. J. Gordon says of Ter Steegen's later ministry:

> No thought of making himself attractive or widely influential seems to have entered his mind. But just when he was most shunned and deserted by the world, then the sin-burdened and sorrowing began to crowd upon him from every direction to crave his spiritual ministrations. Mark it well,

O popular preacher, compassing all art and originality in order to draw the people! Here was one who had no thought of drawing anybody, his heart being set only on the one end of becoming holy unto the Lord, and perfectly doing His will. Indeed, while pursuing his humble calling as a ribbon maker, how little he anticipated being a preacher at all. But like his Master, for whom he lived supremely, "he could not be hid." The people thronged upon him. He tried to withdraw from them, but so much the more they pressed about him. Before he had risen in the morning, fifty or sixty would gather at his lodgings to hear the Word of Life from his lips. While state-church clergymen were jealous of his irregular ministry and complaining of him to the magistrates, he was yielding to the importunity of hungry souls, and consenting to preach. Such crowds gathered that they not only filled every part of the house but climbed on ladders about the windows in their eagerness to catch his words. One totally unknown to him came two hundred miles on foot in bad weather that he may hear the words of this blessed man. But Ter Steegen meantime is strangely amazed at it all, since his discourse is so plain and unstudied. "I cannot think what the people seek from such a poor creature," he exclaims. (from *The Twofold Life*).

Here was a man who did the impossible. Thus the camel passed through the needle's eye. Such things are possible with God. The secret of such infinite wealth and resources is crystal clear to those who, without reserve, embrace what Ter Steegen calls *"the mystery of the inward and outward Cross."*

Whether it be haunting reproach, or bloating pride, or bulging pockets, has my reader met his issue?

CHAPTER XV

The Man With the Withered Hand

S HE HAD been saved, but still she was shy and self-conscious. Once she was a consistent attendant at our services here in Three Hills, but later from her new home in a distant city she wrote us and revealed a growth in grace that had not been without some soul struggles. "God finally got me convicted," she said, "that I should be giving away gospel tracts. I answered, 'Lord, I simply can't do it; if ever I give away any tracts, *Thou* art the One who must do it.' Later while I was doing some business at the bank, the Lord said to me as I faced the bank teller, 'Here is someone to whom *you* can give a tract.' Immediately my heart asked, 'Lord, art *Thou* going to give this man a tract?' Even as I cried to God, *my hand went out*, and I gave him a tract. Since then I have passed on my secret of victory to others, and they too find that it works."

The story of Christ's dealing with "a man who had his hand withered" is found in all three synoptic gospels. Picture that scene in the synagogue. The Pharisees are there, full of craft and cunning. With curious and critical eyes they glance back and forth, first at the crippled man, then at Christ. They may have been whispering, "Is it lawful to heal on the Sabbath day?" Christ takes up their challenge and issues two specific commands to the man with the withered hand — the first, "Stand forth;" the second, "Stretch forth thine hand." Let us take them up in this order.

The first command, "Stand forth," may be rendered, "Arise, and stand in the midst." For the poor self-conscious one this was a severe test. Could he stand this exposure? this coming out from the crowd? this separation? Christ, it would seem, was calling first for this simple trial of faith and obedience. What this man could, he must do. And he did it. Before those green-eyed, long-bearded Pharisees he dared to come out and stand forth, his right hand hanging helpless and limp at his side.

But why all this procedure? Was it not arbitrary and unnecessary on the part of the Saviour? Could not Christ just as easily have healed him where he was seated back in that crowd? He did not have to call him out into such a place of conspicuous exposure. Ah, my reader, let us not be too sure. Let us herein discover divine wisdom again. Souls everywhere are calling for healing and restoration. They sense how limp and helpless they are. They feel their need. Many of them know that their need is Christ. Some of these want to come to Him. By way of a similar illustration consider a young man who suddenly faces some past misbehaviour, some dishonesty, some thievery, some unfaithfulness to his fellows. His definite act of sin stares him full in the face. Yet the issue of his recovery is likely to be dependent on some point of restitution which would most certainly mean exposure and shame. He can and must repent of this act. It will be in vain that he trusts the blood of Jesus to cleanse him if he refuses to obey God in restitution. Such a soul may even cry to God for mercy and profess to believe on the Lord Jesus Christ. Nevertheless, such believing is all in vain if in the one thing needful he refuses to meet God. His repentance demands confession of sin and restitution.

Here is where Christian workers must have wisdom. Of course, we need to beware of creating a lot of secondary issues and bringing up problems which are confusing and extraneous to the one all-important matter of believing on Christ. On the other hand, we must seek to eliminate this mere mental assent so common in many modern conversions. If we are wise to win, we must discern whether there lurks any concealed sin or hidden argument with God. Someone has put it this way: "On the one hand, we have to beware of leading the soul to a supposed faith in the blood of Jesus without any practical repentance toward man; on the other, we need to take heed lest the seeking soul rest satisfied with his repentance and never rests upon the sacrifice of Christ" (Wilkes, in *The Dynamic of Service*).

Let us catch, then, the full import of this first word of command, "Arise, and stand in the midst." Stand forth. Come out into the open. Come on, man. Come out where all men can see you. Fear not the faces of these scowling scribes. Shun not the shame. Let them criticize, as they will, this whole Sabbath-day procedure and recovery. Care nothing for that. Let all the world come and see. This true meaning of Christ's "Arise, and stand in the midst" is scarcely known today because salvation is made so easy.

Next comes the definite command, "Stretch forth thine hand." This called for an impossible thing. If impossible, was it not therefore unreasonable? "Stretch forth thine hand" — how could he? He had perhaps come to the synagogue to have Jesus stretch it out for him. It did seem to call for an impossible and therefore unreasonable thing. "Stretch forth thine hand" — how absurd! It was the one thing he had long desired to do, but it was the one thing he could not do. Now in the presence of that curious and critical crowd he was commanded to do it. Christ picked out, shall I say, his one great and conspicuous incapacity, and there demanded the impossible. Perhaps for many years the shrunken and limp member had hung helplessly by his side, a mere mockery of a hand. Now there rang in his ears the command: *"Stretch forth thine hand."* Impossible? But he did it! And his hand was made whole like unto the other.

You are a Christian. What is your withered hand? the one great impossible? the one thing that Christ commands? Your first consideration may center around your self-conscious fear of public shame and exposure, though you are also conscious of your disability, and feel impotent. Christ first calls you to come out into the open, to stand before the crowd, to go forth unto Him without the camp "bearing His reproach." Come out. Separate yourself. Leave that crowd and company whose faces you fear and whose eyes you feel. There is your first test.

Of course, your real trouble may be that you fear the second command, the command to do the utterly impossible. This is the thing you have already gathered Christ is commanding you — to put your hand to the plow and never look back. It may be that you are to hand out tracts, and "stretch forth the hand" on the street corner while declaring the unsearchable riches of Christ. Perhaps you should stretch forth your hand to your purse; yet there your hand hangs and hugs your side — and your purse. Your trouble, of course, is not in your hand. God is reaching for your

heart — through your withered hand. You sigh: If only the
Saviour had asked me to do something else! But that something
else would not have reached your heart. You could have done that
other thing without faith and without grace; yes, without even being right with God. So, in asking you to do the one impossible
thing, Christ crosses your will through your withered limb.

> *Would God my unbelief uncover,*
> *And my poor inmost heart discover?*
> *He issues one divine demand,*
> *And finds me through my withered hand.*

Do your circumstances seem contrary? your possibilities very un-
likely? your capacities very inadequate? Remember that in Christ's
economy all these handicaps are peculiarly suited to the display of
the divine wisdom and power. In this world of the Spirit, the opposite poles of the human and the Divine meet in an activity of
power. Be encouraged. God specializes in impossibilities. Find
herein, perhaps, the reason that He chose you!

Often God asks ministers and missionaries to step out and attempt the impossible. F. B. Meyer said, "We never test the resources of God until we attempt the impossible." But have some
of my ministerial brethren missed this way? Have you feared some
cost, some consequence, some "killing off"? Perhaps your old
friends have fawned upon you. Others have frowned upon you.
In the face of many forebodings and fears you have failed to break
caste. You have feared to go forth to Christ without the camp,
bearing His reproach. "If I were but five years younger," confessed a minister excusingly, "I would leave all and and go forth
to that impossible task." This confession was a revelation. The
man was still uneasy. Was God continuing, after all these years,
to make His impossible and unreasonable demand? Soon he would
be "ninety years old and nine," too old and withered to beget an
Isaac. That confession was certainly a revelation! We know now
why he became so angry with us five years before, though at the
time we were nonplussed. God must have been "crowding him into the corner." But the man had argued with God. His fierce
burst of unreasoning opposition was not against us but against
Christ's uttermost demand. Of course, his wife was not in agree-

ment with his obeying God, and his church was opposed. The whole hierarchy of the flesh was up in arms. At that point where his will had been crossed, his heart had been discovered, his self-life exposed. Mighty in the Scriptures, he could have been one of God's key men in Canada, but he halted at the "one thing" demanded. Like King Saul, who spared Agag, he lost his kingdom!

Are we inclined to excuse this minister? Do we pity him because Christ demanded the impossible? Does someone insist, This counsel is one of desperation and death. Who can go so far? We can only reply that if the man *could not*, it was because *he would not*. Bishop Moule said, "If you cannot, it is because somehow and somewhere you will not." To excuse ourselves as too weak and sinful and unable to fulfill such high and holy demands is to argue against the sufficiency of Him who issues the command. "Sin weakens man's power of obedience, but the can-not is a will-not and is therefore condemnable" (Strong). Forever Christ's call carries with it all the capacity needed, No word from Him is void of power. Our whole trouble can be summed up in the question asked by the little girl, "Please, sir, how can we be Christians and have our own way?"

Many men of God are forever standing on their heads, i.e., they are depending upon their own understanding. Their self-styled common sense forever binds them, renders them spiritually impotent. They dare not venture to walk with Christ on the water because their understanding knows that no man can walk on the water. Christ's call cannot be heard, therefore, above their common sense; they can see only disaster and drowning. Though they admit readily that Peter's cold, calculating common sense sank him, the truth is Peter's head but betrayed his unbelieving heart. Was Peter's seeing believing? Common sense may say so, but Scripture says Peter *saw* the winds and waves, and — sank.

The writer has always been glad that he "got going" on his particular impossible sea before his common sense caused him to consider too many billows. Aging calculations would know that it would be too contrary to nature to begin to build a school of one thousand to fifteen hundred students on the prairies. Such "new wine" could not have been put into "old skins." But these carnal calculations could not kill the walk of faith as long as spiritual insight could outwit and outrun natural wisdom. Do I hear some sensible man still objecting: "God gave me my reason, and He would never ask me to do that which is contrary to my good common sense"? Come on, man, your trouble is not in your head. Whether the issue be drawn around a withered hand or a withered head, the trouble is still heart trouble. Someone has said that "the citadel of the heart holds out long after every battery of the intellect has been blown to bits." If your reason were perfectly outreasoned, your heart would still argue. "The heart has reasons that reason knows nothing about" (Pascal). In all sincerity and respect let me say that your withered head is as poor an excuse of a hideout as any withered hand. Paul pins your wisdom to the Cross when he cries, "If any man among you seemeth to be wise in this world, let him become a fool [that is, let him begin by recognizing himself as the fool that he is (Way)], *that he may be wise*" (I Cor. 3:18). How long it takes us to unlearn our conceit! We never glorify God until we accomplish the impossible. As long as we measure our obedience and know just how far God should go and how much He should demand, then Heaven must let us blunder on until we "break the neck of our ignorance over some obstacle." Dr. J. H. Jowett said: "I very much like an epitaph which is found upon a woman's grave in New England: 'She hath done what she couldn't.' " Yes, she was only a "weaker vessel"; she had no strength, no power, no might; but "she hath done what she couldn't." Think of weary hours, long tramps to that little Sunday School, long nights of nursing — night after night, day after day. Worldly-wise men cried out to her, "You will never be able to do it. Pity thyself; this shall never be unto thee." But she did it. She spent long hours in prayer, in watchings often. She fought the battles and turned not back in disgrace. "You'll break down!" But she didn't. *"She hath done what she couldn't."* Does not faith laugh at impossibilities and cry, "It shall be done"? Does it forever remain, then, for some weaker vessel to shame us men out of our cold and calculating love for Christ?

Let us not miss the point of emphasis. Christ wants above all else that we come into union with Himself. Since that union can

come only through an act of willing surrender, Christ calls at a
certain point for an act of obedience. He does not confuse us with
a babel of voices. He is specific. He demands an utter abandonment of heart and will. The state of surrender both in its origin
and in its continuance will be realized around some single act of
obedience. At that given point the word of command is: *"This*
do, and life is thine." In that uttered word of His — not *any* words
of His, or His teachings in general, but His uttered and particular
and specific will at the moment — there is spirit and life, yea, "all
the light and might of God." Whatsoever He saith unto you, do
it. It was Martin Luther who said:

> If I profess with the loudest voice and clearest exposition
> every portion of the truth of God except precisely that little
> point which the world and the devil are at that moment attack-
> ing, I am not confessing Christ, however boldly I may be
> professing Christ. Where the battle rages, there the loyalty
> of the soldier is proved. To be steady on all the battlefields
> besides is mere flight and disgrace if he flinches at that point
> (*Kohila,* by Amy Carmichael).

Thank God for the men who have risked their all in obeying the
word of command, and who have come habituated to the program
of the impossible. They know the Shepherd's voice. They have
learned how to love the Lord their God with all their *mind,* as well
as with all their heart and soul and strength. Such men are prepared to hear God speak to them as He spoke to Hudson Taylor:

> Are you prepared to perish with me, to be counted a fool
> and worse than a fool by your own world, your missionary
> world? May I deal with every shred of your reputation just
> as I choose, and will you be silent? Are you willing to obey
> in everything, every time, and everywhere?

Hudson Taylor's "day of march" had come. He began to walk on
new missionary waters — waters unfathomed, waters on which no
man of his day had ever dared to tread. His path was unknown and
untried. Seas of trouble lay before him. How deep were those
waters! One who knows has said that "only Heaven is better than
to walk with Christ at midnight over moonless seas." Hudson Taylor's whole life was an everlasting "day of march." After many

years of tasks impossible and seas impassable, the old warrior said
again:

> We believe that the time has come for doing more fully
> what He has commanded us, and by His grace we intend to do
> it, not try to do it; for we see no scriptural authority for
> trying. "Try" is a word constantly in the mouth of unbe-
> lievers . . . The word of the Lord in reference to His com-
> mand is not "Do your best," but "Do it." We are therefore
> making arrangements . . .

There never was a truer word than this: "The revelation of my
growth in grace is the way I look on obedience." The call to do the
impossible may seem to be the counsel of despair, but as we become accustomed to habitual obedience, such calls come with delight. They inspire us with new zest and new zeal. Such has been
called, "The Glory of the Impossible." George Mueller learned
this rare lesson in the school of faith and obedience. As he faced
a new Red Sea of impossibility, he said, *"I had a secret satisfaction
in the greatness of the difficulties which were in the way. So far
from being cast down on account of them they delighted my soul;
for I desired only to do the will of the Lord in this matter."*

We feel that this chapter should be of special help to God's servants, those who are conscious of their withered powers. They have
become uneasy and dissatisfied with the results of a routine ministry. Dr. Ernest Wadsworth, of The Great Commission Prayer
League, has said:

> The first law of revival is the "withering work of the Spirit."
> This is the law of humiliation. It is the Holy Spirit's peculiar,
> preparatory plan. It holds good throughout all generations,
> It is certain and sure. Some imagine that the Spirit's work
> is always pleasant and comforting. This is far from the truth.
> His ministry is sometimes heart-rending. This unhappy
> work of the Spirit, the prelude to revival, is stated by the
> prophet Isaiah as a withering ministry: "Prepare ye the way
> of the LORD, make straight in the desert a highway for our
> God. Every valley shall be exalted, and every mountain and
> hill shall be made low: and the crooked shall be made straight,
> and the rough places plain: and the glory of the Lord shall
> be revealed, and all flesh shall see it together: for the mouth
> of the LORD hath spoken it. The voice said, Cry. And he

said, What shall I cry? All flesh is grass, and all the goodliness thereof is as the flower of the field: the grass withereth, the flower fadeth: because the Spirit of the LORD bloweth upon it: surely the people is grass. The grass withereth, the flower fadeth: but the word of our God shall stand forever" (Isa. 40:3-8). This humbling work of the Spirit is always the first gleam of a spiritual awakening. Spiritual renewal begins in the depth of the soul. The foundations are laid in repentance. When such a work of withering appears we may conclude with good reason that people are hearing "what the Spirit saith unto the churches." *The first evidence of a God-sponsored revival is humiliation.*

This "unhappy work of the Spirit," this heart-rending "prelude to revival," may also be the experience of my ministerial brethren. Be not turned aside. Seek God's anointing as a "soldier seeks victory in a siege or battle." Let me exhort you to make much of the might and dynamic of the Spirit. It is quite possible that in entering into the accession of power you will find your very bones withered up and dry as the Sahara Desert. Let this condition drive you to nought but a holy and hopeful despair. Let this be your own personal prelude to revival, that you may learn to preach the gospel with the Holy Ghost sent down from Heaven. How utterly imperative it is that you be endued with power from on high to fit you for such holy and heavenly work! Honour, therefore, every least hunger for the Spirit's mighty anointing.

We cannot but think of David Brainerd, whose holy anointing and influence have inspired hundreds to seek for that power which belongs alone unto God. Dr. A. J. Gordon says that one of the last recorded prayers of this apostle to the Indians was "for the influences of the divine Spirit to descend on ministers in a special manner." His dying counsel to his brother was, "Strive to obtain much of the grace of God's Spirit in the heart." Significantly he added, "When ministers feel the special gracious influences of the Holy Spirit in their hearts, *it wonderfully assists them to come at the consciences of men and, as it were, to handle them; whereas without these, whatever reason or oratory we may employ, we do but make use of stumps instead of hands*" (*The Holy Spirit in Missions*).

Oh the pity that we have such withered powers! Do we indeed "but make use of stumps instead of hands"? We have already intimated that in seeking for this heavenly anointing we may indeed find that the Spirit of the Lord will blow upon us until we are so withered and blasted without and within that we feel like Ezekiel's dry bones. Let us not be discouraged. God has something for us beyond our faintest dreams. Listen to Jonathan Goforth after thirteen years of growing dissatisfaction with the results of his work: "Restless, discontented, I was led to a more intensive study of the Scriptures. Every passage that had any bearing on the price of, or the road to, the accession of power became life and breath to me. So much did it become an obsession with me that my wife began to fear that my mind would not stand it. Slowly the realization began to dawn upon me that I had tapped a mine of infinite possibility." The awakenings which immediately began to attend this missionary's ministry confirmed the fact that he had indeed tapped the infinite resources of revival. The accounts read like a new *Acts of the Apostles*. How true it is also that before Jonathan Goforth paid the price of power he was but making use of *stumps* instead of *hands*.

In order that my reader may be encouraged to seek that anointing which belongs to Heaven's own knighthood, let me call in another witness whose after-life and ministry were a glowing testimony to the fullness and power of the Spirit. We refer to Dr. Samuel Chadwick, of Cliff College, England. He says:

> I have written and preached much on the Holy Spirit, for the knowledge of Him has been the most vital fact in my experience. I owe everything to the Gift of Pentecost . . . I came across a prophet, heard a testimony, and set out to seek I knew not what. I knew that it was a bigger thing and a deeper need than I had ever known. It came along the line of duty, and I entered in through a crisis of obedience. When it came, I could not explain what had happened, but I was aware of things unspeakable and full of glory.
>
> Some results were immediate. There came into my soul a deep peace, a thrilling joy, and a new sense of power. My mind was quickened. I felt that I had received a new faculty of understanding. Every power was alert. Either illumination took the place of logic, or reason became intuitive. My

bodily powers also were quickened. There was a new sense of spring and vitality, a new power of endurance, a strong man's exhilaration in big things. Things began to happen. What we had failed to do by strenuous endeavor came to pass without labour. It was as when the Lord Jesus stepped into the boat that with all their rowing had made no progress. Immediately the ship was at the land whither they went. It was gloriously wonderful (in *Power from On High*).

Oh my brother in the ministry, are you blighted and blasted and mildewed? Are you helpless and hopeless? Then you are just the case for Christ. You are shut up to faith. In spite of all your withered hopes, "Arise, and stand in the midst . . . *Stretch forth thine hand.*" "Impossible!" you cry. Quit your complaint. Launch out. Test His resources, leaving the consequences with Him. Then most certainly you will behold the impossible come to pass.

CHAPTER XVI

Salvation and Baptism

"By grace are ye saved through faith; and that not of yourselves: it is the gift of God: Not of works, lest any man should boast" (Eph. 2:8,9).

THOSE who claim there is an inseparable connection between regeneration and baptism evidently confound things that differ and confuse salvation by grace alone with works of the law. To the Galatian converts, who were being led by false teachers to believe that circumcision could in some way perfect their salvation by grace, Paul says, "I do not frustrate the grace of God: for if righteousness came by the law, then Christ is dead in vain." Those, therefore, who insist that regeneration is not complete without the addition of ordinances put themselves in the same class as the Jews who confounded *grace* with the externals of *works*. Paul says, "Now to him that worketh is the reward not reckoned of grace, but of debt" (Rom. 4:4). The only way, then, that one could compel God to justify him on terms of perfect merit would be to have one hundred percent righteousness. Yet, since perfect obedience as a condition of meriting eternal life is entirely impossible, man is shut up to salvation "by grace through faith."

The only possible sources of salvation are two — man's works or God's grace. So essentially distinct and opposite are these that any work of man causes salvation to be "not reckoned of grace." No salvation is a combination or mixture of both. This Scriptural truth is confirmed in the experience of the saved, for the man who comes under complete conviction that he is indeed "ungodly" despairs entirely of works. He then "believeth on Him that justifieth the ungodly" and finds to his heart's ease and full satisfaction that "his faith is counted for righteousness." The Apostle puts the matter beyond all dispute when he says, "And if by grace, then is it no more of works: otherwise grace is no more grace. But if it be of works [whether Jewish rituals or New Testament ordinances, the principle is identical], then is it no more grace: otherwise work is no more work."

The Saviour disclosed the very exact and simple condition on which all salvation rests when He said to a poor, repentant, believing sinner, *"Thy faith* hath *saved* thee" (Luke 7:50). Individual faith is the one indispensable and only requisite to salvation. In this same chapter (v. 42) the Saviour enforced the nature of salvation by faith alone with this explanatory word: "When they had *nothing to pay"* — no works, no good conduct, no rituals, no vows — "he frankly *forgave* them." Full and free remission of their sins came to these poor bankrupts when they had nothing with which to meet their debts.

It was the same with the thief on the cross. That poor sinner was never baptized, but upon a single look of faith, he was promised by the Lord Jesus, "Today shalt thou be with Me in paradise" (Luke 23:43). This case puts the matter once for all beyond doubt. The essence of salvation has no essential connection with the baptismal act (and if not the baptismal act no other external is logically conceivable) but is through personal faith in Christ. The simplest statement about how a man becomes a Christian is in John 1:12, 13: "As many as received Him [Christ], to them gave He power [right, or privilege] to become the sons of God, even to them that believe on His name: Which were born, not of blood (good parentage], nor of the will of the flesh [self-effort], nor of the will of man [any ordinance or human instrumentality whatever, whether of pope, priest, or parson], but of [out from] God." The new birth is *from above entirely*. Not where men direct, and priests control, and parsons administer, but just as the wind "bloweth where it listeth, . . . so is every one that is born of the Spirit." D. M. Panton rightly says: "Over the water (baptism) man has absolute control; and if regeneration is by water, *the wind is tied to the water*, and so is also under human control. On the contrary, says Jesus, the Spirit is independent of all human summons or direction and moves as the wind — in His sovereignty, His loneliness, His mystery. The water (baptism) man directs whither he will, sometimes wrongly; the wind (the Spirit) regenerates only as and where He will." It has always been thus that souls have been saved, whether in Old Testament days before there was any Christian baptism at all, or in New Testament times from the days of the apostles until now.

In this connection Abraham, the father of all the children of faith, is truly a perfect illustration. Years after he believed, "he received the sign of circumcision [similar to baptism as a sign], a seal of the righteousness of the faith which *he had yet being uncircumcised*" (Rom. 4:11). In this phrase is stated the law of all Christian ordinances. They are but outward signs of already received inward grace. Paul's own conversion and baptism followed this same Scriptural order (See Acts 22:16). After he met the Lord on the way to Damascus, Ananias said to him, "Arise, and be baptized, and wash away [in visible sign and symbol] thy sins, calling on the name of the Lord" (lit., *"having called,"* that is, *"after"* having done so; referring to the confession of Christ which *preceded* baptism, as in Acts 8:37") (Jamieson, Fausset and Brown).

What shall we do, then, about texts such as, "He that believeth and is baptized shall be saved"? In those days (even as in much of the heathen world of today), the only sign or badge of Christian discipleship was baptism. It was the ordinance of baptism that spelled death to false religion, death to sin, death to self — yea, death to all the past, and resurrection to newness of life. A man might profess Christ as much as he liked; but until he was baptized, he suffered no offence of the Cross — he bore no badge that he was identified with the Saviour. If such a person should argue that he would believe but would never be baptized (baptism in that case being plainly the issue around which his will accepted or rejected Christ), then until the crack of doom the condition of vital union with Christ for that man must needs be: "He that believeth and is baptized shall be saved." To an unprejudiced mind, however, it must be plain that it is a matter not of *water*, but of *will*.

Naaman was a great man, but a leper. He came to Elisha with all the pomp and ceremony of a great captain. As a mighty man he gloried in his might. He had to be brought low and made to feel that he was unclean in heart — as unfit for God's presence as

any leper was unfit for society. In Israel the leper was excluded;
he was not allowed to pollute the Lord's house. Notice that Jesus
sent His disciples to *heal* the sick but to *cleanse* the lepers, for
leprosy, like sin, stains. Since Naaman's leprosy emblemed his own
heart's corruption, he needed cleansing. In spite of all his leprous
uncleanness and humbling circumstances, he was still full of pride
and selfrespect. No humble beggar was he.

Elisha treated Naaman with not so much as courtesy or respect.
He sent his servant out not to greet him or invite him in but to
give him a humiliating remedy. Alexander Maclaren observed:
"Naaman wished to be treated like a great man who happened to
be a leper; Elisha treated him like a leper who happened to be a
great man." How could this self-sufficient soul be brought down
to the deadly discovery that he was a leper? Jordan's waters were
chosen of Jehovah to reduce the proud captain to a state of submission. "Go and wash in Jordan seven times, and thy flesh shall
come again to thee, and thou shalt be clean" (II Kings 5:10).

Does all this seem strange? Had not Naaman as an expression
of some faith in the Lord God of Israel come all the way from his
country? Did he not already believe? Were there not many lepers
in Israel in the time of Eliseus the prophet, and none of them
cleansed, saving Naaman the Syrian (Luke 4:27)? His recognition of Jehovah must have been beyond that of many in Israel.
However, only "with the heart" does man believe unto righteousness. In spite of his loathsome condition Naaman was still high-
minded, self-important, unbroken. His incurable disease and personal despair plus the report of the little maid had driven him a
long way, but not far enough. The command to go wash in Jordan signified an acknowledgment that before the Holy One of Israel Naaman was as corrupt in heart as he was in body. In principle this law of cleansing for Naaman was not unlike God's law
to Israel: "*This* do, and thou shalt live." Yet how unreasonable!
How cheap! How common and plain! Whoever heard of any
benefit from Jordan's waters? "Are not Abana and Pharpar, rivers
of Damascus, better than all the waters of Israel? may I not wash
in them, and be clean?" (II Kings 5:12). Yes, Naaman, cleansed
from bodily filth you may be, but you cannot be cleansed from

leprosy except in Jordan. You must be willing to do anything, and the last thing you are willing to do is to submit to such a strange and unreasonable prescription.

There was of course neither saving nor healing virtue in Jordan's waters, whether he dipped seven times or seventy times seven. However, in the act of dipping, Naaman's will would be crossed. There he would meet God. It was, again, not a question of *water*, but of *will*. If he refused those seven dips, he could not believe God. Only in Jehovah's Jordan could he come to an obedient faith. Only there could he wash and be clean. To Naaman Jordan's washing meant open exposure and shame and humiliation; yet it was only by such an undoing that he could come in heart-broken submission to the Lord God of Israel. There was no alternative: "This do, and thou shalt live." Naaman would rather die than do it. He had to do both — had to die in doing it, die to his own filthy pride, and rise to newness of life. He did it — and he lived anew.

Can the reader recollect how, before he was saved, he may have said something like this: "If ever I get saved, I'll not go around telling everbody about it; I'll not stand out there on the street corner and make a fool of myself; if ever I get converted, I'll never go down to that mourner's bench"? G. Campbell Morgan gives an account of a personal experience which indicates the wisdom needed in dealing with souls who have such an argument with God. He says:

> I remember years ago conducting a mission, and at the back of the chapel sat a man. In the very first after-meeting, as I moved around speaking to various persons, I came to that man. I found the Holy Spirit of God had gripped him, but he looked at me and said (I had been inviting people to come out into an inquiry-room):
> "Can't I be saved without going in there?"
> Now when a man begins to ask that question, you must deal with him in just one way. So I said, "No; I don't think you can."
> "Why," he said, "is salvation in the inquiry-room?"
> "No, it is in God; but just as long as you sit here and want to dictate terms to God, you are proving that you have not got to the end of self, and there is no salvation for you. That is the trouble with you."

"Then," he said, "if I cannot be saved without going into that inquiry-room, I will go to Hell."

"My brother," I answered, "That is not God's choice for you. If you have chosen it for yourself, I cannot help it."

Every night that man came and sat there. Oh, how gracious God is! He does not take us at our word. He does not leave us alone when we have said some rash, foolhardy thing.

I had warned the workers, "Don't talk to that man. Leave him alone. Let God have His way with him."

I shall never forget the last night of the mission. Before I had time to ask a soul to move, that man came forward over the backs of the seats to the altar. I looked at him and said, "I thought you were going to Hell, my brother?"

He said, "Oh, I have been there all the week."

Praise God! it does a man good to get there that way for a little while sometimes.

(from *True Estimate of Life*)

Charles Finney, the greatly used revivalist, said, "In meetings I always emphasize immediate submission to Christ." This man of God was not contending with the modern easygoing believism. He knew that salvation was through faith alone, but his emphasis was on the *obedience of faith*.

Let us now give brief consideration to the case of the Saviour's dealing with Nicodemus, that ruler of the Jews who "came to Jesus by night." Nicodemus was a Pharisee and also a master in Israel, but he lacked the courage to consult Jesus by daylight — "for fear of the Jews." Not daring to be caught too closely associated with Jesus, he came under cover of night. Through his observation of the miracles, he had been convinced of Jesus' commission; his "we know" indicated he had some mental conviction. He came thinking that if he had a bit more instruction, he might have better insight into the Kingdom. "We know that thou art a teacher come from God."

Jesus halted Nicodemus on the spot: "Verily, verily, I say unto thee, except a man be born again, he cannot see the kingdom of God" (John 3:3). Apart from the new birth, Nicodemus was told, he would have neither sight nor insight into the things of the Kingdom. Nicodemus was mystified — "How can a man be born when he is old?" Now, as a ruler, he was not unacquainted with

the fact that proselytes, when they were baptized from heathenism
into the Jewish kingdom, were said to have been "as a child newly born." This idea, then, of the new birth on the part of the heathen into the Jewish kingdom was not entirely foreign to Nicodemus. However, he and his fellow Pharisees had assumed the self-
righteous position that, for them at least, there was no necessity of
rebirth. Were they not, as sons of Abraham, the already-born "sons
of God"? Yet their Scriptures, such as Deuteronomy 30, Ezekiel 36
and 37, Psalms 32 and 51, had sufficiently disclosed the necessity
of heart conversion that Jesus was not declaring an entirely new
thing when He spoke to Nicodemus of the new birth: — "Art thou
a master of Israel, and knowest not these things?" Nicodemus need
not have been so mystified. His own Old Testament blamed him for
not having known that salvation by grace through faith had always
implied that when a man was saved he had a new heart and was
born of the Spirit.

We have already said that, through the doorway of washings,
proselytes had come into the Jewish economy. Furthermore, at
that very time John the Baptist was requiring of all men a baptism of repentance and confession of sin. Both Pharisees and Sadducees witnessed his baptism. He called them to repentance, warning them to flee from the wrath to come. So impressed had the
Pharisees already been with John that they had sent a delegation to
inquire whether or not he was the Christ. Concerning the reception of John's baptism, Luke gives us a very illuminating paragraph
and side light: "All the people that heard him, and the publicans,
justified God, being baptized with the baptism of John. But the
Pharisees and lawyers rejected the counsel of God against themselves, *being not baptized of him*" (Luke 7:29, 30).

With this in mind let us listen to Jesus' second declaration to
Nicodemus, a statement which has to do not with *insight*, but rather
with *entrance* into the kingdom of God. "Verily, verily, I say unto
thee, Except a man be born of *water* and of the *Spirit*, he cannot
enter into the kingdom of God." There are those who say that the
words "born of water" refer to the physical birth of every man.
Others say that the "water" refers to the water of "the Word," and

for confirmation they appeal to Eph. 5:26. The writer himself once
felt that this was the best explanation that would avoid the Romish
error of baptismal regeneration.* However, we are a long way
toward understanding this passage if we seat ourselves with Nicodemus and let the Saviour speak to us from that standpoint. This
learned ruler was thoroughly acquainted with the mighty pronouncements of John and the meaning of his baptism, viz., repentance.
John's baptism, while it did not secure a remission of sins, was
an acknowledgment of sinnerhood. It represented an open confession of sin and a corresponding need of cleansing. Nicodemus
was one of those Pharisees who could not dream of being classed
on the level with publicans and sinners. He supposed himself already within the Kingdom, and only waiting its visible institution.
Now Jesus confronted him with the awful fact that, first of all, he
had no insight into the Kingdom; and secondly, that he could not
find entrance except he crawl through the doorway of sinnerhood.
Nicodemus had been skirting John and coming as a *pupil* to Jesus — the great *Teacher*. Had he come by way of John and
John's baptism, he would have come to Jesus as a *sinner* need-
ing a *Saviour*. This is plainly the meaning of Jesus' word to Nicodemus that except he be born of water (John's baptism of acknowledged sinnerhood), and the Spirit (Christ's regenerating work
through the agency of the Spirit), he could not find entrance into
the kingdom of God.

---

* The Catholic church says: "The instrumental cause [of justification] is
the sacrament of baptism, without which justification never befell any man";
and, "If any one shall say that by the said sacrament grace is not conferred
through the act performed, but that faith alone suffices for obtaining grace,
let him be accursed" (Quoted by D. M. Panton). Such is the logical and
unscriptural terminus to which the confusion of works with grace leads those
in error. Over at the opposite pole, we hear Paul crying out, "I do not
frustrate the grace of God: for if righteousness come by the law [whether
through the old ritual of circumcision or, since the principle is the same in
both, by the ordinance of baptism], then Christ is dead in vain" (Gal 2:21).
Paul's logical terminus is set squarely over against that of Rome: "If any
man preach any other gospel unto you than that ye have received, let him be
accursed" (Gal. 1:9). It then comes to this: Either water baptism saves,
or one is saved by individual faith (which is by grace alone). There is no
other possible explanation.

It is pathetic that a few Protestant denominations have not escaped this
Romish doctrine but have continued to propagate her Galatian error.

Those who presume that God instituted with Moses a works-righteousness naturally find themselves involved with mental and theological difficulty when they come to understand and explain these New Testament Scriptures in which baptism seems to be set forth as a conditional element in salvation. If, however, one has an unconfused view of salvation by grace throughout the whole Bible, then he finds his way through these difficult passages without forcing interpretations. He observes that certain varying situations and historical backgrounds call for certain conditional elements and contingencies. These do not confuse grace, but lead rather to its fulfillment.

In keeping with the message of this book, our aim has been to set forth in this chapter only certain broad principles. Our intention has been to discuss salvation in such a way as to do justice on the one hand to the ordinance of baptism, while on the other to rescue legalists from a water-works righteousness.

CHAPTER XVII

Beginning in the Spirit—Ending in the Flesh

A GREAT MAN of God and Bible teacher once found himself such a victim of an uncontrollable tongue that he burnt it with a red-hot poker, hoping that he might thereby get the victory over the unruly member. In a most literal manner he was willing to cut off the right hand, pluck out the right eye, burn the tongue loose at both ends. He was zealous. Nevertheless, though his motive was right, his manner was legalistic. Having begun in the Spirit, he was trying to be *made perfect by the flesh*. God taught him better, however, and since his deliverance from fleshly legalism he cannot cease to sound forth the glories of grace. For having now adopted an extreme "not-under-law" position, he may perhaps be pardoned.

A young man who has just graduated from our school once had great difficulty getting over his pride of voice. He was self-conscious and voice-conscious; he could not sing without being proud. Unable to overcome this vainglory, he seemed to have but one recourse, viz., not to sing at all. However, he had to come to see that, whereas for a time such a course might be necessary, it was only a *legal* effort to crucify the flesh.

A few days ago another young man came with a request that he might be allowed to fast for three days. He had read some literature which assured him that fasting would remove his doubts and cure his spiritual problems. Yes, it is true that the church of today is, for the most part, feasting instead of fasting, and needs to learn afresh how to reverse this order; nevertheless, no amount of bodily buffeting can purchase Christian victory.

News just comes to hand of yet another extremist, who has almost killed herself in a forty-one day fast. Would she outdo Moses and Jesus by one day? To each of these legalists Paul would say,

"Beware of the concision;" beware of a mere senseless mutilation of the flesh. Entrance into the victorious Christian life is on the simple condition of faith. As an old writer has said:

> It is the blood of Jesus alone that cleanseth from all sin, not penal sufferings, not mortifications of any sort, not anything we have, not grace already received, not anything we are or can be, not death or purgatory, no, not the purgatory of all our doings and sufferings and strivings put together. He alone forgiveth sins, and He alone cleanseth from all unrighteousness. *Faith is the only condition and shares in the omnipotence it dares to trust* (Quoted by Wilkes in *Dynamic of Life*).

It has been observed that "the spirit of self-righteousness was the prevailing tendency of the carnal mind under the Old Dispensation, as an unconcern about personal righteousness is under the New" (Fairbairn). This book is being written out of concern for the bringing of all God's people to a proper appreciation of the value of the Old Testament and also for the re-establishing of personal righteousness among orthodox believers.

At present the prevailing tendency is an "unconcern about personal righteousness." Therefore, in order rightly to divide the word of truth to this generation of believers, our chief concern should be neither to release God's people to a false freedom nor to cater to their propensity to use liberty for license. At this hour the chief correction called for is to bring God's people back to "the obedience of faith." On the other hand, however, on the part of many saints there is a deep hunger to go on with God. It is among these who are concerned about true righteousness that there is a natural tendency to legalistic self-righteousness. A great deal of Scripture is adapted to meet the need of such souls.* Let us then

---

* The Bible is adapted to meet the need of each heart. It is written *to each man the way he is going.* For this reason theologians often fall into opposing doctrinal camps. To support his doctrine, one man gathers to himself a host of proof texts. To him these Scriptures present *the norm,* to which seemingly opposite Scriptures must bow. Another man proceeds the same way for his quite different doctrinal position. His mass of texts present the only norm to him, and all other seemingly contradictory texts must come over to his norm. Then the deadlock is on. Consider, for example, law and grace in the New Testament. There is the strongest language asserting the abiding character of the righteous requirements of the law; there are equally strong

give attention to our theme topic suggested by Paul's question to the Galatian believers, "Tell me, ye that desire to be under the law, do ye not hear the law?" Paul is dealing in the epistle to the Galatians with the legalistic teachings of the self-righteous Jews, who would pervert the simple gospel and bring Christian converts into bondage. Let it be remembered that the Pharisaic conception of the law was that it consisted in a works-righteousness whereby men might merit acceptance with God. Long after many Jews had accepted Christ as their personal Saviour this propensity to legalism would cling to them. It was perhaps the greatest doctrinal problem to trouble the early church. But when this question had first come up some years before (Acts 15), it had been settled by the Jerusalem council. When the contention of the Judaizers at that time had been, "Except ye be circumcised after the manner of Moses, ye cannot be saved," the decision reached at Jerusalem had settled

---

statements which run in the opposite direction and seem to represent law as the enemy of grace. The solution, inconceivable to natural reasoning, must lie in this: The Bible is written to each man the way he is going. If a man is going east, Scripture is directed to him to meet his need; if a man is going west, Scripture addresses him accordingly. When men are going opposite directions, there should be little wonder that such Scriptures should seem to contradict one another. How could natural reason ever put the two together? There are doctrines more difficult to harmonize perhaps than those of law and grace. In such cases, rather than attempt to show that they can be brought together, we should prefer to "keep the unity of the Spirit in the bond of peace . . . Till we all come in [into] the unity of the faith" (Eph. 4:3, 13).

Dr. R. C. Mc Quilken of Columbia Bible College, a man of clear and scriptural thinking on this subject, makes this observation:

Much of the confusion among writers who discuss Law and Grace is based on their thought that "law" always means the same thing. All are familiar with the fact that the word "law" may refer to the first five books of the Old Testament, or may refer to the whole Old Testament. Likewise it may refer to the moral law of God, or to the Mosaic system as a system from Sinai to the Cross. It is exceedingly important to study the context to know in what sense the word "law" is being used. Thus many times it may not be a case of using the word "law" in the same way. It must be applied differently according to the way the man is going. If the word is referring to the moral law of God, which is an expression of the will of God, — "I delight to do thy will: Yea, thy law is within my heart." — that is quite different from the discussion of law from the standpoint of the inexorable penalty of the law in such a verse as: "For ye are not under law, but under grace." To be under law would mean that we are under condemnation because we have broken the law. It would also mean that we are under the requirement of keeping the law with absolute perfection if we would obtain righteousness "under the law."

the question for all time: No ordinance or ceremony is necessary to make a man Christ's. Thus, when the "decrees" of this council had been circulated among the Gentile churches, in one direction at least the Judaizers had been halted — no longer could they preach circumcision as a condition of salvation. However, they found another way still open, so they thought, to make disciples for themselves: they could zealously seek (Gal. 4:17) the perfection of Paul's converts. The Judaizers would not question a convert's initial acceptance of Christ, but would show to him the pathway to perfection, viz., through circumcision. The Judaizer would admit that Christ crucified was necessary for salvation, but would insist that it was *Christ plus circumcision for perfection.* Paul, therefore, asked the Galatians: "Are ye so foolish? *having begun in the Spirit, are ye now made perfect by the flesh?*"

Paul's argument in this epistle is to show that the whole of our salvation, whether it be justification, or the gift of the Spirit, or the promise of life, or the coming inheritance — all is wrapped up in Christ. There can be no substitute for Christ, nor any addition to Him. In Galatians 3:29-5:6, in the midst of a discussion about the believer's inheritance, Paul breaks out with this question, "Tell me, ye that desire to be under the law," [you who have been attracted to seek your perfection and inheritance through some addition to Christ], do ye not hear the law?" (won't you listen to the law itself?). In order to overthrow the legalists, Paul next sets forth in allegorical illustration an argument from their own Pentateuch:

> Tell me, ye that desire to be under the law, do ye not hear the law?
> For it is written, that Abraham had two sons, the one by a bond-maid, the other by a freewoman.
> But he who was of the bondwoman was born after the flesh; but he of the freewoman was by promise.
> Which things are an allegory: for these are the two covenants; the one from the mount Sinai, which gendereth to bondage, which is Agar.
> For this Agar is mount Sinai in Arabia, and answereth to Jerusalem which now is, and is in bondage with her children.
> But Jerusalem which is above is free, which is the mother of us all.

For it is written, Rejoice, thou barren that bearest not; break forth and cry, thou that travailest not: for the desolate hath many more children than she which hath an husband.

Now we, brethren, as Isaac was, are the children of promise.

But as then he that was born after the flesh persecuted him that was born after the Spirit, even so it is now.

Nevertheless what saith the scripture? Cast out the bondwoman and her son: for the son of the bondwoman shall not be heir with the son of the freewoman.

So then, brethren, we are not children of the bondwoman, but of the free.

Stand fast therefore in the liberty wherewith Christ hath made us free, and be not entangled again with the yoke of bondage.

Behold, I Paul say unto you, that if ye be circumcised, Christ shall profit you nothing.

For I testify again to every man that is circumcised, that he is a debtor to do the whole law.

Christ is become of no effect unto you, whosoever of you are justified by the law; ye are fallen from grace.

For we through the Spirit wait for the hope of righteousness by faith.

For in Jesus Christ neither circumcision availeth any thing, nor uncircumcision; but faith which worketh by love.

—Gal. 4:21-5:6

Here Paul could be misunderstood as meaning to teach that the whole Old Testament is against the New. Yet Paul would be the last man to teach any such thing. He is simply taking the Judaizers strictly on their own ground. For the sake of argument, he assumes that there were "two covenants" in essential contradiction to each other. From the law itself he shows that these legalists are sons of bondage and that they entangle others therein. Did these self-righteous Jews boast that they were the offspring of Abraham? Did they appeal to the Old Testament for support? On Old Testament ground, Paul will unveil to his own converts the bondage into which the Judaizers would lead them. The familiar illustration which sets forth Paul's argument in an allegory can best be understood by considering in detail some of its antitheses.

Hagar and Sarah. These were the two mothers, both of them wives of Abraham. Hagar was but the bondmaid of Sarah, Abraham's proper wife. In these two mothers we behold two kinds of

offspring, both from the old partriarch. Sarah gave birth to Isaac;
Hagar to Ishmael. Even so, both the Judaizers and true Christians
could boast they were the offspring of Abraham. In these two
mothers, Hagar and Sarah, then, the two covenants found their very
nature and effects prefigured.

Ishmael and Isaac. These two sons represent two classes of wor-
shipers. Ishmael, born of the bondwoman, represented the self-
righteous Jews under the yoke of bondage. Isaac, the child of
promise, even in his *natural* birth represented the *spiritual* born-
again ones.

Law and Grace. Herein are the two covenants. Ishmael was the
offspring of a bondwoman and himself was born in bondage. He
answers to all the sons of Sinai. When looked to for life, the covenant of law genders (i.e., brings forth) children doomed to
bondage; whereas the new covenant of grace, represented by Sarah,
begets sons of life and liberty and freedom. Sinai did indeed
bring forth children unto bondage for the simple reason that *the
law was never designed to beget children* any more than Hagar
was designed to beget an heir to the Abrahamic covenant. Hagar
and Sinai, *when looked to for life,* begat only unregenerate bondmen, mere Pharisaic and selfish sons of the flesh. Thus viewed,
law is, in truth, an enemy of grace. Sarah, then, in her supernatural offspring represented not law but grace. Through Isaac
she was the only proper mother of the children of promise. And
the law stood related to the Abrahamic promise just as Hagar stood
related to Sarah; she was but the handmaid, and was never meant
to be the mother.

The Earthly Jerusalem and the Heavenly Jerusalem. Sinai and
Hagar, with their improper offspring, answers, Paul says, to Jerusalem which was then in bondage with her children. On the other
hand, the freeborn and supernatural sons of Sarah are born from
above, with heavenly citizenship. As such they have been delivered
from the law, from its curse and from its yoke of bondage. How
then should they ever expect to inherit through Hagar? Their
birth from above excludes the flesh. Professor Fairbairn, whose
exposition in this connection is very helpful, rightly says concerning the Mosaic covenant:

God never designed it to *be* a mother any more than Hagar, respecting whom Abraham sinned when he turned aside to her, and took her for a mother of children. Her proper place was that only of a handmaid to Sarah. And it was in like manner to pervert the covenant of law from Sinai to an improper purpose, to look to it as a parent of life and blessing. Nor could any better result come from the error. "It gendereth unto bondage," says the apostle; that is, in so far as it gave birth to any children, these were not true children of God, free, spiritual, with hearts of filial confidence and devoted love; but miserable bondmen, selfish, carnal, full of mistrust and fear. Of these children of the Sinaitic covenant we are furnished with the most perfect exemplar in the scribes and Pharisees of our Lord's time—men who were chiefly remarkable for the full and ripened development of a spirit of bondage in religion—who were complete in all the garniture of a sanctified demeanor, while they were full within of ravening and wickedness—worshiping a God whom they eyed only as the taskmaster of a labourious ritual, by the punctual observance of which they counted themselves secure of His favor and blessing—crouching like slaves beneath their yoke of bondage, and loving the very bonds that lay on them, because nothing better than the abject hireling spirit of slavery breathed in their hearts. Such were the children whom the covenant of law produced, as its natural and proper offspring [i.e., when the letter of the law, instead of the Lord, is looked to for life]. But did God ever seek such children? Could He own them as members of His kingdom? Could He bestow on them an interest in its promised blessings? Assuredly not; therefore it was entirely against His mind, when His professing people looked in that direction for life and blessing. If really His people, they already had these by another and earlier covenant [Abrahamic] which could give them; and those who still looked to the covenant of law, only got a serpent for bread—instead of a blessing, a curse (*Typology of Scripture,* Vol. II).

Circumcision and the Cross of Christ. Neither circumcision nor uncircumcision avails anything in Paul's "new creation." The flesh profiteth nothing. Circumcised, it is no better; uncircumcised, it is no worse. To the Galatians he says, "But I, brethren, if I still preach circumcision" — as the legalizers may assert, because in the beginning I circumcised Timothy (Acts 16:3) — "why am I still persecuted? then hath the stumblingblock of the cross been

done away" (Gal. 5:11, R.V.). Paul was not preaching both circumcision and the Cross. However, it needs to be clearly understood that the subtlety of Paul's critics lay not in their open denial
of the Cross, else the converts would not have tolerated them a moment; but rather it lay in their preaching of the Cross *plus circumcision*. Paul saw circumcision, as held by these legalists, to be the
most relentless antagonist of the Cross. Their preaching is law;
his is grace. Theirs is flesh; his is Spirit. Both could not be embraced together.

But was there not a day when Abraham "received the sign of circumcision, [as] a seal of the righteousness of the faith which he
had" (Rom. 4:11)? Indeed, and with no harm to his faith. For
in Abraham's day what did circumcision mean to him? Had he
not already come to an utter end of himself and any confidence in
the flesh? Was he not ninety years old and nine and without the
least hope in the natural of ever having such a son as Isaac? Had
not faith alone been counted to him for righteousness? As far as
Abraham was concerned, there was no hope in the flesh. Circumcision to him meant an end of the flesh, meant that the flesh profiteth nothing, meant that he had renounced all virtue and strength
in himself. Yet in Paul's time the Apostle was forced to treat circumcision as an enemy of grace, for the Jews were saying, "Circumcision is equivalent to all the commandments of the law." What
was the only possible reply? "I testify again to every man that
is circumcised, that he is a debtor to do the whole law" Gal. (5:3).
Circumcision had come to be the badge of a works-righteousness.
Therefore Paul warns the Gentile converts concerning the legalists:
They "desire to have you circumcised, that they may glory in your
flesh" (6:13). Divinely indignant, the Apostle cries: "God forbid that I should glory, save in the cross of our Lord Jesus Christ,
by whom the world [the religious world, including all the flesh
therein] is crucified unto me, and I unto the world" (6:14). Strange
as it may seem, circumcision, though scarcely mentioned in connection with the Mosaic covenant, had come to be identified with
and representative of all legal righteousness. It had come to represent the self-improvement and profit of the flesh. On the other
hand the Cross meant death to the flesh: "They that are Christ's

have crucified the flesh." At Golgotha there had been such an ignominious termination of the flesh that it spelled death to all fleshly merit, and therefore to circumcision. Circumcision's only cure was the Cross.

A friend of the writer was asked by a bishop of the Anglican Church in India to hold a series of meetings with his people. My friend preached for a week, with the blessing of God upon him. God then laid it upon his heart to preach on Hezekiah's destruction of "the brasen serpent that Moses had made" (II Kings 18:4). He showed how the serpent, which had once symbolized the uplifted Substitute "made sin," had become a kind of fetish or idol. Because Israel had been burning incense unto it, Hezekiah broke it into pieces and "called it Nehushtan," i.e., a piece of brass. At the close of his message my friend turned around, pointed to the great, tall brass cross behind him, and cried out: "Friends, this brass cross has come between you and Christ. You will never get back to Christ until you tear this thing out of here. This is *a piece of brass*." And what happened? The bishop walked up and down the aisles of his church, groaning and wringing his hands and crying: "Oh people, we have heard from God today; we've heard from God." The people were so smitten with conviction that they bowed before God's Spirit as trees bow before the wind — so terrible and awful was the hush of God upon their hearts. They had been struck with reality; they had found and faced the living Christ again. They had learned the lesson that that which begins in the Spirit may end in the flesh.

Does not the modernist know Christ after the flesh, as the man of Galilee? as the beautiful Master, the uncrucified Teacher? Listen to Paul: "Henceforth know we no man after the flesh: yea, though we have known Christ after the flesh, yet now henceforth know we Him no more" (II Cor. 5:16). These modernists have taken away our crucified Lord and know where they have laid Him; they have smothered Him with flowers. And does not the ritualist have a cross? a gold cross, a white cross, or a brass cross? (A number of years ago it was said there were enough crucifixes in the United States to fence in the state of Kentucky; ere long the whole nation may be fenced in.) The ritualists too have taken away the

Crucified; they have buried Him beneath some Christless cross. Both of these extremes are, "after the flesh." What a relief then to sing:

> *"A Christless cross no refuge were for me;*
> *A crossless Christ my Saviour could not be.*
> *But O Christ crucified, I rest in Thee!"*

After the Flesh and After the Spirit. In God's kingdom, that is "not first which is spiritual, but that which is natural; and afterward that which is spiritual" (I Cor. 15:46). The birth of Ishmael was "first," was natural, was after the flesh. But the birth of Isaac was "afterward," was supernatural, was after the Spirit. Such a fleshly offspring as that represented by Ishmael could never enter a spiritual kingdom, for that which is born of the flesh is flesh. As far as the kingdom is concerned, the flesh has neither *insight* nor *entrance* nor *inheritance.* Those born after the flesh (the legalists) were simply unregenerate men who had confidence in the flesh and who had perverted the whole Mosaic legislation to one of a works-righteousness. All this was in sharpest contrast with the gospel of grace, by which the Galatian converts had become the free-born, the born-again, those born after the Spirit.

The birth that is natural is after the flesh; the birth that is supernatural is after the Spirit. Those born of the Spirit soon discover that the flesh lusts against the Spirit. Just as Ishmael mocked and persecuted Isaac, even so does the flesh antagonize and war against the Spirit. "The mind of the flesh is enmity against God; for it is not subject to the law of God, neither indeed can it be" (Rom. 8:7, R.V.). God can take no pleasure in the flesh. It is unimprovable and incorrigible. Its nature is unmitigated enmity; its disposition is unchangeable; its mind is death; its only cure is the Cross. Such is the inveterate antagonism of Ishmael against Isaac, the flesh against the Spirit.

In speaking of "the flesh" as contrary to "the Spirit," Scripture refers to the whole of human nature in its fallen condition. We read of the *wills* of the flesh, the *desires* of the flesh, the *mind* of the flesh, the *wisdom* of the flesh, the *purposes* of the flesh, the *workings* of the flesh, the *warring* of the flesh, the *glorying* of the flesh. Scripture mentions those who walk *according* to the flesh, *after* the flesh, make a *fair show* in the flesh (*Born Crucified*).

Having begun in the Spirit, O fellow believer, be sure you continue, go on, persevere *in the Spirit*. Have you learned to say with Paul, "I know that in me (that is, in my flesh,) dwelleth no good thing"? Or, have you no fear or mistrust of the flesh? If you have come to understand somewhat of the treachery of the workings of the flesh, your battle cry will be: "no confidence in the flesh."

So manifold and subtle are the manifestations of the flesh that a ministry begun in the Spirit can very speedily pass over into confidence in the flesh. In his early ministry a Christian worker will launch forth with a deep sense of personal weakness and need of God's power. He begins in the Spirit. But before long, like Jacob of old, he begins to lean on the flesh. He manages, he manipulates, he schemes. We have in mind a certain minister who, in the beginning, was artless and honest and dependent upon the Spirit. Since those days, the schoolmen have adorned him and given him "what it takes" to produce an effect. He is now a popular speaker, an orator, a rhetorician. He is a born-again man, a man who exalts Christ. He will preach nothing but the gospel, but he does it with the atmosphere and swagger of the flesh. He comes home to boast: "Well, I certainly put that over today." The flesh has so reinstated itself in his life and ministry that its works are manifested in all the cupidity and swagger and ostentation of an Ishmaelite. Such is his abounding "confidence in the flesh" that little comes of all his good preaching. The flesh makes the Cross of none effect.

What has happened to this man? There was a day when, in desperate need of the Spirit of power, he found the five smooth stones of God's grace quite sufficient. But since then his teachers have taught him better! They have spared him the pains of having to go continually through the old troublesome and humiliating way of the Cross. They have so fitted Saul's armour on him that he looks like a real warrior. Of course, he is still a hard-working pastor; he is such a busy man, a man after the people's own heart. He now feels so relieved not to have to face the odds each Sunday with the inadequate weapons of David's spiritual warfare. How he can make a fair show in the flesh! How he has fallen from grace! Christ profits him nothing.

Can the reader not sense the worm at the root of this man's life? Self-confidence came in to supplant and to oust dependence upon the Spirit. Paul's only boast was: "We are the circumcision, which worship God in the spirit, and rejoice in Christ Jesus, and have no confidence in the flesh" (Phil. 3:3). This minister's preference for the flesh — perhaps in the form of vainglory or self-sufficiency — spoiled his glorying in Christ Jesus alone. Self began to take over what the Spirit alone can do. Had he but obeyed the Spirit, the Cross would have taken care of the flesh; but now the flesh — filthy and foul and pretentious — glories in God's very presence.

We recall another minister who, in his grey hairs, after the locusts had eaten his good years, finally got back to God. Hear his confession: "Would you like to know when I became a modernist? One Sunday in the beginning of my ministry I saw in my congregation a man of influence. I trimmed my message that day to win that man's approval. There I became a modernist." He had begun in the Spirit, but how easily he had been side-tracked to the flesh.

Self dies hard. It is difficult to say day by day: "Yet not I — Christ liveth in me." Oh yes, we say it. We rejoice in the promises of God. As Abraham, we look to God for a supernatural Isaac. We laugh a great laugh of faith, believing that there shall be a performance of those things which have been told us from the Lord. We are in the Spirit; we see our heavenly Isaac inheriting all; we preach that Christ must in all things have the preeminence. But be careful. The very next minute hear Abraham saying: "Oh that Ishmael might live before thee!" Oh that Ishmael might be remembered! oh that he might come in for some consideration in the inheritance! Then surely we too need to beware lest, after rejoicing in Christ Jesus and holding Him up as Lord and Heir of all, we cry out the next minute: Oh that my Ishmael might live! Oh that *I* might be improved, be recognized, be given consideration! Oh that *I* might come in for part of the inheritance! But what saith the Scripture? Yet not I. Send Ishmael away. As we have said elsewhere, the flesh cannot, *"shall not* be heir"* with our heavenly Isaac. Christ can only live in me the yet-not-I kind of selfless life. Ishmael must go out and stay out. With eternal vigilance let me say: Away with the flesh in all its forms! They that are Christ's have crucified the flesh. Two thousand years ago God consigned the flesh to the Cross. How dare we seek its improvement, or seek to pull the "old man" off the gallows to make a fair show in the flesh? Let the cross kill off and keep forever in the place of death every vainglorious surge of desire that Ishmael might live.

Are ye so foolish? having begun in the Spirit, are ye now made perfect by the flesh? (Gal. 3:3).

CHAPTER XVIII

Not Under Law—Through Grace

WHEN one of our students returning home from Nigeria passed through Lagos, one of the native Christians in that city, eager to ventilate his dispensational depths regarding law and grace, said to the missionary: *"I am under grace; I'm an outlaw."* He probably uttered some truth in that statement. His being "not under law, but under grace" may easily have meant to him just what he said.

We have already emphasized that so many perverted views were held by the early church converts regarding the law that it was necessary to deliver them from legalistic bondage and make plain to them the liberty and riches of divine grace. That New Testament emphasis has doubtless misled many expositors to an unbalanced extreme in the direction of grace.

If ever it is true that the man of God needs to give diligence to present himself approved unto God, a workman that needeth not to be ashamed, handling aright the word of truth (II Tim. 2:15, R.V.), it is in connection with his application of the principles of law and grace. More especially is this important in the relation of Christians to the principles of faith and obedience. The man who "rightly divides" — or better, "handles aright" — holds a straight course in — "the word of truth" finds, as Charles Finney did, that under certain circumstances he must emphasize one set of truths, while on other occasions an apparently opposite class of truths. When the great evangelist found a church where the people had been fed on little but election and sovereignty and consequently had drifted into self-excusing disobedience and antinomianism, then he would launch forth like an old Methodist and preach man's free will and ability. If, on the other hand, he found that the church had enjoyed only Arminianism, he would declare God's sovereign power until he shook those folks out of resting on their own resolutions and strength. With what result? He had revival in both places. He was divinely wise to adapt truth in each instance to the situation. He was God's workman who needed not to be ashamed, in each case "rightly dividing," or better, "handling aright the word of truth" (II Tim. 2:15, R.V.).

In his adaptation of truth to circumstances, Mr. Finney manifested the wisdom of God as practiced by men of God in all ages. He handled aright, held a straight course in, properly apportioned, the word of truth. The New Testament writers followed this line in their adaptation of truth. Their strong representations of law, as though it were almost an enemy of grace, must be considered on the background of the utterly false conceptions of the law held by the conceited Pharisees of that day. Those utterly perverted views of the legalists demanded correction of the strongest kind, demanded emphasis in another and opposite direction, namely that of grace. Today those who handle aright the word of truth are discovering that the present tendency to lawless and loose living demands another emphasis.

Do we forget that it is just as possible now, as it was for the Jews of old in reading their Scriptures, to read our New Testament in the letter and miss the Spirit's meaning and message for us *today?* We can so emphasize certain doctrinal and "happifying" truths — forgetting that truth out of place is error — that the saints are never discovered and routed out of their hiding places. We believe that certain emphases on New Testament privileges and liberty have so successfully eliminated a sense of duty and obligation that the saints have unconsciously drifted into a lazy and irresponsible disobedience. Our "not-under-law" emphasis, aimed at keeping the saints in a state of feeling happy over their assurance, is a new kind of doctrinal "tradition" (as we emphasize elsewhere) that is making great sections of "the word of God of none effect."

The New Testament writers emphasized grace in order to counteract legalistic self-righteousness, so common to Judaism. Although we have on hand, for the most part, the opposite trend in our church life today, we continue to hold up liberty and freedom, thinking we are preaching the New Testament — which we are, but very often in the letter, with little or no application to the present situation. We seem to forget that "the spirit of self-righteousness was the prevailing tendency of the carnal mind under the Old Dispensation, as an unconcern about personal righteousness is under the New" (Fairbairn).

Regarding this much discussed subject as to the relation of the saints to the law, we find apparently contradictory statements everywhere in the New Testament. Only a balanced and illuminated consideration of this vital theme can lead us to know how to handle aright the word of truth for this or any other hour. There are many Scriptures which, if taken either in their context or in their collective testimony, make plain the abiding character and authority of law as a rule of life for the Christian. They seem to establish beyond question that for disciples no less than for our Master: "It becometh us to fulfill all righteousness," to "fulfill the righteousness of the law," to "fulfill the law" of love, to "look into the perfect law of liberty and to continue therein." This is in keeping with the Apostle's God-given ambition to bring the Gentiles to "the obedience of faith." Does the New Testament revelation of grace then "make void the law"? Certainly not. It only avails to "establish the law" (Matt. 3:15; Rom. 8:4; 13:10; Gal. 5:13; Jas. 1:25; Rom. 15:18; Rom. 3:31).

There are again other Scriptures, manifestly of another tone, which state plainly that the saints are "not under the law, but under grace" and that as such they "are dead to the law." To Timothy Paul says most certainly that "the law is not made for a righteous man, but for the lawless and disobedient." How may it be said that we are "not under law," and yet are to "fulfill the righteousness of the law"? that we are "dead to the law," and yet are indeed "not without law to God, but under law to Christ"? Are law and grace essential opposites, contending dominions, contradictory principles and authorities? Many speak of law as though it were an antagonist, an enemy, a sworn foe of grace. Yet, if God is One, the great Unchangeable, and if the God of all grace is also the God of all law, how can law and grace be contending or contradictory authorities? Since they cannot, how then may it be said to us as saints, "Ye are not under law, but under grace"?

It is not necessary to dwell upon the curse of the broken law resting upon the head of every man outside of Christ. The law sets before men life and death, blessing and cursing. To the transgressor of Heaven's laws, "our God is a consuming fire" (Heb. 12:29). The claims of the law are immutable, unchangeable, absolute. They are obedience, or death. Shut up "under law," the sinner's mouth is stopped; he is guilty before God, hopelessly exposed under "the curse of the law." That frightful curse, however, having fallen upon the Sinless "made sin," it has been lifted from off the sinner. Shut up to faith, the sinner is "justified freely" by God's grace "through the redemption that is in Christ Jesus," and has been "made the righteousness of God in Him." The believer has been removed from that old ground of condemnation, where he was hopelessly exposed to wrath under sin's dominion and doom, and out of pure grace is now "justified from all things." His new position is that of "no condemnation." Through Christ's death for him, the trusting sinner has been "declared righteous." Romans 5 takes up the sinner's complete justification in Christ and concludes: "Where sin abounded, grace did much more abound: That as sin hath reigned unto death, even so might grace reign through righteousness unto eternal life by Jesus Christ our Lord" (vv. 20, 21).

Romans 6 opens immediately with the question: "What shall we say then? Shall we continue in sin, that grace may abound?" Paul's "God forbid," or "Away with the thought," reveals first his personal abhorrence; second, the fact that justification by grace was "not an end in itself, but a means to an end" (Moule), viz., that we might be through with sin; third, that the new relationship "under grace" forbids the thought of continuing "in sin." Paul's argument against such continuance is based upon our life-union with the new Adam in His death and resurrection. As surely as He "died unto sin," death therefore having "no more dominion over Him," no less surely is sin to have "no more dominion over" those "in Him." Note, however, that between the statement, "death hath no more dominion over Him" (6:9), and the later assurance, "sin shall not have dominion over you" (6:14), the Apostle lays down certain conditions necessary for the realization of this freedom from sin's dominion.

Before taking up these conditions, observe two lines of thought concerning Christ's death running through Romans 5 and 6. First Paul dwells upon the fact that Christ was "delivered for our offences" (4:25); "died for the ungodly" (5:6); "died for us" (5:8). Then in Chapter 6, the thought of Christ's death still underlying the whole section, he no longer speaks of it as being *"for* sin" but *"unto sin"*: "He died unto sin" (6:10). Note the difference between *"for* sin" and *"unto* sin." In His death *for* sin as our Representative and Substitute, Christ died once-for-all *to* sin. In other words, Christ so utterly settled the sin question, so exhausted its penalty and power, that "death hath no more dominion over Him." In Chapter 5 *Christ died for me.* In Chapter 6 *I died with Him,* i.e., as to sin's dominion. This lays the basis for us to observe the conditions we must meet in order to experience freedom from the dominion of sin.

The first of these conditions is found in the phrase, "Even so reckon ye also yourselves to be dead unto sin, but alive unto God in Christ Jesus" (6:11, R.V.). Through my life-union with Christ in His death and resurrection, I have "died to sin." His death to sin is my death to sin. In my very humanity Christ so took me up with Himself and so fastened me to Himself in death that, when He died unto sin, I too was executed and there died to sin's penalty and power. Has Christ so done away with sin that He has exhausted its every claim and dominion? And do I share with Him His death for sin, and His death to sin? With holy and bold reckoning, then, let me count on my death-resurrection relationship to God through Christ. In Christ crucified I have been discharged from sin's every dictate and dominion.

Once I have so reckoned I can count upon divine grace to "let not sin reign." I can positively present myself unto God as "alive from the dead." Note in summary the three simple conditions: (a) Reckon yourselves dead to sin (6:11); (b) Let not sin reign (6:12); (c) Present yourselves in full surrender as forever alive unto God "in Christ Jesus" (6:13). Having consented to this life-union with Christ, the soul hears the assuring whisper of God's Spirit: "Sin shall not have dominion over you: for ye are not under the law, but under grace" (6:14). In this living word from God we sense the glorious liberty to be holy.

Once we were in Adam "sold under sin," "under the law," and as such were under sin's penalty and power, but now the curse of the broken law has been exhausted to the full. As surely as "death hath no more dominion" over Christ, so surely is it proved that the curse of the law against sin has been exhausted. Christ's "It is finished" exhausted sin's strength and every ounce of its legal power over us. My cordial consent in faith to these facts enables me to believe that I am under such a plentiful provision of "the Spirit of life in Christ Jesus" that every *"have-to"* demand of the law finds the *"how-to"* of fulfillment "under grace." Let me reiterate: My life-union with Christ provides me with a divine sufficiency, assuring me that every possible "have-to" feeling of law finds the "how to perform" (7:18) fully met "under grace."

Here comes to light also an interesting discovery. It has often been perplexing to believers how Paul could set forth the truth of Rom. 6:1-14 regarding the believer's emancipation from sin's dominion, and yet introduce us later to his own double-minded wilderness experience as recorded in Chapter 7. It has long been my personal conviction that the truth laid down in Rom. 6:1-14 by the great Apostle is the Scriptural order of Christian experience; and, were each Christian willing to learn quickly and simply the facts of deliverance from sin's power made plain and available in Chapter 6, each one *could* avoid the prolonged defeat of Romans 7. That is to say, Rom. 7:7-25 is not necessarily Christian experience. It is indeed a true record of Paul's experience subsequent to his conversion (and, of course, it does describe the experience of many), but it was a post-conversion experience. Note that Paul says, "I was alive once apart from the law," and "I delight in the law of God after the inward man" — things which no unregenerate man would dare to say. Much less could the unregenerate say concerning his inward depravity, "It is no more I that do it, but sin that dwelleth in me." Only a new man in his regenerate life could say, "It is no more I." Even in this expression, however, Paul is not excusing himself. He is not an old man and a new man — not two men, with the new man not responsible for the deeds of the old.

He is a single responsible individual. Paul is plagued with the deepest sense of responsibility and debtorship to cease to do evil and learn to do well.

Let us follow the Apostle through his own misery and wretchedness to the point of complete bondage and deliverance. There are those who would tell us that Paul's struggle here with indwelling sin would have been impossible had he only understood that he was "not under law, but under grace." From the standpoint of theory, theology, and position in Christ, that may be technically correct. However, as we enter with Paul into the depths of his own heart-rending soul wretchedness, we are convinced that no amount of neat clarity of objective truth or of position in Christ could have settled "presto" the Apostle's difficulties. In fact, the law functions powerfully in all this experience to produce in him full and conclusive conviction of sin. The tenth commandment, with all its penetrating "Thou shalt not covet," discovered to Paul his inward covetousness of heart. Without this fresh application of the law he says, "sin was dead," i.e., it had no weight on his conscience. For a time he "was alive without the law," i.e., in lively, happy, spiritual experience with no sense of legal condemnation upon his soul (v. 9); but in the light of this commandment sin awakened and became so aroused in its essential antagonism against the holy will of God that Paul says, "I died." He felt, as it were, death-doomed.

In vv. 10-13, the law's exasperation of inward sin gave him a growing sense of all manner of lustfulness. This shows a further and fuller operation of the law upon Paul's inward life: It fulfills the needful purpose of making "sin" itself appear to him "exceeding sinful" (v. 13).

In vv. 14-17, Paul comes to the conclusive conviction that his sinful disposition is itself a transgression of the holy law of God. He realizes that his own absolute inward antagonism is against the "spiritual" law, "holy, and righteous, and good," and that the workings of this inward carnality are in direct opposition to the new Spirit God had given him at regeneration. However, Paul cannot excuse himself. He is responsible. He must oppose sin, and oppose it he does. How desperate the struggle! How bitter the strife! Paul is seeking to fight it out in the energy of the flesh. Oh the wormwood and the gall and the bondage of sin! Will this cease-less condemnation never end? God's death-dealing law, "Thou shalt not covet," has the victory. Even grace already known does not aid the flesh; Paul cannot obey the law, cannot conquer him-self or his sin. However, he must yet be brought to the very end of himself, to the place of despair, to the dust of death. Here the "wretched man" finds that his captivity is complete. Through this long and bitter struggle Paul is finally shut up to faith, and so well does he learn the secret of victory "through Jesus Christ our Lord" that he later writes for our learning: "Reckon ye also yourselves to be dead indeed unto sin, but alive unto God through Jesus Christ our Lord" (6:11). Paul was now prepared to hear the assuring word he has given us: "Sin shall not have dominion over you: for ye are not under law, but under grace."

Concerning this very point there is a manifest need for under-standing in some of our own fundamental circles today. No sooner does a sinner become well justified than he is hastily taught how to "rightly divide the word of truth." This means to many that he must be shown at once how the Old Testament saints were all under law — meaning under a strict covenant of works — but how we today are under grace. Candidly, there is no special occasion to set forth law as an enemy of grace before his eyes, unless such emphasis be called for.* What such a believer needs, as a rule, is to be shown his blessed privileges in Christ, and then given very plain instruction on "Trust and obey"; otherwise such a contrasted emphasis may mean no more to the new Christian than it meant to the African convert: *I am under grace; I'm an outlaw.*

Perhaps one chief reason for the overdone cry today of "not under law, but under grace" can be found right here in the truth of Romans 6 and 7. For a time subsequent to his conversion, the saint can say with Paul, "I was alive without the law once." He is happy and glad and free. The sense of forgiveness and peace brings him such an abounding bliss and joy that he knows no bond-age, no condemnation, nothing but unalloyed happiness. Before

* Should Seventh Day Adventists or any other such legalists (New Testament Judaizers) seek to bring him into bondage, then clear instruction in this connection would be required at once.

long he makes a shocking discovery. He finds another principle working in his members — finds himself proud, selfish, and un-Christlike in a thousand ways. The tenth commandment, "Thou shalt not covet," discovers to him with horror his hidden inner nature. His virtues appear to be but "taught practices grafted upon a corrupt bottom." The stream of his life is mixed and muddy. He is double-minded. His attempt to be humble helps his pride; his good behaviour feeds his sanctimoniousness. His best deeds, in spite of all his efforts to the contrary, partake of this discovered impurity and corruption. Sin, hitherto dormant, so "springs to life" that he fears, he fails, he feels condemned — as well he may. Not knowing what to make of it all, he consults with others. He goes to his Bible teacher or pastor, but maybe these leaders are in the same condition, and therefore are unable to lead him out of the wilderness into the land of rest and unclouded obedience. It is just here that both *teachers* and *taught* are relieved for a time to hear that they are "not under law, but under grace."

God's Spirit all the while is faithful; He keeps pursuing this saint in his misery, lashing him still more severely with the commandment, "Thou shalt not covet." In the meantime this soul may be cautioned by his advisers not to look at himself, for he will never find any good in himself, but to look to Christ and keep his eyes on Him. This advice is good, and he tries to follow it. Nevertheless, in spite of his efforts to believe he has been freed from the law, the death-dealing "Thou shalt not covet" probes him until he is "exceeding sinful." Undiscerning saints become alarmed, feeling that so and so is overserious, too introspective. What he needs is to get his eyes off himself,[*] they reason. Does he not know that it is a high-water mark of sainthood to sense one's sinfulness? He should expect to get out of such a state. His is but a normal Christian experience. He is no different from the rest of us.

---

[*] There are individuals who are temperamentally inclined to be introspective. They are always blaming themselves. Discernment and experience are needed at times to distinguish between those who are temperamentally morbid and those who are in the thralldom and bondage set forth in Romans 7. While there is a vast difference between these two conditions, some leaders who have experienced the miseries of Romans 7 suppose that every morbid Christian inclined to be introspective needs only Romans 6 and 7 preached to him. This is not the case.

In the midst of these well-meant musings and reasonings, such advisers are secretly alarmed at times over their own shallow devotion and halfhearted piety. Their duplicity and their lack of prayer shame them. The book of Acts haunts them, for apostolic experience condemns them — they cannot reconcile Paul's confession in Rom. 7:18, "How to perform that which is good I find not," with his later testimony, "I can do all things through Christ which strengtheneth me" (Phil. 4:13). Never having been awakened to their own deep inward need, and never having felt the death-dealing thrust of the law, "Thou shalt not covet," they set about to deliver this overserious soul from his sense of condemnation and bondage. Their only known remedy is to tell him that he is not under law, that he is complete in Christ, that God does not see his wrongness but looks at him only through the blood. However, they only prove to be Job's comforters to this man in his misery. While he may experience a momentary *lift* through their advice, he will sink to a new low before long. God is faithful, and will reduce this soul to utter self-despair.

Much of this extreme "not-under-law" teaching is directly traceable to a lack of practical and experimental presentation of the truths in Romans 6 and 7. The saints are taken from Romans 5 immediately to Romans 8. Little wonder they find so little practical outworking of the victorious eighth chapter when there has been such a slighting (if not an actual by-passing) of the truths leading up to it. It was only after Paul had been emancipated from the power of indwelling sin that he exclaimed, "There is therefore now no condemnation to them that are in Christ Jesus. For the law of the Spirit of life in Christ Jesus made me free from the law of sin and death" (Rom. 8:1,2, R.V.). Not until saints are brought to conclusive captivity and to personal self-despair are they able to trust Christ for Christian victory.

Do you, my reader, in advising those in the throes of this conflict, simply tell them that they are not under law, but under grace? Do you tell them not to look at themselves, but just to believe that "There is therefore now no condemnation to them that are in Christ Jesus"? And does your supply of technical knowledge as to their heavenly "in-Christ" position free them? Do you see them de-

livered? In fact, do you even tell them *how?* In the face of their
ceaseless condemnation of heart, do they come to experience deliverance through your quoting, "There is no condemnation"? Do
they come to experience Paul's own assurance, "The law of the
Spirit of life in Christ Jesus made me free from the law of sin and
death"?

Recall again Paul's steps leading up to Rom. 8:1, 2. Through
the tanglefoot of his Romans 7 experience, Paul finally cried out
in a paroxysm of despair: "O wretched man that I am! who shall
deliver me from the body of this death?" Out of these abysmal
depths he saw himself delivered through his life-union with Christ.
(In the last verse of Romans 7 he sets forth the cause of his former defeat and bondage.) Then he bursts forth, "There is therefore now no condemnation" — no kind of condemnation, whether
judicial or experimental — "to them that are in Christ Jesus. For
the law of the Spirit of life in Christ Jesus made me free from the
law of sin and death" (R.V.). Romans 8:2 is in sharp contrast with
Paul's determined struggle and tragic defeat as recorded in Chapter
7. "How to perform that which is good I find not," he cried there.
Here that "how" finds abundant solution through the newly experienced power of "the Spirit of life in Christ Jesus." Such an experimental deliverance, through identification with Christ in His
death and resurrection, will bring believers out of bondage into
true liberty, the liberty wherein Christ sets men free.

Let us gather up our thoughts. Our justification freely by God's
abounding grace is revealed in Romans 5. Our standing in grace
underlies Romans 6 and 7, but it is there viewed not in connection
with justification but rather in connection with sanctification —
"that sin might not have dominion." Justifying grace delivers us
from sin's penalty; sanctifying grace from sin's power. Let it be
carefully noted that Paul's introduction of our "not-under-law" position is not in connection with the cancellation of sin's penalty,
but rather in connection with our deliverance from sin's power.
Paul assures the surrendered saint of his freedom from law: "Sin
shall not have dominion over you: for ye are not under the law,
but under grace." Note the thought in 7:4: Ye have been slain

to the law . . . married to another . . . that ye should bring forth fruit unto God.

Paul reveals not only grace abounding for the chief of sinners, but grace astounding and sufficient for the bankrupt saint. Unless we "handle aright the word of truth" at this point, do we not lead the saint to a false liberty, viz., that he may indeed "continue in sin that grace may abound"? Do we not lead him to believe that justification is to make us *safe*, whereas it is meant to make us *sound*? Does God give us our standing in grace to make us sure of heaven, or does He put us "under grace" in order that sin might "have no more dominion"? In fact, Paul's concluding thought in Romans 5, before ever he sets forth his teaching on holiness in Romans 6, is to the same effect: *"That as sin hath reigned unto death, even so might grace reign through righteousness unto eternal life by Jesus Christ our Lord"* (5:21). Grace is no mere favour conferred upon the ungodly, but is to be experienced as a ruling force and sufficiency, reigning in our hearts as the new, living "law of the Spirit of life in Christ Jesus," and enabling us to prove the no-more dominion of sin. Grace *abounding* is to lead at once to grace *reigning*. God forbid that our teaching should lead the saints to feel, "I am under grace; I'm an outlaw."

CHAPTER XIX

Not Under Law—Through Death

"Ye also were made dead to the law through the body of Christ"
(Rom. 7:4, R. V.).

"I through the law died unto the law" (Gal. 2:19, R. V.).

I T IS A FACT that in old Scottish law a man who was put to death for his crime was thereafter spoken of as being "justified." When a man had been executed, the notice was posted that so and so "was justified at 6 o'clock this morning." Justified? Yes, executed, slain for his crime, dead to the law. The law had released him only through execution, i.e., through death. Lord Byron wrote, "Let them be *justified,* and leave exposed their relics in the place of judgment."

Paul says, "Wherefore, my brethren, ye also were made dead to the law through the body of Christ" (Rom. 7:4, R.V.). If "the strength of *sin* is the *law,*" then both have been exhausted in Christ's laid-down and crucified life. The Apostle bids us behold in the crucified "body of Christ" how we have been "made dead to the law." We died to the law's bondage because the old husband died with Christ. "Our old man was crucified with Him." Sin's power, as well as sin's penalty, has been exhausted. The curse of the law has been met to the full and its power spent. What can the law say to the man who has died? Paul says, "Ye have been slain to the law," slain to its curse "by the body of Christ." The corpse of the Son of God represents an exhausted curse.

Back in Romans 6:14, Paul plainly said, "Ye are not under the law." He then took up the parenthetical warning to believers against thinking this liberty could be abused (Rom. 6:15-23). In 7:1 he resumes the thought stated in 6:14 and begins to explain how the believer comes to be "not under the law." "Or are ye ignorant, brethren (for I speak to men that know the law), how that the law hath dominion over a man for so long time as he liveth?" (7:1, R.V.). The law of any land holds claim over a man throughout his whole lifetime; death alone brings him deliverance. Then Paul uses an illustration from the relation of husband and wife; viz., when the first husband dies, the wife is free to be married to another man. Having died with Christ, we were delivered from the past under-law position. The former husband, our old man, received his execution and last rites (yea, rights) at Calvary. There at that place of open shame we leave "exposed his relics in the place of judgment."

In another connection Paul says, "I through the law died unto the law, that I might live unto God" (Gal. 2:19 R.V.). Here again Paul asserts his death to law, but now adds that this dying to the law came to pass *"through* the law." In its relentless dominion over him, the law drove Paul into the very place of death. The law shut him up under its curse. But just where Paul was cursed, right there where the last volley of the law found its sure mark and Victim, there, Paul says, I died to the law — "that I might live unto God." Then Paul immediately explains again (2:20) how his dying to the law through the law has been brought about: "I have been crucified with Christ." When Christ entered into my place under the curse of the broken law, then that law had dominion over Him as long as He lived. *"Through* the law" Christ died; then *"to* the law," no less surely. Hence Paul's burst and boast of freedom: "I am dead to the law . . . crucified with Christ . . . Christ liveth in me . . . that I might live unto God." Hallelujah forever!

Has the law lost me? Indeed it has, but I escaped its grip only through the doorway of death. The law had me; I was shut up under law with no way of escape. Was I utterly without a way? Well, there was one way, but that was through the trapdoor of death. In my escape, as the trap was sprung, I fell at once to a hanged man's doom. The law lost me, but only through my dying. The law lost me, that God might get me and so have me that I might live unto Him. Thus in getting to God I was slain on the way. I was born again in death, born crucified.

How shallow, then, it sounds for men to boast of their actual experimental freedom from law who have none of the deathmarks of their release, not an indication of crucifixion with Christ. They claim to be free from God's law, while yet they flout His commands. Though living for themselves, in a self-centeredness that refuses to be unhinged, they still boast that they are dead to the law. While they remain so much alive, so fussy and touchy, so giddy and greedy, so alive to the opinions and fashions and laws of society — boast as they may of being not under law — let them hear Paul's *ex cathedra*: "Or are ye ignorant, brethren . . . , how that the law hath dominion over a man for *so long time as he liveth?*" Let such souls, and all who have led them into their lax, loose, no-law position, begin to sink themselves into the wounds and death of the Redeemer. Let them sign away their lives, sign on the dotted line, sign their own death sentences.

Paul's assertions that believers are "not under law," that they are "dead to the law," etc., are no more emphatic than similar statements in the same context that believers have "died to sin," and are therefore "dead indeed unto sin." But someone objects that believers are "dead indeed unto sin" only through their life-union with Christ in His death and resurrection. That is true, and no less true in connection with our being "dead to the law." Let teachers who insist on ringing the changes of "dead to the law," no less mightily declare believers "dead to sin." Has God joined these together? Let not man put them asunder. Paul's epistles glow with the power of our death-resurrection union with Christ. He speaks of being *dead to sin, dead to self, dead to the law;* all these are alike true, but only through life-union with Christ. To all three Christ died a once-for-all death. If, therefore, it is heresy for a Christian to boast that he is experimentally "dead indeed unto sin," it must be no less a heresy to boast that one is actually "not under law" as a rule of conduct for his life. *For what is sin if it be not the transgression of law?* Paul knows no escape, whether from *sin* or *self* or *law,* except through death. Through death into life is the law of the kingdom. So fixed is this principle that if a man refuses to be all alive unto God he can only fall back under the practical grip of law.

The story already told in *Born Crucified* comes to mind. The Boxers of China captured a Mission school and blocked all gates but one. Before that gate they placed a cross and bade the students take their freedom, but only as they trampled on the cross. Some seven stepped on it, saved themselves, and went out to a false and foul freedom — rather, they went out *bound*. The eighth kneeled at the cross and was shot on the spot. All the rest of the hundred students likewise found their freedom, freedom from the law of the Boxers — through death! Not one of the hundred could find an independent ground between these two alternatives. Nor can we. The Cross of Christ is before the Christian; it is his only door of escape from law. To refuse the Cross is to be gripped by law. To accept the Cross is to be freed, freed to "live unto God," freed with that freedom wherewith Christ has made us free. "He is not escaped who drags his chain." Oh let us hasten and bow down and escape from the chain of a self-centered life! Let us blissfully leave self exposed at the Cross, leave its relics in the place of judgment.

CHAPTER XX

Not Under Law—Through Righteousness

In THIS DAY of mounting lawlessness, there is a growing dislike and disregard for everything that savours of true obedience. Some men fear any real emphasis on obedience. What is their remedy to prevent the utter worldliness of their followers? They tell us that the way to produce a Christlike people is to exalt the privileges of grace. We grant that there is somewhat of truth in preaching privilege as the motive for stimulating the Lord's people to righteousness. Paul besought the believers "by the mercies of God" to present themselves a living sacrifice. While a vivid realization of mercies, past and present, should furnish the chief motive power for a new service, even Paul himself does not limit his means to this consideration. Note his own exhortation to the Thessalonians to abound in holiness:

> Furthermore then we beseech you, brethren, and exhort you by the Lord Jesus, that as ye have received of us how ye ought to walk and to please God, so ye would abound more and more.
> For ye know what commandments we gave you by the Lord Jesus (I Thess. 4:1, 2).

In this appeal several points call for consideration.
"To walk and to please God."

As those who love God, the Thessalonian believers are besought "to walk and to please God." Paul's epistles first deal with the believer's inner life in Christ and then with his outward walk in the world. As Christians we are to walk worthy of our high calling and destiny. In its positive expression this phrase, "to walk and to please God," is the very end to which we are saved and sanctified. It will be noted that this direction is general, that it does not contain anything about the *manner,* or the *how,* of pleasing our God. We therefore pass on.

"HOW . . . *to walk and to please God."*

In the little word "how" directions are implied. Paul was specific in giving believers directions as to how to walk and how to act. Ministers often fail in directing believers. There is a generalizing which avoids the embarrassment of being particular and pointed. Preachers can avoid this part of their duty by telling believers just to "do all to the glory of God." That kind of direction is too indefinite. When worldly young folks paint and primp and pet (to say nothing of worse indulgences), it is not sufficient to hold up to them their privileges in Christ. These young folks require *precept* as well as privilege. Why should we pretend that the New Testament lays down no rules? Why tell the believer that his sole consideration is: "Whether therefore ye eat, or drink, or whatsoever ye do, do all to the glory of God"? While that is true, the *manner* of doing all to God's glory is not sufficiently defined. The writer knows a radio preacher who gave that very indefinite direction (Do all to the glory of God) to an earnest inquirer from radioland; yet he himself would walk out of the studio after a broadcast and go to the theater. Precepts must have practical and detailed application. It is surprising how much general truth and privilege can be held up to believers without their having the least compunction about their particular sins of disobedience. As a rule they must be pointed out one by one. Paul taught believers "how" to walk to please God.

"How ye OUGHT *to walk and to please God."*

"For ye know what commandments we gave you by the Lord Jesus." Certainly the little word "ought" can mean nothing short of being duty bound and under moral obligation. Ought means "owe it." It means I owe it to God as a moral obligation to walk and to please Him. Is it no more than a beautiful sentiment that we sing: "O to grace how great a debtor"? Paul could not forget his debtorship. Our conceptions of duty and debtorship today are defective because of our low conceptions of grace. Grace, for the most part, means "get off easy." The exaltation of right-arm *privilege* requires the strict application of left-arm *precept*. This double-armed ministry enabled the Apostle to fight "not as one that beateth the air." Note that before Paul goes into the "how" of a holy life, he prefaces such details with this word: "For ye know what *commandments* we gave you by the Lord Jesus."

It is indeed a great and spiritual task to know how to make present obligation felt without breeding bondage. However, the present "not-under-law" extreme, in both pulpit and pew, is largely due to our cringing from conformity to the whole will of God. We labour to keep the saints happy, and about the only means many men employ to make them holy is to hold up Christian privilege.

In *God's Way of Holiness*, Horatius Bonar deals a most powerful blow to the present tendency to release believers from all law. This teacher of the old school had to deal with some of the same no-law difficulties which are rifling the Church today:

> Some will tell us that it is not *service* they object to, but service regulated by *law*. But will they tell us what is to regulate service, if not law? *Love*, they say. This is a pure fallacy. Love is not a *rule*, but a *motive*. Love does not tell me *what* to do; it tells me *how* to do it. Love constrains me to do the will of the beloved One; but to know what the will is, I must go elsewhere. The law of our God is *the will* of the beloved One, and were that expression of His will withdrawn, love would be utterly in the dark; it would not know what to do. It might say, I love my Master, and I love His service, and I want to do His bidding; but I must know *the rules of His house*, that I may know *how* to serve Him . . . Love goes to the law to learn the divine *will*, and love delights in the law, as the exponent of that will; and he who says that a believing man has nothing more to do with law, save to shun it as an old enemy, might as well say that he has nothing to do with the will of God. For the divine law and the divine will are substantially one, the former the outward manifestation of the latter . . . As to the oneness between divine *will* and divine *law*, I need only quote the words of Him who came to fulfill the law, "Lo, I come: in the volume of the book it is written of Me, I delight to do *Thy will*, O my God: yea, *Thy law* is within my heart" (Psa. 40:7, 8; Heb. 10:7).

So perverted have many men become in their conceptions of anything that savours of "Do" or "Do not" — all this being accentuated by progressive education and present day lawlessness — that many good expositors have misread entirely the meaning of the Mosaic legislation. They have vainly supposed that the Israelites forsook the *privileges* of the Abrahamic covenant when they promised to obey the *precepts* of the Mosaic. Had this principle of exalting the privileges of grace been the sole means of bringing God's redeemed people into conformity with His holy will, then the whole divine procedure at Mount Sinai was unwisdom. Instead of giving Israel the law that they might become a holy nation and a peculiar people, the Lord should have given them a bit of advice or instruction. He should have pointed out the privileges of grace already granted them in the Abrahamic covenant. Their King should have appealed to them as His redeemed people to appreciate His having borne them on eagles' wings.* Or did the divine Wisdom know that the "true grace of God" in the Abrahamic covenant would not— could not — be appreciated by that lawless lot of Israelites apart from the Mosaic legislation?

While it is true that God's master weapon in this age to draw men away from their lust and worldliness is to hold up and exalt the Crucified, both Scripture and experience are against this merely one-armed ministry. We must be taught of the Spirit how to make duty and obligation felt among God's people today; for it is especially true in this day that the redeemed of the Lord again need to be hedged in and shut up to "the obedience of faith." They must be taught that gospel freedom "is a freedom only within the bounds and limits of law" (Fairbairn). If gospel privilege is unappreciated, then it is our supreme task to "make the preceptive will of God as dear to the justified as it is terrible to the guilty." If we preach "the true grace of God," our message will lead the saints to delight in the word "obedience" as much as they rejoice in the

---

* Elsewhere we have pointed out that the All-wise based all the giving of the law upon the basis of the grace of the already existing grace relationship, and that He prefaced the actual giving of the commandments with "I am the LORD thy God, which brought thee out of the land of Egypt, out of the house of bondage." The relationship of grace, plus the redemption from bondage, both preceded the requirement of obedience.

word "faith." Who indeed is sufficient for these things? Only the Spirit-taught can possibly qualify.

In the epistle to the Romans, in which believers are told that they are "not under the law" and that they are "dead to the law," much is made of how to "fulfill the righteousness of the law." Paul himself delights "in the law of God after the inward man" (Rom. 7:22). He rejoices that he is the bondslave of Christ. He is emphatic that believers are released from the dominion of sin only that they may become "the servants of righteousness"; and that they are released from the bondage of the law only that they may "serve in newness of spirit, and not in the oldness of the letter." In connection with this release through grace he asks, "Do we then make void the law through faith? God forbid: yea, we *establish* the law" (Rom. 3:31). By this he means that through faith we pursue the path which discovers the power to fulfill every demand of the law. With this agrees all of Paul's teaching to the effect that to be led of the Spirit and to walk not after the flesh is to fulfill "the righteous requirement of the law."

When the Apostle comes to the great practical outworking of the gospel of grace in Romans 12-16, he does not hesitate to assure the consecrated believer how he meets the demands of all law: "For this, Thou shalt not commit adultery, Thou shalt not kill, Thou shalt not steal, Thou shalt not bear false witness, Thou shalt not covet; and if there be *any other commandment* [referring to the Mosaic law as a rule of life and allowing it proper recognition and application], it is briefly comprehended in this saying, namely, Thou shalt love thy neighbour as thyself. Love worketh no ill to his neighbour: therefore love is the fulfilling of the law" (Rom. 13:9, 10). If the Apostle had been given in any degree to lawlessness, he might here have told us plainly, Love is the end of all law, the exemption from law, the cancellation of all commandment. Instead, however, he says love is "the fulfilling of the law." "Love does not supersede law, nor release us from obedience to it; it enables us to obey. Love does not make stealing or coveting, or any such breach of law, *no sin in a Christian* . . . Yes, Christ hath redeemed us from the curse of the law, but certainly not from the law itself; for that would be to redeem us from a divine rule and guide; it would be to redeem us from that which is 'holy and just and good' " (Bonar). Then this same writer refers to Eph. 6:1-3, where Paul says, "Children, obey your parents in the Lord: for this is right. Honour thy father and mother; which is the first commandment with promise; that it may be well with thee, and thou mayest live long on the earth." He then asks this pertinent question, "Was the Apostle, then, a legalist, when he referred the Ephesians to the law as a rule of life? Did they not know that they were 'not under the law, but under grace?' "

The writer has a very warm friend in the gospel ministry who was at one time a close follower of those whose continual boast is that they are not under law, but under grace. He so devoured this "not-under-law" teaching that he carried it to its logical end in practice. He now admits, of course, that in those days of his half-hearted obedience he found it quite a relief to his conscience to be told that he was no longer under law. So far did he carry out this teaching that, even though a minister of the gospel, he deliberately chopped wood all day Sunday — earning $3.50 thereby — boasting that he was not under law, but under grace. The saints did not appreciate his audacity, even though he had followed his teaching to its logical conclusion and to its unwholesome results.

Before me is a thrilling account of a great work of God among the hill tribes of China. The old Spirit-taught leader of that work had furnished his many new converts with a good catechism, which had proved invaluable for them as beginners. In an emergency a zealous and gifted young missionary had been placed on the field. Inexperienced in the practical upbuilding of the converts, he felt that this catechism had a tendency to produce a "do-this-and-thou-shalt-be-saved" effect on the natives, and feared legalism would come into the church. This young zealot determined to combat legalism and to see that the converts were not under law but under grace. He took exception to the way the church was handling cases of church discipline. He even gave out opium as medicine. Upon being told that these Christians were not allowed to have anything to do with opium, he hotly replied, "There is nothing in the New Testament that says that one may not use opium! Nothing to say you may not smoke tobacco or drink wine either!" Some of the weak Christians made his words an excuse to go back to their old sins. One of the old native deacons stood his ground, however, and the native church in that land was saved from a sad rupture. The old deacon's reasoning was: "What will happen to the church if they are allowed to drink, smoke, handle opium . . . ?" The brilliant young missionary had to be removed from the field. Perhaps he was more to be pitied than censured, for he was only following to their logical conclusions the "not-under-law" teachings he had been given in this country.

Just at hand is a letter concerning a young man and his wife who are attending one of America's leading fundamental colleges. These young folks are planning to be missionaries and are preparing for foreign service. The young wife, already a graduate of another school (professedly fundamental), is in full agreement with her husband that there should be a strange absence of rules and regulations in our Christian schools. The reason? "Because the students just observe them as an outward form and not from the heart. If the regulations at school are right, then the students should observe them without being told. But all the standards are man made and everyone has a right to his own opinion." The wife states that in her former school of training the students observed certain rules on the campus but disobeyed them as soon as they got away. Her claim is that "it would be far better if they did not have those rules." In other words, the leaders of the school, who based their rules on Christian precept, were actually causing the students to sin. "What shall we say then? Is the law sin?" Paul replies, "God forbid." However, modern Christians argue: Do away with law; where there is no law, there is no transgression.

These young folks are the product of false educational philosophies. They are victims of our entire social trend toward lawlessness; but it is pathetic beyond measure that Christian candidates for missionary service should be so utterly perverted in first principles of Bible thinking. It seems to us that they regard the Old Testament as containing an obsolete legalism which must be shunned as an old enemy, and that the New Testament contains advice and instruction for Christians, but nothing of rule or regulation. It is still more pathetic that their lawless principles should be further encouraged by the antinomianism of some orthodox leaders. How would such leaders ever properly train and prepare these young people for the foreign service? And, what is still worse, what will the mission stations and the native churches be like when such young people flood the foreign field? On account of their scholastic attainments they may be readily accepted by some society without first being sifted out as to some of these false principles.

In his able review of Prof. Allis' book, *Prophecy and the Church*, Dr. Wilbur M. Smith, although taking issue with his views on prophecy, points out this ground of agreement:

> Some may disagree, but the author of this review agrees with him [Prof. Allis]that it is regrettable in our day "the thunders of Sinai are not heard . . . It is forgotten that in the New Testament as well as in the Old Testament it is declared that God is a 'consuming fire' " (*S. S. Times*, Nov. 24, 1945).

CHAPTER XXI

Not Under Law — Through the Spirit

"But if ye be led of the Spirit, ye are not under the law"
(Gal. 5:18).
*For the law of the Spirit of life in Christ Jesus hath made me
free from the law of sin and death"* (Rom. 8:2).

CLOSELY related to the previous discussion stands this consideration: "Not under law — through the Holy Spirit." Paul assures the Galatians that to be led of the Spirit frees them from being "under law." The disciples stood in danger of being "entangled again with the yoke of bondage." Would the legalizers pin upon them any process of self-improvement? Paul asks, "Are ye so foolish? having begun in the Spirit, are ye now made perfect by the flesh?" (Gal. 3:3). With a godly jealousy the Apostle assures these believers "If ye be led of the Spirit, ye are not under law." While this verse is emphatically an assurance, it implies: If ye be *not* led of the Spirit (not altogether Christ's and not led of His Spirit), ye are under the law — still under obligation to the law because you have not found your true moral freedom in the Spirit.

While Paul's chief message to the Galatians is one of assurance of liberty (and must needs be so to believers under their circumstances) he had also to throw in a word of caution: "Ye have been called unto liberty; only use not liberty for an occasion to the flesh, but by love serve one another" (5:13). The Judaizers were seeking to bring the Galatians into bondage. Paul suggested the alternative: If you will be servants and will be in bondage, then let it be the blessed bondage of serving one another. They had once been in bondage, enslaved to sin; now with real freedom Christ had set them at liberty, had made them the Lord's freemen. In their new-found freedom and liberty, however, let them be warned: "Only use not liberty for an occasion to the flesh." The reader will notice

232

that the little word "use" is not in the text. Let us read the phrase omitting this word: "Ye have been called unto liberty; only . . . not liberty for an occasion (or opportunity) to the flesh." It seems to us that the word "use" does not clarify, but rather misconstrues, Paul's meaning. Liberty from sin's slavery is only liberty to a new bondage, to a new service "under the law to Christ." There is no middle ground, no state of independence between these two slaveries, "no intermediate moral condition between the one service and the other" (Thomas). The flesh and the Spirit are mutually exclusive masters. There is a relentless and undying antagonism between the two — and no man can serve two masters.

In our new position and provision, "not under the law, but under grace," Paul at once senses the danger of such liberty. There is always a danger of becoming intoxicated with new-found liberties, and the Christian is no exception to this rule. Are we to sin, the Apostle asks, "because we are not under the law, but under grace?" (Rom. 6:15). "Perish the thought," is the meaning of Paul's categorical "God forbid!" And the reason? "Know ye not, that to whom ye yield yourselves servants to obey, His servants ye are to whom ye obey; whether of sin unto death," i.e., issuing in death (Fausset and Brown), "or of obedience unto righteousness?" i.e., resulting in righteousness and life for time and eternity (Rom. 6:16). Let us thank God that by Calvary's infinite power we are furnished "under grace" with ability to yield ourselves unto God.

Our liberty in Christ furnishes no release to the flesh. Ours is a release to the Spirit, and the flesh is contrary to the Spirit. How can the man who rejects the reign and rule of the Spirit do aught but fall back under the practical grip of law? The law, which curses the flesh, will handle him roughly with sledge-hammer blows until he becomes broken and contrite and willing to forsake the flesh to be led again of the Spirit. Coming in like a faithful truant officer the law lays hold of the delinquent child and takes him back to the Teacher, to whom alone he will release him. The law knows no release except to the Holy Spirit.

In that great passage, Romans 8:1-4, which is such a compendium of our full deliverance through Christ, much is made of the Holy Spirit. It is "the law of the Spirit of life in Christ Jesus" whereby the believer is furnished with a counteracting fullness and sufficiency of grace to free him from the down-drag of the law of sin and death. We must make more of the Holy Spirit. The Holy Spirit in all His seven-fold fullness comes to us right from the Lamb on the throne. He is the Spirit of life in Christ Jesus, our new Fountain and Supply. It is the Spirit who must be recognized and received and trusted in all His fullness of power and overflow. Would we know victory in Christ? It is the Spirit who takes of the things of Christ and makes them real to us and in us. He is the very Spirit of the all-sufficient fullness of life in Christ Jesus. Have we been baffled and beaten and tortured until we have thrown up our hands in despair under this law of sin and death which wars in our members? How to perform that which is good we have not found. Ah, here it is, all right at hand in this new principle and Spirit of life in Christ Jesus.

While the law of sin and death contaminates the whole stream of our life, for some souls it takes on special forms. Have you, my reader, been tempted to be deceitful, dishonest, pretentious? — altogether deceptive? The Holy Spirit is the remedy. Is He not the Spirit of truth? It is His office to put truth in the inward parts.

> *"Truthful Spirit, dwell with me;*
> *I myself would truthful be."*

Or, perhaps you have a temperamental tendency to be harsh and bitter and censorious, a tendency to set all others right; you have never found grace and sufficiency to counteract and free you from this form of the law of sin and death. The secret again is in the Spirit.

> *"Gracious Spirit, dwell with me;*
> *I myself would gracious be."*

With most of us the crying evil of our carnality comes out in a foul uncleanness and unholiness. We are so vain and proud, so fastidious and selfish, so opposite from our Master in a thousand ways. How shall we ever be like Jesus, the Holy, the Harmless, the Undefiled? The secret is still the same.

"Holy Spirit, dwell with me;
I myself would holy be;
Separate from sin, I would
Choose and cherish all things good,
And whatever I can be
Give to Him who gave me Thee!"
                                        --Thomas T. Lynch

Our fundamentalism has become cold and calculating. Our ortho-doxy is proper but icy. Our unlikeness to the Lord Jesus is astonish-ing to Heaven and amazing to men. Yet at hand is a freedom and fullness and sufficiency in the Holy Spirit to more than meet our every need. If only our need and His great fullness meet we shall find all in Him. Whether it be wisdom or love or grace or holiness, all these perfections and virtues are found in Jesus, and of all these graces the other Comforter is the Spirit.

It is very possible that in order to be led of the Spirit some of my readers may first have to come to a personal recognition and, shall I say, reception of the Spirit. For, until the Spirit presides as well as resides, we shall have little experience of His leading. A part of the testimony of the late Dr. F. B. Meyer, that great Bible exposi-tor, makes a fitting conclusion:

> I had been for a long time a minister in Leicester, with a large church and of considerable influence in the city, but very unhappy. Conscious that I had not received the power of the Holy Ghost, I went to Keswick. A great number of God's people gathered there to seek and to receive the power of the Holy Spirit, and they elected to have a prayer meeting from nine o'clock to eleven and onwards, to pray for the Holy Ghost. A great many people were there agonizing. I was too tired to agonize and I felt that God did not want me to ago-nize hour after hour, but I had to learn to *take*; that God wanted to give, and I had only to take.

> Tomorrow your little girl will come down to breakfast. She is very hungry, and the bread and milk or the oatmeal is on the table. You do not say: "Little girlie, run upstairs and agonize, roll on the floor for an hour, and then come down." You say to her: "Little one, I am so glad you have a good appetite. Now there is your chair; in you get, say your prayer, and start away."

That is what God says to the soul. Those whole nights of
prayer for the Holy Ghost are principally necessary to get
people who pray into a fit condition to receive the Holy
Ghost; for when the people are ready, the Holy Ghost will
come without agonizing.

So I left that prayer meeting, and crept out into the lane,
and away from the town. As I walked I said, "O my God,
if there is a man who needs the power of the Holy Ghost to
rest upon him it is I; but I do not know how to receive Him. I
am too tired, too worn, too nervously down to agonize." A
voice said to me, *"As you took forgiveness from the hand of
the dying Christ, take the Holy Ghost from the hand of the
living Christ."*

I turned to Christ and said, *"Lord, as I breathe in this
whiff of warm night air, so I breathe into every part of me
Thy blessed Spirit."* I felt no hand laid upon my head, there
was no lambent flame, there was no rushing sound from
heaven; but *by faith,* without emotion, without excitement,
I took, and took for the first time, *and I have kept on taking
ever since.*

I turned to leave the mountain side, and as I went down
the tempter said: "You have got nothing. It is moonshine."
I said: "I have." He said: "Do you feel it?" "I do not feel
it, but *I reckon that God is faithful,* and He could not have
brought a hungry soul to claim by faith, and then give a
stone for bread, and a scorpion for a fish. I know I have got
it because God led me to claim it."

CHAPTER XXII

Not Under Law—Through Love

A N OLD MINISTER had been so wonderfully filled with the Spirit that his joy and peace knew no bounds. His life was full to overflowing. Some time later a misunderstanding came in between another brother and himself. Feeling that the other man was to be blamed, he sat in judgment upon him. He sensed very soon that his spiritual fullness and joy had departed. Then God spoke to him with this Scripture: "Grudge not one against another, brethren, lest ye be condemned: behold, the judge standeth before the door" (Jas. 5:9). He saw that he had usurped the throne of judgment, while Christ, the Judge, stood just outside the door ready to enter and judge all believers. What right had he to be in the judgment seat? The Spirit said to him, "Grudge not." God so convicted him that he wrote to the brother confessing that he had been wrong in holding this grudge against him. The brother wrote back expressing his full forgiveness. The old minister now noticed that he had a little renewal of his former joy in the Holy Ghost.

Later on as he was reading one day in Matthew, the Spirit spoke to him through this verse: "So likewise shall my heavenly Father do also unto you, if ye from your hearts forgive not every one his brother their trespasses" (Matt. 18:35). Here the Spirit convicted him that he had expected the other man also to ask to be forgiven, and that he himself had not "from his heart" forgiven the other brother. God made him write again with the further acknowledgment that he had now fully forgiven him. This was some advance over the lower stage of holding a grudge, and as a result the old man experienced some further recovery of the Spirit's fullness of joy.

He was not yet back to his original ground, however. The feeling of his heart was, What lack I yet? God's Spirit had this final word on the matter: "By love serve one another." The Spirit whispered: Now see how you can help this brother; seek by love to serve him. This was the climax. It would have been easy to let the other brother go his own way. Would they not get along better if they did not meet? But the law of love must be fulfilled. "Oh love that will not let me go." God will not let me say, Let the other brother go his own way. He says, "By love serve one another." Such is the impossible law of love. The old minister found that the yoke was easy, the burden light. It was joy, yea, fullness of joy, to seek to serve his brother. What about the other brother and his wrongdoing? you ask. Christ says, "What is that to thee? Follow thou Me." Leave him to Christ. "To his own master he standeth or falleth." God will also bring him to full conviction and repentance in His own way and time.

Two believers have a quarrel. Each claims the other to be equally as guilty as he, if not more. Let us suppose that each one is willing to assume fifty percent of the responsibility. James has a word for such believers when he says, "If ye fulfil the royal law according to the Scripture, Thou shalt love thy neighbor as thyself, ye do well: But if ye have respect to persons, ye commit sin, and are convinced of the law as transgressors. For whosoever shall keep the whole law, and yet offend in one point, he is guilty of all . . . So speak ye, and so do, as they that shall be judged by the law of liberty" (Jas. 2:8-12). Until one is filling to the full love's royal law of liberty, let him know that to come short in only one point — in this case the failure of love — is to fail completely, to become "guilty of all."

Any believer who thus fails and argues as to the degree of his guilt withers up in his spiritual experience. The work of conviction begins, for he has broken the command, "Thou shalt love thy neighbour as thyself." He has not fulfilled the law of love. Since he still argues, conviction must deepen. He knows he is wrong, but he refuses to admit that he is "guilty of all"; he may be leprous, but he is not yet all leper. The Spirit continues to put the pressure upon him, and finally so shuts him up and stops his mouth that he begins to lose sight of his brother's faults and begins to see himself as God sees him. His guilt increases. He ceases to think of his be-

ing only fifty percent responsible for the quarrel. Instead he finds
he is one hundred percent guilty — *for his own sin.* He is all
leper, "guilty of all." Thus the law, as a truant officer, seizes upon
this arguing, quarreling Christian and shuts him up to Christ; nor
will the law release him until he confesses in broken-hearted penitence that he is *all guilty.* A broken and a contrite heart the law
will not despise. The law releases the man to the Holy Spirit, who
sheds abroad the love of God in the man's now contrite heart. The
man is at liberty and is filled with divine ability to fulfill the royal
law of love. Being now led of the Spirit, he is not under the law.
He finds his liberty and freedom in filling to the full the law of
love. What about the other brother? With him the Spirit pursues
the same process. Each one must be brought to one hundred percent guilt for his own sin, and after that each one finds glorious
freedom and liberty to love his neighbor as himself. Professor James
Denney says:

> Liberty, when it does not deepen the sense of responsibility
> to God and to the brotherhood—and it does not always do
> so—is an anarchic and disintegrating force . . . It is this
> which makes Christian education difficult, and church dis-
> cipline often impossible (*Expositor's Bible*).

The Apostle calls love the capstone and crown of the Christian
life, the very "bond of perfection." The apostle John, full of years
and enfeebled, so tradition tells us, could still utter his one-sentence
sermon: "Little children, love one another." He knew that in this
sentence he had comprehended all.

We first taste the love of God in the forgiveness of sin. Yet love
seems to be the last thing we ever learn. As the years roll by and
as the judgment seat of Christ becomes more of a reality, we feel
that nothing tests us more severely than the probing question, Am
I more Christlike in the matter of love? Do those who know me
best know I have grown in love? Do the home folks know it? Does
the world around me sense the sincerity of my love? Or, do I
find it hard to love? Is it a labour, a task, a command that is
grievous? The aged Apostle said, "This is the love of God, that
we keep His commandments: and His commandments are not
grievous" (I John 5:3, R. V.) Then he gives us the reason: "For

whatsoever is begotten of God overcometh the world: and this is the victory that hath overcome the world, even our faith." If I find love a labour, a yoke grievous and heavy to be borne, then, John says, there is in me that which is not yet "*begotten.*" There is an area, a sphere, some "*whatsoever,*" where the life of Christ and the love of God have not penetrated. There is some locality in me where the natural life holds sway and refuses to give way to the reign of love.

While God's commands are, of course, all impossible to the life of nature, these same commands are a delight to "whatsoever is begotten of God." If my brother's weight seems heavy, and if the command to love him is still grievous, then I lack the "begotten" life. I still have an argument with God. I do not want to love the brother. The Cross of Christ must therefore make a new inroad into my self-life. Its cutting and killing power must reach *me*. The law of love can operate only through "whatsoever is begotten," only where "*I*" have been crucified. The only reason it is still difficult to love that neighbour or that enemy is that the Cross has been denied its fresh and death-dealing application to the natural life. Many folks speak of the Cross of Christ being heavy, and of having to bear their cruel and heavy cross; but the Cross is heavy only to that which refuses to die. Christ's yoke is easy; His burden is light. Such resurrection life and love, however, follow the death-dealing power of the Cross. "His Cross," says Samuel Rutherford, "is the sweetest burden that ever I bare: it is such a burden as wings are to a bird, or sails to a ship, to carry me forward to my harbour." When Christ lives in me His own mighty and "yet-not-I" kind of life, then the impossible law of love will be easily and gloriously filled to the full.

We have mentioned the judgment seat of Christ. Before that august and awful tribunal — "the terror of the Lord" Paul calls it — only one thing can avail, and that is supreme love for God and man. John tells us how we may have boldness in the day of judgment: "There is no fear in love; but perfect love casteth out fear: because fear hath torment" (I John 4:18). So many of God's children are reproached with fears and self-condemnation. With many of us this state is, of course, due to known disobedience; but with others such self-reproach and fearfulness may be due to a false estimation of Christian service. Some restless saints feel that if they could but accomplish a certain amount of untiring service for Christ, or if they could but win so many thousands to Christ — all of which is as holy an ambition as ever thrilled an apostle — they feel, I say, that if they could but realize a certain magnificent amount of accomplished service, they would have boldness at the judgment seat of Christ. But, my friend, this is to proceed upon a wrong basis entirely. All our salvation, including all our service, is so entirely of grace that God can allow nothing to satisfy us or to please Heaven but "perfect love." It is perfect love — nothing else, nothing less, *nothing more* — that casts out fear.

Love is indeed the fulfilling of all law. "The fruit of the Spirit is love, joy, peace, longsuffering . . . against such there is no law." What kind of condemnation can there be against the Spirit's own fruit? If then we be led of the Spirit, most certainly we are not under law. The compassion of Christ seizes upon us and carries us captive under the mighty sway and compulsion of love.

> *Need I that a law should bind me*
> *Captive unto Thee?*
> *Captive is my heart, rejoicing*
> *Never to be free.*
> *Ever with me, glorious, awful,*
> *Tender, passing sweet,*
> *One upon whose heart I rest me,*
> *Worship at His Feet.*
>
> —Ter Steegen

All of heaven is wrapped up in love. God is love. The whole Bible, with all its changes of administration and dispensation, has all had as its crowning and supreme objective the bringing of man back into love and harmony with God. Accordingly, the Apostle of love says, "Brethren, I write no new commandment unto you, but an old commandment which ye had from the beginning" (I John 2:7). On these two commandments, love to God and love to man, hang all the law and the prophets. From Paradise lost to Paradise regained, all the divine precepts have hinged on love. Even at the giving of the law, as has been pointed out, the whole administration was in love. "From His right hand went a fiery law for them: *Yea,*

He loved the people." Those with spiritual eyes always saw that love to God and man was "more than all whole burnt offerings." Therefore John says concerning the law of love, "I write no new commandment unto you, but an old commandment which ye had from the beginning" (I John 2:7). Now that we might know the source of all this thousands-of-years-old love, John adds that "the old commandment is *the word* which ye have heard at the beginning." John here tells us that no word of God in all the Old Testament reached its objective except as it produced love in the heart. This law of brotherly love, he reminds us, was first shockingly violated when Cain killed Abel. Then he goes on to say, "Again, a new commandment I write unto you"; but he immediately explains that which constitutes the *newness* of this law of brotherly love: "Which thing is true in Him and in you: because the darkness [of ceremonial formalism which had beclouded true brotherly love] is passed, and the true light now shineth" (I John 2:8). John says that this new commandment is now exhibited in Jesus and in the living epistles "known and read of all men."

It was for this reason that John, in writing of this law of brotherly love, insisted, "I write no new commandment unto you [i.e., not one that is utterly new or was never commanded before], but an old commandment which ye had from the beginning [of divine revelation to man]." All that John or Jesus ever meant by the "new commandment" of love was simply the bringing of the "old commandment" back into bright manifestation. There is an analogy of this in the "new creature," which, although he is born anew, is not another person, but the same identical person only made "new." John Owen once said: "A commandment that is always practiced is always new, and John speaks of that of love." The new covenant, then, written on the heart is not actually the seventh in a succession of covenants. God has had some souls under all dispensations who have been united to Him through their loving and obedient faith, and *on whose hearts has been written the word of the living God.* All God's governing arrangements, whether under one covenant or another, have been for the one unchanging and unalterable purpose of furthering His grace in the hearts of men.

Those who feel that the new covenant is strictly and entirely new, and that the law of love has now supplanted a supposed law of mere works under Moses, might well consider the various testimonies of saint and psalmist in the days of old. Here are a few from the 119th Psalm: "I will run in the way of thy commandments, when thou shalt enlarge my heart" (v. 32); "O how love I thy law! it is my meditation all the day" (v. 97); "How sweet are thy words unto my taste! yea, sweeter than honey to my mouth!" (v. 103); "Great peace have they which love thy law: and nothing shall offend them" (v. 165). Surely God's "blessed man" in Psalm 1, who delighted in the law of the Lord and meditated therein day and night, and who became like a tree planted by the rivers of water, could scarcely have been under a "yoke of bondage" or under a strict covenant of works. If that blessed man were under the mere letter of law, how is it that so few saints of today can even reach the spiritual altitude of David and the other Old Testament examples of faith? Surely these souls, whose examples so shame the saints of today, must have known somewhat of grace while they were under the administration of law. Certainly those who thus found the law of the Lord more to be desired than much fine gold, and who rejoiced therein as those that find great spoil, yea, who knew the blessedness of man "whose transgression and whose sin is covered" — surely these souls could say with David and all others who had found the secret: "I will walk at liberty: for I seek thy precepts" (Psa. 119:45). They served God in newness of spirit and not "in the oldness of the letter."

Though they lacked that brightest of all manifestation of God's love in the incarnate Sun of Righteousness, nevertheless His merciful lovingkindness and salvation were the refrain of song and psalm. With what a burst of joy and jubilation would that "little flock" have joined us in singing:

"Could we with ink the ocean fill,
*   And were the skies of parchment made,*
Were every stalk on earth a quill,
*   And every man a scribe by trade,*

> *To write the love of God above*
> *Would drain the ocean dry;*
> *Nor could the scroll contain the whole,*
> *Though stretched from sky to sky."*

Such souls as these, who walked at liberty and found Heaven's lovingkindness better than life, would also agree with Bishop Moule: "The man who loves cannot possibly wish to be his own law." These illuminated men did not dream of setting love and righteousness at variance. Nor would they understand a dispensational extreme that would seek to make the Sermon on the Mount an enemy of the grace of God. Those old worthies who trusted in the Rock of their salvation, who fed on the true Bread, who experienced the efficacy of the Lamb's blood, and who drank of the spiritual Rock — "that Rock was Christ" — and who esteemed the reproach of Christ greater riches than the treasures of any Egypt — surely these souls would have seen in Christ's Sermon on the Mount such an expression of love and righteousness as is indeed the filling to the full of all law.

In his summary of the relation between love and righteousness in keeping with the inspired commentary that "love is the fulfilling of the law," David Gracey of Spurgeon's College made this balanced observation:

Are we, therefore, to suppose that love can dispense with the precepts? By no means. The propelling power of the engine does not enable it to dispense with the firm metal rails, nor does the swiftness of the vessel render it independent of the helm. On the contrary, the greater the swiftness, the firmer must be the guidance of the helm; the mightier the engine's force, the more need there is for its course to be shaped by the undeviating line. So the sacred passion of Divine love within the heart cannot afford to part company with the precept of the law. To come to such a conclusion would be altogether contrary to our Lord's meaning. Dealing with those who saw only the outside of the law, our Lord opened up the precepts, and showed them what was within. They wanted to know how to fulfill the law of righteousness.

The answer was, to love God and man. But when showing those who did love Him how they were to love Him, He said, *"If ye love Me, keep My commandments"* (John 14:15). Thus *"the commandment is a lamp; and the law is light"* (Prov. 6:23): it is a *"lamp unto my feet, and a light upon my path"* (Psa. 119:105). The conclusion, then, to which we come is that law contains the principle of love, that love is to be guided by the light of law.

CHAPTER XXIII

The Royal Law of Liberty

A MINISTER once met a little Scotch lassie carrying in her arms a baby boy so bonny that she staggered beneath his weight. "Baby's heavy, isn't he, dear?" said the old minister.

"No, sir," replied the little bairn; "he's not heavy; he's my brother."

The royal law according to the Scripture, "Thou shalt love thy neighbor as thyself," is such that, if we fulfill it, we shall "do well." Let us therefore "look into the perfect law of *liberty*, and continue therein," for if we be not forgetful hearers, but doers, we shall be blessed indeed. Such is the blessed bondage by which the Christian is enslaved that "a life of self-renouncing love is his life of liberty." Brother is heavy only when we lack the life-power of divine love. In this day of exaggerated individualism, when preachers and educators have indulged in the wildest extravagance to let us know the liberty that is ours, we do well to heed some of the limits set to our everyday liberty. In matters of right and wrong, liberty certainly must have no more laxity than liberty's laws in other spheres. Law is law, and that needs to be said with a vengeance. If law governs heaven itself, then woe betide the dwellers of earth who think to overthrow law. The angels that sinned violated law, and at once created hell. There can be no such thing as liberty of any kind outside the bounds of law.

A mathematician may say he has a right to draw a five-sided rectangle, but he has no right after that to draw anything. He has forfeited any liberty he ever had as a mathematician, for he did not stay within the limits of the laws of mathematics. In the same way a scientist may say he has a right to believe evolution, but truly great and honest scientists rightly say, "As soon as a man receives the evolutionary theory regarding the origin of man, he forfeits the right to be called a scientist," because science pertains to facts. I may claim I have liberty to drive a car as fast as I like and to drive right through the stop signs, but I will soon forfeit the right to drive at all. Thus it is throughout all the experiences of life; all man's liberties must be within the limits of law.

It ill becomes teachers of grace to become so utterly bent on preaching liberty that they cast off all restraint, break asunder all divine bands, and cast away all Heaven's cords from us. It indicates not only a lack of a true conception of law itself but also a poor understanding of the gospel. What, after all, is gospel freedom but a conferring of grace and freedom to do the will of God? Why preach to selfish and self-indulgent and easygoing Christians that the gospel has set them free from all obligation, thereby further catering to their selfish and self-centered lives? A selfish person is one who thinks that liberty consists in having things his own way, whereas "true freedom consists in having things in the right way — and the right way is God's way." Someone correctly observes that, if you dig deeply enough into the Bible at any place, you will find a "Do right" implied or stated.

About a quarter of a century ago a foremost preacher of New York said:

> One of our most venerated and farseeing citizens recently remarked that in his eighty years of active life, associated with some of the most stirring events in the commonwealth, he had never seen such an orgy of lawlessness as that through which we are living now. Startled into thoughtfulness by this assertion, I made some interesting discoveries: that I could not recall ever having preached a sermon on obedience; that when I searched volume after volume of modern addresses and sermons, I did not run upon any that dealt with respect for and obedience to authority. There were plenty on freedom, on the emancipation of the individual, on the outgrowing of old restraints, but few, if any, upon the necessity and glory of being mastered by what rightfully masters us. The impression began to sink in that our orgy of lawlessness is not an accident, nor merely a post-war psychological reaction, but that

it is the natural fruitage of deep-rooted tendencies in our
thinking which have affected alike our religion and our law
(D. M. Panton).

Today we have a liberty abroad which knows not "the law of
Christ," a liberty which does not deepen our sense of responsibility
and subjection to God. Such liberty fosters loose and lawless living, which breeds anarchy. It is a force, disintegrating, deadly, and
suicidal. Leaders who attempt to exercise church discipline find it
well-nigh impossible, and those of us in Christian education can
understand that much of our fundamentalism has unwittingly developed a tradition which hides its antinomianism. While there is
a professed adherence to Christian ethics, the teeth of those ethics
have been pulled by a "not-under-law" extreme.

It doubtless sounded very pious for the Pharisees of old to exalt
Moses, even though they made his legislation of no practical effect
through their traditions. They were sticklers for the letter of the
law — all the orthodox of today share with them that determined
adherence to the inspiration of Scripture — but they were, after all,
straight antinomian. They claimed to be Moses' disciples, yet they
built up a traditionalism which became a covering under which to
hide their disobedience. Likewise we claim to accept all the ethical
teachings of the New Testament, yet we often promote a "not-under-
law" principle which robs those very teachings of all obligation or
necessity, i.e., we rob them of all authority over us. While we exalt
New Testament ethics, we labour to hold them forth only as privileges and instruction for Christians. We are careful lest the saints
should ever come to feel that these precepts are a duty or a necessity.
We make obedience a *beauty* instead of a *duty*, a matter of *option*
instead of an *obligation*. All the while God's people are left in their
fleshly self-centeredness, listening to additional sermons on liberty.
Many well-meaning ministers seem to be desperately afraid that
some of the dear saints might fall into a feeling of self-condemnation
and bondage unless the blessings and privileges and liberties in
Christ are continually lifted up to them.

Have I confessed Jesus Christ as Lord? Do I belong to Christ? Am I His property? Am I subject to Him and under His government? Am I not then an eternal contradiction to myself and to my position "in Christ" if I be not "under law to Christ"? "Hereby perceive we the love of God, because He laid down His life for us: and we ought to lay down our lives for the brethren" (I John 3:16). The apostles and all God's true people sense the meaning of emancipation from past slavery, and they know that the only adequate return is to lay down their lives for others. Paul cried, "Woe is unto me, if I preach not the gospel," but that word "woe" has little meaning among us today. One who seems to labour incessantly to make the believers feel that they are so privileged as not to be under law of any kind states that unless dispensational teaching walls off the application of Old Testament obligations from New Testament saints, we are in danger of "having the blood of lost souls required at our hands," as were Old Testament men of God (Ezek. 3:17, 18). Having safely walled us off from Ezekiel's sense of responsibility for lost souls, this writer, wittingly or unwittingly, renders Paul's "woe unto me" and other solemn New Testament texts regarding "disobedient" servants, *of little or no effect*. This he does through this comparatively new and popular traditionalism.

Do we fundamentalists forget that every time the Saviour warned against leaven, He first named the Pharisees? "Take heed and beware of the leaven of the Pharisees and of the Sadducees." Both of these classes are still with us, and we are to beware of both. Ernest Gordon once wrote a great exposure of the Modernists entitled, "The Leaven of the Sadducees." Another book has long been due on "The Leaven of the Pharisees." The Sadducees denied the supernatural inspiration of God's Word; the Pharisees contended stoutly for the very jot and tittle of Scripture, but "made the Word of God of none effect through their tradition." The ultra-dispensationalists are developing a new traditionalism, perhaps unintentional, which is subtly and ingeniously making much of the Word of God of none effect. Beware of this new form of the leaven of the Pharisees. It denatures and devitalizes an obedient faith. The words in an inscription in the Lubeck Cathedral are appropriate to us today.

Ye call me MASTER................. and OBEY me not.
Ye call me LIGHT................... and SEE me not.
Ye call me WAY.....................and WALK me not.
Ye call me LIFE....................and DESIRE me not.
Ye call me WISE.................... and FOLLOW me not.
Ye call me RICH.....................and ASK me not.
Ye call me FAIR....................and LOVE me not.
Ye call me ETERNAL................ and SEEK me not.
Ye call me GRACIOUS.............. and TRUST me not.
Ye call me NOBLE..................and SERVE me not.
Ye call me MIGHTY................. and HONOUR me not.
Ye call me JUST....................and FEAR me not.
        If I CONDEMN you......BLAME me not.

Let us return to the question, Have I called Jesus Christ my Lord?
Am I His blood-bought property? Or, do I just call Him, Lord, Lord,
without being in subjection to His government? Paul could easily
combine in one chapter (I Cor. 9) his "woe unto me" and his
boast of being "free from all" and "under law to Christ." Those,
however, who are not yet properly "free" nor truly "under law to
Christ," must seek for some softening of Paul's "woe unto me."
The early Christians, less theological and less trammelled with tradition, were infinitely more practical and obedient. Caesar could
not outdo Christ as King in command; the believers had "another
King, one Jesus." It has been said that when a Roman soldier was
told by his guide that if he insisted on taking a certain journey he
would probably die, he royally replied, *It is necessary for me to
go; it is not necessary for me to live.*" As the Roman soldiers were
subject to Caesar, no less were true disciples "good soldiers of
Jesus Christ," and obedient unto death.

We are reminded of the Roman centurion who protested the
necessity of Jesus' coming to his house in order to heal his servant:
"Speak the word only, and my servant shall be healed." Then the
centurion gave as his reason for such implicit faith in Christ's word
of authority, "I also am a man set under authority." Note that he
did not say, "I am a man set *in* authority," nor "I am a man set
under authority," but "I *also* am a man set under authority." He
was so completely submitted to the central will at Rome that he
could say, "I also am a man set under authority, having under myself soldiers: and I say to this one, Go, and he goeth; and to another,

Come, and he cometh; and to my servant, Do this, and he doeth it" (Luke 7:8, R.V.). This centurion was completely subject to Caesar. Of such men Campbell Morgan says:

> A soldier was not permitted to say that he had a will of his own. His time was not his. His dress was chosen for him. His food was chosen for him. By the law of Rome, no Roman soldier could hold any possessions. Indeed, he could have said he had no will of his own. If he had kith or kin they could make no claim upon him" (*The Great Physician*).

Such a soldier had been truly emancipated from civilian life and order — emancipated to the central will of the throne, for there was no middle ground between civilian life and Caesar's. His complete subjection to Caesar fitted him for his task; he was under authority, so completely under it and obedient to it that he found therein the secret of his authority over his men. The centurion sensed that the Lord Jesus was vested with authority, even though He was a great distance from his sick servant. He knew that His word was with power. He saw that Christ was subject to God even as he himself, on a lower plane, was subject to Caesar; and he recognized that Christ's subjection to the government of God was the basis of His authority over disease and darkness and death, irrespective of distance. He therefore said to Jesus, *I also* am a man *under authority*. I am under authority and am therefore in *authority*; I am in authority only because I am under authority, and I sense that Thou art the same.

This brings us to consider the depths and heights of Christ's supremacy. He who said, "All authority hath been given unto Me in heaven and on earth," also said, "I can *of Myself* do nothing." He would exercise no act of will in word or deed or miracle independent of His Father. We read, therefore, that Jesus could not do His own works, could not speak His own words, could not do His own will. He could not save Himself and save others. Blessed, glorious inability! Such were the limitations set to the liberties of the high and lofty One who inhabits eternity. Is this inability bondage? It is indeed the highest kind of bondage — the bondage of love, the bondage of inability to have our own way to do our own will; it is the liberty to lay down our lives for others, the liberty to sacrifice all and yet never think of sacrifice; it is the royal and all-divine law, the "perfect law of liberty"; it is love's royal law for her loyal few, for love "seeketh not her own."

Watch this royal law lived out in an heir-apparent to the throne of Israel, namely to Jonathan, the prince. Already an experienced warrior, Jonathan was the pride of Israel's fighting forces, and in the eyes of all the common people, the darling successor of Saul. The day came when the Philistines defied the armies of Israel, and the mighty Goliath fell headlong before the stripling lad from Bethlehem, weak and weaponless, fresh from keeping his father's sheep. "And it came to pass . . . that the soul of Jonathan was knit with the soul of David, and Jonathan loved him as his own soul." This language might sound like an indulged extravagance did it not occur again and again in the sacred text. Finally, when David poured out his personal lament and Christlike elegy over the death of Saul and Jonathan, he said of the latter, "Thy love to me was wonderful, passing the love of women." Even as God had found in David a man after His own heart, so had Jonathan; although he was a good many years David's senior, the soul of Jonathan fastened upon the shepherd lad, finding in the son of Jesse his heart's delight.

Jonathan, of course, was devoted and faithful to his father even to the last. Although he was so loyal to "the Lord's anointed" that "in their death they were not divided," he was yet more devoted to David, for "Jonathan and David made a covenant, because he loved him as his own soul." "And Jonathan stripped himself of the robe that was upon him, and gave it to David, and his garments, even to his sword, and to his bow, and to his girdle" (I Sam. 18:4). Here we find this princely son and heir-apparent stripping himself of his royal raiment all in order to seal the kingdom to David, for what else could Jonathan mean by stripping himself of his own royal insignia but that he was leaving himself destitute for the sake of his sworn friend? What is more, when he handed over his sword and his bow, Jonathan stood completely at the mercy of his rival.

Two great generals once met on the field of battle. The vanquished came forward holding out his hand to greet his conqueror. The victorious general said, "I do not want your hand; I want your sword, and the vanquished general was compelled to hand over his sword. How different was Jonathan's surrender! This princely son and successor to Israel's throne, by his act of voluntary self-emptying and humiliation, is surpassed by One only — Israel's own invisible King. The Son of God stripped Himself of all His royal insignia in order that He might clothe us with His own robe and seat us with Himself over all worlds. Jonathan's self-stripping scarcely has a parallel in human history, and it is rather remarkable that we have no more superb illustration even in New Testament times.

Jonathan's light shone still brighter as he continued to fulfill this royal law of liberty. His devotion to David caused Saul's anger to be kindled: "Thou son of a perverse rebellious woman, do not I know that thou hast chosen the son of Jesse to thine own shame, and unto the shame of thy mother's nakedness? For as long as the son of Jesse liveth upon the ground, thou shalt not be stablished, nor thy kingdom" (I Sam. 20:30, 31, R.V.). Apparently Jonathan was disregarding the great object of respect and devotion, namely his mother. By not seeking the throne for himself — it was already his legitimate right — it seems manifest that he was implying his own illegitimacy as the heir-apparent. For David's sake he endured the pain and shame of being reckoned a bastard. This accusation his raging father cast into Jonathan's teeth, and then fell upon him with a javelin. Was there ever a more glorious and voluntary bearing of reproach, the very "reproach of Christ," which Moses also had borne some centuries before? Do we marvel at such willingness to lay down crown rights and wonder how this coming king of Israel could do it? Here is the answer: Jonathan was fulfilling the royal law of liberty, loving his neighbour as himself. Jonathan and David met in Christ. There we find the love that "seeketh not her own," that which is hers by right. Love's royal law removes kings and sets up kings — yea, makes kings out of Jonathan and others like him.

A bit later we find David a fugitive out in the woods, about to lose his faith in God because of the treachery of those he had befriended. Saul was seeking his life, and David was all but in despair. How easily Jonathan could have simply allowed David to lose faith and thereby become unfitted to rule, and the kingdom would be Jonathan's after all. Why not let his rival die? Jonathan, however, seeing David's distress, risked his life and went into the wood to find David and "strengthen his hand in God." Here Jonathan again fulfilled the royal law by strengthening the hand of the man who would soon supplant him completely. Hear the beautiful words of Jonathan to his friend in distress: "Fear not: for the hand of Saul my father shall not find thee; and thou shalt be king over Israel, and I shall be next unto thee; and that also Saul my father knoweth" (I Sam. 23:17).

We would like to have seen David as king and Jonathan seated next to him, but it could not be so. For the sake of the fickle people, and in order that David "in all things might have the preeminence," Jonathan had to pass away. To climax his reproach for Christ and his cross-bearing, as bright as ever shone on the pages of the New Testament, Jonathan died and was "reckoned among the transgressors," even though he died at his post. The throne seat next to David he never saw. Never saw? Let us rather say, as the Lord said to hoary-headed Daniel, "Go thou thy way till the end be: for thou shalt rest, and stand in thy lot at the end of the days" (Dan. 12:13). For his love he seemed to have been cheated completely, but somehow we cannot say with David, "I am distressed for thee, my brother Jonathan." We rather cry, Great and wonderful Jonathan! Thy love passed the love of women! How royal were thy kingly robes that fell upon thy rival! Surely thou wilt yet be seated next to David at the marriage supper of the Lamb! We bow at thy feet and confess that, although our light is greater, our love is less. As Jonathan passed out of sight, we cannot forget how

> *Love took up the harp of life, and smote on*
> *all the chords with might;*
> *Smote the chord of self which, trembling,*
> *pass'd in music out of sight.*
> —Selected

CHAPTER XXIV

God's Weapons

A WARM PRAYER-PARTNER once enclosed a generous contribution to our work with this interesting note:

> This is a contribution which my Father says I should send to you. I trust God will continue to bless and use you for His glory. An old friend of mine used to say that *"God can use a worm to thresh a mountain if He can get all the wiggle out of the worm."*

To His weak, despised captives in Babylon, who were being trampled upon as a thing of nought, God said, "Fear not, thou worm Jacob, . . . Behold, I will make thee a new sharp threshing instrument having teeth: thou shalt thresh the mountains" (Isa. 41:14, 15). What two things could stand in more striking contrast than a worm and a sharp threshing instrument having teeth? In this very contrast is exhibited the way of the flesh and the way of the Spirit. In this figure of a "worm" is reflected a principle of God's working. If the weapon of His choice is a worm, minus the wiggle of the flesh, let every one of us take heart — we may be qualified to be chosen of God. Through Him who for our sakes became "a worm and no man," we can lose the wiggle and energy of the flesh, and yet become His chosen instrument to thresh some impossible mountain.

Gospel principle cuts us all down to one size, flattens us all to the same platform, sets us all in our rightful place. There is no difference — all have sinned and all must be saved by grace alone. The principle holds for the saint as for the sinner, "the flesh profiteth nothing"; whether in salvation or in service, God has so ordered His whole economy "that no flesh should glory in His presence."

"The battle is not yours but God's." In ordering the battle, God has no difficulty in displaying His power. He, who can hang the

world upon nothing and who can by His Spirit garnish the heavens, can suffer no embarrassment manifesting His omnipotence.
When God reveals His might through man, however, He often avoids
the spectacular in order to hide pride from man and guard His
people against the tendency to vaunt themselves.

Recall God's method in the days of Gideon. Israel had been
mightily oppressed for years. An overwhelming horde of no less
than 135,000 Midianites were now massed against her. At Gideon's
bugle call, 32,000 rallied to the front, but God said that there were
too many, "lest Israel vaunt themselves against Me, saying, Mine
own hand hath saved me." That the number might be diminished,
the fearful and faint-hearted were sent home, leaving only 10,000.
Though 32,000 against 135,000 seemed all too few, God nevertheless said that 10,000 were "yet too many"; for with odds thirteen
to one against Israel, should she win, she would still strip God of
His glory. Israel's army had to be further diminished.

This very principle of God's working perhaps explains why, in
spite of the many and urgent demands that we muster all our forces
to meet the inroads of the modern Midianites, comparatively little
yet comes to pass. In spite of the desperate darkness, deepening
into midnight battle, front-line fighters actually dwindle. The fleshly, the fearful, and the faint-hearted cannot tackle the task, for the
odds overwhelm them. God's testings furnish them opportunity to
vanish. All such forces fall out and silently seek the shelter. In
ways simple and inscrutable and fiery God must drain away the
dregs of self-confidence. He must let the flesh fail. Finally, when
all those remaining are convinced that in God alone is their rescue
and remedy, and when those few are so "shut up to faith" that
they carry into their midnight struggle not the weapons of usual
warfare but rams' horns and shouts of Heaven-sent victory, then
God turns the tide and Himself wins the battle. Those 300 become
each a kind of Gideon's lamp, themselves but broken pitchers. There
they stand exposed on the battle field — hazard-loving souls, ha-
zarding their lives, their lamps lighting them up as perfect targets
for the enemy.

Pitchers for the lamps of God—
Hark, the cry goes forth abroad!
Not the beauty of the make,
But ah, the readiness to break
Marks the vessels of the Lord,
Meet to bear the lighted Word!

—Selected

Yet how far from our personal experience all this can be. Gideon's victory is beautiful to write about, thrilling and romantic to read about, but are we almost glad that it happened too long ago to have any practical bearing on our own warfare? Have we wickedly wandered so far from that world of weakness that the lamp and pitcher method frightens us? For example, consider how students for the ministry become paralyzed with fear lest they go forth to battle without having "what it takes" — of letters, degrees, prestige, influence, recognition. Away to Egypt they go, summoning science and philosophy and psychology and what not, in order to escape the stigma of being reckoned among the nondescripts. We greatly fear that in many instances they pursue such a course not to become "willing, skillful workers" — skillful in the word of righteousness — such as Hudson Taylor required for China, but to avoid being among the ignorant and the unlearned. In this day of intellectualism, who would wish to be so extreme as to be

Dead to the world and its applause,
To all the customs, fashions, laws
Of those who hate the humbling Cross.

—Amy Carmichael

Have we forgotten, or do we willingly ignore the fact, that Paul and Timothy and Titus met and faced a world of Roman power and Grecian wisdom without having, to use this modern term, "what it takes"? Paul's successors were to become "thoroughly furnished unto all good works," as was Joshua, by meditating day and night in the Scriptures. Thus they waged their warfare with weapons not of the flesh, but mighty through God to the battering down of all the bulwarks of Grecian wit and wisdom. Was it not John Wesley who said, "Give me one hundred preachers who fear nothing but sin and desire nothing but God, and I care not a straw whether

they be clergymen or laymen; such alone will shake the gates of
hell and set up the kingdom of heaven on earth. God does nothing
but in answer to prayer." After Methodism had been in the field
for one hundred years and had won her greatest victories, "the
Methodist Bishops in 1840 expressed their doubts as to the expe-
diency of establishing schools of divinity" (Ernest Gordon, in
Leaven of the Sadducees). When, therefore, a modern Bible School
Dean gives as one of the reasons why our world is on its way to
certain ruin, "the widespread unwillingness to give to our teachers
the place and prestige in our society which they deserve," then we
begin to see how far removed we are from even wanting to be dead
to the world and its applause —

> *So dead that no desire may rise*
> *To appear good, or great, or wise*
> *In any but my Saviour's eyes.*
> —Amy Carmichael

Let me be honest. Do I wish to become as far removed from
"the worm" method as possible? as far as culture and learning and
prestige can lift me? Do I seek to be lettered, to be elevated, to
have "what it takes" to meet the mountains of modern intellect and
education on their ground? In other words, must I be clad in
Saul's armour? Must I meet wit with wit? Or can I dare with
David to crush every Goliath's skull with one smooth stone? Such
is God's foolishness and weakness, chosen to confound the world's
splendid might; "for it is not 'diamond cut diamond' here, but it
is the lamb that slays the lion, and the dove that outwits the serpent" (Charles Fox).

How we feel for the Christian young people of this generation!
They face an age that well-nigh worships the "god of forces"; they
live in a world of intellect, of science, of military power and might;
and many of them move in an orthodox world that is seeking to
preach the Cross with a wisdom, a cunning, and a genius that can
prove adequate to command the world's respect. Many of these
young people have been converted under a popular streamlined,
high-pressure evangelism, an evangelism with a technique "powerful enough to rebuild the world." We fear that with many of these

methods God is not well pleased, for they mislead God's young folks. Full of natural wisdom, these measures savour of the flesh, and the results soon prove disconcerting and disappointing.

We must turn aside at this point to declare ourselves in favour of every form of honest effort to save our young people. If Christ is preached, we therein rejoice. We have little sympathy indeed with a modern kind of "quietism," which shuts itself away from human need, walling itself off in a kind of quieter and holier-than-thou-worship. There are some fleshly folks today so quiet, so holy, so spiritual that they are forever accusing the brethren who are out in midstream trying to rescue the perishing. They would put the whole responsibility upon the sovereignty of God, while they enjoy their seclusive and exclusive times of worship. They need the rebuke of Charles Spurgeon, himself a great Baptist, who said, "The difference between the Baptists and the Methodists is this: While the Baptists are waiting on God to turn something up, the Methodists go around and turn it up."

In today's Babel of methods, Christian young people stand in a place of desperate need. They must be told with all boldness that God's ways and wisdom run counter to the whole way and wisdom of the world. They must become convinced that God's work is still done by Heaven's worms, that the insignificant and the despised and the weaklings are Heaven's hope of blessed success. Let these young people be made to see the plan and the principle of God's working, for God's solution is as heartening as it is concealed. Set over against the pride and power and wit of the world's wisdom is "the foolishness of God," which is "wiser than men," and "the weakness of God," which is "stronger than men."

If this working principle be questioned, let the whole of our gospel scheme come into review. In Christ is embodied God's secret weapon. All the way from glory to incarnation, to Gethsemane, and to Golgotha, His career was a self-humbling and self-chosen obedience unto death. Such was the disguise of Deity. Hidden in this "root out of a dry ground," with "no form nor comeliness," was the very power of God and the wisdom of God. In His final down-stepping, He gave Himself over to be "numbered with the transgressors" and was "crucified through weakness." In that death

He defeated the whole hierarchy of hell, and became to us the very power of God and the wisdom of God. Is that mere cold theology? Let every human worm be willing to be "planted together in the likeness of His death" — or, as Paul says, become *"weak with Him."* Identification with Christ in His supreme weakness is the secret of all God's mighty working. It is the corn-of-wheat program that insures a harvest of success.

A fundamental preacher goes over this country visiting the various centers of Christian education, and returns to lament "the second-rate men God is using to get His work done." Does this poor fellow not know that God's work has ever been done through weapons of weakness? It has scarcely dawned upon him that the Church may still be full of men "too many, too mighty, and too wise" for God to work deliverance; and Heaven must therefore set about to lessen, to weaken, and to impoverish. This man's surprise over the second-rate men God is using was well rebuked by Professor Denney a half-century ago:

> Perhaps this is not so alarming as the clever people think. There always have been men in the world so clever that God could make no use of them; they could never do His work, because they were so lost in admiration of their own. But God's work never depended on them, and it does not depend on them now.

It is much easier to stand up for Christ than to be identified with Him. Most leaders of God's young people are strong *for* Christ, but they are not yet "weak *with* Christ." His weakness they fear and refuse, yet it is this very weakness that opens the door to Heaven's power. Little wonder that without this power there is such a scramble for the help of the world, the patronage of its princes, the loan of its resources, and the use of its wisdom. Remember, the early church employed none of these. Come to Corinth and listen to the apostle Paul. Facing that carnal and conceited world, he knew that he did not have "what it takes." Hear him confess, "I was with you in weakness and in fear, and in much trembling . . . That your faith should not stand in the wisdom of men, but in the power of God . . . I determined not to know anything among you, save Jesus Christ, and Him crucified" (I Cor. 2:3, 5, 2).

Over against the Apostle's confession, let us set forth the reasonings of modern orthodoxy were it facing the evangelization of Corinth: We need a strong man for Corinth. Paul has been brought
up at the feet of Gamaliel. He has what it takes — is second to
none. He can stand on any Corinthian platform and face the people fearlessly and without apology. Paul is just the man to send
to Corinth. But I hear Paul confess in no mock humility that he
has nothing to prevent much fear and trembling. God has so "unlearned" the Apostle of his worldly wisdom that he fears and trem-
bles lest the people sense anything of the artistic or the oratorical
in his presence or presentation. Paul dared not seek to make the Cross
acceptable to Corinthian taste and preference lest their faith stand
in the wisdom of men and not in the power of God. Paul preached
the Cross in all its bald, unadorned reality — just the mean, plain,
helpless, foolish message of a crucified Nazarene. Paul could say
with heavenly old John Woolman, *"I was jealous of myself lest I
should say anything to make my testimony look agreeable with that
mind in the people which is not in pure obedience to the Cross of
Christ."* Paul would agree with John Calvin that "the knowledge
of all the sciences is mere smoke where the heavenly science is
wanting, and man with all his acuteness is as stupid for obtaining
of himself a knowledge of the mysteries of God as an ass is un-
qualified for understanding musical harmonies."

Paul embodied his message, and therein he had God's secret weapon. As to method and message he followed his Master. He who
preached Christ crucified was himself crucified to the world, to its
ways, to its wisdom — crucified together with Christ. He counted
the world's wisdom but refuse and folly; he feared and trembled
lest he conceal the naked Cross, or so smother its cutting power in
the flowers of oratorical eloquence that he would make the Cross
of Christ of none effect. Paul sank himself into such full fellowship with Christ crucified that he embodied the foolishness of God
and the weakness of God. He was foolishness personified, foolishness two-fold — *"the foolishness of the message and the weakness
of the messenger"* (Fox). The clever Corinthians stumbled over
him and even questioned his apostleship. To them he was only an
ugly little Jew, whose presence was weak and whose speech was

contemptible — a man without purse, without power, and without the art of oratory. To God, however, he was a vessel unto honour, a vessel in which He could conceal His treasure, hide His power, and pour forth His might.

The writer was once asked to speak at a Young People's Camp. It was apparent very early that some of the leaders were fearing the message of the Cross, but, thank God, the atmosphere cleared after the first few days. At the close of the morning sessions, an honest young man was heard to comment upon the message, *"Brutal but necessary."* Such is the message of the Cross. One can be as orthodox as Job, as eloquent as Demosthenes, as fundamental as a Pharisee, and as sublime as Milton, but what is all this except a false glorying in one's own fleshly elegance? How easy to talk about holding the Cross high and about lifting up the Cross in order to make it attractive! Fellow Christians, instead of elevating the Cross, come down and die on it. Forget the elegance and the attraction, and preach the Cross! Christ will take care of the attraction. "I, if I be lifted up from the earth, will draw all men unto Me."

Our fundamental and orthodox world has yet to learn that "if any man will be wise, *let him become a fool in this world.*" Only then will we begin to appreciate Paul's argument to the Corinthians:

> God chose the foolish things of the world, that He might put to shame them that are wise; and God chose the weak things of the world, that He might put to shame the things that are strong; and the base things of the world, and the things that are despised, did God choose, yea and the things that are not, that He might bring to nought the things that are: that no flesh should glory before God (I Cor. 1:27-29, R. V.).

Charles Fox has called this array "God's five-ranked army of decreasing human weakness." Instead of the wise and mighty and noble, God deliberately selects those of ever-decreasing mortal weakness in order that all boasting shall be shut out. It is interesting that, whether foolish or weak or base or despised or are-nots, all God's soldiers Paul calls *things.* So insignificant are God's weapons that they are "scarcely worth calling persons, so that once

possessed by the Holy Ghost, like the Christian warrior, at the battle call they become

> *. . . happy as a love, and attired*
> *In sudden brightness, like a thing inspired.*
> —Charles Fox

In the first rank of God's army we find the fools — fools for
Christ's sake, "such fools that they are not ashamed to be in the
front rank." Next to the fools come the weak things. Do you complain that you are too weak? Then fall in behind the front rank
fools. You are weak in influence? weak in ability? weak in body?
a bit weak in mind? Take heart, little worm, God conceals His
power in weaklings and simpletons; in such He can safely set off
His dynamite. In God's economy, the lamb slays the lion and "the
dove outwits the serpent." Let God's indomitable army pass in review:

> FOOLS—without talents—the *are nots* in sense.
> WEAK—weak in seven ways—the *are nots* in strength.
> BASE—"poor whites"—the *are nots* of low birth.
> DESPISED—without standing—the *are nots* in rank.
> NOTHINGS—nobodies too insignificant even for contempt—
>   the *are nots* of unsuspected existence, "scarce
>   seen, scarce heard, unreckoned."

These nothings and nobodies are yet "the forlorn hope of the
Church, which bursting from their long ambush of obscurity, are
ordered up to charge and break the enemy's line" (Fox).

Is the reader bent on bringing many sons unto glory, bent on being
useable, bent on God's anointing at any cost? Then despise not
your lack in any line. Listen to Martin Luther, the man of abject
and poverty-stricken spirit: "Next to my just cause it was my mean
reputation and mean aspect which gave the Pope his deadly blow;
for the Pope thought — 'Tis but one poor friar; what can he do
against me?' " Luther embodied the hidden power of God. How
foolish it would have been for him to despise his handicaps! He
sank himself into the likeness of his Master's death, embraced his
"mean reputation" and "mean aspect," and thereby dealt the Pope
a deadly blow. In his nothingness was lodged God's concealed omnipotence. "When I am weak," cries the Apostle, "then am I

strong." Seek then, dear servant of Christ, to be weak with Him. "I thank Thee, O Father, Lord of heaven and earth, that Thou didst hide these things from the wise and understanding, and didst reveal them unto babes: yea, Father; for so it was well-pleasing in Thy sight" (Luke 10:21, R.V.).

Dr. A. J. Gordon refers to an address delivered by a man of God before the London Missionary Society. By prayerful study this man had sought to reproduce a true picture of the apostolic missionary. This address created a great tumult when it was delivered, because of the startling contrast it suggested "between the ancient and modern policy of methods and missionary labour." Dr. Gordon says, "He was addressing a society that a little before had greeted with applause the declaration of a speaker who had said, 'If I were asked what is the first qualification for a missionary, I would say prudence; and the second, prudence; and the third, prudence.'" Little wonder that, when this man of God reproduced the apostolic missionary as a man self-abandoned and of sublimely dominant faith, his fleshly brethren were greatly annoyed and aroused to no small commotion. Here is a portion of that eloquent pen-picture of God's Apostolic Missionary:

> Therefore I say, let this type of missionary stand, that he is a man without the care of making friends or keeping friends, without the hope or desire of worldly good, without the apprehension of worldly loss, without the care of life, without the fear of death; of no rank, country, or condition; a man of one thought, the gospel of Christ; a man of one purpose, the glory of God; a fool, and content to be reckoned a fool, for Christ. Let him be enthusiast, fanatic, babbler, or any other outlandish nondescript the world may choose to denominate him. But still let him be nondescript. When they call him trader, householder, or citizen, man of substance, man of the world, man of learning, or even man of common sense, it is all over with his missionary character.
> They must speak or they must die, and although they should die they will speak. They have no rest, but hasten over land and sea, over rocks and trackless deserts. They cry aloud and spare not, and will not be hindered. In the prisons they lift up their voices, and in the tempests of the ocean they are not silent. Before awful councils and throned kings they witness in behalf of the truth. Nothing can quench their voice but

death, and in the article of death, ere yet the spiry flame and
rolling smoke have suffocated the organ of the soul, they
speak, they pray, they testify, they confess, they beseech, they
warn, and at length bless the cruel people.

Be content, dear servant of Christ, to be weak with Him. The
servant is not above his Lord. You may be far from being made
"the filth of the world, the offscouring of all things [of society],"
the very refuse of humanity, and — paralyzing truth — perhaps
as far from being crowned with glory and honour hereafter! God's
way up is still down. In this direction we can go as far and as
fast as we like. By sinking still deeper into the depths of His death,
"weak with Him," we shall become His sharp threshing instruments — worms "having teeth" — secret weapons of His choice.
Such is Heaven's own path and process for prophets and apostles
and martyrs.

Now for our encouragement let one apostle speak for all: "It
seems to me as if God has exposed His apostles to public view, like
the doomed wretches who close a triumphal procession — that we,
like them, have been exposed in the amphitheatre before the eyes of
the world, ay, of angels as well as of men!" (I Cor. 4:9, Way's
Translation). If this way of life in death and death in life be
questioned, or if the offense of the Cross seems too revolutionary,
then let the reader lift his eyes from things present to the "city
which hath foundations, whose builder and maker is God." There
read the names emblazoned forever on the twelve foundations.

APPENDIX A

The Old and New Testament Compared

THE OLD HEATHEN SCHOLAR felt he had a sound argument against Christianity when he said, "You say that Christ came into the world to redeem all sinners. If so, what about the millions of souls who died in this world before the advent of Christ? Did they get salvation or not? Who redeemed them?" Many a missionary might have been nonplussed as to how to satisfy the old scholar. This brings us at once to the source of much failure in reading our Bible aright. There is much haziness in our minds about the Person and presence and redeeming activity of the eternal Son of God in Old Testament times. Even among the orthodox there is deep need of the opening of the understanding that we might understand the Old Testament Scriptures concerning Christ.

In discussing the Old and New Testaments, we are not discussing two books. There is but one Book and one Person, and that Person is the eternal Christ, the center and sum and substance of the one redemption.

I. REGARDING CHRIST IN THE OLD TESTAMENT

(1) *As set forth Declaratively.*

When John would introduce Jesus, he goes back into the dateless days of eternity and traces Him step by step down until "the Word became flesh and tabernacled among us." Note the first five verses of his Gospel. In verses 1 and 2 John declares the eternity of Christ, as well as His distinctness from God the Father. In verse 3 we are introduced to time and creation; here, as in Col. 1:16, absolute creation is ascribed directly to Christ. In verse 4 Christ is set forth as the very Light and Life of men, particularly of our unfallen parents. Verse 5 presupposes the fall, and man is seen "sitting in darkness

266

and in the shadow of death." Behold the invisible and ever-shining Christ in His presence in all Old Testament times, a Presence indeed "rejected of men," but still the Light, the Light personal, persistent, and inextinguishable.

Note that John has introduced this eternal Christ, the Creator and Light and Life of men, as "the Word," that Person of the Trinity apart from whom God has never acted or spoken. Faber sang,

> *"O marvellous, O worshipful!*
> *No song or sound is heard,*
> *But everywhere and every hour,*
> *In love, in wisdom, and in power,*
> *the Father speaks His dear eternal Word."*

God has never been articulate except through Christ, whether in *Creation* or in *Communication* or in *Redemption*. In Bethlehem's Babe, then, we are introduced to no new Person. Micah tells us that His "goings forth have been from the days of eternity" (Micah 5:2, margin). His is an eternal generation; from everlasting to everlasting He is God. God Himself addresses the Son as from dateless eternity when He says, "Thy throne, O God, is for ever and ever." In His relation to redemption, Christ was God's Lamb "verily foreordained before the foundation of the world." Christ's activity, as well as His history, began long before He appeared as Bethlehem's Babe.

(2) *As set forth Predictively.*

(a) In the *covenants,* with Adam after the fall and with Abraham in promise, God has obligated Himself in great agreements of grace. No sooner had man fallen than the Lord God revealed redemption through the blood of "the Lamb slain from the foundation of the world" (Rev. 13:8). To Abraham He promised that "in Thy seed [which is Christ] shall all the nations of the earth be blessed" (Gen. 22:18). One might find Christ, yea, must see Christ, as basic to all covenant realities.

(b) It is very obvious to every orthodox believer today that *prophecy* abounds with specific predictions of the coming One who by the sacrifice of Himself would put away sin. In Gen. 3:15 we have the germ of all Messianic prophecy; herein is the acorn of the mighty oak of all future Messianic prediction. So obvious was it from Old Testament Scriptures that Messiah would come in human form that unbelieving Caiaphas could intelligently adjure Jesus to confess whether or not He was "the Christ, the Son of the living God." So well known were the verbal prophecies of Christ as Son of God and King of Israel that orthodox Jews of Jesus' day needed no instruction in that connection. The whole question was not, Who was Christ? but whether or not Jesus was the Christ. In his very first sermon at Damascus, Saul of Tarsus did not immediately "preach *Christ* in the synagogues that He is the Son of God" but rather, "In the synagogues he proclaimed *Jesus,* that He is the Son of God" (Acts 9:20, R.V.). It was unnecessary to declare to any orthodox Jew of that day that Christ was the Son of God, for he had always believed that. The burning question, the question of all questions with the Jew, was whether Jesus was indeed the very Christ, the Christ already long known to be the Son of God, and predicted to come into the world. The question therefore was not one of *definition* but rather one of *identification.*

Another question which perplexed the Jews was how Christ in His human advent could both die and live forever, some concluding that possibly there must needs be two Messiahs, one to die and another to continue. In his preaching, therefore, Paul showed first from the Old Testament that Christ should both die and rise again, and secondly that Jesus answered to that One.

(c) Old Testament *history* abounds with figures of the great redemption. Israel's deliverance from bondage in Egypt shadows forth deliverance from foes more mighty than Pharaoh. David's reign prefigures that of His greater Son. The uplifted Serpent symbolizes the Messiah "made sin." Jonah images forth His death and resurrection. The smitten rock points to the smitten Christ, the descending manna and the shewbread to the true Bread from heaven, the lamp in the holy place to the true Light that would come into the world.

(3) *As set forth in Vital Presence.*

(a) To spiritual understanding. When the Jews would set Moses over against Jesus, He boldly told them that "they [Old Testament

Scriptures] are they which testify of Me." Did Jesus here mean no more than predictions concerning Himself? Surely He meant that the Old Testament bore testimony to *Him* — His presence therein — to all who had eyes to see Him. "For had ye believed Moses, ye would have believed Me: for he wrote of Me" (John 5:46).

This observation brings us to a very pointed and severe reproof. Our failure to see Christ in the Old Testament is charged to unbelief, and brings us under the accusation of Paul when he said of the legalistic Jews, "Until this day remaineth the same vail [of blindness and unbelief] untaken away in the reading of the old testament" (II Cor. 3:14). Paul asserts that it is heart trouble that blinds us in our reading of the Old Testament. Only the God-anointed eye can find Christ there. Pascal's immortal saying applies here: "One must love divine things in order to understand them." The remedy for the Pharisee of old and for us today is the same: When they turn to the Lord, the vail shall be done away. Remember that Moses and the prophets ministered Christ to those of old even as all Scripture should minister Christ to us. Regarding the Old Testament Scriptures, Professor Denney says:

> We smile sometimes at what seems the whimsical way in which the early Christians, who had not yet a New Testament, found Christ everywhere in the Old; but though it may be possible to err in detail in this pursuit, it is not possible to err on the whole. The Old Testament is gathered up, every living word of it in Him; we are misunderstanding it if we take it otherwise.

We fear that the indictment written by Paul against the Pharisaic Jews can well apply to many of us today: "Until this day remaineth the same vail untaken away in the reading of the old testament; which vail is done away in Christ" (II Cor. 3:14). Notice that Paul does not say "done away in *Jesus*," but "in *Christ*," i.e., in Christ in the Old Testament, for Paul is speaking here not of Jesus in the New Testament (for there was no written New Testament), but of Christ in the Old Testament.

Is Christ the solution to the reader's religious perplexities? Can the Saviour solve every problem and lift the veil of perplexity from your Old Testament? In this connection Professor Denney says,

"Much of the religious doubt and confusion of our own times is due to the preoccupation of men's minds with religion at points from which Christ is invisible. But it is He who is the key to *all* human experiences as well as to the Old Testament." If it is true that we can

> *"Behind Creation's throbbing screen*
> *Catch movements of the great Unseen,"*

it is much more true that the anointed eye can see behind the Old Testament page the living Word. Even the Giver of law becomes visible therein as the Giver of life. A. H. Strong says that "A manuscript of the U. S. Constitution was so written that when held at a little distance the shading of the letters and their position showed the countenance of George Washington." If we are in humble focus, we shall see far more of the glorious face of Christ in the Old Testament Scriptures.

Jesus rebuked the Jews, "Ye search the scriptures, because ye think that in them ye have eternal life [in the mere letter therof]; and these [very Scriptures] are they which bear witness of Me" (John 5:39, R.V.). It is as though He had said: Those very Old Testament Scriptures testify of Me, talk of Me, predict of and point to Me; and My face you should find there.

We need not be too afraid of "the wild extravagance in which some have indulged in spiritualizing Scripture." We need rather bewail being destitute of that illumination which sees beyond the *letter* and discerns the *Lord.* Let us be raptured and ravished with Christ, the Beloved, who throughout the Old Testament "standeth behind our wall, He looketh forth at the windows, shewing Himself through the lattice" (Cant. 2:9).

(b) In historical illustration. In the Old Testament account of Moses' flight from Egypt, we read nothing of Christ or of His reproach, yet in Heb. 11:26 the Spirit says that Moses esteemed "the reproach of Christ greater riches than the treasures in Egypt." Likewise there is no verbal mention of Christ in connection with Israel's multiplied provocations of God in the desert, yet Paul exhorts the Corinthians, "neither let us tempt Christ, as some of them also tempted" (I Cor. 10:9). Historical illustrations almost without number could be brought in to reveal that Christ has always been the "rejected of men." Was He not slain in Abel, sold in Joseph, sawn asunder in Isaiah, and plunged into prison in Jeremiah? In which of the prophets was He not persecuted? Did He not die and rise again in Isaac and in Jonah, and was He not "in deaths oft" as David fled from Saul? Did He not die a thousand deaths before he yielded up the ghost on Golgotha's brow? It is written in the Psalms, "The reproaches of them that reproached thee are fallen upon Me."

(c) In type and symbol. Christ was most vitally set forth, however, to Old Testament believers in the tabernacle with all its furnishings and offerings. The true Israelite saw in the altar, the candlestick, the shewbread, the veil, etc., the deep truths signified therein of the then-present Christ. David in Psalm 51 perceived a deeper hidden wisdom than that on the surface of the law and the ordinances; he saw the truth stated by the writer to the Hebrews concerning the tabernacle and its services: "The Holy Ghost this signifying [i.e., through these Old Testament symbols and sacrifices], that the way into the holiest of all [never other than the Lamb slain from the foundation of the world] was not yet made manifest [in human form]" (Heb. 9:8). Thus until Christ appeared in a greater and more perfect tabernacle, He *was being manifested* to broken and believing hearts through the earthly symbols of the invisible One. The Holy Spirit was there doing His office work of pointing to Christ, as yet preincarnate but about to be revealed.

The law did indeed have "a shadow of good things to come," but the writer to the Hebrews adds that in those ancient sacrifices there was not "the very image of the [heavenly] things" (Heb. 10:1). Dr. Griffith Thomas understands the phrase, "image of the things," as "expressing present reality, though, of course, with its fullness hereafter." Space forbids mention of how those unblemished myriad thousands of sacrifices symbolized the then-hidden, but now revealed, "Passover . . . sacrificed for us." The many and familiar types were all prophetic of the great Antitype, and symbolic of the then-present Redeemer. Those semblances of invisible realities, given to convey light, set forth in substance and meaning the glories of the one and only Mediator. Until He should appear in human frame and form, men were being shut up to Him through that typical form of description and manifestation. By means unmistakable, great doctrines concerning Christ invisible were secured through tabernacle types and testimony, and the Holy Ghost was there "signifying" through those means "the way into the holiest of all."

What shall we more say, for time and space fail to tell of "bloodstained altars more eloquent than words; the lowing oxen, the flashing steel, the dripping blood; the burning flesh, daily, weekly, monthly, yearly. Could ought be more telling and repulsive? To a thoughtful Israelite could anything have spoken more eloquently of the horror and loathsomeness of sin?" (Wilkes). In all these behold the one divine attraction, "the Lamb of God that taketh away the sin of the world." With due reverence, then, let us enter in with the anointed eye, for "in His temple every whit of it uttereth His glory" (Psa. 29:9, marg.).

II. Regarding Salvation
(1) Similarities, Differences, Comparisons.

There is a widespread tendency to contrast the Old and New Testaments instead of to compare them. This tendency may be traced chiefly to the fact that the false views of Judaism regarding the law demanded drastic treatment, and the New Testament writers therefore were obliged to deal with the utterly mistaken conceptions concerning the Old Testament. We must consider that the Judaism of Jesus' day represented a perversion of the Mosaic economy and testimony, and it is to offset these misrepresentations of the Old that the gospel writers are strong in their assertions of an opposite tenor and direction. They were compelled under the circumstances to press home the differences on account of the Jewish abuse of their own Old Testament.

No better illustration of this drastic handling of the Old can be found than that set forth by the apostle Paul in II Cor. 3, where he makes the difference between the Old and the New so great as to seem to be a gulf forever fixed. As a zealot of the law, Saul had shared all the former bondage and formality and legalism which so characterized apostate Judaism. Deliverance from that bondage had been so great that it was a literal passing from death to life, from the letter to the Spirit, from condemnation to salvation. He therefore writes in this chapter with the purpose to deliver his believing brethren completely from every shred of that old legalistic bondage. Professor Denney well says that Paul "here sets the Old and the New in unrelieved opposition to each other . . . He speaks as if the Old Covenant and the New had nothing in common . . . The essence of the Old was the law, written in letters with its uninspiring imperative . . . The essence of the New was spirit . . . The contrast is made absolute, *pro tem.* There is no 'spirit' in the Old at all; there is no 'letter' in the New."

Does Paul always thus contrast the Old with the New? Does He always set forth the Old Testament as though it had no spiritual aspect or as though it revealed no grace? The great Apostle would have been the last to say such a thing when speaking in general or in other circumstances. In Corinth, and in Galatia especially, Paul dealt drastically with certain errors and situations. Under other circumstances he was guided differently. Did he not, along with all the other apostles, appeal to the Old Testament in support of the gospel which he preached? Was it not his boast that he said "none other things than those which the prophets and Moses did say should come"? Both he and Peter preached that "to Christ give all the prophets witness," and that there is "none other name under heaven given among men whereby we must be saved." When the Bereans, more noble than others, searched the Old Testament Scriptures for confirmation of Paul's preaching, "many of them believed." They found, with Augustine, that the New Testament is *en*folded in the Old, and the Old Testament is *un*folded in the New. In his great doctrinal defense of the resurrection, he reminds the Corinthians, "I delivered unto you first of all that which I also received, how that Christ died for our sins according to the scriptures; and that He was buried, and that He rose again the third day according to the scriptures" (I Cor. 15:3, 4).

It is generally admitted by orthodox believers that an essential unity subsists between the old and the new dispensations. Certainly the spiritual realities in both dispensations are found to be identical in their basic inner elements. Few expositors would question that the great truths touching on God, man, sin, grace, faith, forgive-

ness, righteousness, justification, sanctification, redemption, salvation, personal accountability, and final destiny far outweigh some
outer and detailed dissimilarities between the Old and the New. In
comparing the Old and New Testament dispensations, we need to
observe the saying, "On the outside of things look for differences,
on the inside for likenesses" (Hare, in Fairbairn's *Typology of
Scripture*). It is wisdom on our part to seek the distinct unity between the Old and the New in these internal and basic agreements
rather than in the external similarities or differences.

The whole counsel of God's gospel is found in germ in Genesis
3:15. This was the gospel preached before unto Abraham, who, in
New Testament language, is the faith-father of all believers. Concerning that gospel we read that "unto us was the gospel preached,
as well as unto them: but the word preached did not profit them,
not being mixed with faith in them that heard it" (Heb. 4:2). Here,
as throughout the entire New Testament, when the apostles seek to
warn New Testament believers against lust and sin, they draw their
lessons from the failures of Old Testament believers. Now unless
their salvation was similar, wherein would Old Testament believers
constitute "ensamples for our admonition"? The Old Testament
word "salvation" is used in a very personal sense, meaning Jesus
personally (Jehovah-Saviour, or Je-sus). Let us not attach a merely
temporal or carnal meaning to the word "salvation" in the Old
Testament. When the dying Jacob said, "I have waited for Thy
salvation," he was testifying to the reality of eternal life in Jehoshua, or Jesus (i.e., salvation). It is further remarkable that mercy
and salvation form the continuous refrain of Old Testament saints,
the word "salvation" occurring three times as often in the Old Testament as in the New. The set refrain of Israel's singing was, "The
Lord is good, and His mercy endureth forever."

Has the reader ever reflected upon Jesus' reproof of Nicodemus
for not knowing that he should be born again? His reproof of
this ruler of the Jews for his failure to understand the truth of regeneration makes it clear that the doctrine of the new birth must
have been sufficiently revealed in the Old Testament so that Nicodemus was to be blamed for his ignorance. "Nor is it merely a
something that should be experienced under the [New Testament]

gospel that the Old Testament holds it forth — as many distinguished critics allege, denying that there was any such thing as regeneration before Christ" (David Brown). Likewise we must remember that if salvation and forgiveness were not available before Calvary, then the ministry of Jesus Himself was ineffective before His death. Yet where did He drop a hint that anyone had to wait until after His death before he could be saved? Was He not introduced three years before Calvary as "the Lamb of God which *taketh* away the sin of the world"?

(2) *Through Christ, the one and only Way.*

Our previous remarks in connection with the Person and presence of Christ in the Old Testament apply here also to Him in all His redeeming activity. It is passing strange how we can possibly think of any kind of salvation in the Old Testament apart from the Person of the Redeemer. Yet in spite of this self-evident fact, it is not too much to say that the common conception of many orthodox believers today regarding the saints of old is that they, for all practical purposes, were "unitarian" in their thinking, experience, and theology. The unbelieving Jews of Jesus' day could do better than that. We have already pointed out that the wretched ruler, Caiaphas, with only his Old Testament in his hand, understood about Christ and His coming into the world, and therefore put Jesus under oath to confess whether or not He was that Christ, the Son of the living God. Much more then did the little flock of believers "wait for the consolation of Israel."

One of these was Simeon. It had been revealed unto him by the Holy Ghost that he would not see death until he had seen the Lord's Christ. Must he not already have known the Lord's Christ in his heart? With him, therefore, it was not a question of defining the Lord's Christ (who was already his known salvation) but, as has been pointed out, it was a question of identifying Him. When, therefore, Simeon came by the Spirit into the temple, he identified the Christ with the child Jesus, and taking Him up in his arms he said, "Lord, now lettest Thou Thy servant depart in peace, according to Thy word: For mine eyes have seen Thy *salvation*" (i.e.,

Thy *Jesus*). For remember that, whether or not Simeon knew the Child's name, he would have said in the Hebrew, "mine eyes have seen Thy Jehoshua," or Joshua, which is the same as Jesus. (See Heb. 4:8, marg.) Recall also that Simeon was a typical Old Testament believer. Like Moses he esteemed the reproach of Christ. With other saints of old, Simeon drank of the same Rock that had long before been smitten, and from that Rock of their salvation all true Israelites have been sustained.

If "the Spirit of Christ which was in them" — *in* and not merely *on* the old Testament prophets — "testified beforehand the sufferings of Christ, and the glory that should follow," should it seem strange to us to believe that these prophets must have ministered the same Christ to men in days of old? Whether Old Testament prophets or New Testament apostles, they all agreed in Christ. The aim of the Old Testament is (always was) Christ; the aim of the New Testament is Christ Jesus. The end and aim are all the same. The only reason why we might think this to be undue spiritualizing is that we are, as the risen Saviour said, slow of heart to believe all that the prophets have spoken. What is this but to fail to render unto Christ that which has "from of old borne His indelible mark and superscription"?

Take the case of Nathanael, a typical Old Testament character with no New Testament instruction. No sooner had Jesus intimated His firsthand knowledge of this Israelite in whom there was no guile than Nathanael burst out, "Rabbi, Thou art the Son of God; Thou art the King of Israel." Nathanael, tell me, whence this knowledge? Your guileless heart has surely helped your understanding, for you have your ancient Scriptures aright! Notice that Nathanael, with no New Testament teaching, needed no definitions about Christ and God's Son. He needed only spiritual identification with Jesus as that One. Had he not long known that David said, "The LORD [God] said unto my Lord [Jesus Christ], Sit Thou on My right hand, Until I make Thy foes Thy footstool" (Acts 2:34, 35)? Did he not certainly know that David's greater Son would be divine, that He would come from above, that David's Son had been David's Lord, and that the Root of David would one day be born of David's race? Even better than that, Nathanael, along with others like Simeon and Anna — "the poor of the flock" — had a spiritual apprehension that outran and outread any mere verbal prophecies of the Christ, the one and only way of salvation.

No sooner did Je-sus (Saviour) appear in the greater and more perfect tabernacle than Heaven had a new message, the Holy Ghost signifying that "the way into the holiest of all" was now "manifested in the flesh" — the one and only way, so long known by all the regenerated souls of Old Testament times. How did the "little flock" so quickly and instinctively sense the Saviour in Jesus? Was it not that, like Simeon, they already knew in heart "the Lord's Christ"?

(3) *Through Faith Alone.*

"I am Jehovah, I change not." If anyone teaches that there is salvation in any dispensation on terms other than grace, pure unadulterated grace, he has difficulty escaping the charge that he has brought into question the unchanging character of God. The writer was brought up for a time on ultra-dispensationalism, and can bear witness to the effects of this teaching on one's conception of the All-wise. First, God must be different in this present day, when all is given in free grace. A little girl who had been led to believe that God was harsh and severe in those old days could solve the painful mystery only by concluding, "Oh, that was before God became a Christian." In the second place, one might feel very fortunate to have been born on this side of the Cross, when salvation is by grace alone, rather than during those days when God was conducting a works-righteousness experiment on Israel. It will not do for extreme dispensationalists to say that they mean to have no such effect on their listeners, for these are the conclusions to which their thinking followers come. The unchanging character of God suffers at their hands, and Jehovah is not demonstrated to us in their teaching as the Lord that changes not.

In that great classic on righteousness by faith, namely Rom. 3:21-31, Paul clinches his argument by stating that God is the God not "of the Jews only," but "also of the Gentiles." Then he declares salvation can never be otherwise than by faith alone, "seeing it is one God, which shall justify the circumcision by faith, and uncircumcision through faith" (v. 30). The R.V. makes it more emphatic: "If so be that God is one." Paul's argument, then, is that God's unity and unchangeable character confirm His equalization of salvation by faith for all, whether they be Jews or Gentiles, whether of the Old Testament or New Testament times. Beyond contradiction, the consistent unity and unchangeable character of God are at stake in this question.

No sooner has Paul proved the indispensableness of the righteousness of faith for Jew and Gentile alike, and that "the true God is equally the God of all" (Moule), than he proceeds to illustrate this righteousness, the righteousness so long "witnessed by the law and the prophets" (Rom. 3:21). To whom does he now appeal for support but to Abraham and David? Abraham illustrates the righteousness of faith, while David illustrates the blessedness, as well as the righteousness, of faith — both of these men being brought in to illustrate "being justified freely by His grace." Abraham preceded the dispensation of law; David lived during the dispensation of law. Both were justified, Paul says, "not of works." We can therefore understand how Paul would say to his successor, Timothy, "From a babe thou hast known the [Old Testament] sacred writings which are able to make thee wise unto salvation through faith which is in Christ Jesus" (II Tim. 3:15, R.V.). It is quite evident that to Abraham and Moses and David and all the righteous of the Old Testament, faith was indeed the substance of things hoped for and the evidence of things not yet seen.

When we look for characters and lives and deeds to provoke us to faith, do we not find them chiefly in the Old Testament? The New Testament writers often refer to Abraham and to David. Where did the writer to the Hebrews go for his great album of faith heroes but to the Old Testament? And concerning them he concludes, "These all, having had witness borne to them through their faith" (Heb. 11:39, R.V.). Then he adds another significant little phrase to the effect that these all "received not the promise." This does not mean, as W. C. Stevens has so well pointed out, that they had only a prospective, "hope-so" kind of salvation; nor, when it is added that God had "provided some better thing for us," does this imply that we have substance whereas they had only shadows. The better thing is not salvation, or a better salvation; the "better thing" is Christ's having appeared in human frame and form and having "once-for-all" accomplished an eternal redemption, all of which has given us a much wider understanding and grasp of gospel content. We needed some better thing, for the simple reason that the sinking nations were found in a depravity such as is described in Romans 1. Lest we should become conceited, however, let us remember that in the coming millennial age those generations will inherit such a further increase of depravity and apostasy and lawlessness that God will give them a still "better thing." The Son of God will judge the nations, bind the devil, rule with a rod of iron, and force all men to live at least outwardly righteous lives. With no adversary to "deceive the whole world," and with such manifest evidence of Christ's kingship and power, the coming age will indeed have a "better thing."

Perhaps the phrase, "some better thing for us," should not be taken entirely apart from the context which follows: "that they without us should not be made perfect." This signifies that while we have indeed experienced better things in God's program in the now-manifested Saviour, beyond the understanding of Old Testament worthies, yet they of the Old and we of the New are alike waiting for the full consummation of God's program in Christ, "who is *over all*, God blessed forever. Amen." Even as Abraham looked for a city with foundations, we too "seek one to come." When we finally come to the great consummation, when "they with us shall be made perfect," what a beautiful commingling of Old Testament and New Testament features appear in the New Jerusalem! Behold in that final focussing point of the ages of redemption, the beautiful unity of all biblical revelations and dispensations! The Holy City has twelve appointed avenues of entrance, on which gates of pearl are "the names of the twelve tribes of the children of Israel"; this city, with walls so great and high, has twelve foundations, "and in them the names of the twelve apostles of the Lamb." Here, then, has dawned that day when many shall come from the east and from the west, Gentiles of like faith with the Roman centurion, and shall sit down with Abraham and Isaac and Jacob in the kingdom of heaven.

(4) *Vital and Experimental.*

A man of God was once preaching with great liberty and joy on the full blessings of Pentecost. He made it unmistakably clear that "never before that eventful day could such blessings have been realized." Having completed his message upon this premise, he announced that in his next message he would consider illustrations of these hitherto unknown Pentecostal blessings — and in this next sermon what did he do but preach on Hebrews, Chapter 11, finding all his illustrations of this amazing life from the experiences of these who had lived before Pentecost. We have often said that we are sure God blessed both messages, in spite of the fact that in the second he flatly contradicted the first.

Differences among well-meaning orthodox expositors are more often differences of the head than of the heart. Sad to say, however, pride of heart often prevents the head from following the more logical and Scriptural conclusions. Differences of premise are most often the beginnings of differences in exposition and understanding of Scriptures; after that, pride of heart, fear of reputation for fickleness, and the difficulty of breaking caste or of losing cash — all these are determining factors that hold leaders to their traditions (be they old or new) and militate against further teaching of the Spirit.

There are others who see a little further and concede the regeneration of Old Testament saints, but they have a very uncertain conception of Christ as the living, redeeming Agent of such regeneration in those ancient times. Their illumination is therefore still partial, and inadequate to give them exultation and joy in their reading of the Old Testament. Until they come to see the Old Testament Scriptures and the New as one vast panorama of the "common salvation," it will be with difficulty that they come up to the spiritual level of the Old Testament Psalmist who exclaimed, "O how love I thy law! it is my meditation all the day."

With each individual believer there is such a thing as having a "hope" with but little "reason" for the hope. Let us remember that, whereas the *reason* of the hope" may not have been entirely clear to many ancient believers, it is, after all, with the *heart* rather

than with the *mind* that man believes unto righteousness.   Faith
can run where mental understanding and articulate knowledge may
be dim or deficient.   Obedient believing through a heart submission to all God's revealed will is a thing vastly more important than
an articulate and verbal conception of hope's "reason."   This is
not said with any desire to diminish the need today of definite doctrinal statements as to the atoning work of the now-manifested Redeemer.   Any reluctance to declare oneself in such connections today reveals a lack of true submission to all that believers can and
should know in this day of clearer gospel revelation.   Justifying
faith, whether in Abraham's day or in this dispensation, implies a
complete submission to all that one knows of the revealed will of
God.   Such submission produces an exulting and rejoicing faith, the
kind enjoyed by both Old and New Testament saints.   Let us not
limit the vital touch and the experimental reach of the one eternal
atonement.   Rather let us span all the ages as we sing,

> *"In the cross of Christ I glory,*
> *Towering o'er the wrecks of time;*
> *All the light of sacred story*
> *Gathers round its head sublime."*

In summarizing the teachings of this chapter, we would say that
three things are to be emphasized:

1. Christ, the Eternal Word, is God's Agent in creation, communication, and redemption throughout the Old Testament as well as
the New Testament.

2. He is the object of all obedient faith of Old Testament saints.

3. Failure to sense and to see "things concerning Himself" in all
Old Testament Scriptures is chiefly the failure of illumination and
faith.   The failure is not so much a lack of mental acumen as a lack
of heart revelation.   Jesus said to some, "Ye do err, not knowing
the scriptures, nor the power of God," therein revealing their need
— a heart need.   In post-resurrection interview, Jesus corrected two
good orthodox believers and "opened their understanding that they
might understand the Scriptures."   Their trouble was also that they
were "slow of heart to believe," not stupid of mind to perceive.
There is entirely too much knifing up the Scriptures with the keen

edge of human intellect. Heart understanding is, as usual, far behind the mental and hairsplitting distinctions of the ultra-dispensationalists today. We are reminded, in closing, of the heavenly wisdom of Felix Neff, the apostle of the Alps:

> Riches and learning have their dangers for the church. The gospel is a plant of the desert and mountains which degenerates with too much culture, too much fertilizer. It then expands into leafage with little fruit" (*A Book of Protestant Saints*, by Ernest Gordon).

APPENDIX B

The Mosaic Covenant

I. *Its Historical Background*

W HEN THE LORD moved to deliver the children of Israel from their bondage, He assured Moses that He was going to fulfill His oath to Abraham, to Isaac, and to Jacob, and that He was going to bring His own out from under the burdens of the Egyptians, rid them of their bondage, and redeem them with a mighty and outstretched arm. The time had come when these people, now grown to nationhood, were to inherit the land of Canaan. As heirs of the Abrahamic covenant, they must now be redeemed from bondage and taken in to possess their possessions.

Moses was instructed to say unto Pharaoh, "Thus saith the LORD, Israel is My son, even My firstborn: And I say unto thee, Let My son go, that he may serve Me" (Ex. 4:22, 23). As the Lord's firstborn, Israel could recall her origin as the seed of promise. In Isaac, the heir of all, their birth and nationhood had been through the supernaturalness of grace. As heir of all the Abrahamic promises, Isaac was the type of all that was to follow.

When Israel, therefore, came out of Egypt under the blood of atonement and covenant, she had been spared that day "as a man spareth his son." Collectively, the Israelites stood as a redeemed unit; as "the children of the LORD their God" (Deut. 14:1), they had been delivered from the doom which had fallen upon the Egyptian world.

This relationship is reiterated and emphasized when at Sinai a few weeks later the Lord said to the children of Israel, "Ye have seen what I did unto the Egyptians, and how I bare you on eagles' wings, and brought you unto Myself" (Ex. 19:4). Nothing could be clearer than that the Lord here reminds His recently redeemed "firstborn" of the blessed grace relationship that they sustained to

Himself. They had been redeemed and brought out of bondage by the mighty hand of Another.

It is all important that we understand the connection between the redemption of Israel from the land of Egypt and the giving of the law at Mount Sinai. Failure to observe this connection has proved to be a source of much confusion concerning the Old Testament, to say nothing of the damage done to the great body of Old Testament revelation from Exodus 19 onward.

II. *"He was King in Jeshurun," i.e., righteous Israel.*

To fail to see that Christ was here the divine King of Israel is to fail in a simple and first principle of Bible understanding. To say that God never reveals Himself except through Christ should be a mere truism to Bible-loving people. In every communication of God's mind, and therefore in the revelation of law, we are to see the eternal "Word" of God in expression. There has ever been but one King of the Jews. It was He who gave the law on Mount Sinai as well as its positive exposition in the Sermon on the Mount. Recall that it was "as seeing Him who is invisible" that Moses was enabled to esteem "the reproach of Christ greater riches than the treasures in Egypt." Moses proclaimed Christ to be "King in Jeshurun." Isaiah exceedingly feared and quaked when he cried out in self-abhorrence, "Woe is me! for I am undone [cut off, Heb.]; because I am a man of unclean lips, and I dwell in the midst of a people of unclean lips: for mine eyes have seen the King, the LORD of hosts" (Isa. 6:5). That this thrice-holy King of Israel was none other than Christ Jesus Himself, John the apostle assures us: "These things said Esaias, when he saw His [Christ's] glory, and spake of Him" (John 12:41). It would be a great blunder indeed to see only a hard and harsh and distant "unitarian" God dealing with Israel at Sinai and throughout the rest of the Old Testament.

We have long felt that it is just here that those few verses in the biography of the preincarnate Christ, as announced by John in his prologue (John 1:1-13), have specific application. Literally, this sentence reads: "He came unto His own things, and His own people received Him not." In all Old Testament times Christ came again and again to His own created possessions. He came to

His own possessions at Sinai, but His own people received Him not. From the golden calf to Golgotha's brow, He was rejected by "His own." When Israel demanded a visible king, did not Samuel lament that they had rejected their King Divine? Did not the King Himself say to the broken-hearted prophet, "They have not rejected thee, but they have rejected Me, that I should not reign over them" (I Sam. 8:7).

It gives new meaning to the gracious character of the Lord and King at Sinai to realize that the One through whom God is here speaking can be none other — Has He ever spoken through any other? — than our very Christ; and that when He proclaims "the name of the LORD" in all His redeeming activity and intimacy, He does so as "the LORD God, merciful and gracious, longsuffering, and abundant in goodness and truth, Keeping mercy for thousands, forgiving iniquity and transgression and sin, and that will by no means clear the guilty" (Ex. 34:6, 7).

III. *The Approach of the King.*

We must face the fact, however, that in His giving of the law at Sinai the Divine King manifested Himself primarily as One "great and dreadful," whose majesty was terrible to behold. Moses himself did exceedingly fear and quake. This revelation was quite in keeping with the character of the divine administration so necessary at this introduction of Himself to the nation as King.

As He was about to enter into new covenant relationships with His people, He reminded them that He was to them their Redeemer from bondage, who had also brought them to Himself on eagles' wings of purest grace. "Now, *therefore*," — what volumes in these words! In view of your recent redemption and on the basis thereof — "Now therefore, if ye will obey My voice indeed, and keep My covenant, then ye shall be a peculiar treasure unto Me above all people: for all the earth is mine: And ye shall be unto Me a kingdom of priests, and an holy nation" (Ex. 19:5, 6). Although the King here approached His people as Lawgiver, He reminded them first of their relationship to Himself — a relationship of grace. As a nation they were on the ground of the one eternal atonement, viz., that of the "Lamb slain from the foundation of the world." The

"I Am" before Abraham's day was the very "I Am that I Am" who had revealed Himself to Moses as their Redeemer and Deliverer. His relationship to them until then had been that of *Redeemer*. Now the Redeemer comes to them as *King* with *requirement*. First *redemption*, then *requirement*. How like the New Testament this sounds! The Saviour says to "His own" today, "If ye love Me, keep My commandments." So here at Sinai the constraint of their grace relationship is first brought before Israel that they may be encouraged to believe that "their Redeemer is strong" and that He is ready to assist them to obey to the full. Let us repeat: By the constraints of a great redemption they are to be moved to obedience.

They are here at the very outset led to believe that, if they are indeed to fulfill their high calling and inherit that which has been promised them in the existing Abrahamic covenant, they must needs obey His voice. When He comes down upon Mount Sinai to make His rightful claims upon their obedience, He again reminds them of His existing relationship as Redeemer, and prefaces the giving of the law with, "I am the LORD thy God, which have brought thee out of the land of Egypt, out of the house of bondage." It was not by obedience they had been brought out of Egypt, but by redemption and grace alone. Now He claims the right to their full obedience. That claim He bases upon an already existing relationship, viz., that of a redemption. The relationship is that of redemption; the requirement is that of obedience. On the basis of the former He claims the latter. He had redeemed them from the Egyptian world, and had brought them out that He might bring them into the land of their inheritance. Through a grace relationship in the Abrahamic promise, "confirmed before in Christ," the inheritance had been promised them. It was an already promised land. How would they now be able to enter into their promised inheritance, possess their possessions, and fulfill their high destiny? How would they become "a people peculiarly His," "a people for His own possession"? By no other way than the *rugged road of obedience*.

This approach is not different in principle from that reasoned by the Lord Himself when the Abrahamic covenant was confirmed to

Isaac. To this son of promise the Lord appeared and said, "I will perform the oath which I sware unto Abraham thy father; . . . Because that Abraham obeyed My voice, and kept My charge, My commandments, My statutes, and My laws" (Gen. 26:3-5). Do not, my reader, think that such a conditional element is grace confused. This is grace fulfilled. Let us go back a step further. When Abraham, the father of this race of "the firstborn," bound his son upon the altar, Jehovah-jireh, who spared not His only Son, confirmed the covenant with Abraham saying, "By myself have I sworn, saith the LORD, for *because thou hast done this thing,* and hast not withheld thy son, thine only son: That in blessing I will bless thee, . . . And in thy seed shall all the nations of the earth be blessed; *because thou hast obeyed My voice*" (Gen. 22:16-18). Doubtless those who would overemphasize the unconditional element in the covenant with Abraham would like to eliminate the various mentions in Genesis of Abraham's obedient faith, but it is to be noted that it was only after this final testing of Abraham's faith that God confirmed the promise with an oath.

If it is not already unmistakably clear that God blessed Abraham and his posterity because of the patriarch's obedient faith, the matter is put beyond question on the occasion of the patriarch's priestly intercession before the destruction of Sodom and Gomorrah. The Lord says, "Shall I hide from Abraham that thing which I do; Seeing that Abraham shall surely become a great and mighty nation, and all the nations of the earth shall be blessed in him? For I know him, that he will command his children and his household after him and they shall keep the way of the LORD, to do justice and judgment; that [i.e., in order that] the LORD may bring upon Abraham that which He hath spoken of him" (Gen. 18:17-19). It seems clear that Abraham's proper ordering of his household in the steps of his own obedient faith made sure to him the promises of the Lord in the covenant. Those who insistently seek to eliminate any and every human responsibility in their zeal to steady the ark of grace are becoming known by their fruits — their failure to forward the practical holiness and obedient faith of God's people. Only the willing and obedient eat the good of the land.

IV. *The King's Proposal*

When the Lord proposed the requirement of obedience, it was "in order that" as heirs of the promise they might become unto Him "a peculiar treasure above all people, a kingdom of priests, and an holy nation." How otherwise could they be peculiarly His as "a kingdom of priests, and an holy nation" except they be an obedient people? The divine King knew that only as His own became lovingly obedient and loyal subjects could they ever inherit the promises or fulfill Heaven's high destiny for them as a kingdom.

The response of the people to their King's proposal was properly, "All that the LORD hath spoken we will do." Just here we must proceed carefully, for here are hidden rocks where natural reason has often wrecked and gone completely astray. On the presupposition that law, the law which is "holy, just, good," and even "spiritual," is essentially contrary to the grace of God, expositors have missed their way at this point. It has been said that the Israelites "rashly accepted the law," that they here "exchanged grace for law." Another writer and advocate of ultra-dispensationalism says:

> When the law was proposed, the children of Israel deliberately forsook their position under the grace of God which had been their relationship to God until that day; and placed themselves under the law . . . While it is certain that Jehovah knew the choice the people would make, it is equally certain that their choice was in no way *required* by Him . . . Until that hour they had been sustained in the faithfulness of Jehovah and without the slightest reference to their wickedness; but His plan and purpose for them had remained unchanged. He had dealt with them according to the unconditional covenant of grace made with Abraham . . . The surrender of the blessings of grace should have been allowed by these people on no condition whatever, etc.

Leaders of a certain school of thought have agreed together that the Israelites should have declined the proposal of the law. This teacher actually goes so far as to say that Israel, instead of responding, "All that the LORD hath spoken we will do," should have said, "None of these things can we do. We crave only to remain in that boundless mercy of God, who loved us and sought us and saved us from all our enemies and who will bring us to Himself." Then he adds that "such an appeal would have reached the very heart of God." Then he further adds that the Israelites "were called upon to face a concrete choice between the mercy of God which had followed them, and a new and hopeless covenant of works."

Several of these statements call for serious analysis and consideration.

1. "A new and hopeless covenant of works." To presume that the Lord Christ, "the LORD God, gracious and merciful. . . ," here proposed and imposed upon His redeemed people a covenant of mere human works and meritorious self-righteousness is beyond comprehension. What would this be but to keep people under mere law, or to put the matter bluntly, to make them guinea pigs upon which to conduct an experiment for 1,500 years, making them an object lesson to the succeeding ages of "what the law could not do." In fact, an able editor says, "Mankind was put on this footing as a huge dispensational experiment of God." If this be indeed a covenant of hopeless human works whereby is founded a title to the Abrahamic inheritance, then the Lord Himself, "who changeth not," has indeed contradicted Himself in His former covenant of promise. The Abrahamic covenant "confirmed before of God in Christ," wherein is promised life and righteousness, was then nullified and abrogated by God Himself. This, however, is in plain contradiction to the assertion of Paul in Gal. 3:21: "For if there had been a law given which could have given life, verily righteousness should have been by the law." That the covenant of law was never intended as such to convey life is plainly stated in Gal. 3:17, 18: "And this I say, that the covenant, that was confirmed before of God in Christ, the law, which was four hundred and thirty years after, cannot disannul, that it should make the promise of none effect. For if the inheritance be of the law, it is no more of promise: but God gave it to Abraham by promise."

It is pathetically true that the ultra-dispensationalists have taken almost the same position concerning the design of the Mosaic legislation as the degenerate Jews had come to assume by New Testament times. Surely no one should assume that the Judaism of Jesus' day represented the divine intent of the economy as laid down by Moses. Even Saul of Tarsus, the very best specimen of those living within "the righteousness which is in the law, blameless," had to confess that he did many things stubbornly and "ignorantly in unbelief." He needed and "obtained mercy." His ignorance was due to his unbelief, and in this wicked unbelief lay the cause of his blind persecution of the Lord's Anointed. How then can the Pharisaic Judaism of Jesus' day be regarded otherwise than as a misrepresentation of the meaning and message of Moses? If, on the other hand, one regards conceited Phariseeism of that day as the intended expression and natural product of the Mosaic legislation — which it would be if that covenant were one of mere works in contrast to grace — it is not strange if that person lacks a proper spiritual understanding of most of the Old Testament.

The Pharisaic Jews of Paul's day had assigned an utterly wrong place to the law, assuming that it was the divine intention that they should through human works of self-righteousness merit a title to everlasting life. In their degeneracy and blindness they confidently contended that the law had been given to found a works-title to righteousness. We can scarcely imagine the Promiser of life in the Adamic and Abrahamic covenants so changing His method of dealing with His already redeemed people as to disannul the former covenant of promise, thereby making His proposal at Sinai a virtual overthrow of the Abrahamic covenant. It should not be difficult to see that the Pharisaic and conceited Jews of Jesus' day had utterly perverted the meaning of the Mosaic legislation into a dispensation of works-righteousness, which utterly contradicted the Abrahamic promises in Christ. Nor should we rashly presume that He who had manifested salvation by grace ever since the fall of man should suddenly alter the basic condition of entrance into life to that of a hopeless covenant of works. That a fundamental expositor should fall into precisely the same error as that of the carnally minded Jews and reduce the covenant of the Lord Christ at Sinai to a mere covenant of human works, is, to say the least, a revelation of how completely astray we can wander from the Scriptures, once we assume a false premise.

2. "While it is certain that Jehovah knew the choice the people would make, it is equally certain that their choice was in no way *required* by Him." This statement calls for special consideration.

It has already been pointed out that if the Mosaic legislation was a strict covenant of works then Israel's Lord contradicted His former covenant with Abraham. The present statement, that the people's response, "All that the Lord hath spoken we will do," "was in no way *required*" by the Lord, is to impugn the Divine character and wisdom. It is nothing short of charging the All-wise and the All-good with stooping to adopt methods and expedients such as would ill become an earthly king or ruler. Can we imagine the most High, in all His infinite majesty and wisdom, stooping to mock His people and catch them with a kind of practice which no earthly ruler would be guilty of employing? We have long wondered just what answer could have been possible other than that contained in Israel's response to the covenant proposed at Sinai. Whether or not we agree with the eschatological views of Professor Oswald T. Allis we believe he rightly questions whether certain expositors "seriously face the question as to what the result would have been if Israel had refused this gracious offer of God on the ground — there was no other — that they did not wish to 'obey' His voice" (*Prophecy and the Church*).

The already quoted advocate of extreme dispensationalism seeks a way out of the dilemma when he says that upon hearing the law the people should have said, "None of these things can we do. We crave only to remain in that boundless mercy of God, who loved us and sought us and saved us from all our enemies and who will bring us to Himself." Then he adds, "It is evident that such an appeal would have reached the very heart of God." This would have been a polite way of questioning the wisdom of the proposal of law, and presumably it would have been an indication of Israel's cleverness in catching Jehovah's proposal of a mock covenant.

As proof that this teacher actually assumes the proposal at Sinai to have been but a mock covenant, we quote his own words: "The human family had walked before God on the earth for upwards of 2,500 years prior to the imposition of the law. Thus it had been demonstrated that God is able to deal with men in the earth without reference to the law of Moses." Was the law then a mere proposal which Israel should have rejected? Turn to Jer. 7:22, 23.

When the Lord would reprove backslidden Israel for their merely perfunctory ceremonials and hard-hearted ritualism, He said, "For I spake not unto your fathers, nor commanded them in the day that I brought them out of the land of Egypt, concerning burnt offerings or sacrifices: But this thing commanded I them, saying, Obey My voice, and I will be your God, and ye shall be My people: and walk ye in all the ways that I have commanded you, that it may be well unto you." It is as clear as noonday from this portion, as well as from the proposal Jehovah made at Sinai, that it was no mere option with them whether or not they would promise to obey Him. It is very plainly stated that at Sinai they were commanded, "Obey My voice." Most certainly, then, the Holy One did not descend to the indignity of bargaining with His people about matters of such practical consequence. Much less did He stoop to entrap them into a hopeless covenant of human works in order to conduct a mere experiment which offered to its victims no title to life or grace or glory. To suppose so is to misapprehend and impugn the Divine wisdom and goodness. There is no possible way out of the dilemma which those create for themselves, who state that this was a proposal of human works, but to question the wisdom and motives of the Lawgiver Himself. Such false premises and conclusions at this point finally trace themselves up to the character of the One who gave the law.

The best homely illustration we have found to make Sinai's proposals plain is one in connection with acceptance of students. We accept only those who are already saved — already redeemed and brought out of the bondage of Egypt. In our application form for admission to the student body (which might be likened to "a peculiar people," a "holy nation" and a "kingdom of priests"), we ask the question, "Will you abide by the rules and discipline of the Institute and cheerfully obey those over you in the Lord?" While we know that most of these applicants are quite ignorant of all that is contained in the "book of regulations," nevertheless, like every other such institution that intends to have a well-regulated household, we want the signature of all applicants carte blanche to ascertain whether or not they will conform to the kind of life which will make them real students and prospective workers for Christ.

Now let us suppose that some self-confident and clever student detects in this proposal a kind of catch question, and in order to avoid getting "under law" and to prevent his falling from grace, he writes back:

> DEAR SECRETARY OF P. B. I.
>
> You perhaps have not quite understood that I have been saved from bondage and have been carried hitherto on eagles' wings of grace. I have heard it said that "the Dispensation of Promise ended when Israel rashly accepted the law." I crave only to remain in that boundless mercy of God, who has loved me and sought me and saved me and who will bring me to Himself.
>
> I am sure, Mr. Secretary, that such an appeal will reach your very heart. I prefer not to choose a hopeless covenant of works; and in order to prevent my getting into bondage, will you kindly accept me without asking me to do a lot of impossible things.
>
> _Yours very sincerely,_

We can assure the reader of this book that such an appeal would indeed reach our very heart, and we would know at once what kind of student he would make. How could such an individual ever enter into his promised inheritance of service?

The response of all bona fide applicants is (in substance) as follows: "All that the P.B.I. staff has spoken will we do and be obedient." While it is often true that there is some unwarranted self-confidence, as well as some ignorance of all that is entailed, in that affirmative response — nevertheless, such is the only proper reply, unless they intend, indeed, to be disobedient.

Our inquiry as to whether each applicant intends to obey the rules of this Institute is neither a catch nor a mockery. We know that if students are to become workmen who need not be ashamed they must understand the rules and undergo the discipline of our necessary regulations. Sometimes these regulations are felt to be impossible to the undisciplined and fleshly-minded young people of the present day.

The transactions at Sinai would never have produced such confusion and error had expositors been more practical and sensible. Do such men fear the bondage of responsibility and obedience?

It appears that in fearing bondage more than sin, they have bred disobedience, and as a result have robbed many Christians for all practical purpose of the blessed and eternal principles of obedience enjoined in the Old Testament.

Note the whole tenor and teaching of Israel's King at Sinai: You have seen how I have so graciously redeemed you out of bondage and have brought you unto Myself. Now all the earth and her peoples are Mine, and I would have you to be a kingdom of priests, standing in priestly capacity between the other nations and Myself. If, therefore, you are to fulfill this high calling and realize your Abrahamic inheritance and destiny, you must be peculiarly My possession, i.e., you must become a nation of holy people. I want to know now whether you will be implicitly obedient. Your relationship to Me is already that of a redeemed people; now My requirement of you is that you be obedient. If you love Me, you will keep My commandments. All My dealings with you thus far should lead you to trust and obey.

3. "Until Mount Sinai Israel had been sustained in the faithfulness of Jehovah, and without the slightest reference to their wickedness; but His plan and purpose for them had remained unchanged."

Such a statement is pathetically antinomian and does, when followed, only breed the worst type of lawlessness. In the first place, it is not the tone and tenor of Scripture that God does not change His purposes when men turn against Him. Common sense and Scripture agree on this point. In the second place, what is this but to answer the question, "Shall we continue in sin that grace may abound?" not with Paul's categorical "God forbid," but rather with, "Yes indeed, for God's purposes remain unchanged without the slightest reference to wickedness." In the third place, such a statement presumes that, if by the law comes "the knowledge of sin," then let Israel remain ignorant; give her no law that she may never learn her sin; let "grace reign," but not "through righteousness." Upon the basis, presumably, that "where there is no law there is no transgression," let Israel continue to be borne upon eagles' wings of grace "without the slightest reference to their wickedness."

It is presumed that, although Israel is steeped in sin and destined to become increasingly worse through ignorance thereof, the Lord's purposes of inheritance for her will remain unchanged. The Scripture concerning the corrupt Canaanites flatly contradicts such a presumption. Their "cup of iniquity" was by this time full to the brim, and the Lord Himself says, "The land is defiled: therefore I do visit the iniquity thereof upon it, and the land itself vomiteth out her inhabitants" (Lev. 18:25). The warning to Israel was to take heed "that the land spue not you out also, when ye defile it, as it spued out the nations that were before you" (Lev. 18:28). How then can anyone dare to say that compliance with Heaven's proposal for implicit obedience was "in no way required" by the Lord? Candidly, we feel that this betrays an astonishing misunderstanding of and reflection upon the character of the Lawgiver Himself.

V. *The Giving of the Law*

In the midst of an amazing display of His majesty and royalty, the divine King—who else could He be but our very Christ, as yet in the glory "form of God"? — descended upon Mount Sinai in all His unapproachable and infinite holiness. The preparations preceding His grand and terrible descent were all calculated to impress the people with their desperate need for purity. There had been the washings, the abstinence, the barriers about the mount, and the danger of being thrust through with a dart from the divine quiver. Then followed the eventful day when Moses ascended into the mount. The lightning, the thunder, the smoke, the altogether unparalleled display was so marvelous that even Moses exceedingly feared and quaked. To the people, however, carnal and corrupt and inquisitive, this was all a matter of curiosity; they rushed in where angels fear to tread. Moses was bidden to hasten back down lest the Lord break forth upon the gazing, presumptuous rabble. While Moses was at the foot of the mount, "the Lord of glory" thundered the Ten Commandments, indeed "a fiery law." It suddenly dawned upon the curious and carnal crowd that this divine display, so terribly grand and overwhelming, carried with it an awful demand for holiness. They cringed in mortal fear, their curiosity giving way to consternation and terror; but in their inmost souls it was "the

Voice," the Person back of those "ten words" that they could not endure.

Immediately the heads of the tribes of Israel said unto Moses, "Speak thou with us, and we will hear: but let not God speak with us, lest we die. And Moses said unto the people, 'Fear not: for God is come to prove you, and that His fear may be before your faces, that ye sin not'" (Ex. 20:19, 20). Here then at once we find the reason stated why "the law was given *through* Moses." The sinning Israelites could not tolerate the voice of "the Lord of glory." Not able to stand the direct giving of the law, they demanded that Moses mediate the law. On this background the prediction was given of "a prophet like unto Moses," viz., an approachable, "veiled," and gloryless One, a root out of a dry ground without form or comeliness. Whereas the law was *given* through Moses, because the people would not take it directly, it is said later by way of comparison and contrast, "grace and truth *came* by Jesus Christ."

When the King of Israel, the glorious Lawgiver of Sinai, later came in human frame, He laid aside "the form of God," coming not full of glory but full of "grace and truth." This made Him approachable by sinful men without their cringing in mortal terror. Furthermore, it is profitable and clarifying to remember that He who thundered the law from Mount Sinai in its negative form was the same Person who republished the same in the Sermon on the Mount in a more positive exposition. In this beginning of Israel's national history "was the Word," and by Him God gave the law "through Moses." Fifteen centuries later, when the same "Word became flesh and tabernacled among us," three inner-circle disciples "beheld His glory" and were as sore amazed as any Israelite at Sinai. When "He came unto His own" at Sinai as Lawgiver and King, it was appropriate that He should manifest such a majesty and holiness as would make "His own" conscious of their deep sinfulness.

In a recent conference where we were together, Dr. P. W. Philpott emphasized the need once again in this lawless generation of a return to forthright preaching on the Ten Commandments. Dr. Philpott is not an armchair professor, but a great preacher and pas-

tor of exceptionally wide experience. On this occasion he only expressed the growing feeling among hard-headed and consecrated
men concerning the remedy for this disobedient generation.

Those who consider that Israel's invisible King and Redeemer
was only bargaining in His proposal at Mount Sinai should be
afraid thus to trifle with the All-wise. Do they presume that the
omniscient One, whose supreme desire is to bring His own people
to a spiritual condition where they may show forth the praises of
Him who called them out of Egyptian darkness into His marvellous
light — do they presume, I repeat, that He could ever be guilty of
prescribing a law other than that which is in harmony with His own
unchanging divine nature, and which aims at the regulation of the
disposition and the heart? Someone may object that God's people are much more inclined to respond to privilege placed before
them than to external command laid upon them. Hold a moment.
The divine Wisdom is one in all ages. The Lord first gave Adam
life and then gave him command. He also gave the gospel before
unto Abraham in covenant, promise, and symbol, and it was confirmed in Christ. The same exact order follows when Israel came
to Sinai: redemption from Egypt preceded the requirements from
Sinai; their relationship the Lord Himself states to be that of "My
son," and the plea with Pharaoh had been, "Let My son go, that
he may serve Me." It became manifest, however, in their march
through the wilderness and in their unceasing complaints, that the
Lord's redeemed people had very little appreciation of their privileges in the Abrahamic covenant. Privilege alone was not a sufficient constraint. *They demanded compulsion plus privilege.* Little
did they care for the Rock of their salvation, and much less did
they know *how* to serve Him. And *how* was Israel to serve Him?
They must serve Him in holiness and righteousness all their lives.
If, however, they are to serve Him in holiness, they must first know
their unholiness; by the commandment their sin must become "exceeding sinful." It was not surprising, then, that at Sinai the Lord
should have given Israel

A law which unfolds the clearest views of God's character
and service—which denounces every form and species of
idolatry as inconsistent with the spirituality of the divine

nature—which enjoins the purest worship and the highest
morality, and in its very form is a model of perfection and
completeness" (*Typology of Scripture*, Vol. II, by Fairbairn).

As a transcript of the divine mind and will, the moral law is
immutable. It represents the character of Him who "changeth not."
In its revelation to Israel, it expressed the divine nature and the divine will. In its general principles, therefore, it is of eternal and
universal obligation. Professor David Gracey of Spurgeon's College appropriately said:

> For all the changing phases of the Divine Administration,
> there has been no change in the principles of the law. The
> expression may have altered, but not the precepts. These have
> been one and the same both in Eden and outside its guarded
> gates; the same to the world before the Flood and in Patri-
> archal times; the same from Sinai to Calvary; the same from
> Calvary right onward till the Great White Throne appears, and
> then the same for ever. This law, that comes from above, is
> the true objective counterpart to that which is within the
> human breast, and is subjective in the conscience (*Sin and
> the Unfolding of Salvation*).

When, therefore, the Divine Voice uttered the commandments,
the Divine Writings already in the bosom of every Israelite could
not but recognize the claims of the most High. These Ten Commandments had disclosed the secrets of their inmost hearts, and the
Israelites were compelled to own the authority of the divine King
and Legislator. Bowed in awful fear before "the Judge of all,"
Israel begged not to hear the Voice again. Our first parents had also
fled from that Presence and Voice, as moral darkness always shuns
the light. The Israelites sensed their innate tendency to corruption.
Their inner aversion to holiness had been discovered.

We fear, therefore, that the persistent attempt to eliminate law
and belittle the authoritative value of the divine legislation in the
Old Testament is a subtle removal of the very foundations of righteousness. If, indeed, "justice and judgment are the habitation of
His throne," and if it is predicted that in the yet-future Christ will
"magnify the law and make it honourable," then we should recognize in God's eternal and unchangeable love of righteousness
"the firm foundation of moral order and bliss throughout the uni-

verse." In this day of increasing lawlessness and juvenile delinquency, many of us must cease to be echo men and must begin to think for ourselves whether or not we may be reaping what we have sown.

Lest one feel that because Sinai's code is couched in the negative and prohibitive form it is for that reason so far beneath New Testament standards and teaching, we should listen to our Lord Himself, who showed us the inmost nature of the law. In answer to the question, "Which is the great commandment in the law?" He said, "Thou shalt love the Lord thy God with all thy heart, and with all thy soul, and with all thy mind . . . And the second is like unto it, Thou shalt love thy neighbour as thyself. On these two commandments hang all the law and the prophets" (Matt. 22:36-40). How apparent it is therefore that the whole sum of truth and obedience, whether in the Old Testament or in the New, is supported by and summed up in love to God and love to man. It must be apparent that love and righteousness are not contrary principles, and that the law was given in grace for the conviction of sin — that Israel might come, as a holy nation, to love righteousness and to hate iniquity.

APPENDIX C

The Purpose of the Law

I. Its Immediate Design

WHEN THE LAWGIVER approached His people, as has been pointed out, He reminded them that as a redeemed unit they were His "sons" (Ex. 4:22, 23), and that as such He was leading them to the land of their inheritance. He approached them as "children of the Lord" (Deut. 14:1) in order to secure their obedience and to prepare them to serve Him in holiness and righteousness all the days of their life. The whole legislation, therefore, was intended to reveal the divine righteousness and standards expected of a holy people. The whole divine direction and intention could be summed up thus: "Be ye holy, for I am holy."

The holy land which lay ahead of Israel was already spewing out its unholy people. As a "peculiar people of His own possession," the Lord's redeemed were to inherit His holy land; as a "holy nation," they were to abide by His law; as "a kingdom of priests," they must show forth His righteousness and praise in the midst of the nations. While the Abrahamic promise had already been "confirmed before of God in Christ," nevertheless *it was only as they bore the image and superscription of Christ that they could share with Him in His inheritance.* The law therefore set forth the righteousness required of the heirs of the Abrahamic covenant, the righteousness which they were certainly expected to manifest as a redeemed people. If they would enter into and abide in their Abrahamic inheritance, it would be only as they would abide by His expressed will. How would they ever show forth the praises of Him who called them out of Egyptian darkness into His marvellous light unless they learned, by kindness and by terror, somewhat of His character, His requirement, and His holiness?

300

The fact that these blessed designs were not more thoroughly realized in the after history of the Israelites should not reflect on the divine administration at Sinai, nor bring into question the divine wisdom and purpose in having given this law, which is "holy, just, and good," and "spiritual." Had the Israelites, like Joshua, meditated therein day and night, then they would indeed have become a peculiar treasure, a kingdom of priests, and a holy nation. They would have become like a tree planted by the rivers of water, that bringeth forth fruit in its season; their leaf should never have withered, and whatsoever they did would have prospered.

As a valuable side light on the parental care manifested all the way from Egypt, the Lord says in Hosea's day, "When Israel was a child, then I loved him, and called My son out of Egypt . . . I taught Ephraim to go [i.e., walk]; I took them on My arms" Hosea 11:1-3, R.V.). Here at Sinai we are to witness a kingly Father beginning to train His princely sons and subjects to walk. In still closer connection with this giving of the law, let us listen to the "blessing, wherewith Moses the man of God blessed the children of Israel before his death." In holiest reflection upon that sacred descent of the King upon Mount Sinai, Moses said, "The LORD came from Sinai . . . He came with ten thousands of [angelic] saints: from His right hand went a fiery law for them. Yea, He loved the people; all His saints are in Thy hand: and they sat down at Thy feet; every one shall receive of Thy words" (Deut. 33:2, 3). In wholesome imagination and appreciation of this scene, someone has quaintly summed up this portion in these words:

> *"In His heart—*
> *In His hand—*
> *At His feet—*
> *At His command."*

How seldom do we in our thinking couple phrases as Moses did in his deathbed blessing: "From His right hand went a fiery law for them. Yea, He loved the people." With one arm He embraces His own, while from the other proceeds "the fiery law." What blessed compounding of divine faithfulness and love! What a faithful Parent was Israel's King! His love did not shrink from giving

them the necessary discipline on "a law of fire." Let us not forget, moreover, that this is the Christ who is the same yesterday,
today, and forever. Today He still speaks from that glory world
in all the sternness of love, "As many as I love, I rebuke and chas-
ten."

These simple and self-evident findings reveal the Mosaic economy in harmony with, rather than disannuling, the previous Abrahamic covenant of life and blessing; for it should be remembered
that it could not possibly have been the divine intention at Sinai
to invalidate the previous covenant of "promise" with Abraham.
To say that "the dispensation of promise ended when Israel rashly
accepted the law" is an astounding premise to assume. In fact, it
is a conclusion flatly contradicted by Paul in Gal. 3:17, 18. This
conclusion would also cause God to contradict Himself through over-
throwing in this covenant His previous promises to Abraham.
Furthermore, it seriously questions the divine wisdom by virtually
denying that Israel needed the law, and, which is worse, implies
that the All-wise was stooping to a "wretched expedient" right in
the midst of the most terrorizing phenomena this world has ever
seen. To say that the Mount became thick with black darkness and
divine anger because the children of Israel had "rashly" promised
obedience is strange exposition.

Those who miss their way at Mount Sinai by conceiving of that
economy as only the introduction of a hopeless covenant of human
works finally find themselves involved in the strangest and most
contradictory conclusions. The able but, we believe, bewildered
brother already quoted seems forced to multiply words in order
to extricate himself from his own arguments. In one place, for
example, he says, "In the case of Judaism, God forgave sin and
renewed His fellowship with them on the ground of His own cer-
tainty that a sufficient sacrifice would be made in due time by His
Lamb" (*Bibliotheca Sacra*, Vol. 93, p. 418). But he at once reverts
to his premise that the Mosaic dispensation is strictly one of human
works and carnal sacrifices: "The Jews, being a covenant people,
were, when injured by sin, given the sacrifices as a basis for Divine forgiveness." Here the ground is shifted from God's Lamb
to that of animal sacrifices. In his comparison of the Mosaic dis-

pensation with that of Christianity he says, "Judaism required an animal sacrifice; Christianity looks back to the sacrifice already wrought." There are two errors in this one sentence. The first is the assumption that the entire Mosaic dispensation was one of legal works similar to that represented by apostate Judaism of Jesus' day. This mistake into which this Bible teacher has fallen through an erroneous and Pharisaic conception of the Mosaic economy is no small one. The second error, similar to the first, is in representing the Old Testament requirement as a contrast with the New Testament requirement — namely, the Old being "an animal sacrifice" and the New, Christ's sacrifice. Elsewhere the same writer says, "Any person is a dispensationalist who trusts the blood of Christ rather than bringing an animal sacrifice." Surely one does not need to go into the New Testament to prove that the blood of bulls and of goats could never take away sins. Spiritually-minded Israelites knew that God would provide Himself a Lamb, that to obey is better than sacrifice, and that "the sacrifices of God are a broken and a contrite heart."

In the same article this teacher comes to some astounding conclusions:

> What is identified as a spiritual remnant in Israel, seen in all her generations from Moses to Christ, is none other than those who through personal faithfulness claimed the immediate blessings which the Law provided. Some Israelites did live on a very high plane and were in very much personal blessing (*Ibid.*, p. 441).

Note here that it was "through personal faithfulness," not through grace alone, that Old Testament saints from Moses to Christ established a claim upon the divine blessings. Next he goes on to take up souls like Nicodemus, Saul of Tarsus, and other typical Old Testament characters found living during the days of Jesus Christ:

> When looking back upon his experience in Judaism, the Apostle Paul could say that he had then been as "touching the righteousness which is in the law, blameless" (Phil. 3:6). This did not imply sinless perfection, but rather that he had always provided the requisite sacrifices. On that basis the faithful Jew lived and was accepted of God in the Mosaic system. Who, indeed, are the "ninety and nine just persons

who need no repentance" cited by Christ according to Luke
15:7? And why were other covenant people classified as
"publicans and sinners"? After a new order is established
through the death and resurrection of Christ, men like Nicodemus, the Apostles, and Saul of Tarsus were saved by a new
birth, not because they were utter failures in Judaism, but
because a new and vastly different relation to God was provided (*Ibid.*, p. 441).

Space forbids a proper analysis of these strange conclusions, but
it seems plain that the writer feels driven to say that there was a
human-works righteousness which sufficed from Moses until the
death and resurrection of Jesus Christ. Only thereafter did Saul
of Tarsus need to be born again. And did the ninety and nine actually need no repentance? Or have we not always understood that
in the case of such persons Jesus simply took the Pharisees on their
own ground and revealed to them their conceited hypocrisy in assuming themselves to be "just persons" who needed "no repentance"? If these needed no repentance and no new birth as yet —
amazing conclusion! — then what of the case of Nicodemus, who
has already been dealt with? (Chapter XVI). Why did Jesus reprove this blind leader of the blind for not knowing he should be
born again? Did He not make it plain that the Pharisees, even the
best of them who sought to work their way into the kingdom of
God through a righteousness of their own, had utterly mistaken
their Old Testament and were to be blamed for such error? And
where did Paul ever seek to exonerate himself for his deeds done
"ignorantly in unbelief"? Had he not, with Nicodemus, needed
a new birth long before he fell on the Damascan road? Or had
these zealous and self-righteous Jews of former times been accepted
through their own morality and "the requisite sacrifices"? In that
instance what a scaling down of the divine requirement to suit the
"filthy-rags" righteousness of the best of men! Professor Fairbairn's
comment in this connection is very much to the point:

> How were it possible for men, laden with sin and underlying
> the condemnation of Heaven, to earn anything at God's hand
> or do what might seem good in His sight, till they become par-
> takers of grace? Can they work up to a certain point against
> the stream of His displeasure, and prosecute of themselves the

process of recovery, only requiring His supernatural aid to perfect it? To imagine the possibility of this were to betray an utter ignorance of the character of God in reference to His dealings with the guilty (*Typology of Scripture*, Vol. II).

Such reasoning is solid and conclusive and spiritual. Surely those fundamentalists who interpret the Mosaic legislation as the introduction of a self-help program of recovery find themselves strangely in collision with their own thinking and conclusions as Christians. They know already, or ought to know, that human nature can never earn a title to eternal life. The teacher with whom we take issue knows that salvation is by grace alone, but at times he seems to sense that he is on dangerous ground and seems to be driven to extricate himself from an almost impossible dilemma. However, his faulty premise (assumed at Mount Sinai) forces him to this still stranger conclusion regarding Israelites of the Old Testament:

> Since human faithfulness of whatever degree could never be the exact compensation for the values of eternal life or for unending blessings in the kingdom, there is a very large measure of divine grace to be seen in the salvation of the elect earthly people (*Bibliotheca Sacra*, Vol. 93, p. 441).

This paragraph is both hazy and contradictory. The first part thereof could be taken to mean that some souls through "human faithfulness" almost merited eternal life; the latter part, that their salvation was mostly of grace. In all fairness let us ask: Does this expositor actually believe that from Sinai to Calvary, salvation was fifty percent earned and fifty percent grace? fifty percent achievement plus fifty percent bestowment? Does he himself believe that Saul of Tarsus and Nicodemus, having done the best they could and having prosecuted their own recovery up to some seventy-five percent perfection, needed only twenty-five percent grace to win their salvation? If that be so, since the Divine character is unchanging and knows no shadow of turning, may not the same false ground of salvation obtain now? In fact, do not the great masses of the unregenerate, within and without the churches today, believe that the New Testament evangel is a kind of combination of Christian ethics sprinkled with a measure of grace and faith to make up for men's shortcomings? Such is the everlasting propensity of human nature to fall into a program of self-improvement in spite of all that God can do to persuade men otherwise. That evangelical expositors should fall into precisely the same error and charge the most High with having indulged in such a program for 1500 years is a mischievous and wretched confusion of grace and works. Where in all the Bible is there a remotest hint of such a commingling of utterly contradictory principles? If salvation be by grace, whether in the New Testament or in the Old Testament, it is no more of works. When was it ever of works? Obviously all this confusion in the mind of expositors is the inevitable result of their having missed God's plan at Mount Sinai, of having missed Christ there, of having missed the ends of grace God had in view even in the midst of Sinai's thunders.

The multiplied prohibitions of Moses were designed to prick and probe and condemn men's hearts into a consciousness of sin and bring this "kingdom of priests" to a despairing sense of their need of purity. "The law entered, that the offence might abound" — and thank God, "*where* sin abounded, grace did much more abound." *Where*, then, did grace abound? All the way from Sinai to Calvary.

Let us return for a moment to Mount Sinai. In closest connection with the immediate giving of the law, God said: "If thou wilt make Me an altar of stone, thou shalt not build it of hewn stone: for if thou lift up thy tool upon it, thou hast polluted it" (Ex. 20:25). Here is an exquisite gem of truth embedded beside the prohibitions of the inexorable law. Had men but read this portion with care they could scarcely have misread the meaning of Moses as having instituted only a dispensation of works. It is remarkable that, in the very chapter where (according to some teachers) God instituted a works-righteousness, the Lord Himself completely condemned the touch of the flesh upon the very stones of the altar of worship. There and then He refused to allow so much as a hammer of the human to touch the same. If, therefore, the human hand would so pollute the stones of the altar of approach to the most High, what chance had the human heart of building a Babel of its own self-righteousness whose tower and top might reach unto heaven? We repeat: If a hammer or chisel in the hand of a human dare not hew one stone of the altar of acceptable sacrifice, what prospect had the Israelites (the human heart in any age) of winning the reward of eternal life in the energy of the flesh? Candidly, then, we query: What likelihood is there that the all-wise and all-gracious Lord would launch out a whole nation on a program of self-recovery based upon the filthy rags of their own human righteousness? This brings us to consider a still further purpose of the law.

II. Its Nature

"Wherefore then serveth the law?" Or, why then the law? Paul anticipated the sputtering Jew, now shut up to Abraham and to faith, spitting out the question, Why then the law? If no man can be justified by works, if no man obtains life by law, and if Moses did not give us a works covenant, then why the law? The answer is that "it was added because of transgressions." It came in alongside. It did not add to the promise, but, as Paul stated in Rom. 5:20, "The law entered," or came in beside the promise as a handmaid, "that the offence might abound." We need not tarry here to dwell upon that which is well known, viz., "By the law is the knowledge of sin." Paul said, "I had not known sin, but by the law." For the same reason he also said, "The law worketh wrath." The offenders of the law could expect nothing but condemnation and vengeance for having transgressed the divine will.

So tremendous was the sweep and depth of the law that it anticipated the very points at which men were inclined to go astray. It was for this reason that it was given in the negative or prohibitive form. Anticipating the evil inclinations of men's hearts, the law stubbornly said at each point, "Thou shalt not," thereby opposing man in his every willfulness and disobedience. It is divine wisdom to cross man's path and oppose his self-gratification in the very points where he is most inclined to wander. Of course, conscience had already tried in vain to tell Israel these things; these laws were already, in measure, "written on their hearts." The terror from Sinai found its counterpart in conscience. The Psalmist testified to the sweep and depth of the law when he said, "I have seen an end of all perfection: but thy commandment is exceeding broad" (Psa,

119:96). It was, therefore, to be expected that by the law would come "the knowledge of sin," considering the stringent demands of the law upon the conscience for righteousness and the opposition it raised against the current of man's sinful propensities. It has always been recognized that there was among the Jews a far greater sense of sin than there was among the heathen. In any heathen land, "sin and insensibility to sin go together." It was doubtless with this excellent purpose of the law in mind that the East Indians requested of Dr. Claudius Buchanan: "If you send us a missionary, send us one who has learned your Ten Commandments" (Fairbairn).

That preachers can so lightly esteem the benefit and wisdom of such a holy and sweeping expression of the Divine will as was given at Sinai, belittling its precepts and berating its prohibitive character, is a sad reflection upon those who should be ministers of righteousness. Do we ignore the fact that in both the Old Testament and the New Testament "our God is a consuming fire"? In this gay and giddy world, when a thousand passions are clamouring for expression and when lawlessness is rampant in the land and worldliness is rifling our churches, it is high time that some John the Baptists arise before that great and notable day of the Lord to cause men once again to fear before Sinai's terrors and tremble before the Lord God of Elijah.

It must be kept in mind that it was not the divine purpose in Heaven's "thou shalt nots" to reduce the people to a mere lot of slaves and hirelings who would set about to establish their own righteousness. How could the King, "merciful and gracious," delight in serfs labouring through the mere ritual and letter of the law to gain Divine favour? In the course of time, the carnal Jews did indeed mistake the true purpose of the law, to the extent that they at last reduced the whole economy to a mere bondage of human works and meritorious self-righteousness. Patrick Fairbairn, an old theologian who had a deep heart-insight into the relation between law and grace, says:

> It was the fond conceit of the Pharisaical Jews . . . that they might, by obedience to law, work out a righteousness and acquire a title to life and glory which did not naturally belong to them. It is simply against this groundless and per-

verse notion, which had come latterly to diffuse its leaven through the whole Jewish mind, that our Lord and His apostles are to be understood as speaking, when in a manifold variety of ways they endeavour to withdraw men's regards from the law as a source of life, and point them to the riches of divine grace (*Typology of Scripture*, Vol. II).

III. Its Relation to the Abrahamic Covenant

(a) *To Shut Men up to Faith.*

When this phrase, "shut up to faith," is considered in its context, we find that the Apostle likens the law to a jailer who shuts men up and closes every door of escape from condemnation — except one, the door of faith. Behold the law, jailer-like, go down the stern, grim corridors of a prison with many doors on either side, which seem to be exits. There is the door of self-righteousness, the door of good resolutions, the door of religious duties, the door of strict behaviour, etc.; but the law, vigilant and inexorable, has locked and barred every door so that man may escape through none of these. No matter which way he may turn, he is confronted with "Cursed is every one that continueth not in all things which are written in the book of the law to do them" (Gal. 3:10). The writer once confronted a splendid young man, clean and punctilious in his church life, with this verse of Scripture. Finally in desperation he cried out with conviction, "Well, whatever is a man going to do then?" He could see no way out, could find no door of escape. He was shut up; his mouth was stopped; he was guilty and condemned and in the grip of the jailer. When once shut up to faith, he was soon saved.

While this is all plainer to our intellect under New Testament explanation, we are inclined to forget that the same principle obtained in Old Testament times. In fact, when Paul seeks confirmation of his gospel of grace, he brings forth the Old Testament method of salvation, viz., "The just shall live by faith." It has already been pointed out that New Testament writers find their Westminster Abbey heroes of faith in the Old Testament; Abraham is the faith-father, the "father of us all."

Now when "the law entered," or "came in beside," it came in as a means which was intended indirectly to shut men up to the Abrahamic faith, viz., faith in the coming Christ. Did Abraham rejoice to see Christ's day? And did he see it by faith? Did Moses endure "as seeing Him who is invisible"? The law, then, came in jailer-like to "keep them in ward," releasing Israelites only upon condition of faith. To most fundamental expositors today, it is not customary to think of one of the weighty matters of the Mosaic law as being "*faith.*" Yet the Saviour's own accusation of the conceited Pharisees was that along with their evasion of justice and mercy, they had omitted *faith* as one of "*the weightier matters of the law.*"

No sooner had the moral law been given, with its uncompromising terms of obedience or death, than there was also arranged the elaborate ceremonial system, which imaged forth the pathway of cleansing into the holiest of all. Thus the law, pursuing the transgressor with "ten thousand curses," shut a sinner up to faith as shadowed forth in the sacrifices. The guilty soul, condemned and conscious of his just desert, placed his hands upon the head of the flawless substitute and prayed, "Now, O Lord, I have sinned, I have committed iniquity, I have rebelled: thus and thus have I done. But I return in repentance to Thy presence, and be this my expiation." With a broken and contrite heart the sinner could draw near by faith to Israel's own mercy-seat to "obtain mercy and find grace to help in time of need." Thus the moral law had in closest conjunction therewith its complementary counterpart in the ceremonial law, the two together aiming at producing the righteousness of faith in every penitent Israelite. In this connection Fraser, as quoted by Fairbairn, appropriately says:

> God did never make a new promulgation of the law by revelation to sinful men, in order to keep them under mere law, without setting before them, at the same time, the promise and grace of the new covenant, by which they might escape from the curse which the law denounced. The legal and evangelical dispensations have been but different dispensations of the same covenant of grace, and of the blessings thereof. Though there is now a greater degree of light, consolation, and liberty, yet if Christians are now under a kingdom of

grace, where there is pardon upon repentance, the Lord's people under the Old Testament were (as to the reality and substance of things) also under a kingdom of grace.

(b) *Shut up to Christ.*

This phrase, "shut up to Christ," is slightly different from the title of the previous paragraph, "shut up to faith," and calls for separate consideration. This can best be given by an exposition of Gal. 3:17-25, where the relation of the law to the Abrahamic covenant is set forth.

> And this I say, that the covenant, that was confirmed before of God in Christ, the law, which was four hundred and thirty years after, cannot disannul, that it should make the promise of none effect.
>
> For if the inheritance be of the law, it is no more of promise: but God gave it to Abraham by promise (vv. 17, 18).

It had already been observed that it was not the Divine intention in the giving of the law to abrogate or to render ineffective the previous promise given in pure grace to Abraham. If the Mosaic covenant is a mere *ad interim* economy of works, then, Paul says, the Abrahamic promise has been made void:

> For if the inheritance be of the law, *it is no more of promise*: but God gave it to Abraham by promise.

God had so freely granted the promise of grace "in Christ" to Abraham that, Paul says, "no one maketh it void, or addeth thereto." No covenant could either supersede or suspend it. Had not God promised grace in Christ, and had not Abraham and his seed already partaken of this in faith? Paul says, How inviolable then, the covenant! Would the Judaizers interpret Moses as having added or supplemented legal conditions of merit to the Abrahamic promise? Paul says, No one "addeth thereto." So that God did indeed give the law, but neither *instead of* the promise, nor *in addition to* the promise.

Such reasoning incenses the Judaizer. The cornered Jew cries out against Paul: Why then is the law? Since the law can supply no Spirit, can justify no sinner — since it can neither take the place of the covenant or add to it, why then the law? Was God merely mocking His people when He proposed the Mosaic covenant? Did He conduct a mere experiment for 1500 years? Would you, Paul, make the law useless, and make God purposeless in having given it? Paul anticipates and answers these counter reasonings of the Judaizer:

> Wherefore then serveth the law? It was added* because of transgressions, till the seed should come to whom the promise was made . . . Is the law then against the promises of God? God forbid: for if there had been a law given which could have given life, verily righteousness should have been by the law (vv. 19-21).

The law did not stand contrary to the promise; it "was added" — it was a reinforcement, "because of transgressions," i.e., to bring sin to light and make the Israelites feel their need of the Lord as their Light and Salvation. There may have been few Israelites who at this time felt their need of Jehovah-Tsidkenu. Of the Rock that begat them they were unmindful; of the Rock that followed them they were unready to drink. For the true Bread — symbolized daily in the manna that came down from heaven — they were not hungry. Perhaps no great majority of them, like Moses, "esteemed the reproach of Christ greater riches than the treasures in Egypt." Few of them "endured as seeing Him who is invisible." Furthermore, the Abrahamic promise of a Divine Seed was dim and unappreciated by the Israelites. That promise therefore required reinforcement, demanded an assistant.

This economy, being only a handmaid, was not the original promise of life, nor was it the final dealing of God. For how long was this special administration intended? "Till the Seed should come to whom the promise was made." Men needed to be shut up to Him who would yet appear in the flesh. "Wherefore then serveth the law?" "By the law is the knowledge of sin"; and on account of sin "the law worketh wrath" (Rom. 3:20; 4:15). The law clearly worked wrath in Israel. "The law, which they so glibly promised

---

* In v. 15 Paul says the law was not an addition in the sense of supplementing a new meritorious condition of inheriting "the promise" of grace. Here he explains in what sense it was an addition.

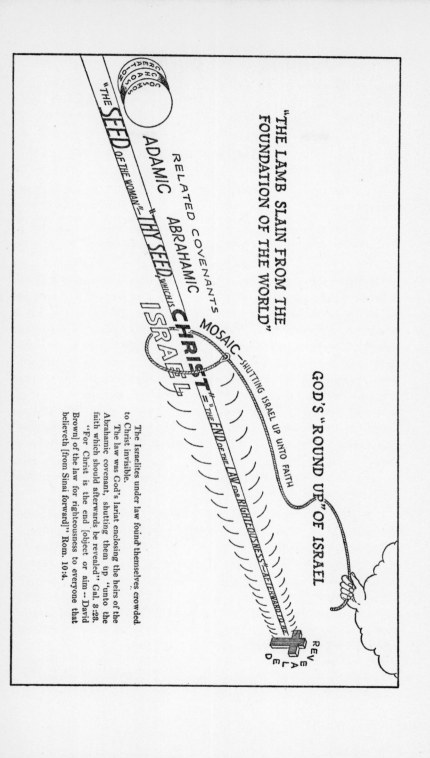

GOD'S "ROUND UP" OF ISRAEL

"THE LAMB SLAIN FROM THE FOUNDATION OF THE WORLD"

RELATED COVENANTS

ADAMIC   ABRAHAMIC

"THE SEED OF THE WOMAN" — "THY SEED, WHICH IS CHRIST"

ISRAEL

MOSAIC — SHUTTING ISRAEL UP UNTO FAITH

"THE END OF THE LAW FOR RIGHTEOUSNESS" — AFTERWARD TO BE

REVEALED

The Israelites under law found themselves crowded to Christ invisible.

The law was God's lariat enclosing the heirs of the Abrahamic covenant, shutting them up "unto the faith which should afterwards be revealed" Gal. 3:28.

"For Christ is the end [object or aim — David Brown] of the law for righteousness to everyone that believeth [from Sinai forward]" Rom. 10:4.

to obey, they straightway flouted — notwithstanding the thunders
of Sinai. But, lo, the shattered tables, the angry Lawgiver's flashing eyes, the draught of water impregnated with the powder of the
golden calf, the fall of 3000 Israelites under the consecrated sword of
the Levites — all prepared Israel to hear and feel the words of
Moses as recorded in Exodus 32:30: 'Ye have sinned a great sin' "*
(W. C. Stevens). Wherefore then serveth the law? Again comes
the answer:

> But the Scripture hath concluded [shut up and shut in] all
> under sin (v. 22).

Does this mean that their case was hopelessly fatal? that they
were left under condemnation, as in a prison? Indeed not. This
was all done in keeping with the gracious provision and purpose
"that the promise by faith of Jesus Christ (the promise which
pointed to the coming Christ in Jesus) might be given to them that
believe" (v. 22). God's law, then, might be likened to God's lariat
to "round up" rebellious and roaming Israelites and shut them in on
every side and bring them to an obedient faith in the Abrahamic
promise of the coming Seed. (See diagram on page 313.)

Before Christ appeared in the flesh — after which time the uplifted One could be preached as the object of faith — God found
it necessary to shut men up to the faith, i.e., faith in the Coming
One.

> But before faith came, we were kept under the law, shut
> up unto the faith which should afterwards be revealed (v. 23).

The phrase, "before faith came," cannot mean that there was
no faith in God's people before the death and resurrection of Christ,
else how account for the faith heroes of Hebrews 11? Rather, before Christ appeared as the object of faith, the Israelites were kept —
not "kept under," but "kept in ward" under the provision of the
law. Stiff-necked Israelites were mercifully and yet forcibly "shut
up" or imprisoned, that they might learn the meaning of the already promised grace of the Abrahamic covenant — "shut up unto
the faith which should afterwards be revealed." Herein, then, is at
once both the marvel and mystery of grace during the dispensa-

---

* See Appendix D for further treatment in this connection of Exodus 32-34.

tion of law. By measures fearful and forceful, Israel's King shut His people up to Himself while He was as yet unrevealed. Thus the law was a marvellous assistant to grace until the day when He should be "made *manifest* unto Israel." Paul concludes this portion of his argument regarding the ministration of the law:

> Wherefore the law was our schoolmaster to bring us unto Christ, . . . But after that faith is come, we are no longer under a schoolmaster (vv. 24, 25).

These verses require care, for they confirm all we have said about Christ in the Old Testament. While it is Paul's purpose here in confounding the Judaizers to present more forcibly the contrast between the imprisonment of the Old and the subsequent freedom in the New, he manifestly avoids saying what many present-day expositors think he says in this portion. Was the law Israel's "tutor" or truant officer "unto Christ"? The thought of the phrase, *"unto Christ,"* does not mean *"until Christ"* (as a certain reference Bible wrongly indicates in its margin). Jesus once said, "The law and the prophets were *until* John," clearly meaning length of time, or continuation *"until"* John. But Paul does not here say that the law was our schoolmaster *"until Christ."* The aim, or telic, of the law, all the way from Sinai to Calvary, was Christ — and not merely a distant, coming, and yet-to-be-revealed Christ, but rather the living, present Jehovah-Jesus invisibly in their midst as the Rock of their salvation.

We know of no more illuminating illustration of the law as a means of grace than that set forth in John 8:1-11. Therein is dramatized the law as a marvel of grace. The scribes and Pharisees had seized on a woman taken in sin and had forcibly brought her to Jesus. In so doing these officers unwittingly, but perfectly, functioned as though they had been the truant officer, or the law itself. By their legal hands this poor guilty and despairing woman was forcibly imprisoned, "being shut up unto the faith about to be revealed" (Gal. 3:23, Roth.). Behold her as a poor, pursued, condemned, and hard-pressed soul crowded *"unto Christ,"* the hope set before her. Thus shut up unto Christ, the object of faith, she illustrates perfectly Moses' "ministry of condemnation." If we fail as fundamental ex-

positors today to see the designs of grace veiled in the Mosaic legislation, do we not come under the accusation of Jesus levelled against
the Pharisees, namely that they omitted "*faith*" as one of the weightier
matters of the law? When this guilty and condemned woman presently called Jesus "Lord," we find the true meaning of that much
misunderstood text: "Christ is the end [aim or objective] of the
law for righteousness to every one that believeth." In this simple
illustration of the salvation of the woman taken in sin, we see how
the law functioned for 1500 years as God's lash and lariat in His
great "roundup" of wild and unbroken sinners, shutting them up to
faith in Christ.

An Exposition of Romans 9:30-10:10

"What shall we say then? That the Gentiles, which followed not after righteousness, have attained to righteousness, even the righteousness which is of faith" (9:30).

THE GENTILES had long been in the far country. Disobedient to the law of conscience and corrupted by the moral condition described in Romans 1, they made no pretence to pursue after righteousness. Yet now they have achieved righteousness, and no mere legal righteousness, but the righteousness of faith.

But Israel, which followed after the law of righteousness, hath not attained to the law of righteousness (v. 31).

Israel, on the other hand, ostensibly pursued hard after righteousness. They set out to meet the law's heavenly standards, hoping thereby to arrive at acceptance with God. But as mere fallen men full of the filthy rags of their own self-righteousness, they missed the way — could never "arrive."

Wherefore? Because they sought it not by faith, but as it were by the works of the law. For they stumbled at the stumblingstone (v. 32).

The great blunder of the Jews was to misread Moses as having instituted works-righteousness as a basis of meritorious acceptance with God. Having failed to seek righteousness by faith, they had only the righteousness of the scribes and Pharisees. Holding to the letter of the law, they rejected the Lord of life. Throughout their history they stumbled against the stone of stumbling — meaning Christ invisible in the Old Testament. When He finally appeared as the incarnate object of faith, the great Anti-type prefigured by all Old Testament types, they rejected Him and still asserted their righteousness independent of Him.

As it is written, Behold, I lay in Sion a stumblingstone and rock of offence: and whosoever believeth on Him shall not be ashamed" (v. 33).

Paul is here quoting phrases from Isaiah concerning Christ invisible in the Old Testament — phrases sometimes mistaken for predictions. Isaiah speaks of "a stone of stumbling" and "a rock of offence" in Isa. 8:14. At this time the wicked king Ahaz was bent on a confederacy with Assyria rather than trust in the Lord. He refused the very present help of Immanuel (God with us). See Isa. 8:8-10. Ahaz had already been rebuked for his unbelief by the God-given prediction of the virgin-born Immanuel. When he and his people still refused to make the Lord their "sanctuary" — a place of abiding worship and resort as well as a Rock for their shelter and safety — Isaiah warned them that in their blind unbelief their Rock would prove to be a stone of stumbling, over which they would fall and be broken.

Paul quotes the last part of Romans 9:33 from Isa. 28:16. The time is a few years later in the days of Hezekiah. All Jerusalem was in consternation, for Sennacherib, king of Assyria, was demanding Judah's surrender. A strong political group in Jerusalem was making haste to flee to Egypt for assistance. The Lord's word again was, "Behold, I lay in Zion for a foundation a stone, a tried stone, a precious corner stone, a sure foundation: he that believeth shall not make haste." Again Israel's sure foundation Stone was "despised and rejected of men." But two believing statesmen, Isaiah and Hezekiah, refused to lean on Egypt. They relied upon the King and Rock of their salvation, and bore His reproach in the midst of God's unbelieving people. Nor were they confounded or put to shame.

To humble and believing hearts Christ was always Israel's Rock of salvation, but to those who rejected Him He was ever a "stumblingstone and rock of offence." What prophet ever proclaimed Him, the coming Just One without being persecuted? Was it not Isaiah who was "sawn asunder" — so the Jews tell us — for having said he had seen Jehovah-Jesus in all His glory? (John 12:41). When Christ was finally nailed to the Cross, it was but the climax of His rejection all the way from the golden calf to Golgotha.

Brethren, my heart's desire and prayer to God for Israel is, that they might be saved (10:1).

This fervent prayer in the spirit of mercy for the salvation of Israel shows that their present fallen state excludes no individual from gospel privileges. Incidentally this verse (as well as the last part of Chapter 9) indicates that the sovereign election of Chapter 9 has to do not with the personal salvation of individual souls, but with the choice of God's instrumental channel of blessing to others. It was only when faith failed that Israel fell — for this age — from her special place of privilege. Heaven still weeps, therefore, over their having stumbled over the Stone.

For I bear them record that they have a zeal of God but not according to knowledge (v. 2).

Israel was still zealously reading Moses, but with blinded minds — "which veil is done away in Christ." With their backs upon the Lord, the veil remained — yes, still remains — upon their hearts. Like Saul of Tarsus they were sincerely zealous, so zealous they were "not afraid of a world in arms." What a mixture of motives animated their zeal — still blindly pursuing but never arriving!

For they being ignorant of God's righteousness, and going about to establish their own righteousness, have not submitted themselves unto the righteousness of God (v. 3).

Israel stubbornly persisted in setting up their own righteousness to establish a claim for themselves that would stand in the judgment. Bishop Moule well says, "They aspired to acceptance. God bade them submit to it. In their view, it was a matter of attainment; an ascent to a difficult height where the climber might exult in his success." But instead of building up a great Babel of human righteousness, whose tower and top might reach unto heaven, they should have submitted themselves to the righteousness of God. God's righteousness is for paupers, not for the proud. Israel's blindness is no mere misfortune or an excusable ignorance. It is a blindness based upon proud unbelief. A great theologian once said, "Blindness precedes unbelief and is the cause of it." It is rather the opposite. Unbelief precedes blindness and is the cause thereof. Unbelief is nonsubmission — the collision of the human will with the will of God.

Ever since the fall of man the great question has been one of righteousness. "How can a man be just with God?" has been the supreme problem from the beginning until now. Both conscience and law should bring man to the plea of the Psalmist: "Enter not into judgment with Thy servant: for in Thy sight shall no man living be justified" (Psa. 143:2). Viewed from this standpoint, righteousness means rightness with God, harmony with heaven and the divine will.

The old patriarchs, including Abel, Enoch, Noah, and Abraham, all made the discovery of divine peace, not through their own works and merit. Among all these Abraham stands out as the shining example, the man who believed God and whose faith was reckoned to him for righteousness. What is the whole of Hebrews 11 but a testimony to the all-sufficiency of faith as the sole condition of righteousness? New Testament gospel righteousness was confirmed as being in Scriptural harmony with the Old Testament standard, "The just shall live by faith." Man must, of course, either make himself righteous before God by his own works, or be made righteous by God's grace and power through simple faith in the Redeemer. One is man's method; the other is God's. Scripture makes God's method crystal clear. Righteousness by faith through grace is God's original, universal, and effectual method of justifying the ungodly. It was against this method that the self-righteous Jews rebelled and perverted all their Old Testament, including Moses, when they set about to build up "their own righteousness." In this, therefore, they exercised a stubborn refusal to submit themselves to the righteousness of God.

Paul's phrase, "the righteousness of God," stands over against man's self-righteousness. Paul contrasts these two elsewhere when he says, "not having mine own righteousness, which is of the law, but that which is through the faith of Christ, the righteousness which is of God by faith" (Phil. 3:9). Concerning this righteousness of faith, let us here insert a brief consideration of Romans 3:21-31. Paul has just climaxed his long previous argument (1:18-3:20), regarding man's guilt and need of a free justification, with the conclusion that "by deeds of the law there shall no flesh be justified." Man's mouth is stopped. He is guilty. It is impossible for him to meet the demands of violated law. In blissful contrast with man's hopeless and death-doomed condition, Paul breaks out in 3:21: "But now the righteousness of God without the law" — altogether apart from deeds of self-righteousness — "is manifested, being witnessed by the law and the prophets." How clear he makes it that true righteousness is not God's exaction from man, but His gift to man! It may prove helpful to summarize the last eleven verses of Romans 3 under the heading, "True Righteousness."

(a) Its *source*—-God, not man, (v. 21).
(b) Its *condition*—faith, not merit (v. 22).
(c) Its *agency*—grace, not law (vv. 21, 24).
(d) Its *channel*—the redemption in Christ Jesus, not works (v. 24).
(e) Its *ground*—the blood of propitiation, not behaviour (v. 25).
(f) Its *warrant*—it leaves God "just," not man "boasting" (vv. 26, 27).
(g) Its *subjects*—man universal, not classes (vv. 23, 28-30).
(h) Its *history*—witnessed by law and prophets in the Old Testament, and now "manifested" and "declared" without shadow in Jesus Christ (vv. 21, 26).

Such is the glorious gift of righteousness, the only righteousness that can ever be approved or accepted in high heaven.

> *"Our faith receives a righteousness*
> *That makes the sinner just."*

Let us now note the sweep and history of this method of justification. This righteousness, as already observed, leaves God "just." The Bishop of Durham is right when he says that God's Righteousness is God's Justification, for only thus could He magnify His own law and make it honourable. Christ satisfied the divine righteousness when He bore the penalty due to sin. Paul says (3:25, 26) that when Christ "put away sin by the sacrifice of Himself," it was "to declare His [God's] righteousness for the remission [pretermission, or passing by] of sins that are past, through the forbearance of God; To declare, I say, at this time His righteousness: that He might be just, and [as well as] the justifier of Him which believeth in Jesus." It was indeed through "the forbearance of God" that He "passed by" sin before Christ manifested the great "once-for-all" atonement. In olden days God had warned men of their doom, but seldom had He exacted any part of the penalty due to sin. Only on rare occasions — at the Flood, at Sodom and Gomorrah, and during the plagues in Egypt, etc. — did God give men a foretaste of the final doom of sin. For the most part He "passed by" in forbearance the sin of the ungodly.

Not only the ungodly did God forbear, but also the godly. Paul presently introduces Abraham as a sinner of old who was "justified freely by God's grace." The Psalmist rejoiced in personal redemption as *"plenteous."* David, the man of scarlet sins, sang of the happiness of the man whose iniquities are forgiven and whose sins are covered. Still the question as to *how* God could be at the same time "a just God and a Saviour" had not been cleared up. Heaven's throne was not above suspicion. Even Moses needed to be brought to understand the existing redemption grace whereby God could carry forward His covenant people. When that Lawgiver actually beheld the calf-worshipping people at the foot of the mount, he dashed the tables of stone to fragments in token of the broken covenant (Ex. 32:19). So great and grievous was this offence that Moses cried, "Ye have sinned a great sin: and now I will go up unto the LORD; peradventure I shall make an atonement for your sin." Moses instinctively felt that only on such a just basis of atonement could there be any future arrangements of the Lord with His people. Listen to Moses as he lays the situation before the Lord: "Yet now, if thou wilt forgive their sin —; and if not, blot me, I pray thee, out of Thy book which Thou hast written" (Ex. 32:32). Moses knew there had to be an actual and available ground for forgiveness. He had seen the Lord in all His holiness. He knew that Heaven could not overlook sin. So determined was he that, if necessary, he was willing to offer himself as a fresh atoning sacrifice. He could not possibly understand how the Lord could freely forgive and overlook such flagrant disobedience.

In his grasp of essential justice, Moses was right, but the Lord knew that Moses needed to be brought into a further revelation of the grace relationship which already obtained through the one eternal Redemption. At length the Lord so revealed Himself as

"The LORD, The LORD God, merciful and gracious, longsuffering, and abundant in goodness and truth, keeping mercy for thousands, forgiving iniquity and transgression and sin" (Ex. 34:6, 7), while not altogether forgetting iniquity, that Moses became satisfied that there was an available and already existing ground — a ground so sufficiently inherent in the Rock of their Redemption that no other or additional atonement was called for. Herein is made clear to Moses (and to us) the fact that the covenant at Sinai was not proposed on any other ground than that of an already existing grace relationship, and that this ground itself was the very substructure of the Abrahamic covenant "confirmed before of God in Christ." No sooner had Moses seen this good ground than he hastened to say, "Let my Lord [redemptive, gracious, forgiving], I pray Thee, go among us [such an One we need]; for it is a stiffnecked people; and pardon our iniquity and our sin, and take us for Thine inheritance" (Ex. 34:9). In the Lord Christ's redemptive Person and Presence Moses sensed the solution as to *how* the King all-gracious could continue in covenant relationship with the people and carry them forward. Let the reader also carefully study Num. 14:11-24.

Until Calvary, however, God's righteous basis for "passing by" Old Testament sins had never been *declared*. God's righteous character seemed impaired. How long could He thus continue? Had His holiness been compromised? How had He dealt *justly* with David in forgiving him in his ungodliness? How could He thus be at once a "Saviour" and a "just God"? One purpose of the propitiation in Christ, Paul tells us, was to declare, i.e., openly publish, God's righteousness. God's Lamb, which was "foreordained before" and "slain from the foundation of the world," solved the paradox. David Gracey well says in this connection:

> It became needful that the rule of God should be cleared from every shadow of suspicion . . . The apostle declares the propitiation of Christ was the righteous foundation on which were based these acts of forbearance and these acts of justifying grace. It results, therefore, that Christ satisfied righteousness in bearing the penalty due to sin; He satisfied righteousness in respect of divine forbearance of the unrighteous; and above all, Christ satisfied righteousness in respect of the sinners who were made the righteousness of God in Him.

Now that all this was in full force under the Old Testament economy and that the pulse of Calvary was felt as soon as the sinful
pair exchanged their fig leaves for God's righteousness by substi-
tution is evident in all the saints of old. In fact, the Apostle has
just said (Rom. 3:21) that the provided righteousness of God
through faith in Christ, which has been "now . . . manifested," has
all the way along been "witnessed by the law and the prophets." This
righteousness, which is apart from all human works of law, is new
only in that it is "now manifested." As David Brown states it:
"This justifying righteousness is at once *new*, as only now fully
disclosed, and *old*, as predicted and foreshadowed in the ancient
Scriptures." Very true! Law, as well as prophets, only bears witness to this law of faith for righteousness. The law never demanded
a sacrifice as a meritorious work on man's part, but only as an expression of faith, a faith which at once became "the substance of
things hoped for, the evidence of things not [yet] seen." Not only
Samuel but all discerning saints sensed from the law itself that
"to obey is better than sacrifice." Broken-hearted David expresses
the true sentiment when he says, "Thou desirest not sacrifice; else
would I give it: Thou delightest not in burnt offering. The sacrifices
of God are a broken spirit: a broken and a contrite heart, O God,
Thou wilt not despise" (Psa. 51:16, 17). Then David immediately
expresses his own approval of the offerings as expressive of faith
when he adds, "Do good in Thy good pleasure unto Zion: build
Thou the walls of Jerusalem. Then shalt Thou be pleased with the
sacrifices of righteousness, with burnt offering and whole burnt
offering; then shall they offer bullocks upon Thine altar" (Psa.
51:18, 19).

The prophets were continually seeking to deliver the people from
a mere formal worship and point them to Jehovah-Tsidkenu, i.e.,
Jehovah our righteousness. For years we have been impressed with
the Psalmist's continual mention of Heaven's righteousness and salvation: "My mouth shall shew forth Thy righteousness and Thy
salvation . . . I will make mention of Thy righteousness, even of
Thine only" (Psa. 71:15, 16). While enjoining obedience to the
law of Moses, the prophets in the Old Testament had no other obedience in mind than that which is the fruit of faith. David says,

"Offer the sacrifices of righteousness, and put your trust in the LORD" (Psa. 4:5). The words "faith" and "believe" in the New Testament find their counterpart in the Old Testament word "trust." The giants listed in Hebrews 11 for our edification were those who lived "by faith." Those who had their eyes opened to behold wondrous things out of God's law saw that one of "the weightier matters of the law," as Jesus said, was "faith." It was for this reason that Moses in his song of witness against apostate Israel referred to them as "a very froward generation, children in whom is *no faith*" (Deut. 32:20).

It ought to be clear that the justifying "righteousness of God" by grace through faith has always been Heaven's one and only method of saving lost men. Let us return to the unfolding of that righteousness in Romans 10.

> For they being ignorant of God's righteousness, and going about to establish their own righteousness, have not submitted themselves unto the righteousness of God.
>
> For Christ is the end of the law for righteousness to every one that believeth (vv. 3, 4).

The little word "end" is interpreted by many in accordance with a doctrinal premise already assumed. The ultra-dispensationalist and the antinomian take the word to mean that Christ is the end of all law, "the law's disappearance from the scene"; in other words, the old dispensation, a dispensation of mere works-righteousness, has been abruptly terminated, and a new dispensation of faith-righteousness has come in with Christ's death and resurrection. But this view collides, as will be noted later, with Paul's own quotation from the law itself to support the claims he makes for righteousness by faith.

Careful regard to the context will help us to arrive at the correct meaning of the word "end." In our above quotation we have purposely put verses 3 and 4 together. The meaning of "Christ is the end of the law for righteousness to every one that believeth" must be considered in closest connection with the two righteousnesses, viz., man's and God's, in verse 3. Man's righteousness, as we have already seen, is in sharpest contrast with, and in opposition to, God's righteousness. In the concluding verses of Chapter 9, we saw that the Jews failed to arrive at the law of righteousness because they sought it as though it had been by works. In their stupid and stubborn self-righteousness, they clung to the letter of the law and refused to submit themselves to the righteousness of God. "For Christ is the end [the object or aim (David Brown)] of the law for righteousness to every one that believeth." The law reached its end in Old Testament times only when it brought individuals to believing confidence in Christ. In Old Testament language, that would be to "trust in the Lord" and to find in Him alone the Rock of their salvation, the LORD their righteousness.

The law, as we have observed in Galatians 3 (Appendix C), was the truant officer to bring men unto Christ, to shut them up unto the faith which should afterwards be revealed. "Wherefore the law was our schoolmaster to bring us *unto Christ*" — not *until* Christ, as it has been misunderstood and mistranslated. The law was God's means from Sinai to Calvary to shut men up unto Christ invisible until such time as He would come in visible form and put away sin by the sacrifice of Himself. Just as the Pharisees dragged the poor adulteress taken in sin to Jesus, so had the law been conducting and crowding men to Christ, "the end," or objective in view. It was the divine design of the law to drive men to despair in order that they might flee to the mercy seat. David Brown quotes Bengle as saying: "The law hounds a man till he betakes himself to Christ; then it says to him, Thou hast found an asylum, I pursue thee no more; thou art wise, thou art safe."

Those Jews, however, who mistook the *means* for the *end* and went about to establish their own righteousness were faced with the alternatives, viz., obedience or death. Charles Simeon has an appropriate word in this connection:

> Tell me, then, ye who desire to be under the law, do ye not hear the law? Does it say anything to you but "do this and thou shalt live"? Does it set before you any alternative but "cursed is he that continueth not" (Gal. 3:10)? "Do this," this wrath-working law proclaims, "do it all—all without exception—continue in it from first to last, and you shall live; but a curse, an everlasting curse, awaits you if you offend in one particular." Plead what you will, these denunciations are irreversible — its terms cannot be changed. You may say,

"I wish to obey"; and it answers you, "Tell me not of your wishes, but do it."

"I have endeavoured to obey."

"Tell me of no endeavours, but do it or you are cursed."

"I have done it in almost every particular."

"Tell me not what you have done almost; have you obeyed it altogether? Have you obeyed it in all things? If not, you are cursed."

"I have for many years obeyed it, and but once only have I transgressed."

"Then you are cursed; if you have offended in one point you are guilty of all."

"But I am very sorry for my transgressions."

"I cannot regard your sorrow; you are under a curse."

"But I will reform, and never transgress again."

"I care nothing for your reformation; the curse remains upon you."

"But I will obey perfectly in the future, if I can find mercy for the past."

"I can have no concern with your determination for the future; I know no such word as mercy; my terms cannot be altered for anyone. If you rise to these terms you will have a right to life, and need no mercy. If you fall short in any one particular, nothing remains for you but punishment!"

Thus the law came in alongside — "was added" — as a reinforcement to the already existing Abrahamic covenant of grace. The law was not intended to give *life*. That was already promised in the Seed of the woman, which Seed was to come through Abraham's God-given Isaac. This promise of life in Christ was the "end" which the law had as its objective for righteousness. The law had done its work when any poor despairing and guilty soul of Old Testament times cried out, "God be merciful to me a sinner." Soon that soul was numbered among the "every-one-that-believeth" and went down to his house "*justified*." While the law, therefore, could not confer life, nevertheless, "the commandment was ordained to life." It definitely promoted the purpose of bringing men to an end of themselves that they might find life through "the promise" in Christ.

It has long seemed clear to the writer that expositors need never have been confused and perplexed regarding God's designs in the Mosaic legislation had they but followed through the long-recognized principles of law in conscience and circumstance, principles both beneficent and necessary in order to bring men to blessedness in Christ. As we have already emphasized, what a melancholy reflection it is upon our fallen human nature that we have to be "shut up" to all the mercies of God! If we could evade them and avoid them and cheat ourselves of them, notwithstanding their gracious freeness, we would. God is still shutting men up to faith. It should be natural for us to trust in God, but it is not. God must employ severe measures to reduce us to despair and root us out of our self-confidence and self-righteousness. All of Heaven's wisdom is brought to bear upon us through circumstances and disappointments in order to drive us to confess that our "help cometh from the Lord."

As we scan the centuries, faces of great saints come before us, men who were saved only after being utterly subdued. Luther sought righteousness by fastings and prayers and night vigils until he almost wasted away. Finally, in utter despair, he was shut up to the faith that was so graciously revealed to him. We have already referred to Abraham Poljak — one of hundreds of Jews who have learned to say: "I thank God for all the strokes with which I was driven from darkness to light. It is better that we arrive beaten and bleeding at the glorious goal than that we decay happily and contented in darkness. Hitler's arrows and our misery have led us . . . On the bitter ways of emigration we have found Jesus, the riches of all worlds."

In this connection another beautiful illustration from that interesting little country of Korea comes to hand (from D. M. Panton). A half century ago a Korean scholar and aristocrat was plunged into prison for two years by his autocratic king. Then at the outbreak of the Russo-Japanese War he was arrested on an unnamed charge, and was again imprisoned.

In my distress, unconsciously I lifted up the corner of the coarse reed-mat that covered my prison floor, when, lo, what should I see beneath it but a little book with red cover and a Chinese inscription. I looked at it and it said, "The Gospel According to St. John." Had I found the elixir of life I could not have been more overjoyed. Here was a book, and I could read, and such a book. I read it through that day. Yes, read it through, twenty-one chapters, and like a breath of life it was to me. The next day I read it again, and as I read I prayed that God would open my eyes. Would you believe it, as I read it and continued reading Jesus rose before me, divine, the Great Saviour. I had been wholly wrong in my estimate of Him. He was God indeed. After I had read it through about thirty times, one morning word came that I was free.

"Free?" asked I of the officer. "Why was I arrested in the first place, and why am I let go now?"

"I don't know," said he, "but you are free."

So I returned home and on my way I asked myself, Who locked me up in prison? My soul answered, God. Why did He lock me up? That I might have a vision of Jesus, the Divine One. Who put the little book under the mat? The Holy Ghost, the Comforter. Thank God for all His goodness.

Such is the divine wisdom in shutting men up to Christ. This process holds good not only in the beginning of the Christian life, but also in its continuance. It is by the pathway of despair that we come to fresh exercises of faith. How many are the illustrations from Scripture which come before us, almost all of them to the discredit of the saints themselves. After three days and three nights in the whale's belly, Jonah finally confessed, "Salvation is of the LORD." Job suffered a thousand deaths, as it were, before he was shut up to an overwhelming revelation that brought him to abhor himself and to repent in dust and ashes. After nearly a quarter of a century, Abraham came to the end of all natural power, and looked upon his "as-good-as-dead" body, not to the weakening of his faith, but rather to the strengthening thereof and to the fulfillment of the promise of God to give him seed of an entirely supernatural order. Moses was shut up in the backside of the desert that he might learn the way of faith. The great Apostle tells us that he came to an entirely new knowledge of God as "the Father of mercies, and the God of all comfort" through a set of circumstances such as he had not before experienced. To the Corinthians he says, "For we would not, brethren, have you ignorant of our trouble which came to us in Asia, that we were pressed out of measure, above strength, insomuch that we despaired even of life: But we had the sentence of death in ourselves, that we should not trust in ourselves, but in God which raiseth the dead" (II Cor. 1:8, 9). Did God seem cruel in thus bringing His beloved Paul once again to the dust of death and reducing him to utter despair? Such is the cruelty of a love that has a blessed end in view. As he looked upon himself, Paul too was as good as dead — and in that very extremity he found a new and superhuman hope, a "faith born of despair." He had the sentence of death in himself that he should cease all self-confidence and put his trust in God. Thus the Apostle "in deaths oft" experienced a whole series of resurrections and discovered that he could always triumph in Christ.

Have you, my reader, like the Apostle himself, tried to live a holy and pure life? Have you spared yourself no pains in the struggle to live a life pleasing to God? — yet failed the worse the more you have striven and fought? — In your desperation you cry out, "O wretched man that I am! who shall deliver me from the body of this death?" If you have indeed come to complete despair, to the end of yourself, then listen to the blessed secret of faith: "I thank God through Jesus Christ our Lord." How is it you have finally come to discover your all-sufficiency in Christ? Is it not by the pathway of failure and defeat and despair? Finally — blessed *finally* — you have been shut up to find your all in Christ. Think not, however, that you have attained. The process holds good throughout life. But we must return to our context.

> For Christ is the end of the law for righteousness to every one that believeth.
> For Moses describeth the righteousness which is of the law, That the man which doeth those things shall live by them.
> But the righteousness which is of faith speaketh on this wise, Say not in thine heart, Who shall ascend into heaven? (that is, to bring Christ down from above:) (Rom. 10:4-6).

Many expositors have missed their way in these verses. The Apostle has just stated that Christ has ever been the one aim of the law for righteousness "to every one that believeth." Now he finds confirmation for this provision of true righteousness by quoting from Moses himself, "*For* Moses describeth the righteousness which is of the law." Verses 4 and 5 are closely connected by the casual conjunction "for," indicating that Moses also had Christ in view as

"the end of the law for righteousness." Do not be misled by reading this phrase, "the righteousness which is of the law," out of its
context. In another connection Paul once denounced what he termed
"mine own righteousness, which is of the law" (Phil. 3:9) ; and
here in our context (Rom. 9:30-10:3) he has condemned his own
people forever having gone about by the works of the law to establish their own righteousness, for in so doing they were guilty of
nonsubmission to the righteousness which is of God. Now Paul
brings in Moses as a witness to this true righteousness. The question
is: When Moses described "the righteousness which is of the law,"
did he write of a works-righteousness or the righteousness which is
of God? He must have had in mind one or the other, but certainly
not a mixture of the two. Furthermore, if the Mosaic covenant set
forth a works-righteousness, an opposition righteousness, a righteousness contrary to the righteousness of God, how could the Apostle
call in Moses to confirm his argument for the true righteousness?*
Paul has already condemned such a contradictory scheme of self-
recovery. We repeat the question: How then can Paul introduce
Moses as describing a mere legal self-righteousness when he calls
on him to confirm the true righteousness which the law has always
had in view for "every one that believeth"? We must conclude
that Moses likewise wrote to bring men to the end of the law for
righteousness. Moses is not contradicting Paul, nor Paul Moses.
When, therefore, Moses describes the righteousness which is of the
law — which the law always had as its objective — he can have
nothing else in mind than the "one righteousness" in Christ.

When Moses wrote of how to realize "the righteousness which
is of the law," he merely added, "The man that doeth those things
shall live by them," thus summarizing the method of the law to bring
men, not to self-righteousness, but to the true righteousness. How

---

* Those who conceive of the law as having instituted a form of legal righteousness find themselves bogged down in this passage. They are, therefore,
driven by compulsion, rather than by exposition, to conclude that the phrase,
"Christ is the end of the law for righteousness," must mean the dispensational
termination of that economy. Whereas it is true that the foreshadowings and
ceremonials have found their fulfillment in Christ crucified, nevertheless the
context of Romans 10:3-5 forbids the thought that Paul's chief meaning had
to do with chronological termination. Most stoutly he contended that the law's
aim was ever to bring men to Christ and that Moses confirms that contention.

then are we to understand such a phrase? Some presume that this "living" refers only to social and temporal blessings; others conclude, as did the carnal Jews, that the law presented only a covenant of legal works. Such views obviously fall far below this present context, and do violence both to Moses and to Paul, as well as to almost all of the Old Testament. While words may seem on their surface to put the matter of life on the plane of pure human merit alone, we ask again, How could Moses have introduced an economy that would have sanctioned self-righteousness? or that would have countenanced for a moment the nonsubmission of the Israelites to the righteousness of God? This would be to pit the Mosaic covenant against the Abrahamic, and to make Moses contradict Paul. Furthermore, to imagine such a possibility betrays a woeful ignorance of the depravity of the human heart, as well as ignorance of the character of God in His dealings with fallen men. While the most High knew that no law could give life, He also knew that man must be brought to despair before he would appreciate and embrace God's mercy. Without apology or explanation, therefore, the Lord said: "The man that doeth those things shall live by them."

While Chapters XIII and XIV deal at length with the principle involved in the phrase, "This do and thou shalt live," let us observe also here that the Mosaic economy (as summarized in v. 5) at no time purposed that a man by piling up punctual performances and fulfilled duties could thereby attain to life. The design of the law was to make Israel more deeply conscious of sin and to bring them to the need of repentance and forgiveness. The law, therefore, laid upon the sinner a burden of commandment which, if resisted, would crush him to death under a sense of guilt, and bring him perchance to a deep need of mercy through the Redeemer. The claims of law were simply obedience or death. To the sinner the summary of law is this: "Cursed is every one that continueth not in all things which are written in the book of the law to do them" (Gal. 3:10). The outraged law places upon him a yoke which no man "in the flesh" can bear. The law works wrath against transgressors. The trouble is not with the law — for it is "holy, and just, and good" — but with the transgressor, who is bound by his sin. And how strong is that sin? "The strength of sin is the law." Under the wrath of Heaven and bound by chains of sin, what chance had the sinner to free himself or earn a title to life? David Gracey puts it thus:

> If the sinner tries to sever the connection, he finds it impossible. His *abhorrence* will not break the link; his *resolves* will not remove the tyranny; his *scrupulous care* cannot guard against surprise; his *struggles* will not overcome it; his *mortification* will not stay it; his *confessions* will not banish it; his *tears* will not wipe it out; his *penances* and *sacrifices* cannot atone for its wrong. Affliction hardens, and prosperity inflames it. It flourishes under the brightness of earthly joy, and thrives beneath the shade of human sorrow. It keeps on its course, through disquiet, through fear, through sore travail of spirit, in apprehension of the great disquiet in the dread unknown.

How pitiful that the Jews ever came to view the law as having provided them with a mass of duties by which they might build up their self-righteousness and fortify themselves against the righteousness of God! And yet equally fatal is it to our reading of the Old Testament to conclude, as a great Bible teacher says, that "The righteous man under law became righteous by doing righteously; under grace he does righteously because he has been made righteous." To come to such a conclusion is to assume that the law was strictly a covenant of works and in this respect to read the Old Testament with the same misapprehension as the conceited Pharisees. On the contrary, the divine design in saying, "The man that doeth those things shall live by them," was to bring a man down, to undo him, to undermine his ego, to bring him to an utter end of himself. The carnal Jews, however, instead of viewing the Heaven-high standards of the law as something to reduce them to despair, made each detail thereof the rung of a ladder whereby they might ascend those heights and obtain the reward of eternal life. Viewed in this way, most assuredly "the law is not of faith." Such a "law of works" contradicts and excludes the "law of faith."

It was the method of the law to drive men to the dust of death in order that out of that depth men might cry to the Lord of life and live. Thus Christ would be found by "every one that believeth" to be the blessed end Moses had in view when he laid down the un-deviating and impossible condition, "The man that doeth those things shall live by them."

It is well to remember in this connection that no sooner was the impossible law laid upon the Israelites than specific directions and provisions were made relative to the sacrifices, which not only foreshadowed the coming of the once-for-all redemption but also symbolized a present and substitutionary righteousness. While it is true that the blood of bulls and of goats could never take away sins — what spiritual Israelite ever thought so? — those sacri-fices did bespeak the provision of the most High, who, while mer-ciful and gracious to forgive, could by no means clear the guilty. Here let us remind ourselves again that the Holy Ghost was there and then signifying through these very means that "the way into the holiest of all was not yet made *manifest*" (Heb. 9:8). In the meantime the law was shutting men up to *the faith* — invisible but real — which should afterwards be revealed. It must therefore be true that the Old Testament believer who had come to the mercy seat and had found grace to help in time of need was indeed de-livered from the condemnation of the law and must then have been, in spiritual experience, under grace. Although living under the external administration of law, he no longer conceived of it as a yoke unbearable, but rather it became his delight and he meditated therein day and night. He experienced, as did David, that where sin abounded, grace did superabound.

Next we come to contrast and similarity. In v. 6 Paul says, "*But* the righteousness which is of faith speaketh on this wise . . ." The little word "but" indicates contrast, in a certain sense, between "the righteousness which is of faith" and "the righteousness which is of the law." Again let us move cautiously. Has not Paul already shown us that the end of the law was not realized until a man was brought to faith in Christ? Did not the law shut the sinner up to that faith? Likewise is not New Testament righteousness through faith in Christ? There can be no contrast in this passage then as to the one divine righteousness, called "the righteousness which is of God."

It remains that the contrast implied is one of Old and New Testament methods in bringing men to that righteousness. The Old Testament economy shut men up to faith in Christ; the New Testament economy preaches the uplifted Christ as the object of faith. In vv. 5 and 6 the righteousness which is of the law is contrasted with the righteousness which is of faith only with respect to the dispensational economy under which men are brought to the one righteousness in Christ. The law's method was largely that of an external compulsion which crowded men to Christ; the New Testament method is especially that of holding up the Crucified that men may be drawn unto Him. Moses' method was primarily that of driving men to Christ pre-incarnate. Nevertheless, whether it be *driving* men to Him *invisible,* or *drawing* men to Him *"manifested"* and uplifted — whichever of these stands out the more prominently — the end is the same, viz., righteousness through Christ.

> But the righteousness which is of faith speaketh of this wise, Say not in thine heart, Who shall ascend in heaven? (that is, to bring Christ down from above:)
> Or, Who shall descend into the deep? (that is, to bring up Christ again from the dead.)
> But what saith it? The word is nigh thee, even in thy mouth, and in thy heart: that is the word of faith, which we preach;
> That if thou shalt confess with thy mouth the Lord Jesus, and shalt believe in thine heart that God hath raised him from the dead, thou shalt be saved.
> For with the heart man believeth unto righteousness; and with the mouth confession is made unto salvation (Rom. 10: 6-10).

Here, with Deut. 30:11-14 before him, Paul runs his New Testament "word of faith" concerning the immediate nearness and availability of salvation in Jesus, into the framework and language of Moses. Let us therefore first take a glance at the passage in Deuteronomy.

> For this commandment which I command thee this day, it is not hidden from thee, neither is it far off.
> It is not in heaven, that thou shouldest say, Who shall go

up for us to heaven, and bring it unto us, that we may hear it, and do it?

Neither is it beyond the sea, that thou shouldest say, Who shall go over the sea for us, and bring it unto us, that we may hear it, and do it?

But the word is very nigh unto thee, in thy mouth, and in thy heart, that thou mayest do it.

In these words Moses let the people know that the multiplied laws which he had just laid down were all comprehended in what he calls "this commandment," i.e., a single comprehensive commandment. It was all the word of the Lord, a word very nigh, a word immediately powerful and easily accessible, even in the mouth and in the heart, that they "may do it." After having rehearsed to Israel the length and breadth and depth and height of all the law, Moses anticipated the Israelite groaning and sighing and beginning to excuse himself on the ground that the law was too high in its demands — "Who shall go up for us to heaven, and bring it unto us, that we may hear it, and do it?" — and that it was beyond his reach in its breadth — "Who shall go over the sea for us, and bring it unto us, that we may hear it, and do it?" Moses' answer is simple and plain: "For this commandment that I command thee this day, it is not hidden from thee [not too hard for thee, R. V.], neither is it far off. It is not in heaven [so high that it must be reached by attainment] neither is it beyond the sea [so distant that it requires your effort to go and fetch it] but the word is very nigh unto thee, in thy mouth, and in thy heart, that thou mayest do it."

The true summary of the law, Moses tells them, is not in a mere mass of external details, but in the word spoken from the living and omnipresent God — a word so "nigh" that it need but be embraced for them to find immediate divine ability to "do it". Moses is saying: Be not faithless, but believing. Doubt not your God's presence and ability in His word. The divine utterance is neither distant nor difficult. It is so nigh unto you that your inability may easily and immediately give place to the divine enablement. Hear this commandment as "the voice" of the living God, and you will find in it the power and presence of Him who speaks it. Faith comes by hearing and hearing by the word as the voice of God. Hear the word as from God. Let the Lord thy God "circumcise thine heart" (v. 6) to love the Lord thy God, and thou shalt discover that He speaks and it is done; he commands and it stands fast. No word of His can be void of power. This commandment is not too hard for thee, not beyond thee. Make no excuses. "This is the love of God, that we keep His commandments; and His commandments are not grievous."

The man who thus heard the word of the Lord as "spirit and life" and became believingly obedient thereto would rejoice in the Lord his God and would be forever thankful that the law had shut him up, had stopped his mouth, had rendered him excuseless, and had brought him into utter submission to the righteousness of God. Such was the righteousness Moses had in mind. To this passage in Deuteronomy Paul appeals for support of the very "righteousness which is of faith" which he would emphasize to New Testament believers. Right here in the heart of Moses' "righteousness which is of the law" Paul finds hidden the true righteousness which Moses would crowd the believingly obedient to embrace.

Into this very framework and thought-form of Moses Paul runs his New Testament word of faith concerning the crucified and resurrected Jesus. Was the word of the Lord through Moses (a word very nigh unto man, in the mouth and in the heart) to be believingly obeyed? Paul's word of the Lord concerning Jesus crucified and risen is also very nigh unto men: "Say not in thine heart, Who shall ascend into heaven? (that is, to bring Christ down from above:) Or, Who shall ascend into the deep? (that is, to bring up Christ again from the dead.) But what saith it? The word is nigh thee, even in thy mouth, and in thy heart." At this point Moses added "that thou mayest do it"; but Paul finishes the phrase calling it "the word of faith, which we preach." Did Moses know that Israel needed only to become believingly obedient to the word of the Lord to find divine ability to do the impossible? Of course Paul knows that the word of the Lord concerning Jesus Christ is no distant word; in the power of the living God that word is immediately present in the mouth and in the heart, to be believingly submitted to by any and every soul of man: "Because if thou shalt confess with thy mouth Jesus as Lord, and shalt believe in thy heart that God raised Him from the dead, thou shalt be saved: for with the heart man believeth unto righteousness; and with the mouth confession is made unto salvation" (Rom. 10:9, 10, R.V.). The word of the Lord Jesus is near, living, dynamic, requiring only the believing submission of the heart. All that Christ has done, and is now doing at the throne, He is able to do within us — this very hour. All is within our reach, here and now — "Today." The word of faith means simply hearing and doing what God says.

In commenting upon the word of Jesus, "Every one that *heareth* these sayings of mine and *doeth* them," Dr. R. V. Bingham brings out this valuable sidelight from the foreign field:

> In translating the Scriptures into many of our African languages, it is hard to find words that set forth abstract terms such as "faith" and "hope" and even "love." And in more than one language the term "faith" has been rendered in the very words which our Lord uses here, "hearing and doing."

This comment is in harmony with Paul's word of faith regarding the crucified Jesus, viz., that confessing Him with the mouth, which is the proper expression of the believing heart, is the sole condition of salvation.

Is this conditional element a new kind of works? Perish the thought! It is but the confident appropriation and proper expression of God's freely-offered righteousness and salvation. Furthermore, it helps us today to be delivered from a mere mental assent, which carries with it no corresponding submission to the lordship of Christ. Elsewhere we point out that there is an easygoing "believism" abroad today which glibly speaks of sinners believing on Jesus as their Saviour and then at some indefinite and later date coming to full submission to Him as "Lord." One is called salvation; the other is called full surrender. Scripturally speaking, these two cannot be divorced. It is believing submission to "*Jesus as Lord*" that Paul holds out here as the condition of salvation. Was it not the sin of the carnal Jews that in going about to establish their own righteousness they did not submit themselves unto "the righteousness of God"? There is an amazing amount of "Just be-

lieve" today that knows nothing of submission to "Jesus as Lord."
It might assist us to recover the true meaning of faith to note the
Revised Version of John 3:36: "He that believeth on the Son hath
eternal life; but he that *obeyeth not the Son* shall not see life, but
the wrath of God abideth on him."

The spiritual harmony between Moses' "righteousness which is of
the law" and Paul's "righteousness which is of faith" — the fact
that both refer to the one "righteousness which is of God" — is
well illustrated in the following incident,[*] told by Dr. H. C. Mabie:

> I call to mind a bashful young farmer in the West, who
> had grown up far from the atmosphere of the church and to
> whom the habits of religious meetings were unfamiliar, saying
> to me when I urged upon him to come to the prayer meeting
> that night in a neighbouring farmhouse, and openly confess
> with the mouth his need of Christ, "I never could stand up
> and talk in that way before people, even though I wanted to;
> it would kill me to do it."
> "Well," I replied, "die then: I know how hard it is for
> you, but Christ commands the impossible. He told Peter to
> come to Him walking on the water, and as long as Peter kept
> his eye on the Lord, he also walked the waves. He commands
> you to confess Him before men and I shall expect you to do
> it tonight, even though you die in doing it."
> To the meeting this timid man came. When he rose to
> speak he laboured as if he were Atlas lifting the world on his
> shoulders. The effort crushed the cowardice out of him; for
> before he sat down he sang the song of the new life. By
> faith he attempted the impossible: he seized the ideal he knew.
> Christ met him in the act, and he came into a saved state
> (from *Method in Soul-Winning*).

Was this young man saved by works or by grace? By grace
alone, of course. Yet the principle of law — the compulsion the
young man felt that he must meet the simple command of open confession — crushed and crowded him to Christ. Submitted to the
righteousness of God — "with the heart man believeth unto righteousness" — he confessed with his mouth "Jesus as Lord." Moses
and Paul agree.

---

[*] Further comment on this illustration will be found in Chapter XIII.

The Seventh-Day Sabbath and the Lord's Day

WE HAVE SOUGHT in this book to safeguard and promote eternal principles of righteousness — principles which are as unchangeable in their character as the Nature and Will from whom they proceed. The laws of God, in their great basic underlying character, are of necessity of abiding and universal obligation. Let it always be borne in mind that, while in various dispensations the technical expression of divine law may have altered, its abiding principles are the substructure of all changing phases of divine administration. Back of each of the Ten Commandments is the whole of the divine righteousness, of which each command is a particular expression. Therefore, while the law of the Sabbath given in the fourth commandment is in its very nature ceremonial, none the less it contains for all men of all ages a fundamental and abiding principle of righteousness. It simply recognizes that the very constitution of man's nature requires physical rest and spiritual recreation. This principle — one day in seven — must therefore stand as much today as ever. It cannot be otherwise than it was in the beginning, viz., "the Sabbath was made for *man*." Such a provision simply subserves the need of man's physical and spiritual being.

In seeking to adhere to these unchanging principles of righteousness as expressed by God in Old Testament law, we cannot avoid giving brief consideration to the question, "Ought Christians to keep the Sabbath?" Since, however, many excellent exposures of Seventh-day Adventism are already in print, we shall seek to confine our sphere of observation to the message of this book.

The claims of some Seventh-day advocates are false when they assert that Sunday was instituted by Constantine or by the Pope as the Christian's holy day. The facts of history contradict these claims. Neander, reckoned as one of the greatest of all church historians, said:

> The opposition to Judaism early led to the special observance of Sunday in place of the Sabbath . . . As the Sabbath was regarded as representing Judaism, Sunday was contemplated as a symbol of a new life consecrated to the risen Christ. Because it was grounded in His resurrection, Sunday was distinguished as a day of joy.

To confirm this historian's statement from the writings of the "Church Fathers" (church leaders immediately succeeding the apostolic age), we find many evidences. Justin Martyr, writing before the middle of the second century, said:

> On the day called Sunday all who live in cities or in the country gather together in one place, and the memories of the Apostles or the writing of the prophets are read as long as time permits.

Eusebius, the "Father of Church History" (about 260-340 A.D.), informs us:

> From the beginning Christians assembled on the first day of the week, called by them the Lord's Day, for the purpose of religious worship, to read the Scriptures, to preach and to celebrate the Lord's Supper.

Perhaps the statement of Tertullian, written about 200 A.D., summarizes with fairness the prevailing practice in the early church:

> The Lord's Day is the holy day of the Christian church. We have nothing to do with the Sabbath. The Lord's Day is the Christian's solemnity.

Turning to Scripture, it is manifest that the first day of the week was observed in the very earliest days of the Christian church. While Jewish Christians may have continued for some time to observe the seventh day on account of their tendencies to legalism, there is no indication at all that the Gentile Christians gave heed to the seventh day. In fact, there is evidence to the contrary. In the fifteenth chapter of Acts, where the question of circumcision and the law of Moses came before the Jerusalem Council, among the "necessary things" which the Gentile Christians were exhorted to observe, there is no mention of the Sabbath. Nor will it do for the Adventist to claim that this omission was because the Gentiles were already keeping the Sabbath, for in the two special instances in which church gatherings are spoken of among the Gentile Christians, the first day of the week is mentioned as a time of meeting (Acts 20:7; I Cor. 16:1, 2).

One of the common questions voiced by Adventists is this: Where do you find in Scripture that the Sabbath day was changed to the first day of the week? Our answer is, It never was; the Sabbath is still the seventh day of the week. Another question is, Where is there a command in the New Testament to keep the first day of the week? The answer is, There is none, as such. Would not a better question be, Where is there in the New Testament the least command either from Christ or the apostles to keep the Sabbath? Dr. R. A. Torrey has pointed out that "every one of the Ten Commandments is expressly reaffirmed in the New Testament except the Sabbath law, and there is not one syllable in our whole New Testament suggesting that the Sabbath is binding on the Christian." He then refers to Rom. 13:8-10; Eph. 6:1, 2; James 5:12; and I John 5:21 to show how "every commandment written on the tables of stone except the Sabbath law is explicitly declared in the New Testament to be binding on Christians. But the one commandment upon which the Seventh Day people lay all their emphasis is neither by explicit statement nor hint said to be binding upon Christians in any verse in the New Testament."

Perhaps it would be of profit to call in an ex-Adventist, D. M. Canright, and listen to his own statement:

> After keeping the seventh day for twenty-eight years; after having persuaded more than a thousand others to keep it; after having read my Bible through, verse by verse, more than twenty times; after having scrutinized to the best of my ability every text, line and word in the whole Bible having the remotest bearing upon the Sabbath question; after having looked up all these, both in the original and in many translations; after having searched in lexicons, concordances, commentaries and dictionaries; after having read armfuls of books on both sides of the question; after having read every line in all

the early church fathers upon this point; after having written several works in favour of the seventh day, which were satisfactory to my brethren; after having debated the question more than a dozen times; after seeing the fruits of keeping it, and after weighing all the evidence in the fear of God, and of the judgment day, I am fully settled in my own mind and conscience that the evidence is against the keeping of the seventh day.

Turning again to Scripture, we note that there is explicit declaration to the effect that the Sabbath is not a binding obligation upon the Christian in this age.* There is the plainest statement possible in Col. 2:16, 17 in confirmation of this fact: "Let no man therefore judge you in meat, or in drink, or in respect of an holyday, or of the new moon, or of the sabbath days: Which are a shadow of things to come; but the body is of Christ." Let not the Sabbatarian claim that Paul did not here refer to the Sabbath of the seventh day. Such would be dishonest dodging of Paul's use of the plain word "Sabbath." Since no divine word authorized the Christian's observance of the first day instead of the seventh, there must surely have been a deep, underlying wisdom which, considering the facts and circumstances, would not allow the Church of that age to become a graft on Judaism. (By Judaism we mean that utter perversion of

---

* Does some one urge that in Romans 14 Paul actually does away with all days and that every man is only to be "fully persuaded in his own mind"? Such a point as this must be considered with care for the simple reason that Paul himself met with believers on "the first day of the week." Yet, under the existing circumstances, what could the Apostle say but "let every man be fully persuaded in his own mind" when converts were closely associated with those who had Judaistic scruples regarding foods and drinks and days? So especially confusing and difficult of solution were the conditions of the hour that they would scarcely admit of rule or of specific directions. In general they were advised: Let not the strong despise the weak; let not the weak judge the strong; but especially let no man go contrary to his own "conscience" in these matters. "Let each man be fully assured in his own mind" (Rom. 14:5, R. V.). Certainly the Sabbatical obligation, whether of the first or the seventh day, is, *pro tem*, not recognized. And among the orthodox of today such a question of scruples finds little or no analogy. We doubt, however, whether the all-Bible principle of one day of rest in seven should now be swept aside by the directions necessary at Paul's time. The question that should distress us in this hour is not an overmuch regard for the Lord's Day but rather our utterly lawless disregard of one day in seven. In other words, today church conditions are more akin to the looseness that characterized God's ancient people in Moses' day, when they demanded some principles of obedience.

God's Old Testament legislation so prevalent in New Testament times.) The fact is that the Judaizing teachers early sought in two ways to fetter the Gentile saints: first and chiefly by circumcision, and secondly by Sabbath keeping. "Moses' disciples" of Jesus' day gloried in circumcision and the Sabbath. Yet it is well to recall that both these institutions preceded Moses. How then did these two ordinances come to be the two great signs of the Abrahamic covenant?

The first of these covenant-signs to be given the Israelites was circumcision. "God said unto Abraham, Thou shalt keep My covenant therefore, *thou, and thy seed after thee in all their generations.* This is My covenant, which ye shall keep, between Me and you and thy seed after thee; Every man child among you shall be circumcised. And he that is eight days old ["a son of eight days," Heb.] shall be circumcised . . . and my covenant shall be in your flesh for *an everlasting covenant*" (Gen. 17:9, 10, 12, 13). It is perfectly plain that this was a perpetual sign, sacred and blessed to Israel as a seal of national distinction and calling. To this day it is practiced by them, and in this sense belongs to no people but to the seed of Abraham.

Circumcision as instituted in the original purpose of God signified the utter unprofitableness of the flesh. Righteousness had been reckoned to Abraham when, in the face of his self-despair of ever having a son, he believed God. The old patriarch turned from himself and trusted the promise of God for a supernaturally begotten son. Thereafter he received circumcision as the sign and seal of the righteousness which God reckoned to him after the failure of the flesh. In its deepest meaning, therefore, circumcision signified the circumcision of the heart to believe God (Deut. 10:16 and 30:6). It was meant to be *the cutting off and cure* of all self-righteousness. Who can doubt that many an Israelite entered personally into this signified purification in "putting off" the sins of the flesh? On the contrary, when Paul sought in New Testament times to deliver the Galatian converts from bondage, he had to treat circumcision as the symbol of all self-righteousness. He declared that those who submitted to circumcision became debtors to do the whole law. In

Paul's time circumcision, instead of its being a *cure*, had become a *curse*.

It is remarkable that there was foreshadowed the passing away of the old creation in the very ordinance of circumcision to be observed on "a son of *eight* days." As rest at the first creation was on the seventh day, so rest in the new was to be on the eighth, i.e., the first day of the week. When the Judaizers (contrary to the circumcision of the Cross) sought the improvement of the flesh, Paul cried out, "In Christ Jesus neither circumcision availeth any thing, nor uncircumcision, but a new creature [creation]" (Gal. 6:15). In circumcision itself (observed on the eighth day), Paul discerned the doing away of the flesh and the beginning of the Spirit. Just as there was a proper connection between the old creation and God's having rested on the seventh day, so Paul discerned a vital connection between the new creation and our resting in Christ on the eighth day. Those who have been baptized by the Spirit into Christ "are the circumcision," and similarly those who have believed into Christ risen have entered into the eighth-day "sabbath of the soul." As believers we "are circumcized with the circumcision made without hands, in putting off the body of the sins of the flesh by the circumcision of Christ" (Col. 2:11). Thus we have the inner content and meaning of circumcision through the Cross of Christ, while the rite itself continues to belong to Israel as one of her covenant signs.

The other great Israelitish covenant sign never yet revoked, never changed as to the day, and never transferred from Israel to others, is the Sabbath of the seventh day of the week. It was not only part of the body of law given on Sinai, but it was a covenant sign for Israel, as exclusive as circumcision. In Exodus 31:12-17, the record is found of the giving of the Sabbath as a perpetual sign of an irrevocable covenant with Israel: "And the LORD spake unto Moses, saying, Speak thou also unto the children of Israel, saying, Verily My sabbaths ye shall keep: for it is a *sign between Me and you throughout your generations;* . . . Wherefore the children of Israel shall keep the sabbath, to observe the sabbath throughout their generations, for a *perpetual covenant. It is a sign between Me and the children of Israel for ever.*" It must be manifest that this covenant sign was irrevocably ordained for Israel. Having been incorporated into her national life, it is just as plainly disallowed as a condition of Christian obedience in this dispensation as circumcision. Doubtless the recognition of this covenant sign as "perpetual" for Israel led the Jerusalem Council, when giving directions to the Gentile Christians as to the "necessary things," to give no least hint of Sabbath requirement (Acts 15:28, 29).

In the Old Testament there is another typical observance which shadows forth the first day of the week with special application to this dispensation. We refer to Leviticus 23:9-21, where it is manifest that a far better day than the Sabbath of the commandment was to supersede the seventh day. The Jews were directed during the Passover to bring in a sheaf of firstfruits (a plain type of the risen Christ, I Cor. 15:20). This was presented "on the morrow after the sabbath" (v. 11), i.e., the eighth day, or the first day of the week. Notice carefully that after the Sabbath was past, the sheaf was brought; even as after the Sabbath was past, the women came to the tomb; and after the Sabbath was past, Jesus rose from the dead, the firstfruits of the resurrection harvest. It becomes plain, then, that those who are "risen indeed" with newness of life in Christ Jesus on the morrow after the Sabbath rejoice that old things have passed away, that all things have become new. This passage in Leviticus goes on with the further direction that from this "morrow after the sabbath" Israel was to count ahead seven Sabbaths, and then on the fiftieth day (the morrow after the seventh Sabbath) was to "offer a new meat offering unto the LORD." This Old Testament feast of Pentecost looked forward to the New Testament outpouring of the Spirit through the resurrected and glorified Son of man. Observe that these Old Testament feasts looked not backward to the old Sabbath and the old creation, as do the Sabbatarians, but looked forward to the dawn of a new day, "the morrow after the sabbath," which was to supersede the seventh. Therefore it is not surprising that in the early church there should forthwith arise the recognition of the first day of the week as one of deepest spiritual significance, a day associated with the risen Christ and with newness of life and with the fullness of His outpoured Spirit.

Let us now turn to the question of the first day of the week, the Lord's Day, and its proper observance. We are at once confronted with the fact that the Apostle, who met with believers on the first day of the week, was forced also to grapple with delicate and difficult situations regarding the Judaistic observance of days and months and years. When he wrote of the consideration due from "the strong" (those who enjoyed their full gospel liberties) to "the weak" (those who had imbibed or retained special scruples as the result of Judaistic influences), he placed days on the same footing with drinks and meats. See Romans 14. Are we to conclude from this chapter that Paul laid down a rule as applicable to the Lord's Day as to meats and drinks when he said: "Let each man be fully assured in his own mind"? Can we concede that the Lord's Day is one of those "days" of which it can be said: "One man esteemeth one day above another. Another man esteemeth every day alike"? We believe not. In dealing with the problems of meats and drinks and days and months and years the Apostle was referring to things in connection with the ceremonial law. Of course, Paul did at times show how the weekly Sabbath, with other days, was a "shadow" of things to come. Elsewhere we have dwelt upon the spiritual realities as shadowed forth by the weekly Sabbath. But in Romans 14 Paul is dealing with the difficulties of the ceremonial law to which he refers in Gal. 4:8-11 and Col. 2:16-23.

During former generations there was a tendency in some Protestant circles to fall into a legalistic observance of the Lord's Day. But our prevailing tendency is in the opposite direction. Our chief trouble lies rather in an unscrupulous unconcern about personal righteousness. Today the trend is to disregard the Lord's Day, each man doing "that which is right in his own eyes." A discerning teacher of this hour makes this valuable comment:

> Present dispensationalists seem to take the view that we say to the Lord: "We realize that we have nothing to do with the Jewish Sabbath. We are not under law. We are not to observe 'days.' However, we have observed that there might be great blessing in the Old Testament plan of having one day in seven for rest and worship. The Old Testament passages show that great and rich blessing resulted therefrom. Therefore, out of our love for the Lord we are going to suggest that the Christian

church might observe one day in seven. Also we think it would be appropriate to choose the first day of the week." I do not believe that this is the case at all. It was God that gave us this blessing of the Lord's Day as well as all other blessings. We have the sanction of His law. The whole ceremonial law was done away and, therefore, if there were ceremonial features connected with the one day in seven such as the extra sacrifices, we have nothing to do with them except to carry out the spiritual truth symbolized by them. But I believe it is a great mistake of the present-day fundamentalists to take for granted that the Sabbath had anything to do with the ceremonial days and months and years.

It was Tholuck who, while relaxing Christians from the proper obligations of the Lord's Day, deplored the prevailing neglect thereof as destructive to the life of Christian piety. Listen to his plea for a stricter observance:

> *Spirit, spirit!* we cry out. But should the prophets of God come again as they came of old; and should they look upon our works, *Flesh, flesh!* they would cry out in response. Of a truth the most spiritual among us can not dispense with a rule, a prescribed form, in his morality and piety, without allowing the flesh to resume its predominance. The sway of the Spirit of God in your minds is weak; carry, then, holy ordinances into your life (quoted by Fairbairn).

Jesus made it plain that in the beginning the Sabbath was made *"for man."* From such a statement it can scarcely be concluded that the Sabbath was merely or distinctly a Jewish institution. Although the Sabbath was incorporated into Jewish national life and economy, the original Sabbath, as hallowed by God (Gen. 2:3) at the conclusion of creation, was intended as a recurring day (once in seven) of spiritual rest and bodily refreshment. That the Israelites prior to the giving of the law were not utterly ignorant of the seventh day Sabbath seems evident from Exodus 16:28, 29. Furthermore, when Israel was given the fourth commandment (Ex. 20: 8-11), the reason laid down for the observance of the Sabbath was the great fact of God's original creative relationship to the whole world: "For in six days the LORD made heaven and earth, . . . and rested the seventh day." From this passage it cannot be advocated that the Sabbath was merely Jewish or ceremonial or instituted by arbitrary enactment. Circumcision could be rightly so regarded, but not the Sabbath. The latter was based upon the constitutional law in the very nature of man, and therefore abides in principle for the Christian no less than for Jew or Gentile. The Sabbath was made for man to meet his spiritual and physical need.

Some dispensationalists of today conclude what the Jewish Sabbath *should have been* from what Jesus *found it to be* in His day, a mere cold, dead formalism — not the Sabbath made for man, but man for the Sabbath. However, as we turn from Judaism's distortion of the original meaning of the Sabbath, we learn from Isaiah its deep spiritual design and blessedness: "If thou turn away thy foot from the sabbath, from doing thy pleasure on my holy day; and call the sabbath a delight, the holy of the LORD, honourable; and shalt honour Him, not doing thine own ways, nor finding thine own pleasure, nor speaking thine own words: Then shalt thou delight thyself in the LORD; and I will cause thee to ride upon the high places of the earth, and feed thee with the heritage of Jacob thy father: for the mouth of the Lord hath spoken it" (Isa. 58:13, 14). Such indeed was the original intent of the Sabbath as made for man. One could scarcely desire a better description of the proper observance of the Lord's Day. Yet how completely the Israelites missed the meaning and joyous delight of their Sabbath! No less to us today does Isaiah reveal how we are turning our one day in seven into the very revelry he condemns. The Lord's Day is for the most part a time for pleasure trips, excursions, picnics, athletics, social gatherings, concerts, theatricals, automobile rides, and recreations in general. Isaiah especially condemns these very practices when he says, "not doing thine own ways, nor finding thine own pleasure, nor speaking thine own words." It was Bishop Andrewes who said, "To keep the Sabbath in an *idle* manner is the Sabbath of oxen and asses; to pass it in a *jovial* manner is the Sabbath of the golden calf, when the people sat down to eat and drink and rose again to play; to keep it in *surfeiting* and wantonness is the Sabbath of Satan, the devil's holiday" (Fausset).

It is refreshing in these days of growing laxness to read what Dr. R. A. Torrey wrote years ago concerning the liberty of the Lord's Day:

> Though it is privilege and not law, woe be to the man who despises this privilege. He will suffer. Woe be to the man who makes this day of holy privilege a day of secular activity, of work or hilarity or amusement, and forgets he has a soul to refresh by the study of the Word of God and prayer and work for Christ. No man can despise the Lord's Day with its holy privileges without suffering grievously in spirit, soul, and body . . . Each of the ten commandments is an expression of an eternal principle, and the eternal principle stands under the new dispensation as well as under the old.

In this connection an interesting bit of correspondence with a missionary to Manchuria furnishes information much to the point. This man of God had been brought up as a strict Presbyterian to consider that the first day of the week, the Lord's Day, "is to be sanctified by a holy resting all that day, even from such worldly employments and recreations as are lawful on other days; and spending the whole time in the public and private exercises of God's worship, except so much as is to be taken up in the works of necessity and mercy." When he went to Manchuria, he was surprised to note that, apart from the fact that church services were held on the Lord's Day, there was little difference, even among the Christians, between that day and any other day of the week. Very few missionaries took the Lord's Day seriously. He says:

> Early in my experience in Manchuria I was shocked when a large sack of flour was delivered to our door on Sunday afternoon. It turned out to be a gift from the leading Christian of the city who wished in this way to welcome the missionaries who had recently come to live and work there. He had sent out to a grocery store, purchased the flour and had it delivered on the Lord's Day. This man was one of the most earnest, faithful Christians I have known in China. It never occurred to him that it was wrong to buy and sell on the Lord's Day. When such questions were raised, Chinese Christians would wave them away with the simple assertion, "We are not under law, but under grace."

Even the missionary's landlord, a leading member and officer of an indigenous Chinese church in the city, allowed his store with a dozen clerks to remain open on the Lord's Day for the simple reason that he was not under law, but under grace. Then this pioneer and veteran missionary goes on to say:

One day a remarkable document met my eye — a rather long tract composed and published by a Chinese Christian in the far north of Manchuria, quite beyond the region worked by missionaries. This tract raised the question: "Why is the Lord's blessing being withheld from the Church?" By a long and devious argument the author arrived at the conclusion that the Lord's blessing was being withheld from the Church for two principal reasons, to wit: (1) Failure to observe the Lord's Supper every week; (2) Observance of the first day of the week as the Christian Sabbath. The writer of this tract was not a believer in the seventh-day Sabbath; he recognized the first day of the week as the Lord's Day, but held that observance of it as a *Sabbath* — that is, by abstention from work and worldly business — was a symptom of an unspiritual legalism which must interfere with the true progress and revival of the Church.

In this Chinese tract was the Antinomian teaching fairly gone to seed. This man not only ignored the Christian Sabbath; he actually opposed it as something contrary to true Christian living and spirituality, something from which the truly spiritual Christian is emancipated. I never knew any missionary to take such an extreme position; yet the real germ of this man's Antinomianism was to be found in the teachings of some missionaries on the subject of the Christian's relation to law and grace. This Chinese Christian had only taken those doctrines and followed them out further than the missionaries had done.

In visiting Korea I was impressed with the contrast to conditions in Manchuria. Korean Christians, in general, were very careful and conscientious in matters of first-day Sabbath observance. To disregard the Lord's Day, among Korean Christians, seemed to be the exception rather than the rule. Among Presbyterians in Korea, at least, a church member who disregarded the Lord's Day by doing ordinary business was subject to church discipline. In Manchuria, I am sorry to say, beyond attendance at church services, an almost complete neglect of the Lord's Day was the prevalent condition among Chinese Christians. I am convinced that one "secret" of the spiritual strength of the Korean Church has been the insistence upon conscientious Sabbath observance since the days of the early missionaries in that country. Apparently that insistence did not exist in Manchuria nor most parts of China.

Apart from the right or wrong of the matter, it is obvious that no church can be truly spiritual and make real progress when the majority of the members are working at secular jobs seven days a week. Such a condition leaves hardly any time for Christian education and worship. Under such conditions any church is bound to be a weak and compromising church, and the pastor or missionary associated with it must do his work under a terrific handicap. The careful observance of the Lord's Day as "the Christian Sabbath" as taught in the Westminster Shorter Catechism is *not* "legalism," but simply Christian ethics; and it is really necessary for the spiritual nurture and growth both of the individual Christian and of the Church as a body.

We can do no better in closing this chapter on the seventh-day Sabbath and the Lord's Day than to quote the following from Dr. G. Campbell Morgan, that prince of Bible expositors: "The Sabbath idea, as now embodied in the resurrection day, must be defended from all attacks, and by the joyousness of worship and the readiness of service, demonstrate its delight."

Acknowledgements

The writer acknowledges the great kindness of various authors and publishers who have granted permission to use extracts from their copyrighted publications. Among these are:

The Society for Promoting Christian Knowledge, London, England, for selections from the works of Miss Amy Carmichael.

Zondervan Publishing House, Grand Rapids, Michigan, for quotations from *By My Spirit*, by Jonathan Goforth, and the writings of F. J. Huegel.

Moody Bible Institute of Chicago, for selections from *The Twofold Life*, by A. J. Gordon (now out of print); *A Book of Protestant Saints* and *The Leaven of the Sadducees*, by Ernest Gordon (out of print); *Born Crucified*, by the author; *The Atomic Bomb and the Word of God*, by Wilbur M. Smith (out of print); and *Grace*, by Lewis Sperry Chafer.

The Moody Press of Chicago for selections from *God's Way of Holiness*, by Horatius Bonar.

Fleming H. Revell Company, New York City, for quotations from *The Great Physician* and *True Estimate of Life*, by G. Campbell Morgan; *Method in Soul Winning*, by H. C. Mabie; *Memoirs of Charles G. Finney*, by Charles G. Finney; *George Muller of Bristol*, by A. T. Pierson; and *Ought Christians to Keep the Sabbath*, by R. A. Torrey.

Funk and Wagnalls Company, New York City, for excerpts from *Typology of Scripture*, Vols. I and II, by Patrick Fairbairn.

American Tract Society, New York City, for a quotation from A. J. Gordon's Introduction to *Uncle John Vassar*.

Christian Publications, Inc., Harrisburg, Pennsylvania, for selections from *The Way of the Cross*, by J. Gregory Mantle (now out of print); *The Holy Spirit in Missions*, by A. J. Gordon (out of print); *Revelation, the Crown-Jewel of Biblical Prophecy*, by W. C.

Stevens (out of print); and *Through Fire and Through Flood*, by F. B. Meyer (now out of print).

Bible House of Los Angeles, Los Angeles, California, for quotations from *The Bible Basis of Missions*, by Robert H. Glover.

Evangelical Publishers, Toronto, Ontario, for a brief quotation from *Matthew the Publican*, by Rowland V. Bingham.

Oliphants Ltd., London, England, for brief quotation from *The Dynamic of Service* and *The Dynamic of Redemption*, by Paget Wilkes.

Van Kampen Press, Wheaton, Illinois, for excerpts from *Except Ye Repent*, by Harry A. Ironside.

Oriental Missionary Society, Inc., Los Angeles, for excerpts from *Streams in the Desert*, by Mrs. C. Cowman.

The Presbyterian and Reformed Publishing Company, Philadelphia, for a brief quotation or two from *Prophecy and the Church*, by Oswald T. Allis.

Bibliotheca Sacra, Dallas, Texas, for quotations from *Bibliotheca Sacra*, Vol. 93, No. 372.

The Sunday School Times Company, Philadelphia, for quotations from *Will Revival Come?* by Ernest M. Wadsworth.

Where we have made only brief quotations of a sentence or two, we have not felt it necessary to secure special permission from the publishers. However, we have aimed not to take advantage of the generosity of any copyrighted material without securing proper permission.

We are also indebted for very brief excerpts from the writings of various great saints and theologians such as Gerhard Ter Steegen, William Law, W. H. Griffith Thomas, Robert Murray McCheyne, Paget Wilkes, Andrew Murray, A. B. Simpson, C. A. Fox, T. C. Upham, James McConkey, Charles Spurgeon, Samuel Rutherford, John Calvin, Adolph Saphir, Charles Simeon, Madame Guyon, J. H. Jowett, A. S. Ormsby, Hudson Taylor, David Gracey, James Denney, Charles Hodge, John Woolman, Oswald Chambers, Alfred Edersheim, Bishop H. C. G. Moule, Samuel Chadwick and A. H. Strong. We feel especially grateful to D. M. Panton for illustrations from *Dawn*, an evangelical magazine published in England.